Grassroots

STUDIES IN EARLY AMERICAN ECONOMY AND SOCIETY
FROM THE LIBRARY COMPANY OF PHILADELPHIA
Cathy Matson, *Series Editor*

Grassroots Leviathan

*Agricultural Reform and the Rural North
in the Slaveholding Republic*

ARIEL RON

Johns Hopkins University Press
Baltimore

© 2020 Johns Hopkins University Press
All rights reserved. Published 2020
Printed in the United States of America on acid-free paper

Johns Hopkins Paperback edition, 2023
2   4   6   8   9   7   5   3   1

Johns Hopkins University Press
2715 North Charles Street
Baltimore, Maryland 21218-4363
www.press.jhu.edu

The Library of Congress has catalogued the hardcover edition of this book as follows:

Names: Ron, Ariel, 1978– author.
Title: Grassroots leviathan : agricultural reform and the rural north in the
slaveholding republic / Ariel Ron.
Description: Baltimore : Johns Hopkins University Press, 2020. | Series: Studies in
early American economy and society from the Library Company of Philadelphia |
Includes bibliographical references and index.
Identifiers: LCCN 2020002937 | ISBN 9781421439327 (hardcover) | ISBN
9781421439334 (ebook)
Subjects: LCSH: Agriculture and state—New England—History—19th century. |
Agriculture—Economic aspects—New England—History—19th century. |
Agriculture—Government policy—New England—History—19th century.
Classification: LCC HD1773.A3 R66 2020 | DDC 338.10974/09034—dc23
LC record available at https://lccn.loc.gov/2020002937

A catalog record for this book is available from the British Library.

ISBN 9781421446721 (paperback)

*Special discounts are available for bulk purchases of this book. For more information,
please contact Special Sales at specialsales@press.jh.edu.*

To the memory of my grandparents, who lived history more than most

CONTENTS

In this latest title in the series Studies in Early American Economy and Society, a collaborative effort between Johns Hopkins University Press and the Library Company of Philadelphia's Program in Early American Economy and Society (PEAES), Ariel Ron provides a groundbreaking study of farmers in the northern states between the American Revolution and the Civil War. *Grassroots Leviathan: Agricultural Reform and the Rural North in the Slaveholding Republic* challenges head-on the long-standing arguments about a declining rural population in the face of advancing industrialization. Instead of a receding "yeoman" presence in the shaping of the American national identity and growing state and federal powers over the republic, Ron's compelling narrative places northern farmers at the core of economic and political development. Rather than portraying farmers as the premier voice for reducing the power of government, he urges us to see that agricultural Americans were deeply enmeshed with the rise of state institutions and shifting political economy in the decades before the Civil War.

Indeed, northern American farmers built a massive agricultural reform movement in the early republic. Made up of northern middle-class farmers, rural businessmen, local political leaders, and publicists, the reformers cast off references to self-sufficient yeomen and traditionalist farming strategies. Instead, a new discourse of "scientific agriculture" gained strength. The new vision foresaw an active role for government in reshaping the countryside into locales of intensive, technologically innovative, and profitable farming. And the movement enlisted a massive popular base to build and energize institutional reforms to meet such goals, a "grassroots leviathan" that hailed not from factory manufacturing or canal building but from the countryside.

Ron has read an impressive array of agricultural journals and reports, individual farmers' diaries and account books, and agricultural organizations' internal records stretching across dozens of county archives. These sources provide the basis for arguments that shake up our long-standing perspectives about northern farmers and demonstrate their deepening influence on the national state over the decades before the Civil War. That influence could not have been achieved if farmers had been withdrawn from emerging markets or unconcerned with policy development. Agricultural reformers, argues Ron, were in fact enthusiastically engaged with improving agriculture and demanding policies that would fundamentally change how rural America was governed. Farmers were readers; a rising agricultural press reached throughout the northern states and helped consolidate an otherwise dispersed population of rural people into networks with common needs and projections for the future. The agricultural press spread information about recent scientific research on crop yields and livestock breeding, news about geologic surveying, advertisements for seeds and saplings, and outlets for new farm implements or fertilizers.

Farmers were also joiners; they formed over a thousand agricultural organizations that brought together experts in new farming strategies and reformers who were willing to take farmers' demands through political channels. And farmers were engaged with their communities and regions; every fall, rural fairs brought together huge crowds of producers, sellers, and customers to display and market the fruits of "scientific agriculture." Fairs were sites for sharing ideas about innovation, showcasing the results of new chemical and mechanical experiments, and building enthusiasm for the next new policies reformers would take to state and federal governments.

Most far-reaching of all, and right in the midst of news about slaves' emancipation during the Civil War, the federal government created two massively influential institutions with the backing and pressure of the agricultural reform movement: the United States Department of Agriculture and the Morrill Land Grant Act. Both of these would lay the foundation for networks of agencies and policies that would bring the federal government into the countryside as never before, at the urging of the grassroots leviathan itself.

Cathy Matson, Series Editor
Richards Professor of American History Emerita, University of Delaware
Director, Program in Early American Economy and Society, Library
Company of Philadelphia

ACKNOWLEDGMENTS

Where to begin? I owe the most to the incomparable Robin Einhorn, the best dissertation adviser I could have asked for. David Henkin was a huge influence throughout my time at the University of California, Berkeley. Brian DeLay arrived late in my graduate career but has given me invaluable feedback and advice at many stages of this project. Richard Walker rounded out my committee and made several valuable suggestions. Of my other teachers at Cal, I'd particularly like to thank Martin Jay, Irwin Scheiner, Andrew Brashay, Marion Fourcade, and Margaret Weir for course material that has stuck with me and worked its way into my research in various ways. My graduate peers influenced me as much as anyone else, maybe more, especially Daniel Immerwahr, Corey Brooks, and Anna Armentrout.

For research support I am indebted, in addition to the Berkeley history department, to the Program in Early American Economy and Society (PEAES) at the Library Company of Philadelphia; the Yale Center for the Study of Representative Institutions (YCSRI) with funding from the Jack Miller Center; the Gilder Lehrman Institute for American History in conjunction with the New-York Historical Society; and the Center for the History of Business, Technology, and Society at the Hagley Museum and Library.

At PEAES, Cathy Matson encouraged my early research and profoundly shaped the transition from dissertation to book, particularly the addition of material on the early national period. Jim Green, Connie King, Wendy Woloson, and the staff of the print department directed me to essential primary sources. Archivists at several other area institutions, including John Pollack at the University of Pennsylvania's Kislak Center for Special Collections, likewise aided my research. During two years in Philadelphia I also benefited from an extensive community of scholars, principally those connected with Penn's McNeil Center for Early American Studies, where director Dan Richter was kind enough to extend visiting researcher privileges. Among those I met in Philly, I owe an extra debt to Emily Pawley, Noam Maggor, Hannah Farber, Mary

Summers, and Andrew Shankman for vital discussions and comments on written work.

At YCSRI, Steven Smith and Keith Wrightson provided me with precious freedom and encouragement, while Yiftah Elazar was a friend and an interlocutor. My time at two Jack Miller Center Summer Institutes proved valuable for having met Pamela Edwards, Michelle Schwarze, Jonathan Gienapp, Nora Slonimsky, and Randall Hendrickson. Two years at Yale gave me the opportunity to attend and present research at various workshops, including a graduate colloquium of the Program for Agrarian Studies, a joint session of Yale Environmental History and the Yale Early American Historians, and workshops with the Race and Slavery Working Group and the American Political Development group. In these various sessions and surrounding conversations, comments by Gavin Wright, Joanne Freeman, Paul Sabin, Ryan Hall, Alejandra Dubcovsky, Michael Blaakman, Stephen Skowronek, and Sam DeCanio stand out. Naomi Lamoreaux deserves special thanks for her unbounded intellectual generosity and acuity. With New Haven in mind, I could not fail to mention Howard Stern, Hannan Hever, and Stephen Poland, who always help me think new things.

Others shaped this book in ways large and small. I met Gautham Rao and Stephen Meardon at the 2010 Policy History Conference and have been benefiting from their generosity, advice, and collaboration ever since. At that meeting, Richard F. Bensel gave my early work its first reading outside of Berkeley and left me with valuable comments to ponder. Monica Prasad affected my thinking in several hard-to-specify ways. Eric Foner read my dissertation and gave me valuable feedback. Richard R. John offered essential tips on both primary and secondary sources. Dael Norwood, Matt Karp, and Catilin Rosenthal joined me in a writing group that was both fun and helpful. Simon Vezina has been a consistently insightful interlocutor concerning Henry C. Carey and theories of economic development. At various times I presented work in progress and received valuable feedback in the following venues: the Bay Area Seminar in Early American History, Harvard's History of Capitalism Dissertation Workshop, the Early American History Seminar at Ohio State University, the Columbia University Seminar in Economic History, and the CUNY Graduate Center's Early American History Seminar.

A manuscript conference at Southern Methodist University (SMU) in 2018 was an exceptionally valuable privilege. My special thanks to James Oakes and Reeve Huston for providing detailed reader reports that were both encouraging and incisive; to Andrew Graybill and Ruth Elmore for organizing the event; and to all of the other participants, each of whom helped me understand my own work better than before: Neil Foley, Tom Richards, Ed Countryman, Aaron Crawford, Crista DeLuzio, Alexis McCrossen, Stephen Maizlish, Chris Morris,

Andrew Torget, Michael Wise, and Kyle Carpenter. I am equally grateful for the support and encouragement of the entire history department at SMU.

Yet more thanks to those who helped bring this book over the finish line: to Laura Davulis and Esther Rodriguez for their efficient and no-nonsense handling of things at Johns Hopkins University Press, to Beth Gianfagna for her scrupulous copyediting, and to the anonymous manuscript reader, whose detailed report and excellent advice guided the final revisions of this book. Thanks also to Audra Wolfe for valuable developmental editing at a slightly earlier stage, and to Cornell University's Society for the Humanities, where this manuscript was completed.

Finally, a huge debt of gratitude to my partner, Nataly Abramovitch, for abiding with me through the work for this book, and to my mother, father, and extended family, who cultivated my interests and aspirations.

Grassroots Leviathan

Introduction

The United States was an overwhelmingly rural society before the Civil War and for some time afterward. There were cities and factories, of course, especially in the northern seaboard states. In 1860, Manhattan's population was nearing a million. Brooklyn, which had been farmland at the time of the American Revolution, was itself home to 250,000. New England's mill towns were already proverbial, and Chicago's growth elicited awe. But these were exceptions. In the same year, eighty percent of Americans lived in rural places of 2,500 inhabitants or fewer. Fifty-nine percent of the labor force worked in agriculture, only fifteen percent in manufacturing. As the farm editor Jesse Buel put it, agriculture remained "the great business of civilized life."[1]

National numbers obscure regional variations, but shearing away the almost entirely agricultural South and looking only at the North, the focus must remain on the countryside and the farm, not the city and the factory. In the North as a whole, three-quarters of the population remained rural in 1860. Even in the Northeast, the nation's most urbanized and industrialized part, the proportion stood at nearly two-thirds. Despite the abiding myth that the Civil War pitted an industrial North against an agrarian South, the truth is that agriculture continued to dominate the economic, social, and cultural lives of the majority of Americans well into the late nineteenth century. Most contemporaries assumed it would always be this way. Abraham Lincoln took it for granted that farmers were, "in the nature of things . . . more numerous than any other class."[2]

If the majority of the people were in the country and agriculture was at the base of their lives, it must be the case that agricultural history is somehow central to the formative period from roughly the founding of the United States to its rupture in the Civil War. Farmers, in other words, must have played an essential role in the making, unmaking, and remaking of the republic. This statement, straightforward as it may seem, invites reflection. What exactly does it mean to speak of *farmers* in this period? And what does it mean to speak of them *as* farmers, to stress their occupation in agriculture?

In recent years, historians have devoted tremendous attention to a particular class of antebellum "farmers": the slaveholding planters of the Old South. The new work has radically changed received views. Planters were once thought of as would-be feudal lords standing athwart history. They now appear as brutally innovative capitalists whose aggressive drive to make the United States an expansive slaveholding republic was every bit as modern as the industrialization of Lancashire. The change of mind comes from new analyses of southern commodities, social relations, and cultural practices through theoretical lenses ranging from neoclassical economics to poststructuralist literary studies. Disparate as they are, these approaches have aligned in refocusing the study of slavery on the category of property. By shifting the perspective from labor to the "chattel principle," scholars have tied planters to global capital flows and financial innovation, upending the old view that planters were essentially premodern. A familiar class of historical actors has thus been recast in a new mold.[3]

Much less work has gone into reimagining northern farmers. The point of departure still seems to be the "yeoman" and his "agrarian" ideal. In the classical accounts of Thomas Jefferson and J. Hector St. John de Crèvecoeur, the yeoman farmer—implicitly white, male, and heterosexual—wants nothing more than to secure an adequate farm on which to raise a family and found his civic independence.[4] The disappearance of this way of being has motivated more than a century of historical narratives. According to Frederick Jackson Turner's frontier thesis, the struggle to wrest civilization from wilderness produced the yeoman values of self-reliance and egalitarian democracy, while the closing of the frontier at the approach of the twentieth century signaled a changed and presumably diminished American character.[5] For Richard Hofstadter and the historians of the consensus school, the yeomen were real enough, but the agrarian ideal was mostly a useful myth that, ironically, the yeomen themselves undermined by their pursuit of material progress.[6] More recently, historians of the "market revolution" have elucidated a complex process through which yeoman independence was eroded and gradually destroyed by increasing trade, which tied farmers' fates to distant, uncontrollable markets.[7] Each of these paradigms has been generative. Each has also been subjected to important revaluations by historians of gender, Native America, and the environment. But even in the revaluations, much of the basic analytic framing remains intact. A common narrative thread tends to prevail: the small, independent, agricultural social unit of American settler colonialism dissolves into the modern, industrial, mass society of American global empire.

The necessary complement of rural declension, whichever way understood, is urban ascension. Although scholars have long since moved on from taking the Industrial Revolution (capital *I*, capital *R*) as history's central thing-to-be-explained, much of the scholarship remains colored by the presumption that early urbanism and industrialism heralded the significant part of the American future. The cost of this framing has been a tendency to view agriculture as a declining sector rather than as a developmental and dynamic one.[8] It is true, of course, that urban ways of life and industrial manufacturing eventually came to predominate. This does not mean, however, that insisting on the nineteenth century's essential rurality is merely an exercise in excavating forms of life buried by the sands of time. For well over a century after the American Revolution, as the modern city gradually triumphed, rural communities constituted the main currents of American life. They did not do so in isolation, nor in a blind stupor. They pursued their own modernities and, in the process, prescribed key terms on which the rest of us have come to inhabit ours.

The mythic image of the yeoman farmer is one of these. Seemingly a quaint survival of a bygone era, it is really a symbolic pillar of the American nation-state. Its continuing relevance is attested by such twentieth-century inventions as the "family farm" and the "heartland," words that evoke the supposed essence of American identity while projecting it backward in time.[9] The general pattern is hardly confined to the United States. For instance, the Japanese novelist and literary critic, Kōbō Abe, observed after World War II "that, even in the advanced industrial countries . . . the *image of authentic citizen* still remains that of the good farmer."[10] Rooted and therefore patriotic, productive economically as well as reproductive demographically, independent because self-reliant, the figure of the farmer appears as the very type of the modern nation-state. It is a figure that leans heavily toward the nation rather than the state side of the conjunction, involving the belief that the nation is distinct from and more fundamental than the state. If the trope of farmer self-reliance suggests a homology with national independence and even autarky, it also signifies a bulwark apart from and against the state's overdevelopment. Farmers remind us to get government off our backs. Yet even a passing familiarity with the agricultural policies of modern developed countries reveals this conceit to be absurd. Agriculture is deeply entangled with state institutions, perhaps more so than any other economic sector.

Actually, even as the yeoman myth took hold, many farmers pursued tangible governing power in ways that came to alter the institutional structure of the American state. Scholars know this well about the late nineteenth and early twentieth centuries but have rarely looked for farmers as agents of state development before the Civil War.[11] It is hard to imagine antebellum farmers in such a role. It must have taken a direct confrontation with industrial modernity—an independent development occurring elsewhere, in the factories and cities—to have made them so. They had been yeomen, after all, builders of homes rather than states. But then, there is a mystery. In 1862, even as pressing war measures confronted it, Congress created the US Department of Agriculture (USDA) and the land-grant university system. These agencies constituted the most significant departure in American agricultural governance since the Constitution and the Northwest Ordinances codified the slaveholding settler-colonial state in the 1780s. Yet no one seems to have asked, how is it that in the midst of a total war against slavery, Congress found time to fundamentally reorient the federal government's relationship to the country's major occupational category, or how these two things might have been related?

The yeoman myth is as much about the American state as about American farmers. Until recently, scholars regarded the early nineteenth-century social structure of propertied independence as constitutive of weak governing institutions. In place of the state, they saw a dominant two-party system that mediated between voting citizens and limited government powers. Because the substance of this system was the distribution of patronage coupled with the production of partisan identity, the state appeared as merely a vessel for the social forces that the parties coordinated.[12] In this view, the Civil War was not the deep, historical rupture that it was thought to be. Instead, the better part of the nineteenth century was a unitary "party period" in which parties constituted American politics as, on the one hand, a high-flying ideological debate about what "self-government" actually meant, and, on the other hand, a grimy insider contest for money and power. Since the Civil War did not seriously disturb this pattern, slavery was understood more as aberration than structure—a bug, not a feature. The yeoman republic endured, only to be engulfed by the inexorable tide of industrialization.

Yet much as scholars have revolutionized older understandings about slavery, they have overturned the party-period conception of the nineteenth-century American state. They have shown that it was more administratively robust than previously thought.[13] And they have retheorized law and associationalism as constructive of state power rather than as brakes on it.[14] The upshot is a new perception of the nineteenth-century American state as powerful and ubiquitous long before the Progressive Era brought changes in form. In this respect, US historiography has followed a much broader move to denaturalize free markets and the ontological priority of society by revealing their institutional and therefore political underpinnings. Consequently, slavery has appeared increasingly important to understanding the nature of the early American state. A market in human beings did not just happen. If the new history of slavery and capitalism is one side of the shift, another is the even newer history of slavery and the state.[15]

With the old periodization swept away and slavery looming large, the Civil War reappears as a deep historical break.[16] And it is in this context that one must again wonder why a new national agricultural state was founded at the precise moment that slavery was destroyed. The USDA and the Morrill Land-Grant Act of 1862 laid the groundwork for a matrix of new agencies that would fundamentally change the governing of rural America, establish a core piece of the developmental state that emerged from the Civil War, and, in the twentieth century, serve as a model for US interventions abroad.[17] These things came from somewhere. They were the culmination of a decade-long campaign powered by a massive agricultural reform movement that had been building up in the North since the early national period.

The story remains little known or appreciated, in part because the reigning conception of northern free labor ideology focuses attention elsewhere. Rooted in labor history, the free labor synthesis explains not only why northerners broke irrevocably with southern slaveholders, but also the terms on which they confronted postbellum industrialization. The payoff is double, grounding the causes of the Civil War in the emergence of the all-northern Republican Party coalition and explaining the retreat from Reconstruction with reference to that coalition's fracturing in the face of industrial labor strife.[18] Northern farmers are mostly audience in this drama rather than players. The usual view of labor has always been problematic for dealing with them because the sharp distinction from capital, on which it depends, was not typical of their situation. To bring agricultural change into focus requires a different lens.

This book shifts attention from industrialization to agricultural development. It shows how northern, middle-class farmers and rural businessmen built an enormous agricultural reform movement, keyed to the slogan of "scientific agriculture," that they used to institutionalize their presence in a reimagined state apparatus. The upshot was a grassroots leviathan, a popular state-building machine in—of all places—the countryside. The story of who made this apparatus, how it worked, and what it ultimately did challenges standard accounts of the nineteenth-century political system and necessarily pertains to the coming of the Civil War. In confronting the "Slave Power," agricultural reformers became key players in the Republican Party's assault on the slaveholding republic and in the construction of a new American developmental state that took its place.

Agricultural Reform and American State Development

The agricultural reform movement emerged in the decades after the American Revolution as a mass social movement that connected millions of mostly northern farmers through a triad of novel rural institutions. The first was the agricultural society. By the end of the antebellum period, more than a thousand such organizations coordinated a growing range of agricultural reform and improvement activities at the local, state, and national levels. The second was the farm press. Its enormous readership consolidated geographically dispersed farmers into a networked agricultural public that redefined the imagined boundaries of rural life. The third was the agricultural fair. Repeated each fall, these constituted uniquely rural instances of mass society, astonishing contemporaries with their crowds and cornucopian displays. The societies, journals, and fairs together catalyzed deep changes in rural America and, perforce, in the country as a whole.

At one level, the changes were economic. After the Revolution, Euro-American agriculture faced a confluence of circumstances that forced farmers to alter their day-to-day practices in fundamental ways. Depleted soils from generations of overcropping called for new, intensive soil-maintenance regimes. A deteriorating pest environment, intensified by the Revolution's troop movements and shifting trade patterns, led farmers to alter their crop mix and search out new, pest-resistant crop varieties. Indian dispossession and western settlement, urban growth and immigration, and the industrialization of Britain transformed commodity markets and predicated new migrations. The antebellum agricultural economy was thus highly dynamic, presenting farmers with a range of challenges and opportunities. In this context, agricultural reformers argued for a "scientific agriculture" to modernize the countryside. The new farming would be intensive, sustainable, and profitable, its practitioners market and technology savvy.

New institutions proved essential for diffusing the practices of scientific agriculture. The reform project began in the United States shortly after independence as a patrician effort to strengthen the nascent republic's economic power. But the sweeping social transformations that eventuated in Jacksonian white male democracy meant that this paternalistic vision foundered. The renewed agricultural reform movement that began to emerge during the 1830s encouraged farmers' participation in a way that the old patricians had not, and consequently it cemented a principal role in shaping agricultural practice. Reformers designed agricultural fairs as sites where farmers could learn from one another and, by competing for prizes, achieve the social distinction that was thought to motivate innovation. They published agricultural journals that offered primers on basic scientific concepts; promoted new chemical, mechanical, and biological technologies; and exhaustively discussed farming's prosaic details. They organized societies to coordinate these activities and to branch out into new ones, including scientific research, geologic surveying, standardization of crop nomenclature, and systematic testing of implements, fertilizers, and the like. In these ways, the agricultural reform movement built a particular path of rural economic modernization.

But economics is only one part of the story. The agricultural reform movement innovated in politics. It was, in fact, itself a kind of novel political technology. In *The Federalist Papers*, no. 10, James Madison famously argued that an extended republic made "it less probable that a majority of the whole will have a common motive . . . or if such a common motive exists, it will be more difficult for all who feel it to discover their own strength, and to act in unison with each other."[19] The institutions of agricultural reform vitiated this check precisely where it should have been most secure: among rural people whose geographic dispersion impeded coordinated action. Societies, journals, and fairs allowed farmers to imagine themselves as both the nation itself and as a distinct class within it in order to lobby government like never before, transforming the "agricultural interest" from a quasi-aristocratic voice of the rural patriciate— claimed especially by southern planters—into a quasi-democratic voice of the mostly northern rural middle class. Reform movement leaders wrote editorials, organized conventions, circulated petitions, and pressured legislators to enact an increasingly ambitious program of government-sponsored agricultural education and research. These efforts gradually led state and federal officials to adopt entirely new ways of governing rural America.

All this was born of a distinctive mode of advocacy that I call nonpartisan anti-politics.[20] Agricultural reformers insisted that farmers had a uniquely legitimate claim on the collective resources of the republic but shunned the partisan arena that contemporaries equated with politics itself. According to Jesse Buel, farmers were the one class fully "identified with the welfare of the state."[21] They practically *were* the state and ought to enjoy a governing capacity unmediated by parties. Nonpartisanship was more than a slogan, it was an organizational imperative. Bringing farmers together required occupational solidarity, which meant that divisive, preexisting partisan loyalties had to be put on a separate plane from that of the "agricultural interest." Since partisanship largely defined the boundaries of the political in the nineteenth-century United States, agricultural reform had to be something other than politics. "Political ambition . . . abides not on the farm," Buel claimed. Only three years earlier he had himself stood as the Whig nominee for governor of New York.[22] But Buel the politician and Buel the agricultural reformer were two distinct personas. Party politics never appeared in Buel's agricultural journal, where farmers' demands were presented as the unvarnished will of the people. Nonpartisan anti-politics did not so much repudiate political action as displace and transfigure it.

Although Buel and other reformers claimed an identity of farmers with nation, in practice they positioned agricultural societies as the representative organizations of just another special interest group jockeying for a piece of the state within a pluralistic society. Later, they sought to insulate new government agricultural agencies from partisan control by fostering bureaucratic expertise and autonomy. These developments are usually associated with a later period of American history. Yet already by the eve of the Civil War, the agricultural reform movement's considerable success amounted not only to an increasingly hegemonic agenda for rural America but also to an incipient restructuring of the American state. The significance of this timing is that it intersected, at a crucial moment, with the politics of slavery.

Agricultural Reformers and the Republican Party against the Slave Power

Because it invoked an identity with the people, agricultural anti-politics was, at bottom, a form of nationalism. Like all nationalisms, it involved a matrix of judgments about what was and was not proper to the national community. These judgments were decisively shaped by northerners' proportional domination of the agricultural reform movement. Compared with the South, the northern free states had a larger population, denser hinterlands, and more egalitarian rural society, all of which contributed to much greater participation in the movement. When it came to the number and size of agricultural reform institutions, the North often enjoyed an advantage of an order of magnitude. Consequently, northern voices dominated the discourse of agricultural reform, infused it with their worldview, and steered it toward their priorities. Northern numerical superiority turned the movement into an incubator of a specific vision of the nation. This meant that, notwithstanding the movement's avowed nonpartisanship, its pursuit of state-building initiatives in the midst of the sectional crisis of the 1850s aligned it with the embryonic, antislavery Republican Party.

Agricultural reformers rarely acknowledged their northern tendencies, instead presenting their movement as truly national. The ideology of agricultural reform nevertheless evidences northern predisposition in a number of ways. Most obvious was the frequent invocation of free labor principles. But this was ultimately just one part of an expansive economic nationalism. Central, too, was the "home market" idea, according to which domestic urban and industrial growth were integral to agricultural development. Cities, the thinking went, made for dependable markets that nearby farmers were uniquely positioned to supply. Manufacturers, in turn, would provide farmers not just with consumer goods, but also with revolutionary producer technologies such as mechanical reapers and chemical fertilizers. In the context of a profound reorientation of the northern economy from colonial transatlantic trade to domestic development, these points amounted to a powerful case for industrial policy. Rural nationalism in a northern register was also evident in the belief that small rather than large farms were most conducive to scientific agriculture. The outstanding contemporary example of large-scale agriculture was the southern plantation, which by the 1830s was firmly linked in northern minds with economic stagnation and environmental decay.[23] Small owner-operators were supposed to have better incentives. Equally important, they collectively formed dense and developmentally favorable hinterland markets.

During the 1850s, leading Republican Party ideologues adopted these positions more or less wholesale. Agricultural reform allowed Republicans to project a vision of national progress that could be articulated with other sectors of the economy and still appeal to the northern rural majority. It simultaneously provided a set of standards by which to judge slave agriculture as backward. Men who would emerge as Republican leaders echoed agricultural reformers' economic vision, often when speaking at agricultural exhibitions. At the 1852 Vermont state fair, for instance, Lincoln's future secretary of state, William Henry Seward, insisted that "a constant and uniform relation must always be maintained between the state of agriculture (and, indeed, of society itself) and the cotemporaneous state of invention in the arts."[24] He thereby acknowledged agriculture's identity with "society itself," even as he stressed technological innovation emanating from the manufacturing sector. This proposition was greatly elaborated in the work of Henry C. Carey, the early Republican Party's most important economic theoretician. Given the North's rural character, it only makes sense that the agricultural reform movement heavily shaped Republicans' worldview.

Ideological affinity with Republicans was strongly reinforced by southern hostility to agricultural reformers' national policy agenda. According to southern Democrats, the new federal agencies that reformers demanded were unconstitutional. But as shown by examples ranging from the Fugitive Slave Act of 1850 to the lesser-known Guano Islands Act of 1856, southern politicians deployed the principle of constitutional strict construction to limit only specific forms of national power. The problem for agricultural reformers in the 1850s was that their essentially northern perspective made southern politicians suspicious of the vision they sought to institutionalize at the national level. Precisely this made agricultural reform initiatives attractive to Republicans. Besides informing how Republicans understood the world, they offered popular, ostensibly nonpartisan issues with which to dramatize the obstructionism of the "Slave Power."[25]

These points are essential for understanding how Republicans actually governed once in power. It is well known that secession allowed Republicans to enact a comprehensive economic program during the Civil War, a "blueprint for modern America."[26] The key features and logic of that program, however, remain misunderstood. Historians know, for instance, that the Homestead Act aimed to settle the West with free farmers and to provide a "safety valve" for eastern labor. But they do not typically stress that, in accordance with the logic of the productive small farm, it was also thought to be the best way to develop the nation's landed resources. Similarly, when historians discuss tariffs, they tend to emphasize Republicans' use of the "pauper labor" argument to appeal to urban workingmen. According to this idea, tariffs protected American workers from low-wage foreign competition. But because the Republicans' social base was in the rural and small-town North, not in the largest cities, the more important appeal was the "home market" idea, which stated that protectionism benefited farmers by enlarging their domestic markets. Meanwhile, the origins of the USDA and the Land-Grant Act—major policies that have received attention only in specialized historiographies—have largely escaped analysis by political historians because they were formulated in agricultural rather than in partisan circles.

Economic and environmental change in the antebellum rural North fostered new governing imperatives that ultimately clashed with the makeup of the slaveholding republic. If slavery was the negative referent for the Republican vision of American national development, agricultural reform supplied much of the positive content. That vision was enacted in a burst of wartime legislation that, alongside slavery's destruction, shaped the country's trajectory for decades to come and defined basic aspects of American nationality.

Sketch of the Chapters

The book is organized into four parts of two chapters each. Part 1 establishes the origins and development of the agricultural reform movement, including the creation of a robust and wide-ranging discourse of scientific agriculture. Everything follows from this. The first chapter shows that agricultural reform in the United States began as a project of postcolonial nationalism. Initially directed by rural patricians, it was a didactic effort to acquire knowledge from Europeans and adapt it to American conditions. The operative principle was the Enlightenment concept of "emulation," which worked on both the national and individual levels: the United States had to emulate the techniques of the European powers if it were to gain true independence, and this required ordinary farmers to emulate the farming standards of their social betters. The annual agricultural fair emerged as the key mechanism to set these processes in motion. But as fairs became popular and won public funding, they also became enmeshed in the era's broad challenge to patrician dominance. By the mid-1820s, a backlash against agricultural societies' elitism caused a general abrogation of state subsidies. Scientific agriculture would not get far in the free states as a quasi-aristocratic project.

Deference-to-democracy politics cleared the ground for a new, mass agricultural reform movement to take shape during the antebellum period, as shown in chapter 2. The rise of an independent agricultural press in the 1830s constituted farmers as a distinct public. Rhetorically accessible and even populist, the journals redefined agricultural reform as the common interest of the rural majority, now imagined as an undifferentiated mass of citizen-famers. This conception retained the patricians' economic nationalism and faith in science, but sought to foster farmers' occupational solidarity by detaching agricultural reform from the political sphere. As what contemporaries understood by "politics" took the form of two-party competition, agricultural editors engaged in a nonpartisan anti-politics that drew on rural norms of consensus to identify farmers with the nation. A large number of American farmers, now linked through the agricultural press, came to constitute a well-networked social formation that redrew the boundaries of rural community. A new generation of agricultural reformers then activated this network by mobilizing press coverage, petition drives, and conventions to demand renewed subsidies for agricultural societies. During the 1840s, these efforts succeeded in state after state. By 1850 or so, publicly supported agricultural fairs dedicated to the Baconian slogan, "knowledge is power," were among the country's largest mass gatherings. Agricultural reform had been remade as a social movement.

Importantly, the constituencies and methods of these campaigns were distinctly northern. The implications of this sectional predisposition are developed in part 2 by exploring how agricultural reform shaped northerners' understanding of broader transformations in the national economy. The chapters in this section are concerned with relating northern developmental ideology to actual economic patterns. An encompassing ideology—a worldview—does not spring directly from social experience. It has to be fashioned by assembling pieces of life that have already been interpreted at more local levels. In other words, no patterned experience finds its way into an ideological synthesis without prior mediation. The agricultural reform movement—more precisely, the discourse of scientific agriculture that it sponsored—was what mediated between the day-to-day realities of farming and the big-picture theorizing of northern economic nationalists.

Chapter 3 introduces two key concepts for seeing how a distinctly northern

economic nationalism articulated agricultural reform with industrial development. The first of these I call the "Greater Northeast," an expanding geographic
space centered on New England and the Mid-Atlantic states and characterized
by the combination of urban growth, dense rural hinterlands, the absence of
slavery, and mixed agriculture bound for domestic rather than export markets.
The second is the "home market" thesis, as described above. By showing how
actual economic development in the Greater Northeast plausibly corresponded
to the home market idea's linkage of agriculture and manufacturing, this chapter explains why many northern farmers supported a protective tariff as one part
of an integrated national developmental program. That alignment, in turn,
helped position northern agricultural reformers in opposition to southern slaveholders committed to staple exports.

Chapter 4 carries these themes forward in time and expands on them through
a detailed examination of the writings of Henry C. Carey, widely regarded as
the early Republican Party's leading economic theorist. It begins by situating
Carey in a transatlantic conversation about political economy in which inherent limits to agricultural productivity appeared as inherent limits on overall
economic development. To counter this view, Carey drew heavily on scientific
agriculture to argue for the transformative power of science and technology.
In Carey's work, the home market's reciprocal trade between the agricultural
and manufacturing sectors collapsed into a single, concentrated cluster of varied domestic exchanges that spurred innovation and made the most efficient
possible use of natural resources. Other Republican ideologues with links to
agricultural reform, notably George Perkins Marsh, Erasmus Peshine Smith,
and even Ralph Waldo Emerson, told a similar story, indicating the emergence
of a northern economic vision that I call the "Republican developmental synthesis." This vision drew farmers deeper into the developmentalist coalition,
augmenting the existing program with a new emphasis on government science
and education. It also drew the line more sharply with the South by insisting
that technological innovation was an emancipatory historical force directly at
odds with slavery.

Whereas parts 1 and 2 describe the general aims, structure, and influence of
the agricultural reform movement as it emerged during the antebellum period,
parts 3 and 4 delve into the nitty-gritty details of policymaking. These chapters
show why a federal agricultural department and federally funded agricultural
colleges became key policy goals for reformers in the 1850s. Reformers thus
shifted their attention decisively to the national level in the midst of a deepening sectional crisis and consequent partisan realignment.

Part 3 presents two case studies that show how agricultural reformers moved
from private and state-level initiatives to federal ones. Chapter 5 tells the story
of James Jay Mapes, a well-known farm editor who lent his name and expertise

to the country's first venture in the manufacture of superphosphates, a break-through chemical fertilizer. Mapes's bombastic style, possibly fraudulent busi-ness practices, and quixotic scientific theorizing led to a controversy in the 1850s that illuminates a key difficulty of the agricultural reform program. Achieving a scientific agriculture meant introducing newfangled products, such as chem-ical fertilizers, whose efficacy was premised on technical claims that farmers were poorly positioned to evaluate. The agricultural press proved unable to adjudicate such matters, so reformers came to call for the establishment of gov-ernment research institutions that could settle the science and test new tech-nologies. The general thrust was toward a federal agency on the order of what would become the USDA.

Scientific agriculture also indicated the need for founding agricultural schools, a tricky project examined in chapter 6. Early national reformers envi-sioned state-sponsored and forthrightly elite institutions to train the gentry. Their program foundered predictably in the Jacksonian era. During the 1830s and 1840s, agricultural education came to occupy a significant place in the curricula of many rural academies that served the middling class of landown-ing farmers who formed the core constituency of the emerging agricultural reform movement. When reformers renewed calls for specialized institutions, they initially hoped to establish them privately on the model of the academies, but the inability to secure anything close to adequate funding quickly led to intensive efforts to lobby state governments. Several state legislatures responded, but the finances remained shaky at best, in large part because the demand for scientific research raised costs immensely. Reformers therefore turned their attention to the federal government. This was the background for proposals to fund state agricultural colleges with grants from the federal public domain, the basis for the Morrill Land-Grant Act.

Part 4 shows what happened when agricultural reform, ostensibly a national movement but actually dominated by northern voices, took its agenda to Wash-ington, DC. There it ran squarely into the prerogatives of southern planters and the political structures of the slaveholding republic, driving an alliance between agricultural reformers and Republican partisans. Chapter 7 details reformers' efforts to build an effective national lobby modeled on their successes at the state level. Critical to this story was the simultaneous growth of a de facto fed-eral agricultural agency within the Patent Office. From 1849 to 1852, reformers were stymied in their effort to convert this agency into an official agricultural bureau. But they came out of the campaign with a strengthened commitment to building lobbying power through the newly formed United States Agricul-tural Society. Opening a permanent office in the nation's capital, the society created a forum for linking agricultural reformers with legislators and adminis-tration officials. Despite the intent of its top leaders to remain neutral on slavery and to disavow sectional bias, the organization's own membership and the responsiveness of Republican members of Congress drew it increasingly into the Republicans' orbit.

The inevitable and increasingly open clash with the slaveholders becomes apparent in chapter 8 through a comprehensive look at the campaign for the Morrill land-grant bill toward the end of the 1850s. I take considerable pains here to demonstrate that the defense of slavery was the unstated cause of fierce southern resistance. Some readers may find this overkill, but the predominance of slaveholder interests in the antebellum political system remains surprisingly controversial. A comparison of congressional roll call votes in 1858 and 1859, when the bill narrowly passed Congress only to die by presidential veto, with the vote in 1862, when southern Democrats no longer controlled their northern colleagues, clears away any suspicion that partisanship rather than sectionalism determined the course of national agricultural policy. The congressional debates also bear witness to the hegemony of agricultural reformist ideas by this time, as politicians regurgitated reformers' views and paid homage to their influence. On the face of things, this influence promised disproportionate advantage to the South, where agriculture constituted almost the entire economy. Southern obstructionism therefore shows especially clearly how committed most southern leaders were to safeguarding slavery over any other goal. The destruction of the slaveholding republic proved a necessary condition for the creation of new federal agricultural agencies and for the founding of a national developmental state of which they were exemplary parts.

A Note on Sources

Linking agricultural and political change in the antebellum North poses a methodological challenge. The period's political historiography alone is enormous and based on a correspondingly large corpus of primary documents. One could spend a lifetime working through this record. Yet, if one dispenses with the image of the yeoman farmer—traditional and presumably well-understood—there is a lot to learn about agriculture. This study begins by trying to understand agricultural practices and conversations. My primary research has been in agricultural journals and reports, individual farmers' diaries and account books, and agricultural organizations' internal records, often found in obscure archival collections at county historical societies and town libraries. In line with the premise that farmers must have fundamentally shaped the era's political economy simply because they were many, I have been guided by the supposition that understanding agricultural changes would reveal important patterns of power and interest that would remain invisible by pursuing only political sources.

As an illustration of what I mean, consider Lincoln's address at the 1859

Wisconsin State Agricultural Fair. This document is typically read for the way that Lincoln articulated core principles of free labor ideology in reply to southern critiques of northern wage labor.[27] Little attention is paid to the first half of the address, in which Lincoln discussed agriculture. Since he had never much liked farming, Lincoln was conscious that his audience might find much of what he had to say old news "and a large part of the rest possibly already known to be erroneous." Nevertheless, he plowed ahead, and to a modern reader, it might seem that he was too modest. He discussed wheat yields with some precision, noted the perennial problem of fencing costs, explained the benefits of intensive farming on small tracts of land, and made an especially detailed examination of the steam plow, a subject about which he had "thought a good deal, in an abstract way."[28]

This portion of the talk was largely unoriginal but not inept. In a rural society, even a man disinclined to farming knew a good deal about it. It was also thoroughly future-oriented. Lincoln referred only to new ways of farming, and he apologized ahead of time for the possibility that his remarks were out of date. We can infer that general knowledge about agriculture in Lincoln's North was not merely traditional. Instead, it focused on reform, improvement, and change, what Buel called "the new husbandry."[29] Finally, the scope of the imagined change was huge. Lincoln maintained that "the soil has never been pushed up to one-half of its capacity."[30] He next suggested that "educated labor," an impossibility under slavery, would allow northern farmers to intensify their mastery of nature by deploying the benefits of science and technology.

But Lincoln never quite spelled out the connection between slavery in the South and agricultural reform in the free North, and he entirely ignored key agricultural policy proposals. He shifted abruptly from the steam plow to free labor, suggesting his discomfort with the subject of agriculture. Politics was the real point of the address, farming merely a requisite of the occasion. We can surmise, then, that the agricultural reform and improvement Lincoln invoked, which was directly related to the day-to-day activities of the majority of Americans, had some relevance for the deepening sectional crisis. But—and this is where the methodological problem comes into view—we might also conclude that, while a person in Lincoln's position can offer some hints, the full story has to come from other sources. Lincoln knew a fair amount about agriculture "in an abstract way," but he did not much care for the mucky details. He said as much when he declared himself "in some sort a politician, and in no sort a farmer."[31] Buel made the point explicitly to William Seward years earlier. "Your business as a professional man, and as a politician," he observed, "will not have led you much into agricultural reading, or indeed a taste for it."[32]

Perhaps because we are (post)industrials ourselves, our ability to perceive the substratum—the muck—of nineteenth-century politics has been hampered by the reflexive tendency to see the rural and the agricultural as local, traditional, and insular, as forming ways of life somehow always passing from the scene.[33] Generations of critical scholarship have shown, however, that speech and action deemed political are conditioned by other things not accorded the same status. This book proceeds from the premise that we can learn about American politics and governance and the sectional crisis that occasioned their transformation by examining antebellum agriculture with fresh eyes. It draws on sources from the likes of Buel to get at what Lincoln could not quite articulate. The speeches of antebellum politicians are littered with references to farmers and agriculture, but these are only the tip of a buried mountain, platitudes and conventionalities atop a huge mass of agricultural discourse that remains relatively unknown. Only after recovering that discourse, the social movement that produced it, and the political economy in which it was embedded will it be possible to make proper sense of the politicians' actions and rhetoric without falling into timeworn clichés about Jeffersonian agrarianism.

In Medias Res

On a hot and dry September day in 1849, plumes of dust could be observed along a road leading east from the city of Syracuse to a small elevation. Thousands of people were passing on foot and on horseback, in private carriages and public omnibuses, making their way to the ninth annual state agricultural fair. Although only exhibition officials and society members would be admitted on that first day, the grounds were already packed. As many as five thousand new members joined the society at the gates, which entitled them to come in with their families and, it was reported, allowed them to sneak in a few neighbors, too.[1] "But if the first day had witnessed a crowd," a local magazine commented, "what shall we say of the second? Every street and public place was literally crammed with human beings."[2] Overnight thousands more visitors had arrived in all manner of vehicle "loaded to repletion."[3] Among them was the young farmer Benjamin Gue. He had walked eight miles to the train station at Canandaigua, traveled in "cars . . . as full as they could be," and observed "a complete jam" on the Erie Canal, the boats without "a spot on deck or below."[4] As the hotels in Syracuse filled up, town residents opened their homes to visitors, canal boats remained moored to provide makeshift quarters, and special trains conducted the spillover to Oswego, Auburn, and even Utica, over fifty miles away.[5]

Every account of the three-day event stressed the incredible number of

Landscape view of the 1849 New York State Agricultural Fair. Published in *Transactions of the New York State Agricultural Society* 9 (Albany: Weed, Parsons & Co., 1850). Courtesy of the Library Company of Philadelphia.

people—a "dense mass," an "immense assemblage"—and estimates of total attendance ranged from sixty thousand to two hundred thousand. If the published ticket sale figures are near accurate, the actual number was certainly over one hundred thousand, nearly five times Syracuse's population.[6] The New York State Agricultural Society (NYSAS) was highly gratified by the turnout. Its annual report bragged of "a throng beyond the population of a great city—a representation, almost by their individual presence, of the farmers of the State."[7] Others seemed less enthusiastic. "Such a mass of human beings never was collected together before," complained one observer, "and I hope never will be again."[8] Yet just such a mass—perhaps an even larger one—assembled the following year when the state fair came to Rochester. According to the NYSAS report, "although, for the time, they speak of the crowd as so great that they will not again attend, yet, after they return to their homes, it is one of the great events of their lives, and they refer with the deepest interest, to the fact that they were present at the Great Fair, the greatest ever held."[9]

Benjamin Gue was exemplary, devoting to the Syracuse fair several pages of a diary otherwise characterized by perfunctory notes on chores and the weather.[10] It may seem unsurprising that a farm boy like Gue would find the scale of the event astonishing. But so did the famous editor of the *New-York Tribune*, Horace Greeley, who came to report on it personally. The big city newspaperman was stupefied. "After passing three or four hours in wandering among and gazing

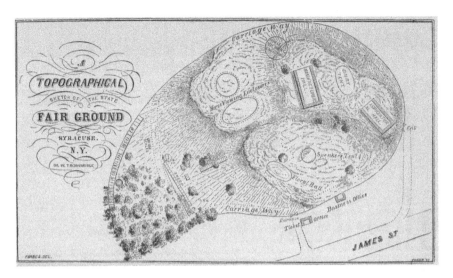

Overview and map of the 1849 New York State Agricultural Fair. Published in *Transactions of the New York State Agricultural Society* 9 (Albany: Weed, Parsons & Co., 1850). Courtesy of the Library Company of Philadelphia.

at this bewildering mass of Live Stock, Implements, Farm Produce, Inventions, &c.," he wrote to his legions of readers, "I have brought away little more than a headache and a more vivid conception of the wonders of Nature and Art, and a more lively idea of that beneficent Future to which Industry is now hastening."[11]

The fairgrounds outside Syracuse enclosed more than twenty acres. The first thing one saw upon entering was the speakers' tent. Just beside it was another, called Floral Hall, which proved among the fair's great attractions. Gue had never seen anything like it and was simply amazed by its "dazzling splendor."[12] Continuing on to the right, one came to three more "halls," two of them long, wooden structures housing the mechanical and agricultural exhibitions; the third, a large tent containing the dairy display. One might then proceed counterclockwise to a pair of rings where judging committees put horses through their paces. Further on still, a series of pens, coops, and stalls displayed various breeds of "improved" livestock. Other animals sought relief from the heat in the shade of a four-acre grove. Surrounding the whole grounds, just inside the fence, was a carriage way affording "a very pleasant drive."[13]

The livestock and implement displays generated tremendous interest. In a typical statement, the *New England Farmer* averred that "the cattle show may, without exaggeration, be said to have been the greatest exhibition of fine stock ever held on this continent."[14] Agricultural editors generally singled out the herd of Devon cattle as the best and most extensive, but the Short Horns, Ayrshires,

Floral Hall at the 1849 New York State Agricultural Fair. Published in *Transactions of the New York State Agricultural Society* 9 (Albany: Weed, Parsons & Co., 1850). Courtesy of the Library Company of Philadelphia.

Herefords and even the native grades were also said to be impressive.[15] The merino sheep belonging to a Vermont breeder drew particular attention. One observer was startled to discover a creature on whom "the wool stood out each side full a foot," obscuring almost all of its features.[16] For some city dwellers, the fair was a rare chance to witness not the machine age, but the latest phase in humanity's ten thousand–year project to redesign animal biology.[17]

Many visitors found the "vast display of improved implements" especially striking.[18] Mechanics' Hall "was filled to overflowing," exclaimed the editor of the *Ohio Cultivator*. "The plows, harrows, cultivators, sowing machines, rollers, horse rakes, straw cutters, reapers, thrashing machines, mills, and cook stoves, might be estimated by *acres*."[19] Greeley considered "this altogether the most important feature of the Fair. A great ox may be reared by a greater fool; but no man who ever worked a year at farming can spend a day among these implements and invitations without being stimulated to *think*."[20] Gue noted that several implements "displayed much ingenuity." Having purchased a name brand plow (the "Cayuga") the previous spring as well as having constructed his own cultivator (a relatively novel device at the time), Gue undoubtedly felt himself competent to give an opinion.[21] Though he did not buy anything, others did. One farm journal editor, at any rate, endorsed the fair precisely because "farmers see, and have an opportunity to purchase, hundreds of new contrivances for abridging human toil."[22]

The fair was more than its official displays. Henry Clay, the "man of men"

Merino sheep at the 1849 New York State Agricultural Fair. Published in *Transactions of the New York State Agricultural Society* 9 (Albany: Weed, Parsons & Co., 1850). Courtesy of the Library Company of Philadelphia.

for Gue, was only the most prominent of such attending notables as Vice President Millard Fillmore and Governor Hamilton Fish.[23] The traditional plowing match and "Floral Ball" added spectacle and entertainment.[24] More edifying were the scheduled discussions of sheep husbandry and agricultural schooling. The latter, Greeley thought, "cannot fail to awaken a general and lively attention to the great topic it presented."[25] The annual address was delivered by Professor James F. W. Johnston of Edinburgh, one of the world's foremost agricultural chemists. Though he lectured on technical subjects for nearly two hours toward the end of an exhausting exposition, Johnston drew such a large audience that Greeley and many others could not get close enough to hear. Afterward, the various award committees announced their decisions, winning animals were paraded before spectators, and, finally, a sale of stock, implements, and grain closed the fair. Even then events had not quite concluded. The next day, the North American Pomological Society convened its second annual meeting on the grounds.[26]

Just outside the enclosure, an army of "publicans, porters, and purveyors" supplemented the official program. Fanny Kemble Butler, the English actress recently returned to the United States to finalize a high-profile divorce, gave dramatic readings of Shakespeare, while a kind of Ferris wheel provided fairgoers with dramatic views of the surrounding country. Some agricultural reformers denounced the juxtaposition of such "spurious broods of auxiliaries" with the fair's official program. The result, they complained, was an "incongruous mass of utility and nonsense, things befitting the occasion and things utterly

View of the 1854 Pennsylvania State Agricultural Fair (detail). Courtesy of the Philadelphia History Museum at the Atwater Kent.

subversive of it." Yet most visitors presumably enjoyed it all without qualms.[27] The *Albany Evening Journal*, one of New York's most important political newspapers, deemed the exhibition "more than successful—it was triumphant." A local magazine declared it "undoubtedly the greatest gathering of the kind ever known in the New World."[28]

Similar gatherings soon followed with regularity. The Indiana state fair of 1851 reprised events at Syracuse almost exactly, the town of Lafayette suddenly peopled to overflowing.[29] The 1854 Pennsylvania state exhibition reportedly attracted a hundred thousand visitors.[30] In 1859, a young man tramping about eastern Ohio observed a train "presenting the appearance of a mass of human beings"; arriving later at Zanesville, he witnessed streets "very much crowded with visitors, 40,000 being the estimated number inside the fair grounds today."[31] That same year, the exhibition of the United States Agricultural Society in Chicago featured more than forty enclosed acres, 150,000 square feet of roofed display space, two steam-powered presses, a telegraph office, and $20,000 in premiums—the combination attracting a single-day attendance of fifty thousand.[32] Meanwhile, the NYSAS fairs continued to grow apace even as, across the state, the annual exhibitions of the American Institute of the City of New York, which included plowing matches, cattle shows, and substantial displays of farm products and agricultural implements, had been drawing crowds in the hundreds of thousands since the mid-1840s.[33]

The state agricultural fairs of the 1850s were major events akin to revivalist camp meetings and "monster" partisan rallies. According to one farm editor, they were "justly looked upon as the most important gatherings of our citizens."[34] It is true that the absolute numbers are not so impressive compared with the millions who would visit world's fairs only a few decades later. But the ways that contemporaries described these midcentury agricultural exhibitions suggest an almost overwhelming subjective experience, a common encounter with superlative bigness. How did these events come about? Who organized and attended them? What did they mean? Above all, what did they do?

PART ONE

RISE OF THE AGRICULTURAL
REFORM MOVEMENT

CHAPTER ONE

The Limits of Patrician Agricultural Reform

Forty years before the New York State Agricultural Society's Syracuse fair, the patriot and agricultural reformer, David Humphreys, staged an event more modest in form but no less ambitious in vision. Humphreys had been an aide-de-camp to George Washington during the American Revolution and afterward a diplomat to Portugal and Spain. He returned in 1802 to Connecticut, where he wrote lyric odes to national economic development and established a woolens manufactory supplied by merino sheep specially shipped from Iberia. In 1810, if the newspaper report can be believed, his employees asked to celebrate Independence Day by doing something "useful." Humphreys decided on a plowing match, an old English custom that would soon become central to American agricultural fairs. Accordingly, on July 4, farmers commenced the ceremonial plowing early in the morning while woodworkers erected a "shepherd's lodge," some forty apprentices "dressed in neat and comely uniforms" performed "other agricultural operations," and unspecified persons, perhaps the wives of the laborers, prepared a feast. Among all the busy people—"each at his station, co-operating without noise, as if animated with the same spirit"— not a single name was mentioned other than Humphreys, who appeared as the moving will behind this near-literal performance of nation building. With an ironically pointed toast, Humphreys closed the day: "*Independence. Deeds—*

not words.—Let those who appear to love their country prove it by actions rather than by toasts and declamations."[1]

It would take both deeds and words to remake American agriculture. The Humphreys plowing match was a step, but a halting one, not quite the right combination. Independence had transformed the colonial elite into a national leadership class deeply conscious of the gaps that yawned between their nascent republic and the imperial metropoles of Europe.[2] The sense of backwardness implicated agriculture as much as anything else. Writing in 1786 to a renowned English agricultural improver, George Washington deprecated American farming as "unproductive" and even "ruinous." Conversely, the Pennsylvania patrician George Logan was "astonished" by the farming "perfection" he observed in Britain.[3] For these men, American nation building required adopting and adapting the techniques of the European agricultural revolution. Doing so also promised to buttress their own personal wealth and standing. If there was a conflict of interests here, they failed to see it, accustomed as they were to managing both public and private affairs. That failure would prove the political undoing of agricultural reform's first phase.

The patricians began by establishing agricultural societies modeled on British counterparts. These organizations tried to disseminate technical information about farming by publishing occasional volumes of essays, but they were largely restricted to elite circles. During the 1810s, however, several societies began holding agricultural fairs where improvement could be demonstrated, not just discussed. The Humphreys plowing match was an early and partial iteration of this development. The fairs proved a critical institutional innovation that created a new type of popular festival designed to harness individual ambition to larger goals of national economic development. Ordinary farmers responded with considerable enthusiasm. For the first time, the agricultural societies had real influence.

Almost immediately, however, they fell victim to their own success. Popularity led state governments to provide modest subsidies for the fairs, but it also brought scrutiny of the tensions between reformers' private interests and their claims to public service. Those at the head of the reform project failed to grasp the new situation, continuing to expect a deference that ordinary people were less inclined to give. In an emerging democracy undergoing rapid capitalist development, the entire agricultural reform project came to look like an elitist scheme to leverage government resources in support of privilege. The deference-to-democracy politics that characterized the transition from the early national period to the Jacksonian era thus killed the patricians' agricultural reform project. But the patricians had not failed entirely. They had hit upon the agricultural fair as the key institutional innovation, and they had positioned agricultural reform as a matter of national development grounded in the promise of science and technology. The popular movement that began to emerge in the 1830s built on these foundations.

Agricultural reform thus constituted a basic facet of American economic nationalism throughout the nineteenth century. Less visible than "internal improvements" to roads, canals, and harbors, it offered a deeper measure of transformation. As one agricultural society argued, "It is vain to give facility to transportation, unless the products of the country are increased by good husbandry."[4] In a nation of farmers, national development had to begin on the farm.

The Early National "Promoting" Societies

Agricultural "promotion" societies began to appear shortly after the Revolution. Membership in these groups was highly selective. The founders of the Philadelphia Society for Promoting Agriculture (PSPA), established in 1785, included four signers of the Declaration of Independence as well as several senators, congressmen, and army officers. The New York Society for the Promotion of Agriculture, Arts, and Manufactures—later renamed the Society for the Promotion of Useful Arts (SPUA, 1791)—was directed by powerful landholders such as Chancellor Robert L. Livingston and Stephen Van Rensselaer. By 1803, "scarcely a State in the Union" lacked a comparable organization.[5]

Social exclusivity limited rather than enhanced agricultural societies' reach in the United States, unlike in Britain. The early American organizations acted much like private scientific societies. Working within the tradition of polite Enlightenment science, members read about European practices, conducted experiments, and reported their findings in learned papers that were occasionally collected and published. "To the extent that they reached out to the public," one historian finds, "it was to encourage those enlightened people who happened to fall outside their circle of acquaintances."[6] Elite Europeans who did this sort of thing tended also to control vast estates on which large-scale developmental experiments could be initiated by command. In Scotland, for instance, agricultural improvers engaged in what Frederik Albritton Jonsson calls "civic cameralism," the use of civic associations to coordinate massive socioenvironmental projects.[7] But in the United States, only slaveholders possessed a comparable degree of social control, and even they rarely possessed the land, capital, and political power of high-ranking aristocrats.

The PSPA exemplified the ambitions of patrician agricultural reformers and also the obstacles that they encountered. The organization was conceived by John Beale Bordley, a man groomed for public office who decided instead to establish a model plantation on Maryland's Eastern Shore. Bordley was a classic Enlightenment type. When not reading about the serious business of history, science, and agriculture, he "amused himself with geometry and algebra." After early efforts to communicate his agricultural insights to popular audiences proved disappointing, he sought out "men of property and education" for more elevated conversation. The class of people he had in mind is suggested by his essay advising landholders on the management of hired laborers and tenants.[8]

The men who joined Bordley in founding the PSPA were, like him, patricians accustomed to leadership. Most were also staunch Federalists. Richard Peters, who would soon emerge as the organization's leading figure, earned a reputation for agricultural expertise by experimenting with crop rotation schemes and pioneering the use of gypsum as a soil amendment. Having served on the Board of War during the Revolution, he later worked to suppress democracy's perceived excesses while upholding paternalist privileges and obligations.[9] Similarly, Timothy Pickering, who held cabinet appointments in both the Washington and Adams administrations, was a Federalist don and a committed agricultural reformer. An early and active member of the PSPA, Pickering would later return to his native New England, where he remained a bitter foe of all things Jeffersonian long after retiring from politics.[10]

Not everyone in the PSPA was a Federalist. In 1788, for instance, the society heard an "ardent democrat" deliver a paper on farming practices in Delaware.[11] The invitation had perhaps come from George Logan. Like Peters, Logan was a wealthy landowner known for his work adapting British crop rotation principles to American conditions. Unlike Peters, he was an arch-Jeffersonian who affected the style and politics of a plain yeoman. During the 1790s, he authored fiery denunciations of Federalism in leading Jeffersonian papers. By this time, he and his allies had broken with the PSPA and formed an ostensibly more inclusive agricultural society for the county rather than merely the city of Philadelphia.[12] In the wake of this departure, Logan espoused a newly politicized agricultural reform that seemed pitched to popular audiences. He now argued that "the yeomanry" should organize "not only for promoting agricultural knowledge . . . but to stimulate and encourage each other to support their rights as men."[13] He thus proposed a democratic vision of agricultural reform.

In practice, however, Logan seems to have been more concerned with his own quixotic rendering of republican virtue. He is best remembered for taking it upon himself to personally negotiate a resolution to the Quasi-War with France, an act that only a man who regarded public policy as his personal domain could have contemplated. Congress responded with the Logan Act, which to this day bars private citizens from interfering in foreign relations. Logan's efforts toward agricultural organizing were better founded, but they too could seem incongruous. For instance, his alternative to the PSPA averred that "no man shall be eligible as a member, but a farmer."[14] Yet Logan was himself a physician trained in Europe, not to mention the proprietor of an estate that William Penn had personally granted to his grandfather—he was hardly a farmer in the plain sense of the word. The term thus functioned as a kind of republican credentialing device.

In contrast to Logan's virtue politics, the PSPA's Federalist establishment of Bordley, Peters, and Pickering proposed a thoroughly paternalist vision of agricultural reform. In 1794, they authored a petition calling on the Pennsylvania legislature to charter a state agricultural society that would keep the government "informed on a subject so important to the prosperity of the country." The new organization, headquartered in Philadelphia, would open branch offices integrated with local schools. "Thus the youth in our country will effectually, and at a cheap rate, be grounded in the knowledge of this important subject," which would not only improve agriculture but "assist good government."[15]

The state legislature ignored this visionary effort at panoptic state building. Despite its elite connections, the PSPA's divided leadership and lack of a popular base gave it little capacity to exert political influence. The organization was, in fact, on the point of dissolution, its membership rent by the break with Logan and harried by the seasonal yellow fever epidemics that devastated Philadelphia starting in 1793. Having already ceased regular meetings in that year, it suspended operations entirely soon after the petition, not to reconstitute itself for over a decade.[16]

When the society regrouped in 1805, the national political landscape had changed dramatically. Federalists were on the retreat and ascendant Republicans had begun to factionalize. Although George Logan never rejoined the PSPA, his place within the splintering Jeffersonian coalition indicates that he remained as much a "political squire" as his Federalist peers. In 1798, Logan must have shocked his well-bred friends when he spoke before Philadelphia's radical Tammany Society. Four years later, however, he worked to block the nomination of the Tammany congressional candidate, who represented the interests of artisans and tradesmen. Like other Jeffersonian agricultural reformers who indulged in the rhetoric of radical democracy, Logan chose the "Quid" brand of Democratic-Republicanism, "an alliance of politics and enterprise" that rendered economic development in populist terms while perpetuating the leadership of gentlemen.[17] In the first decade of the 1800s, then, agricultural reform remained more or less where it had been twenty years earlier, a patrician's game struggling for an audience.

Merino Mania

A sudden craze for imported sheep helped agricultural reform move beyond patrician circles. Contemporaries called it "merino mania," a mad rush to purchase the Spanish breed known for its fine and bounteous wool. The spread of the merinos, the press generated to publicize their value, and the novel ways they were exhibited in public made the agricultural reform project newly visible. The episode engaged ordinary farmers in ways the promoting societies' learned essays and enlightened paternalism never could. The same promotional logic, however, exposed the inherent conflicts of interest within a developmental program that promised an unproblematic alignment of individual and national benefits.

Merinos were a sought-after biological technology. The shifting center of woolens manufacturing had long tracked political power in Europe, from northern Italy to the Low Countries to England. Spain, meanwhile, kept a lock on a unique form of the raw material, exporting its merinos' fine wool while barring the sale to foreigners of the animals themselves. During the eighteenth century, the Hapsburg monarchs made occasional royal gifts that allowed a handful of small merino flocks to become established elsewhere in Europe. In a mercantilist age, these sheep, too, remained closely guarded. But the wars of the French Revolution disordered the continent and loosened restrictions, allowing several Americans to obtain merinos for shipment home. Napoleon's subsequent invasion of the Iberian Peninsula then led desperate Spanish officials to authorize the export of tens of thousands of merinos, commencing a historic scattering of the country's treasured flocks to the outer edges of the Anglo-settler world. From the United States to South Africa to Australia, the production of a raw material long associated with a critical phase of European economic development began to migrate away to the imperial margins.

Merino mania in the United States began with David Humphreys and Robert R. Livingston. Serving as diplomats to Spain and France, respectively, in 1802, each took advantage of official connections to circumvent restrictions on merino exports. Back home, they bred sheep for sale, let rams for stud services, and manufactured their own cloth. A few others did likewise. For example, the French émigrés E. I. DuPont and Peter Bauduy obtained merinos through their own ties to European elites.[18] But Livingston and Humphreys added a public promotion campaign. In a letter published by the Massachusetts Society for Promoting Agriculture (MSPA), Humphreys argued that "every civilized nation in the world" understood the need for domestic woolens manufacturing. "How long are we to continue thus like colonies dependent on a mother country?" he demanded.[19] This and similar missives by Livingston were widely reprinted.[20] By 1809, the pair had gotten President James Madison and other public figures to set a conspicuous example by wearing "elegant suits" made from their fabrics.[21]

Interest in the merinos grew quickly. Purebred animals were probably too expensive for ordinary farmers to purchase, but they could be had on shares or crossed with native breeds. The PSPA's Reuben Haines III, for instance, bought several merinos that he immediately "put out to the halves" with a nearby farmer.[22] Wealthy gentlemen sometimes lent out merino rams without charge in order to promote local agricultural development, especially if they planned to build a woolens mill and wished to have a steady supply of wool. State bounties, arranged by merino promoters, could also help. In one case, a New York farmer paid fifty dollars to hire a full-blooded ram from a breeder in Vermont, then immediately recouped the cost by collecting a bounty offered by his own state "to the person who should introduce the first Merino buck into each county."[23]

The mania took off in 1807 with President Jefferson's embargo. By shutting down much of the country's trade with Europe, the policy redirected capital into domestic textile manufacturing, thus promising to conjure new markets for raw wool. Merino prices skyrocketed. In only three years, the value of a purebred ram rose tenfold and a true asset bubble formed, driven by expectations of rising sheep prices rather than by any underlying demand for wool. The bubble began to deflate in 1810 when another American diplomat took advantage of the war in Spain to ship thousands of merinos home. Others followed his example, and by the end of 1811 as many as twenty thousand had disembarked in American ports (figure 1.1). With the market suddenly flooded, prices collapsed. Reuben Haines apparently thought this an opportune time to

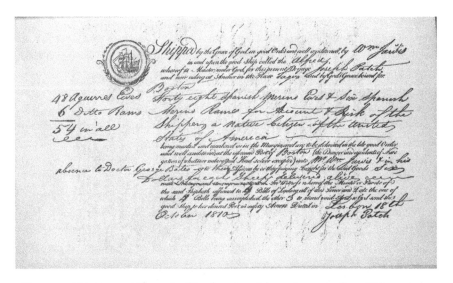

Figure 1.1. Shipping certificate for fifty-four Spanish merinos sent from Lisbon to Boston. At the height of the merino mania in 1810, the American merchant and consul in Lisbon, William Jarvis, purchased and shipped thousands of the Spanish sheep to the United States. The ones enumerated here may have been destined for his own operation in Vermont, which helped turn the state into a center of wool production and sheep breeding. Courtesy of the Library of Congress.

buy. "I should much prefer seeing all thy estate invested in Merino sheep than Bank stock," he advised a cousin in 1813.[24] But two years later, the Peace of Ghent brought a second flood, this time of cheap British textiles, which undercut American manufacturers, reduced domestic demand for wool, and further depressed merino prices. Reports soon appeared of farmers butchering their stock for mutton.

The mania, while it lasted, was driven by a cascade of print. The famed Virginia agricultural reformer Edmund Ruffin recalled later that during the craze "there were more discussions, and more pamphlets—to say nothing of newspaper out-pourings, than enough to elicit all the information on the subject."[25] The MSPA, for example, reprinted an English lecture on "The History of the Merino Sheep in Europe" and sponsored the translation of a French work on the subject.[26] Around the same time, Chancellor Livingston authored his own manual, aiming to "combine information and amusement . . . in a style . . . to satisfy a plain farmer."[27]

This promotional literature casually mingled patriotism and self-interest. Livingston assured his readers of "the advantage that would accrue both to themselves and their country" from investing in merinos. "What is all farming but an advance made with a view to future profit?" he added.[28] A pamphlet from the Merino Society of the Middle States of North America simply declared that "public spirit appears to be nothing more than another name for the enterprize [*sic*] of individuals." Though it explicitly declined "to say what we will do to introduce national improvement," it promised that "if we gain it for ourselves, we will share it with the nation."[29] After the bubble burst, these kinds of claims were easy to ridicule. "Merino sheep at 1500 and 2000 apiece," commented one newspaper, "is a story that savours of something besides patriotism."[30] All the same, the merinos had come to stay and made a valuable upgrade to American livestock. It seems that in 1860 most of the country's sheep descended in part from the importations made during the mania.[31] Throughout the rural North, this progeny could be seen on grassy hillsides once covered by forests, an unmistakable sign of economic, ecological, and social change.

One index of the transformation was the renewed interest in taxing dogs. Canine depredations became costlier after merinos raised the value of American sheep flocks. New laws levied poll taxes on dogs and authorized the summary killing of unlicensed, "worthless" animals, in the process raising funds to compensate sheep owners for losses. Thomas Jefferson, among others, supported these measures, avowing his "hostility to dogs" and his readiness to "join in any plan of exterminating the whole race."[32] Remarkably, dog tax politics roiled farming communities across the country for more than a century. Petitions for and against the duties inundated county governments and state legislatures, which responded by passing and repealing them, raising and reducing them, extending and contracting them—in short, by going back and forth on the matter.[33] The controversy was an occasion of endless parody—"the humble petition of sundry Puppies," etc.—but it was also a real dispute pitting sheep owners against a cross-class assortment of rural folk who kept dogs for hunting, companionship, and guard duty. The geographical sweep and historical endurance of the matter hints at how agricultural reform initiatives, such as the upgrading of livestock, entailed ramifying social changes.[34]

The most important development to come out of the merino mania was the agricultural fair, which would quickly become a basic institution of northern rural society. Like other aspects of the reform project, agricultural exhibitions originated in Europe and became known to Americans through the reports of diplomats, merchants, and travelers. Most influential were the festive sheep shearings put on by prominent English aristocrat-improvers. Several members of American agricultural promotion societies attended these events in person during the 1790s. Though rooted in long-standing rural traditions, the sheep shearings were distinguished by the awarding of prizes, or "premiums," for excellent specimens. They thus aimed to leverage promotional display for commercial agricultural development.[35]

Similar events soon appeared in the United States. Livingston and George W. P. Custis, the favorite grandson of George Washington, established famous annual sheep shearings on their respective estates. Celebrated in the press as patriotic endeavors, the shearings remained grounded in their hosts' private wealth and personal interests.[36] This was true in a straightforward pecuniary sense: one visitor recalled being led by Livingston "ostensibly to the Sheep Shearing tho in reality to an extensive sale of Sheep at the tune of ten thousand Dollars in One hour."[37] But it was also true more indirectly, for patrician leadership was as much on display as the sheep (figure 1.2). It was hardly a coincidence that the shearings were introduced on the two great bastions of lordly prerogative in the early United States, the Virginia Tidewater plantation and the Hudson River Valley manor. Custis and Livingston presided over these festivals as quasi-aristocrats, treating their guests to "sumptuous" feasts prepared "with a liberality approaching almost to profusion."[38] Not coincidentally, patrician power meant that New York and Virginia remained among the least democratic states of the early Republic.[39] The rhetoric of national improvement worked to legitimize that fact by coloring patrician leadership in patriotic hues. Custis, for instance, framed the shearings as acts of public virtue by staging them under "the tent of Washington . . . this memorable canvas commemorative of the revolution and its immortal hero."[40]

In an 1809 letter to PSPA secretary James Mease, Livingston spelled out a scheme that exemplifies how thoroughly he identified the general good with his own financial interests. Mease had asked why prices for merino wool were higher

Figure 1.2. Chancellor Robert R. Livingston, patrician agricultural reformer. Courtesy of the New York Public Library.

in New York than in Delaware. Livingston answered that a "small and irregular" supply could not justify investment in the manufacturing technology to create demand. In turn, farmers would not invest in the skills to increase the supply. How to escape this classic underdevelopment trap? "It may be useful to mention to you," Livingston continued nonchalantly, "one of the great causes of the anxiety to have fine wool, which is now diffusing throughout this state." A year earlier, the New York legislature had created a system of premiums to encourage raw wool production at the behest of the Society for the Promotion of the Useful Arts, which would select the winners. Conveniently, Livingston was president of the society. No surprise, then, as he related modestly, that "last year, the first prize for domestic manufactured cloth was adjudged to that made from my ¾ bred wool," while "the first manufacturer's prize was taken by one to whom I sold my half-bred wool." No surprise, either, that Livingston thought the legislature had acted "very wisely." In one fell stroke, he had set the machinery of state to making him a market and promoting his personal brand. Livingston never betrayed a misgiving that something might seem improper about his orchestrating public expenditures for private gain. Neither did Mease. Himself the owner of many merinos, Mease published Livingston's letter "in the hope that the wise example exhibited by the state of New-York, will be followed by every state in the Union, and especially by our own."[41]

In both an economic and a social sense, then, early agricultural reform exemplified the knot of private and national interest that John Lauritz Larson has characterized as the "designs of the monied gentry."[42] Nowhere was this more apparent than in the merino mania. But the very success of the merino campaign allowed those designs to slip their bounds. The result was a sudden flowering of popular interest in agricultural reform that was sustained by the critical organizational innovation of the agricultural fair.

The "Modern" Agricultural Fair

The first "modern" agricultural fair took place in 1811 in the Berkshire hills of Massachusetts. Its self-proclaimed inventor was Elkanah Watson, a classic "projector" type forever chasing new visions on future horizons. During the Revolution, Watson associated with important people in Europe and also won, then lost, a fortune in trade. Afterward, he wound his way to Albany, where he immersed himself in projects without end. He advocated for schools, canals, and rural industries, pushed aggressively for urban improvement, and earned himself the epithet of "that dam'd paving Yankee." He rarely met a developmental plan to which he could not sign on.[43] The agricultural fair was of a piece with this activity.

In his early efforts to shape public affairs, Watson succeeded through sheer indefatigability and canny use of the press, authoring numerous opinion pieces under a welter of pseudonyms. At the same time, he attached himself to a series of powerful patricians. Initially siding with Federalists, he later aligned himself with Quid Republicans, whose penchant for coalition building around development projects suited him perfectly. Watson was a man perched between eras. On the one hand, he understood the new power of the anonymous printed word for hustling popular support behind a developmental agenda. On the other hand, he wanted nothing more than to be a country squire, a man from whom authority flowed as irresistibly as a spring freshet. To be sure, Watson stood high on the social ladder. But in an era when fine grades of social distinction still mattered, he was not quite on the upper rung.

By 1807, Watson found himself "completely infected with the Spanish Sheep mania."[44] He obtained a pair of purebred merinos from Livingston's flock, moved to Pittsfield, Massachusetts, to establish a woolens manufactory, and followed Livingston's playbook by attempting to organize an agricultural society that would encourage local farmers to supply him with merino wool. But Watson was not really on Livingston's level, and his plans provoked apathy or open scorn. "How truly laughable it is to hear those who are daily dashing in all the pomp of Eastern pageantry," observed a local, "recommending . . . a plain and simple *home-spun* garb."[45] To turn public opinion in his favor, Watson decided to display his merinos for all to see the breed's advantages. That he did so "under the great elm tree in the public square" rather than on his own estate underscores the distance between him and the likes of Livingston. But this, too, failed. Watson now realized that he needed to allow the community a real role in the proceedings. The next event, organized under the auspices of the newly founded Berkshire County Agricultural Society, included cattle, which were more important to the local economy. The success of this exhibition led Watson to claim the title of agricultural fair inventor.[46]

In reality, Watson was just one among many moving toward the emerging model of the county agricultural fair. According to the MSPA's John Lowell, "many of us had visited the European shows, and the subject of introducing them had been discussed" years before the Pittsfield fairs.[47] In 1811, for instance, the Bucks County (PA) Society for Promoting Agriculture and Domestic Manufactures held an exhibition of cattle, horses, and sheep.[48] Between 1809 and 1812, the Columbian Agricultural Society held half a dozen semiannual exhibitions in the District of Columbia that drew the attendance of members of Congress and considerable press coverage. Reports in the *National Intelligencer* and other newspapers circulated widely, reaching Pittsfield in the summer of 1810—after Watson's initial sheep shearing but before the larger exhibition.[49]

Watson's signal contribution to this broader movement was his talent as a showman and publicist. Introducing a measure of spectacle, ritual, and "éclat," he gave the fairs an appealing cultural coherence. This included an opening prayer, a procession, and a formal address; music, singing, and dancing aimed at attracting the young; a variety of contests—from plowing matches to horse races to trials of oxen's hauling strength—that appealed to male farmers; premiums for household manufactures and cooking designed to gain women's participation; and a bevy of sideshows and diversions that would culminate decades later in the phenomenon of the midway.[50] Watson also missionized tirelessly. He authored a series of articles and pamphlets to promote what he called the "modern Berkshire system," helped organize several county societies in New England and New York, and visited others to lend his personal imprimatur to their efforts. Though some resented his self-importance, most recognized his effectiveness. "You have hearers," the PSPA's Richard Peters wrote him in 1819, "whereas I have been for some fifty years a stationary preacher and until lately have delivered discourses to empty benches."[51]

After the War of 1812, the trend toward fair-holding agricultural societies took off, and the dynamics of agricultural reform began to change. Between

1817 and 1819, local agricultural societies were founded and held fairs in New York's Otsego, Jefferson, Albany, Rensselaer, Queens, Cayuga, and Oneida counties.[52] At about the same time, the MSPA initiated two decades of its popular Brighton "cattle shows," and the PSPA started planning its own event.[53] Fair-holding societies also appeared in Pennsylvania, Ohio, Maine, Connecticut, and New Hampshire.[54] In 1821, an agricultural exhibition in New York City drew six thousand attendees. The PSPA's Philadelphia show of the following year brought an estimated ten thousand.[55] By 1825, the MSPA estimated nearly fifty agricultural fairs throughout the country, some of them already well-established annual rites.[56] "We do not suppose, at this time," commented the *Connecticut Courant* ahead of the fifth Hartford County fair in 1821, "any thing need be said to convince the public of the beneficial tendency of this institution."[57]

These agricultural exhibitions differed from colonial market fairs. Rather than facilitating exchange, they were designed as public displays with an expressly didactic, developmental purpose.[58] The heart of the distinction was the concept of "emulation." According to the great compendium of Enlightenment thought, the *Encyclopédie*, emulation was a "noble and generous passion which, admiring merit, beautiful things and the actions of others, attempts to imitate them, or even to surpass them, striving to this end courageously and with honorable and virtuous principle."[59] It was a kind of collegial rivalry that spurred great achievements, melding the glory of the individual with that of the community. The idea went back to antiquity, but as early as the seventeenth century it came to be seen as a mechanism for aligning individuals' behavior with larger aims of state.[60] It was a powerful concept in early national America. John Adams believed that "emulation next to self-preservation will forever be the great spring of human action."[61] Various institutions applied the principle. For example, as new rural academies sprang up after independence, educators argued that the innate thirst for distinction could be made to redound to the common good by fostering a culture of praise and reward for acts beneficial to the nation. This joining of personal ambition to national purpose validated the aspirations of teacher and student alike in rural settings where individual drive could conflict with traditional familial expectations.[62]

Agricultural societies mobilized emulation similarly. Offering medals, certificates, silver plate, cash prizes, and other "premiums," they created a system of public distinctions intended to awaken spectators' impulse for social recognition. Whereas the old promoting societies simply advertised occasional premiums without much additional hoopla, the fairs turned the premium system into a social and media event. As one reformer observed, without an exhibition, "the agriculturist has rarely a witness of his labours to excite his pride."[63] The fairs drew spectators and generated press coverage. By thus making farming into

"an object of public attention, and a means of obtaining celebrity," they constituted a new mechanism for reaching the "retired and unknown farmer."[64] In
turn, argued Timothy Pickering, "exciting emulation among our farmers will
lead to important improvements in our husbandry."[65] Fairs on the emulatory
principle were to be a mainspring of rural development.

Premiums required funds, which agricultural societies sought to obtain
from state governments. The Massachusetts General Court proved especially
responsive. It contributed heavily to the MSPA's endowment, which by 1813
amounted to $20,000, then added an annual allowance to finance the society's
Brighton exhibitions, and later extended benefits to county agricultural societies.[66] Other state legislatures, though not nearly so munificent, also kicked in
funds for premium lists. New Hampshire granted $100 in 1817 to each of two
county agricultural societies, enlarging and extending the grant to five societies
the following year. Though a meager subsidy, it was enough to draw up a premium list and bring out local farmers in significant numbers. New York's agricultural reformers pulled off the biggest coup. In 1818, the state legislature
created a Board of Agriculture composed of delegates from county societies and
provided the combined network with $20,000 over two years.[67]

The following year a major financial panic brought the national economy
to a standstill, but, surprisingly, states did not reduce agricultural aid. In the
midst of the worst depression on record, New York actually extended the Board
of Agriculture for another four years and pledged the "staggering sum" of
$40,000, while Pennsylvania enacted agricultural subsidies for the first time.[68]
The continued support was due to the fact that northern agricultural societies
had become prominent venues for articulating a program of economic recovery
through government-sponsored promotion of the "home market," a topic covered in chapter 3. Here it is important to note two things. First, agricultural
reform was now widely understood as an essential component of national economic development. Wool had a special place in this vision because it so clearly
linked agricultural improvement with domestic manufacturing. Second, government support, even if modest, strongly encouraged interest in agricultural
reform and led to the founding of many local agricultural societies. By the early
1820s, then, the success of the fair with the infusion of subsidies meant that the
agricultural reform project seemed poised to take off.

The Patrician Project Falters

Public fairs and public subsidies drew agricultural reform out into the open,
where it could become popular and effect widespread changes in American
farming practice. But the reform project's new leaders were, like Watson, still
wedded to a patrician imagination of personal authority. Consequently, they
failed to recognize how publicity and the decline of deference in postrevolu-

tionary America would subject their affairs to new kinds of critical scrutiny. In short order they squandered the public mandate they had briefly won for agricultural reform.

Grievances against the ways that agricultural societies awarded premiums fueled an almost immediate backlash against state subsidies. The main complaint was that most of the premiums invariably went to the richest farmers. Especially galling were the prizes won by country gentleman who obtained results by lavishly uneconomical means. This subverted the premiums' ostensible purpose, turning them into mere displays of social power. In a few cases society officers seem to have been guilty of outright fraud by conspiring to distribute premiums among themselves. Some society members understood that if greater inclusivity were not quickly achieved, public repudiation was sure to follow. Having taken government money and encouraged popular participation, gentlemen reformers could not expect the kind of deference they had once taken for granted.[69]

The New York Board of Agriculture soon came under attack as an elitist institution of little use to ordinary farmers. The charges hit home because the board appeared to be merely a reorganization of Livingston's patrician SPUA, clothed with state authority and paid for out of the public treasury. Patronizing statements by board president, Stephen Van Rensselaer, the closest thing in New York to a genuine aristocrat, that the board "elevated the condition of the yeomanry in their own estimation," could not have helped.[70] The new party politics taking shape in the 1820s would not support the public funding of what looked like a network of gentlemen's clubs. In 1823, a New York Assembly dominated by Martin Van Buren's Bucktail faction overwhelmingly voted to repeal the board's authorizing legislation. Senate inaction prevented the board's immediate elimination, but two years later the legislature simply declined to renew it.[71]

The story in Pennsylvania paralleled the one in New York, with an ironic twist. In 1823, a merchant-turned-cattle-breeder named John Hare Powel, upset that the PSPA had failed to reach beyond its elite membership to a wider audience, established a rival organization called the Pennsylvania Agricultural Society (PAS). Like Logan before him, Powel portrayed himself as an anti-elitist, promising that this new organization would be "composed of practical farmers" and reject "abstruse scientific disquisitions."[72] He soon convinced the legislature to redirect appropriations slated for the PSPA to his own group. The PAS then put together a well-attended fair in Chester County and published a compilation of practical farming essays. Yet the supposedly egalitarian association was quickly unmasked. Not only was its membership wealthier than its rhetoric suggested, but Powel himself kept winning most of the premiums. At one exhibition, every single one of the prize-earning neat cattle either belonged to

TABLE I.I.
New Members in the Middlesex (MA)
Agricultural Society, by Decade

	New members
1820–29	441
1830–39	62
1840–49	276
1850–59	238

Source: Bound manuscript membership book,
1819–61, MAS-CFL, series 3, box 2, item 1.
 Note: The membership book records the names
of members and the date on which they received
their "diploma." The figures for the 1850s are
probably understated, as the dates are listed less
precisely for this decade, and many members are
listed with no date at all.

Powel or originally came from his herd. It was Livingston's wool premium scheme
in a new guise. But times had changed, as the fall of the New York Board indicated. With nearly $4,000 of state funds already expended, farmers became
incensed at a policy that seemed to transfer tax dollars out of their pockets and
into the accounts of wealthy gentlemen. By the end of 1825, a massive wave of
petitions convinced the Pennsylvania legislature to abrogate agricultural funding entirely.[73] A broadly similar scenario played out in New Hampshire, where
in 1824 the legislature rescinded aid to the state's agricultural organizations
amid charges that they were political vehicles for "great agriculturists."[74]

Only in Massachusetts did subsidies and fairs continue without interrup-
tion. But even here there is evidence that elitism undermined agricultural societies' popularity from the mid-1820s through the subsequent decade. In 1823,
Theodore Sedgwick warned of "a lurking jealousy and ill will toward these
societies" as a result of their tendency to attract "the more opulent farmers."[75]
This resentment appears on the books of the Middlesex Agricultural Society
as a sharp decline in new memberships (table 1.1). The society added hundreds
of members in the 1820s, most of them in two large batches during the fall of
1820 and the fall of 1824, presumably around fair time. Thereafter, however,
new memberships slowed to a trickle until a revival occurred in the 1840s and
1850s. Perhaps in response to this downward trend, the society's trustees decided in December 1829 to introduce a premium category "for the best cultivated Farm, regard being had to the quantity of produce, *manner and expense*
of cultivation, and general appearance of the Farm." By creating an award for
cost-effective farm management, the trustees may have sought to open competition to middling as well as "opulent" farmers.[76] Yet the move did nothing to
change the stagnant rate of new members until broader conditions became more

favorable to a resurgent agricultural reform movement roughly a decade later. From 1823 to 1839, no new county agricultural societies were established anywhere in Massachusetts, clear evidence of stalled progress.[77]

Agricultural societies relied heavily on state subsidies in their initial years. When public aid was withdrawn, most simply ceased to exist.[78] At this point, the patrician agricultural reform project faltered irrevocably. What remained was a general impulse toward agricultural reform in search of new organizational and rhetorical structures that could reconcile developmental nationalism with emerging democratic norms.

During the 1830s, the creation of the Second Party System shaped agricultural reform's comeback in important ways. Anti-elitist rhetoric and small-government policy principles infused the Democratic Party. While many individual Democrats fully supported the objects of agricultural reform and even called for renewed state aid, their party's position in the new political order tended to militate against taking a strong stand in favor of government spending, no matter how little. It was therefore the Whigs, with their marriage of electoral appeal and economic nationalism, who would sponsor the resurgence of agricultural societies in the 1840s.

But party ideologies were ultimately secondary to the way that the party *system* contoured the political landscape. Once the agricultural reform project entered the public arena, some kind of politics had to follow. Wrangling was inevitable with government funding at stake. As a century of dog tax controversies showed, no reordering of social relationships through fiscal policy was too small to fight over. The patrician project proved unable to navigate a political sphere being transformed by democratization through partisanship. Its failure ultimately gave rise to a mass social movement that innovated a distinctive, if unacknowledged, strategy for circumventing party politics altogether.

CHAPTER TWO

Agricultural Reform as a State-Building Social Movement

Within a generation of the elimination of the New York Board of Agriculture, a new organization, the New York State Agricultural Society, had gained significant public funding and influence. In 1849, its outgoing president, Lewis F. Allen, bragged that it occupied "a position . . . of state, nay, of national importance." Allen averred that the old board had been undone by its failure "to enlist the affections of the farmers generally," whereas the subsequent movement for agricultural societies had become "deeply grounded . . . in the affections of our people." The success was so complete that it would now take "a hardy legislator" to challenge the societies' public standing. Somehow, then, agricultural reformers had turned it all around.[1]

Although the 1830s proved the low tide for agricultural organizations, that was not true of agricultural reform in general. The same period witnessed an explosion in specialized farm journals. Employing a more popular style than the old promoting societies, the agricultural press broadened the range and deepened the reach of agricultural reform, creating a new agricultural public. From this base, reformers launched a series of campaigns to renew government funding for their organizations. Those campaigns began to succeed in state after state during the 1840s, providing subsidies that revived the old agricultural societies and catalyzed the founding of hundreds of new ones. By the 1850s, the societies and their annual fairs were settled institutions of rural life, and agricultural reform had been reborn from the ashes of the patrician project as a mass social movement.

The version of agricultural reform that arose in the 1830s and 1840s was diffuse and led by individuals who might have been prominent in certain circles but were otherwise obscure. The dearth of manuscript sources left by even the most important of them testifies to their status as second-tier elites at best. Agricultural reform did generate an immense amount of print, but in media that have been underexamined. Similarly, the period's massive agricultural exhibitions have received relatively little attention, and the true extent and significance of public funding for agricultural societies has not been understood. The assembled evidence indicates that by the 1850s the agricultural movement comprised a network of hundreds of agricultural organizations and journals; a physical presence in state office buildings, county fairgrounds, and countless farm improvements; and a pervasive discourse of "scientific agriculture" that shaped broader conceptions of the American political economy and its future.

To achieve all this, agricultural reformers eschewed conventional politics and instead developed a distinctive mode of advocacy that I call nonpartisan anti-politics. Like an antihero who subverts generic expectations, anti-politics can be thought of as a kind of advocacy that deliberately avoids established political forms in order to appear beyond the realm of politics. In an era that equated politics with partisanship, this meant assiduously submerging partisan identities while presenting advocative action as a matter of common sense, objective need, and popular consensus. Starting with the campaigns for state subsidies, reformers organized local meetings and petition drives, called statewide conventions, lobbied legislators, and adopted populist rhetoric to enlist government backing for an increasingly ambitious agenda. In doing so, they mobilized many of the same techniques commonly associated with contemporaneous moral reform movements such as temperance and abolitionism. But agricultural reformers insisted that none of this amounted to politics. They understood that rural communities favored decision making by consensus (or its appearance), knew that appealing to farmers as a class required avoiding divisive partisan identities, and believed that women's participation in agricultural fairs ruled out electioneering. The movement therefore developed an organizational and media infrastructure entirely independent of the party system.

An important effect was to mask sectional disparity within the agricultural reform movement. By any conceivable measure, the movement skewed heavily to the North. In addition to both relative and absolute superiority of numbers, the North featured the most influential journals, the most active societies, and the most spectacular fairs. As a result, northern voices steeped in northern conditions dominated the discourse of agricultural reform and determined the main lines of its national agenda. The style of anti-politics meant that overtly sectional rhetoric was rare. Yet precisely because of the reluctance to acknowledge sectional cleavage, it became easy to miss the fact that agricultural reform was nationalist in theory, northern in substance. This became politically salient when agricultural reform was merged into a broader northern program for national economic development that slaveholders found unacceptable.

Emergence of the Agricultural Press

An independent agricultural press emerged in the United States in the 1820s and 1830s. The importance of this development cannot be overstated. Part of the explosion of print that transformed rural society over the course of the nineteenth century, the agricultural press fundamentally changed the shape and content of reform discourse as it had existed in the early republic. New farm periodicals expressed the reform agenda in a vernacular idiom and opened a discussion forum by soliciting reader contributions. They fostered a more inclusive, interactive, and impersonal public space than had existed before the 1820s. In this way they began to define a distinct agricultural public that could deliberate on issues and mobilize in pursuit of its interests. The emergence of these new media thus marked a critical difference between the abortive agricultural reform project of the 1820s and the institutionalization of the new movement in the 1840s.

The agricultural press grew so rapidly that an elite readership alone could not possibly have sustained its rise. Table 2.1 shows that the number of distinct farm journal titles more than quadrupled from the 1820s to the 1830s, while the ratio of such journals to free rural inhabitants more than tripled. Many of these journals were short-lived, yet by making a serious attempt to put a new title on the market, the failed publishers as well as the successful ones gave evidence of the growing popular interest in agricultural reform. In the 1840s, both the number of farm journals and their ratio to free rural inhabitants continued to rise, if more slowly. In the next decade, the absolute number of new titles rose yet again while the per capita rate flattened out. These trends likely reflect the rapid initial growth and subsequent consolidation of the farm journal business. Successful early forays into the field during the 1820s, in the context of a general expansion of print media, encouraged a proliferation of new entrants. As time passed, the more profitable journals merged with or bought up their competitors. Hence the rate of new journals slowed even as overall circulation, for which there is no precise measure, continued to increase. Something like four hundred specialized agricultural periodicals came into existence over the course of the antebellum period. By the 1850s, thirty to forty active journals enjoyed a total circulation variously estimated between 350,000 and

TABLE 2.1.
Distinct Agricultural Journal Titles per 100,000 Free Rural Inhabitants, by Decade

	Distinct titles	Per 100,000 free rural inhabitants
1820–29	19	0.195
1830–39	90	0.707
1840–49	141	0.857
1850–59	181	0.851

Sources: Compiled from S. C. Stuntz, *List of the Agricultural Periodicals of the United States and Canada Published during the Century July 1810 to July 1910*, ed. Emma B. Hawks (Washington, DC: US Department of Agriculture, 1941); *Historical Statistics of the United States, 1789–1945* (Washington, DC: GPO, 1949).

Note: The column "Distinct titles" measures the number of different agricultural journal titles to appear in that decade. Titles that persisted from one decade to the next were counted once in each decade. The rate in the right-most column was determined by dividing the number of distinct titles in a decade by the free rural population as calculated from the federal population census at decade's end and then multiplying by 100,000. The free rural population was estimated by subtracting the entire slave population from the entire rural population for each census. This procedure slightly underestimates the free rural population and therefore slightly overestimates the ratio of agricultural journals to free rural inhabitants.

500,000. The effective circulation was certainly much larger, owing to the prevalence of joint subscriptions and borrowing in contemporary reading practices.[2]

Reprinting expanded the reach of the farm press further. The weekly edition of the *New-York Tribune*, which circulated widely in the immense rural hinterland of New York City, frequently published agricultural items before adding a regular department in 1853 under the editorship of the popular farm journalist Solon Robinson. The *New York Times* did similarly by employing Luther Tucker and later Orange Judd, two of the period's most influential agricultural editors.[3] Small-town papers repeated the trend at the local level. The *Semi-Weekly Eagle* of Brattleboro, Vermont, for example, usually included an "Agricultural" section with articles reprinted from leading farm journals.[4] Similarly, the *Germantown Telegraph*, which served farming suburbs north of Philadelphia, provided a "large amount of original Agricultural Information of great value."[5] Such items were popular. Announcing the addition of an agricultural department in 1849, a religious journal noted the "singular . . . avidity with which articles on agricultural interests are read."[6]

The demand for agricultural literature encompassed more than periodicals. The catalog of agricultural monographs, many pirated from European editions but increasingly authored by Americans, steadily expanded through the antebellum era. Although books were expensive, farmers often clubbed together to establish subscription libraries that purchased books on a variety of subjects, including agricultural reform and improvement. In 1847, C. M. Saxton & Company responded to the demand by becoming the first American publishing firm to concentrate exclusively on agricultural subjects. By comparison, the first domestic publisher specializing in technical industrial matters appeared only several years later and did not hit its stride until after the Civil War.[7]

Historians usually date the advent of the farm press to 1819, when John S. Skinner established the *American Farmer* in Baltimore and Solomon Southwick established the *Ploughboy* in Albany. Actually, there had already been some experiments with a periodical format oriented to farming.[8] The journal of the Massachusetts Society for Promoting Agriculture (MSPA), begun in 1813, was an attempt to open "a channel of communication between the several Agricultural Societies in the Commonwealth, and between individual farmers," but the society characteristically blotted this effort with reflexive condescension, expecting gentleman to speak and farmers to listen.[9] The journal was not really a periodical, either, but more of a transitional medium. It lacked a standard format and typically ran to a hundred pages of erudite prose. Its editor saw himself as belonging to "a *middle* generation, between the revolutionary patriots, & the *modern* man."[10]

The "modern" men, in this case, were the agricultural editors who followed.[11] Most cut their teeth as partisan political printers. The *Ploughboy*'s Southwick was at one time a leading Democratic-Republican spokesman known especially as a prose stylist. Brought low by a rhetorical intemperance that lost him the state printership while earning him a record-setting libel judgment, Southwick shifted his attention from politics to agriculture. To appeal to a popular audience, he adopted the pen name Henry Homespun, striking a folksy note while evoking reformers' fixation on domestic woolens manufacturing. The gesture may have proved too cute. Despite support from the New York Board of Agriculture—or perhaps because of it—the journal failed within a few years. It had become "engulfed in politics," according to Lewis Allen, and "died of its own inanition."[12]

Jesse Buel and Luther Tucker, two influential early agricultural editors, also began their professional lives as political printers. Buel edited several political newspapers before coming to Albany in 1813. There he founded the *Argus*, which became the leading organ of Martin Van Buren's political organization. This put him in an awkward position. As a Van Burenite, he was required to attack the governor's economic program, including the reviled Board of Agriculture, which, however, Buel himself supported. Forced into contorted pro-agricultural reform, anti-administration positions, Buel at last left the *Argus*. Within a few years he had built up a famously productive farm in the "Sandy Barrens" west of Albany and earned himself a reputation as a farming expert.

During the 1830s, he began to write widely on agricultural subjects, helped edit Luther Tucker's *Genesee Farmer*, and then, with Tucker as publisher, founded and edited the *Cultivator*, which instantly became the country's best-known farm journal.[13]

Tucker, like Buel, came from a New England farming background, learned his trade as a printer's apprentice, and escaped a life of rural poverty through ambition and self-directed reading. In 1826, he founded the *Rochester Daily Advertiser*, which became the city's Van Burenite mouthpiece. After a bruising political battle with the future Whig Party mastermind, Thurlow Weed, Tucker began to shift his attention to agricultural reform, founding the *Genesee Farmer* in 1831. When Buel died at the end of that decade, Tucker sold his political paper, moved to Albany, and took over the *Cultivator*, which he eventually merged with another of his farm journals. By the 1840s, he was one of the most important figures in American agricultural reform. In addition to publishing several important agricultural periodicals, he served for many years as the New York State Agricultural Society's treasurer and recording secretary. During this time, he trained the editors of at least ten other agricultural papers.[14]

The move from political to agricultural journalism was common. Isaac Hill, known to historians as a pugnacious printer-editor and Democratic Party power broker, founded the *Farmer's Monthly Visitor* after retiring from active politics. He had once employed Luther Tucker in his shop. Samuel Sands, who took over the *American Farmer* in 1834, and Simon Brown, who edited the second iteration of the *New England Farmer* in the 1850s, began as apprentice printers during early national battles over the role of newspapers in politics.[15]

Most of these editors had been Jeffersonian partisans rhetorically committed to democratization. They carried that sensibility over to agricultural journalism. Even as they encouraged the racing and gendering of what became Jacksonian democracy, they sought an otherwise inclusive public sphere, bringing the idealized model of enlightened inquiry down to ground level for white men. They vowed to eschew "the unintelligibleness of technical science" in order to present "interesting and useful facts . . . in the unstudied attractions of native plainness." They also asked their readers "to become *correspondents* and send us the results of their experience and observations in farming." The *Cultivator*, for instance, boasted of some three hundred published correspondents in its 1844 volume, "almost all of them practical farmers." Whereas the older promoting societies, exemplified by the MSPA, had assumed distinct roles for gentlemen and ordinary farmers, the new press presented agricultural reform as the common project of an undifferentiated, though implicitly white, agricultural mass public.[16]

What the editors *did not* carry over from party politics mattered as much as what they did. The experience of intense partisan conflict seems to have left some with a bad taste, or at least a determination to draw a firm distinction between party politics and agriculture. In this way they actually affirmed gentlemanly conventions they had disavowed with their democratizing rhetoric. Early national patrician reformers often spoke of agriculture as an escape from the "vortex of politics" into the peaceful repose of "rural retirement," where they could experience the harmony of a supposedly organic social order.[17] This was not, of course, a simple withdrawal from politics. It was a studied performance of transcendent love-of-country drawing on the "agrarian patriotism" of eighteenth-century English country Whigs.[18] Editors invoked something of this tradition by appealing to nonpartisanship, nationalism, and rural norms of consensus. Hence the fierce partisan, Isaac Hill, opened the first issue of the *Farmer's Monthly Visitor* with a letter from a political rival pledging that "in this thing you shall have my hearty cooperation." As the *American Farmer* urged, "let politicians quarrel for place or principle, but let all unite in agricultural exertions."[19] Demarcating the category of the political is itself a political act. Agricultural nonpartisanship thus shifted rather than abandoned the political ground. When editors and their correspondents defined the technologies, policies, and values they associated with rural progress as matters of the common national interest rather than of political contention, they established a discursive base from which to demand that the political system respond to farmers' ostensibly objective needs.

The emergence of the agricultural press occurred in the context of changes to the antebellum print market. A number of factors converged in the decades after the American Revolution to vastly expand the American reading public. Among these were postal policies that subsidized newspapers and expanded mail access, rising rates of literacy and general education, improved interior lighting and eyewear, and the emergence of a middle class for whom reading formed a way of life. As the market grew larger, it also grew more specialized. New genres of periodicals that simultaneously appealed to and conjured up discrete reading publics came on the scene: religious papers, women's magazines, the flash press, and, soon enough, agricultural journals.

The *American Farmer*'s John S. Skinner was well positioned to grasp these changes. Skinner belonged to a Maryland planter family and enjoyed the social standing to climb high in government before venturing into agricultural journalism. Beginning as an inspector of mail during the War of 1812, he eventually rose to third assistant postmaster general in the Harrison and Tyler administrations. Given the close association between journalism and the post office during this era, Skinner's work gave him an insider's view of print market developments. Socially connected and culturally savvy, he scored an immediate hit with the *American Farmer*. He would later repeat the feat with a groundbreaking sports journal, the *American Turf Register and Sporting Magazine*.[20]

Other farm papers were linked to commercial suppliers of agricultural inputs. By the early 1800s, nurseries, seed stores, fertilizer dealers, and implement manufacturers competed for farmers' attention. As the commercial vanguard of agricultural improvement, they often dealt in new technologies that required extensive description and promotion. Agricultural periodicals were well suited to this purpose. Thus, for instance, the first *New England Farmer* was an "advertising arm" of the New England Warehouse and Seed Store. Similarly, the Allen brothers' *American Agriculturist* was closely connected to their warehouse, implement manufactory, and breeding businesses.[21] Even when agricultural suppliers did not directly control a journal, they provided content and advertising patronage. If many in the farm press migrated horizontally from politics to agriculture, others moved vertically from selling agricultural tools to selling agricultural words.

Editors appealed directly to farmers but also shaped the general public's understanding of American agriculture. By publishing a steady stream of material that addressed the same basic themes of soil maintenance, livestock improvement, market discipline, technological innovation, and the like, the editors crafted a discourse of "scientific agriculture" that resonated in the wider public sphere. Editors and correspondents shared a broad frame of reference even if they often disagreed about technical details. As echoes of their views found their way into mainstream media—through reprintings, quotations and vague references—the underlying premises of agricultural reform acquired a sense of accepted truth independent of any particular source. Agricultural reformers thus gained discursive clout, the power to be heard and taken seriously in the public sphere.

Journal offices became critical nodes for establishing committed reform networks that provided the social foundations of this influence. As early as 1837, the *Cultivator* reported receiving twenty inquiries in only two days regarding specific varieties of seeds, implements, and livestock. Because editorial staffs tended to reply by referring farmers to nurserymen, stock breeders, implement dealers, seed distributors, and improving farmers, they established ties among those most interested in agricultural reform. At the same time, editors contacted postmasters and solicited local agents to manage groups of subscribers. In some cases, higher-order "special agents" coordinated regional networks of subscription managers. Editors not only reprinted each other's material but also acted as each other's agents, giving them overlapping lists of contacts. Even a small journal could count on the assistance of its "brethren of the 'Corps Editorial.' "[22]

Strategically located and speaking a language of vernacular improvement, farm editors forged an agricultural public.[23] But who really composed it? Evidence is fragmentary yet points unsurprisingly toward middle-class farmers (table 2.2). In the fall of 1837, for example, members of the Silver Spring Farmer's

TABLE 2.2.
Farmers' Presence in the Agricultural Reform Movement

Group	State	Year(s)	No.	No. with known occupations (% of total)	No. of farmers (% of known occupations)
Publishing Committee of the *Practical Farmer*	PA	1837	17	9 (52.9)	9 (100)
Cultivator subscribers in Oxford	NY	1839–65	132	119 (90.2)	87 (73.1)
Executive Committee of the Fairfield County Agricultural Society	CT	1843	77	48 (62.3)	39 (81.3)
Petitioners for a federal agricultural bureau from Turbot	PA	1850	45	34 (75.6)	27 (79.4)
Fairgrounds fund contributors from Concord	MA	1853	29	23 (79.3)	17 (73.9)
Founding members of the Octoraro Farmer's Club	PA	1856	23	23 (100)	22 (95.7)
Shareholders in the Bucks County Agricultural Society	PA	1858–59	148	86 (58.1)	69 (80.2)
		Totals	471	342 (72.6)	270 (78.9)

Sources, in order of table rows: *Practical Farmer* 1 (Oct. 1837): 1; Sally McMurry, "Who Read the Agricultural Journals? Evidence from Chenango County, New York, 1839–1865," *Agricultural History* 63 (Autumn 1989): 5–6; meeting minutes, Oct. 18, 1843, FCAS-FMHC, series A, folder 2; petition from Northumberland County, PA, referred to House Committee on Agriculture, May 28, 1850, RG 233 (HR 31A-G1.1); "Report of the Committee to Purchase Land, &c.," Oct. 4, 1853, MAS-CFL, series 5, box 5, folder 3; Sanders P. McComsey, ed., *A History of the Octoraro Farmers Club, 1856–1946* (Manheim, PA: Sentinel Printing House, 1948), chap. 2; stock certificate book of the Bucks County Agricultural Society, 1858–1867, ASBS-MMSL.

Note: Occupations were determined mostly from manuscript census records for 1850 and 1860 obtained through Ancestry.com. Some additional determinations were made with the help of local histories and genealogies.

Lyceum in Cumberland County, Pennsylvania, formed a publishing committee to issue the monthly *Practical Farmer*. Nine of the committee's seventeen members can be identified in the 1850 manuscript census records, and all of them were farmers. The average value of their real estate ($5,614) slightly exceeded farmers' average for the township ($5,234). The richest among them was the committee's president, yet his wife was apparently illiterate. These were no patricians. They nevertheless believed themselves fully capable of pursuing scientific agriculture. "Let every one contribute according to his ability to aid in the general diffusion of useful knowledge," the journal's editor avowed, "and wonders will be accomplished in a short time."[24]

Other evidence suggests much the same picture elsewhere.[25] Studies of a rare surviving farm journal subscription list find that two-thirds of the subscribers were farmers, that they were distinguished by their commitment to education, and that they seem to have produced larger crops and to have adopted modern implements earlier than their neighbors.[26] Diaries, ledgers, and other personal papers indicate how seriously some farmers engaged with agricultural reform. Thomas J. Aldred of Chester County, Pennsylvania, a well-off but basically ordinary farmer, kept numerous clippings and handwritten transcriptions of agricultural articles in his personal journal.[27] In one case, Aldred copied out an essay on crop rotations; in another, he meticulously reproduced the illustrations from Thomas Jefferson's famous essay applying mathematical principles to the design of a plow's moldboard. Another document records ownership of several implements designated by their brand, such as a "Harper Plow No. 1," implying a habit of distinguishing implements by make and model, which in turn suggests exposure to the marketing commonly found in the agricultural press.[28]

A more detailed portrait is possible in the case of Charles Colfelt, who is interesting because of his minor contributions to agricultural print. A country merchant who turned to farming, Colfelt settled during the 1850s on five hundred acres of relatively inexpensive land in Bedford County, Pennsylvania. There he employed a combination of tenants, hired hands, and family labor, in addition to such novel labor-saving technologies as a mechanical mower. His papers, which record crop experiments and purchases of various fertilizers and implements, attest to his interest in scientific agriculture.[29] In 1844, the *Cultivator* published a summary of his letter reporting an experiment with potatoes and, the following year, it published the full text of another letter detailing a homemade mixture of fertilizers applied to a corn crop. "Some of my neighbors rather quizzed me about the compost," he wrote, "but when husking and hauling in time came, they were amazed. The corn grew surprisingly." With only two brief appearances in print, Colfelt nevertheless reached a wide audience through reprinting. At least one farmer—hundreds of miles away in St. Lawrence County, New York—reported positive results after trying Colfelt's fertilizer mixture on his own corn crop.[30] The exchange epitomizes what a farm journal correspondent called a "liberal commerce of thought and knowledge among agriculturists."[31] It illustrates how the agricultural press extended the boundaries of rural life even in that most rooted of endeavors, the day-to-day practice of farming.

Revival of the Agricultural Societies

The emerging agricultural public mobilized during the 1830s and 1840s to renew state funding for agricultural societies. The campaign in New York achieved its basic aims when, in 1841, the legislature allocated $8,000 in annual subsidies, enough for the state's farm organizations to establish themselves and proliferate.[32] As in the early 1820s, the appropriations came in the midst of a severe economic downturn. Unlike the earlier era, they were never rescinded.

Instead, the reach and influence of agricultural reformers grew, and fiscal support was gradually increased in various ways. By the 1850s, the New York State Agricultural Society was operating as a quasi-governmental agency.

The general trajectory of the New York case seems to have characterized developments elsewhere. The campaign for the 1841 law began a decade earlier when the state's farm journals called an agricultural convention. Among the delegates to the first meeting was William Seward, then a state senator, who would prove a critical ally when he became governor in 1839. The delegates established a state agricultural society as a coordinating body for county societies, few of which actually existed yet because of lack of funding.[33] Over the next decade, the convention continued to meet annually to agitate for renewed public subsidies, with a "vigorous agricultural press" providing support throughout. In 1834, after the governor endorsed the idea in his annual message but the legislature did nothing, Lewis Allen led a protest by the "friends of agriculture." Later that year, when the senate agriculture committee rejected subsidies on the grounds that the Board of Agriculture had been a wasteful failure, Luther Tucker published a series of articles in the *Genesee Farmer* offering point-by-point rebuttals. The real issue, according to Tucker and others, was that agricultural reform served no specific partisan agenda. It was therefore easily cast aside to the detriment of the public interest.[34]

Partisan commitments mattered. Agricultural reformers were both Whigs and Democrats, but reform could and did produce partisan fault lines when public funding was at stake. Although many Democrats supported limited public sponsorship of agricultural societies, the hardline "Radical" faction viewed subsidies and delegations of state authority as precisely what the party ought to fight.[35] In New York, small-government Democrats such as Samuel Young and Jehiel Halsey successfully fought off the renewal of state support for agricultural organizations throughout the 1830s.[36] Reformers continued the pressure by getting up petitions, writing editorials, and lobbying in Albany, but the breakthrough only came when Whigs took control of the state government, a change conditioned by the financial crises of the late 1830s. In line with the Whig agenda, agricultural reform was again pitched as key to a recovery plan premised on a long-term commitment to domestic economic development.

Lewis Allen anticipated the shift when he introduced a bill for agricultural subsidies in February 1838. Allen was already a regular contributor, under the pseudonym of "Ulmus," to Tucker's *Genesee Farmer*.[37] Having begun as a Buffalo businessman and town booster, he thought in broad developmental terms and pursued two related policy goals: expansion of the state's internal improvements and of its agricultural reform initiatives. He believed both essential to developing the agricultural potential of the entire region between the Great Lakes and the Ohio River. As he explained in a report for the New York Assembly, "Agriculture constitutes the broad base upon which the whole super-structure of society depends."[38] Although he introduced his bill too late in the session to bring it to a vote, Seward's gubernatorial election in the fall indicated success was just ahead. Allen immediately wrote to Seward that subsidies for agricultural societies formed "a subject of paramount importance in promoting the wealth and prosperity of our state." Moreover, it was "popular with the people."[39]

Jesse Buel echoed these efforts, deploying the political skills he had once honed as a partisan editor.[40] In the pages of the *Cultivator*, Buel published essays calling for "patronage to agriculture." At the same time, he lobbied Seward personally. Meeting with him sometime in December, Buel urged reestablishing the Board of Agriculture. In a follow-up letter, he informed Seward that he and other agricultural reformers had distributed several hundred petition forms, which would soon be raining down on the legislature. "Pardon me for saying," he concluded, "that I consider this branch of labor . . . merits the fostering care of government and that it must ultimately *command* it."[41] This was a warning. Farmers, Buel reminded the ambitious politician, constituted a majority of the electorate, although that bare fact meant little. The question was whether the farmers were awake to their interests as determined by the likes of Buel and Allen. For this reason, Buel enclosed the latest issue of the *Cultivator*, in which Seward could peruse such pieces as "Serious Suggestions Addressed to the Interests and Honor of Farmers," which advocated a "more liberal state policy" for agricultural improvement. The point here was not merely to forward a set of persuasive arguments, but to call attention to those arguments' publicity. Buel was inviting Seward to imagine thousands of farmers reading Buel's editorial, to participate in the "mass ceremony" of the imagined farmers' community, and then to reimagine the farmers as voters at the polls.[42] Allen similarly assured Seward that "a vast many" farmers desired renewed subsidies for agricultural societies. Meanwhile he sent letters to the *Genesee Farmer* declaring that "farmers have only to will it and they can COMMAND all the sources of improvement."[43] This was a kind of inside-out game, shaping public opinion "out of doors" to strengthen influence in the halls of government. Seward learned the lesson well. Years later he could be heard avowing at an agricultural fair that "the electoral body, the farmers," should have "chief control of society and government."[44]

Sweeping Whig victories in the 1840 elections overcame lingering opposition from Radical Democrats. The roll call vote on the 1841 "Act to Promote Agriculture" reveals the partisan and regional determinants of legislators' support for subsidizing agricultural societies (table 2.3). Whigs backed the measure three-to-one, while those opposed included the author of the "Stop and Tax" law of 1842, the Democrats' signature fiscal retrenchment policy. But the fact

TABLE 2.3.
Voting on New York's 1841 "Act to Promote Agriculture"

	Whig		Democrat		Overall		Abstaining	
	For	Against	For	Against	For	Against	No.	%
Erie Canal corridor	22	1	5	0	27	1	8	22.2
Remaining areas	12	10	16	15	28	25	38	41.8
Overall	34	11	21	15	57	26	46	35.7

Source: *Journal of the Assembly of the State of New-York*, 64th sess. (Albany: Thurlow Weed, 1841), 198–99, 240–41, 760–63.

Note: Party affiliations were determined by reference to the Assembly's voting on nominees for state comptroller (198–99) and surveyor general (240–41). This procedure produced no discrepancies but left two assemblymen who voted on the agriculture law unaccounted for. Both were from the "remaining areas" region. The counties making up the Erie Canal corridor are Cayuga, Erie, Genesee, Livingston, Madison, Monroe, Niagara, Onondaga, Ontario, Orleans, Oswego, Seneca, Tompkins, Wayne, and Yates.

that a majority of Democratic legislators voted for the law suggests that partisanship was not the key issue. A regional breakdown clarifies this. The bill's support base was heavily concentrated in the growing counties of western New York linked to the Erie Canal. Not only did assemblymen from this region back the bill almost unanimously—including all five Democrats—but a higher proportion showed up to vote than in the rest of the state. As might be expected, rapidly developing commercial farming districts favored government support for agricultural modernization. In contrast, the rest of the state split more-or-less evenly along both regional and partisan dimensions, providing only a bare majority for passage.

Agricultural reformers scored their next big victory in Ohio with the creation of a state Board of Agriculture. Things there were broadly similar to New York except that the Whigs proved more essential. Ohio's reformers had been calling for state support for some time, leading to an 1833 law authorizing small disbursements from county treasuries to local agricultural societies. That law largely turned into a dead letter. Subsequent public meetings and the formation of a state agricultural society failed to prompt any changes.[45] After 1844, however, Whig control of the state government, the example set by New York, and the establishment of the state's first agricultural journal, the *Ohio Cultivator*, inspired reformers to mount a serious lobbying campaign. In June 1845, reformers convened a two-day meeting in Columbus, leading to the introduction of a new funding bill, and legislators were treated to almost daily petitions in its favor during the ensuing winter.[46] By the end of January, one Whig paper was claiming that "the Agricultural interest of Ohio imperatively demands" the measure.[47]

When the bill finally came up for consideration, stark partisan divisions emerged in two key votes, the first on the public funding provision, the second

TABLE 2.4.

Voting on Ohio's "Act to Encourage Agriculture" (1846)

	Funding agricultural organizations		Final passage	
	For	Against	For	Against
Democrats	3	18	2	19
Whigs	34	1	30	1
Unidentified	2	1	1	1
Overall	39	20	33	21

Sources: Journal of the House of Representatives of the State of Ohio 44 (Columbus: C. Scott and Co., 1846): 3–5, 706, 720–21; *Annual Reports for 1875, Made to the Sixty-Second General Assembly of the State of Ohio at the Regular Session, Commencing January 3, 1876* (Columbus: Nevins & Meyers, 1876), 1:298–300.

Note: Party affiliations were determined by reference to two sources: (1) vote totals for governor in each assemblyman's district (because voting was likely by ticket, gubernatorial and assembly voting should correlate very closely) and (2) a symbolic partisan roll call vote on whether to bar the House speakership from going to any representative who was also a bank officer. This procedure resulted in several discrepancies. Those that could be resolved by adding the abolitionist gubernatorial vote to the Whig candidate's vote were recorded as Whigs. The few remaining discrepancies are recorded as "unidentified."

on final passage (table 2.4). Unlike in New York, the Ohio results leave no hint of ambiguity, with Democrats overwhelmingly opposed and Whigs all but unanimously in favor. The legislature's Whig majority thus assured the Board of Agriculture's establishment and its financing from a "state agricultural fund" that netted several thousand dollars per year. As in New York, state monies prompted a spate of organizing, so that, from 1846 to 1850, fifty-two county societies appeared or reappeared after a period of dormancy.[48]

It might seem, then, that the renewal owed more to the Whig program of state-sponsored economic development than to agricultural reformers' own efforts. But the Whigs really played only a facilitative role. Whigs tended to be friendly to agricultural subsidies, but they never campaigned on the issue nor included it in their platforms. Moreover, many leading reformers remained Democrats. The economic depression that helped bring Whigs to power gave them a popular mandate to enact economic reforms, and this provided the occasion for renewing agricultural subsidies. But it was the farm press's multi-pronged lobbying campaign that put agricultural reform back onto the public agenda to begin with. As a correspondent for the *Ohio Cultivator* urged, "Let us go to the capitol OURSELVES, and take the business into our OWN hands."[49] In Ohio, as in New York, the mobilization of reform networks was the essential factor.

The agricultural reform movement's independence from the party system grew out of its operations at the local level, especially the production of annual town and county fairs. These exhibitions usually took place in the fall, lasted one or two days, and revolved around the display of livestock, farm products, agricultural implements, and local manufactures.[50] Typical in its arrangement was the Middlesex (MA) Agricultural Society's fair in September 1859. It began at nine o'clock with a plowing match, followed an hour later by a "Trial of Strength and Discipline of Working Oxen," and then a horse exhibition. After several hours for visitors to observe the displays and enjoy the offerings of "Peddlers, Auctioneers, Showmen, and Caterers," the society's officers, members, and guests formed a procession that marched to town hall for the annual address, additional speeches, the reports of the judging committees, and the awarding of premiums. With almost seven hundred members and their families potentially participating, the procession must have been impressive. Reports of the previous year's exhibition, at any rate, described large crowds. At four in the afternoon, the society's annual meeting for the election of officers was held in the courthouse, and, after that, a dinner was arranged, with more speeches and toasts.[51]

Public funding and democratic organizing were essential to producing such spectacles, as illustrated by the founding of the Fairfield (CT) County Agricultural Society. Fairfield had no agricultural society when Connecticut legislated a $200 annual subsidy in 1840, so a group of citizens met to form one. Among them was Eli T. Hoyt, a local businessman who had retired to a farm. Clearly a member of the county elite, Hoyt understood that the society's survival depended on ordinary farmers. The first fair, he believed, would make or break the organization. To ensure its success, he fretted over location, called for many small premiums rather than a few large ones—it was "not so much the *amount*" that generated interest "as the fact of getting the *premium at all*"—and constantly reminded fellow organizers to promote the event through personal channels as well as the press. "Procure by direct invitation the attendance of as many farmers as possible," he advised. "Be particular," he urged again, by contacting "known individuals" who could be counted on to get neighbors involved. The strategy paid off. A well-attended first fair led county towns to compete to host subsequent exhibitions. By 1843, there were effectively two Fairfield societies, one for each state senatorial district, each directed by a large, farmer-dominated executive committee (figure 2.1; see also table 2.2).[52]

Fairs were occasions for edification and entertainment, sociability and the affirmation of communal ties. "Never felt we so proud of our citizenship in the good old County of Windham," Vermont, wrote the editor of the *Semi-Weekly Eagle* in 1851, "as when we looked upon the multitudinous array of fair women and brave men, who were assembled at Fayetteville, on the farmers' festal day." With all of 3,800 people in its largest town, Windham County was almost entirely rural. Hence the *Eagle* argued that "the value of a well-established and prosperous Agricultural Society, in this county, may be easily made of substan-

Figure 2.1. A plowing match at the 1852 Fairfield County (CT) Agricultural Fair. Published in *Gleason's Pictorial Drawing Room Companion* 3 (Nov. 6, 1852): 297. Courtesy of the Library Company of Philadelphia.

tial interest to not only every farmer but to every man."[53] Local fairs quickly became favorite institutions that represented rural society as "an organic, corporate community made up of productive households."[54] Contemporary county histories situated them within triumphant chronicles of local progress from pioneer "wilderness" to civilized modernity. Typically teleological is the 1859 account of a Pennsylvania county historian who marveled that the original agricultural society of six members had grown into "a noble and expanded institution" visited "annually by thousands."[55] In accounts like these, the trope of the disappearing Indian elided continued Native American presence and helped construct agricultural reform as progressive and implicitly white.[56]

If the fairs aimed to display a kind of social harmony, they inevitably also manifested fault lines. For instance, agricultural reformers favored plowing matches as didactic demonstrations of skill and coordination, "the magic powers of a well directed community of labour," as one well-to-do observer put it.[57] But many farmers preferred trials of brute oxen strength, which reformers criticized as mere spectacles cruel to animals, devoid of instructional value, and retrograde in their association of manhood with raw physicality.[58] Class and sometimes ethnic divisions are registered in the practice of awarding premiums to the farm owner even if others performed the labor. In 1853, the ostensible competitors in a spading match each had an Irish gardener do the actual spading.[59] Class and gender divisions can also be discerned in the changing emphases of premiums for women's work. Growing attention to decorative needlework at the expense of functional items such as rugs and blankets evidences how reformers' bourgeois gender norms, in which home was separated from work, differed from many farmers' lingering understanding of the household as, first and foremost, a site of productive labor. Finally, fairs were occasions for illicit erotic encounters and other transgressive behaviors.[60]

The fairs' popularity therefore drew on many sources, some of them "utterly subversive" of reformers' intent, as Lewis Allen's brother, Richard, put it.[61] Consider, for instance, the layered meanings one might plausibly ascribe to the following description of a wildly successful exhibition in 1859: "Newtown was soon literally jammed with crowds. . . . For hours people poured through the several gates. . . . The fair sex were out in their strength, and in the jam hoops were demolished or compressed without the least consideration."[62] The last line presents a vivid image of the crowd's immensity. Does it also evidence historians' finding that separate spheres ideology was looser in rural than in urban settings?[63] Does it instead disclose a sub-rosa critique of women's fashions and perhaps their presence in public?[64] Or does it indulge in sexual titillation by evoking a crush of bodies promiscuously pressed together? No doubt there is much cultural ground to work over here.

When it comes to political influence, what matters is that agricultural reformers were able to orchestrate these occasions and then leverage the diversity of attendees' motives to present an image of robust social support for the agricultural reform program. There was enough genuine farmer interest in the substance of agricultural reform to make this presentation plausible and appealing to a middle-class audience: if not literally every farmer was on board, surely the best were. Crowded fairs endowed the agricultural public with the feel of a mass movement and gave reformers a discursive power that underwrote their growing clout in state capitals.

Reformers obviously could not afford to divide their communities along partisan lines. On the contrary, they imagined fairs as places where "friendships are formed by which party and personal animosities are worn away, and the people are brought to look, unbiased, at those principles which concern their welfare."[65] The very first Berkshire fair illustrates the point. At the head of the opening procession, the town's oldest living Federalist and oldest living Democratic-Republican cooperated to drive a team of fifty oxen pulling a plow in a symbolic ritual of community consensus.[66] Women's involvement, which was essential to any exhibition's success, further militated against partisanship, because party politics were supposed to be a masculine domain.[67] Nonpartisanship was therefore baked into the agricultural societies' organizational logic. And so, despite Whiggery's obvious ideological affinities with and substantive support for agricultural reform, the movement's leaders never abandoned their nonpartisan stance, nor did Whig politicos try to claim the movement for their own purposes. Instead, agricultural reformers projected the local onto the national, envisioning rural social harmony in the flow of economic progress as the essence of American nationalism.

A State-Building Social Movement

Operating outside the party system, agricultural reformers came to exert an oblique yet increasingly substantial influence on government over the course of the 1840s and 1850s. Reformers occasionally urged farmers to elect representatives friendly to their interests, but an electoral strategy absent a partylike organization was unrealistic and never really tried. Instead, reformers worked to build a self-aware farming constituency and to shape broader public opinion in order to legitimize a form of political pressure that looked a lot like special interest lobbying. "Agriculture occupies four-fifths of the laboring population of the land," Lewis Allen said, but the farmer was "the least benefitted at the hands of those he elects to govern him, of all others." Farmers needed to coordinate advocacy "by *association*," just as other groups promoted their own interests. Here Allen called attention to the practical reality of a pluralist polity in which many interests jockeyed for a measure of state power. Even as they identified farmers with the nation, reformers also lobbied pragmatically much like everyone else.[68]

The strategy gradually led state governments to lend more and more support to the agricultural reform movement, which in turn derived new strength from its association with public authority. Bit by bit, agricultural reform became an official endeavor, one that tended toward bureaucratic forms enjoying state backing but partially insulated from short-term partisan imperatives. This trajectory foreshadowed wide-ranging shifts in American governance that are typically thought to have really begun only toward the turn of the twentieth century. Stressing policy over politics and the government's administrative over its legislative functions, the agricultural reform movement augured a basic restructuring of the American state.

Reformers began by pushing for a variety of state-level measures that solidified agricultural societies' legal and financial standing. During the 1840s and 1850s, many states followed New York and Ohio by providing agricultural societies with subsidies and tax exemptions.[69] In Massachusetts, meanwhile, an uninterrupted system of appropriations encouraged agricultural organizations to establish substantial permanent endowments, and in 1852 the General Court recognized as official a state Board of Agriculture convened the year before by leading reformers.[70] Although even here the appropriations were basically small, public funding was sufficient to establish durable state-level agricultural bodies and to ensure the rapid proliferation of agricultural fairs. Rising fair revenues, in turn, augmented organizational budgets. In several states, the combination of public funding and fair receipts allowed central organizations to be staffed by full-time salaried secretaries who devoted undivided attention to the cause.

Other measures also promoted agricultural reform. In 1853, for instance, New York enacted a general incorporation law for county and town agricultural societies to facilitate acquisition of real estate.[71] Although societies had existed for years without incorporation, many began raising large sums during the 1850s for permanent fairgrounds, making new legal arrangements desirable. The state further aided this kind of effort by exempting agricultural fairgrounds from taxation. Local towns, which often competed to become the permanent sites of county fairs, added another measure of public subsidy.[72]

A critical source of funding came in the form of printing subventions budgeted separately from, and often exceeding, direct appropriations. Year after year, state printers turned out an astonishing quantity of agricultural reports. Ohio ordered fifty thousand total copies of the Board of Agriculture's annual reports for 1855, 1856, and 1857, and added to that over seven thousand copies of the board president's separate statement. These documents were far and away Ohio's most heavily printed state papers and were specifically exempted from the law governing general public printing expenditures. Their cost far surpassed what the board earned from its agricultural fund in the best of years.[73] The legislature of New York supported the publication expenses of not one but two major agricultural institutions, the state society and the American Institute of the City of New York. By my calculation, it ordered a combined total of about thirteen thousand copies in 1858 and similar amounts in other years.[74] The volumes were no lightweight affairs. The state society's annual report exceeded eight hundred pages throughout the 1850s and cost some $8,000 each year, equal to the annual direct appropriation for all of New York's agricultural organizations combined.[75] Other state organizations benefited from similar legislative largesse.[76]

The revival of government support for agricultural reform thus flooded the countryside with hefty official reports from agricultural societies. These documents vastly increased the volume of available agricultural literature and were used by the societies to arouse latent energies in their support. Yet the tens of thousands of reports that came off state presses each year paled in comparison to the output of the federal government. Between 1851 and 1860, Congress ordered the printing of roughly 2.2 million copies of the Patent Office's annual *Agricultural Report*. In 1859 alone, the Government Printing Office produced more than 326,000 copies of the six-hundred-page tome, a figure comparable to the record-breaking first-year sales of *Uncle Tom's Cabin*.[77] Easily the federal government's leading year-to-year printing expense, the *Agricultural Report* was a perennial bestseller. "Probably most of the members of this House, who represent rural districts," stated one congressman, "are almost daily reminded of the estimate placed upon these reports by their constituents."[78]

State support for agricultural publications went beyond even the annual reports. In 1839, New York paid for a school district library series that included several monographs on agriculture, including Jesse Buel's two-volume *Farmers' Instructor*.[79] Several years later, it began publishing the five-volume *Agriculture of New York*, a part of the monumental (and monumentally expensive) *Natural History of New York*, which was distributed to most of the state's approximately two hundred Regents academies.[80] These two acts, therefore, supplied virtually every district school and academy in the state with works in the emerging field of agricultural science. At least one other state, Vermont, similarly subsidized agricultural textbooks for local school districts.[81] In other cases, states subsidized publications on special agricultural topics.[82]

Altogether, while direct public funding of agricultural societies was modest, printing subsidies and other aids helped make the discourse of agricultural reform ubiquitous. By the late 1840s, even the technical jargon of agricultural chemistry had become commonplace.[83] During an 1856 congressional debate, for instance, one senator casually described the nitrogen content of an imported fertilizer with notable precision: "It is given in the analysis as 13.50 including the crenates and humates of ammonia, oily matter and lithic acid."[84] Discussions of agricultural reform topics, including even the precise chemical compositions of specific fertilizers, had gone mainstream.

State publication added authority to ubiquity. "Scientific agriculture" became the official future of American farming. This implied that the government bore responsibility to respond positively to the alarming information about declining crop yields, parasitic infestations, and other urgent problems detailed in its own reports. Officially sanctioned investigations, reformers and politicians understood, easily became calls for state action. Indeed, as Oz Frankel shows, the publication of official documents was a major means of state-making in the nineteenth century.[85] State agricultural reports played a significant part in this process—a circumstance that might, after all, be expected in a predominantly agricultural country.

Yet the relationship between state governments and their agricultural organizations was, by later standards, ill-defined. State boards enjoyed a closer formal association with their respective governments than did state societies, but there was no significant difference in functions or funding. Over time, agricultural organizations tended to take on more official responsibilities and gradually encouraged the creation of full-fledged state agricultural agencies. During the antebellum period, however, state boards and societies operated as bodies that were semiofficial, semiautonomous. The advantage of this arrangement was that there was little direct political oversight. In particular, agricultural organizations could avoid becoming patronage institutions beholden to whatever party happened to be in power. On the other hand, they had to fight to define their policy aims as proper affairs of state.

The New York State Agricultural Society, for example, worked diligently to secure its official status. It established its central office in Albany's "Old State House" and drew attention to the fact that its annual transactions appeared "under legislative authority." To cultivate influential connections, it invited legislators to regular public meetings of its executive committee. Meanwhile, it leveraged its ties to county farm organizations to strengthen its position with both the legislature and its own rural constituency. It solicited not only the formal county reports required by law, but also "the names of *many* active practical farmers" and "any newspapers containing articles calculated to promote the interests of the Farming Community." It thus built a record of public endorsements and a central list of statewide contacts. Its officers also visited county fairs to urge local counterparts to use "their influence in promoting the purposes of the State Society."[86] The cumulative effect was evidenced when the legislature paid to erect a new building for the society's offices and museum alongside the state cabinet of natural history (figure 2.2). The society also gained a special appropriation to fund entomological research on crop pests.[87]

Most important, the society's efforts resulted in spectacularly crowded state fairs. The power of such organizations ultimately derived from their ability to mobilize a very large, if dispersed, constituency of farmers and a small but influential set of men in state capitals. If county fairs staged progressive local communities, state exhibitions displayed the potential power of the larger agricultural public by dramatizing the magnitude of farmers' scattered numbers. Commentators' amazement at the crowds hints at the impact of these uniquely visible instances of rural mass society. Hence, the 1849 Syracuse fair was said to contain "a throng beyond the population of a great city." Only a few months later, an editor wrote that the farm press "*begins* to feel that it is of some account in the *commonwealth*" and able to stir "the farming class to a sense of its rights in the state." Lewis Allen was more direct. "We hold the power of the state by our numbers. We can control the halls of legislation."[88]

At this point, agricultural reformers' clout derived from the strength of their movement rather than from any real governing authority. State boards and societies had no capacity to compel even the county and town societies that were in some sense subsidiary to them. They instead "respectfully requested" information from their local counterparts and appealed to the "welfare of the Cause" to motivate action.[89] While most county organizations complied willingly, annual reports frequently complained that some were delinquent or failed to respond at all. The county societies, in turn, depended on their ability to gener-

Figure 2.2. "Agricultural Rooms" of the New York State Agricultural Society in Albany's "Old State House." Published in *Transactions of the New York State Agricultural Society* 14 (Albany: C. Van Benthuysen, 1855). Courtesy of the Library Company of Philadelphia.

ate popular interest in their annual fairs. The farm press, too, relied on a subscription base of popular support. The whole agricultural reform enterprise therefore resembled a social movement much more than a political machine, a narrow special interest lobby, or a bureaucratic organization. It had a flexible network structure whose unifying bonds were shared ideology and interest rather than, say, patron-client relationships or a rational hierarchy of functions. These shared commitments defined agricultural reform's core institutions and made for something like a "movement culture."

Social movements are often thought of as inherently oppositional, their paradigmatic acts figured as highly charged moments of struggle: marches, demonstrations, strikes, civil disobedience, and the like.[90] In their oppositional nature, they instance a clear dichotomy between state and society. But the antebellum agricultural reform movement does not fit this mold. Instead, it identified agriculture as a distinct domain of practice, constituted a corresponding public, defined problems, debated solutions (or performed such debates), and worked to endow government with the requisite capacities to respond. It was a state-building social movement, and because it generally sought to avoid open confrontation, it favored a linked strategy of agenda-setting in the public sphere and lobbying at the seats of power.

It worked remarkably well. By the outbreak of the Civil War, agricultural reformers were exerting influence at all levels of government, with an established presence in county seats, state capitals, and even Washington, DC. Having gained public funding to expand their movement, they began taking on official responsibilities that drew them ever-closer to the state. Quite independently of the parties, the agricultural reform movement was beginning to construct novel ways of governing.

The Sectional Distribution of Agricultural Reform

This trajectory soon brought agricultural reform to the national level, where its course was critically determined by the movement's pronounced sectional unevenness. The move from state- to national-level politics and the accompanying sectionalization of the reform movement's policy agenda are detailed in later chapters. Here it is necessary to demonstrate and account for the degree of sectional disparity, which was rooted in the relationship between agricultural organization and rural social structure.

Analysis of an 1858 national survey of agricultural societies indicates that they were heavily concentrated in the northern free states in both absolute and relative terms. Table 2.5 establishes three measures for gauging the relative extent of agricultural societies. The first (column 2) gives the distribution of organizations relative to total population, showing the incidence of agricultural societies in each region. The second (column 3) attempts to approximate farmers' organizing propensity by excluding the urban and enslaved populations. The last column gives a region's number of agricultural organizations relative to its number of farms, providing an alternative measure of the propensity for agricultural organizing. Each of the measures strongly favors the North.

It is not that southerners were entirely indifferent to agricultural reform. Yet although they read journals, adopted new planting and management methods, and formed some societies, southerners proved far less active organizers than did northerners.[91] J.D.B. DeBow, a leading observer of southern agriculture, believed that planters were simply uninterested in "agricultural societies among themselves." As a committee of the South Carolina State Agricultural Society admitted, "the habits of the planters are those of separate action. . . . Each regards his plantation as his empire."[92] Certainly no southern state agricultural society ever achieved the national stature of the New York, Massachusetts, or Ohio state organizations. Nor, before the Civil War, did any southern state other than Maryland go as far in establishing independent institutions of agricultural education and research as did the states of New York, Pennsylvania,

TABLE 2.5.
Agricultural Organizations by Region in 1858

	Agricultural organizations	Organizations per 100,000 inhabitants	Organizations per 100,000 free rural inhabitants	Organizations per 1,000 farms
Midwest	411	5.29	6.11	0.63
Northeast	279	2.63	4.10	0.50
Southwest	119	1.71	2.85	0.26
Southeast	78	1.45	2.68	0.31

Sources: Report of the Commissioner of Patents for the Year 1858: Agriculture (Washington, DC: William A. Harris, 1859), 91. Free rural population was estimated from the 1860 federal census as in table 2.1, thus somewhat overestimating the South's rate of agricultural organizing.

Notes: Midwest: Illinois, Indiana, Iowa, Michigan, Minnesota, Ohio, Wisconsin. Northeast: Connecticut, Maine, Massachusetts, New Hampshire, New Jersey, New York, Pennsylvania, Rhode Island, Vermont. Southwest: Alabama, Arkansas, Kentucky, Louisiana, Mississippi, Missouri, Tennessee, Texas. Southeast: Delaware, District of Columbia, Florida, Georgia, Maryland, North Carolina, South Carolina, Virginia. The territories and Pacific states were excluded.

The table displays a substantial divergence *within* the North that reflects artificially inflated midwestern figures. The Patent Office's distribution of reports and seeds operated as a de facto national subsidy for establishing agricultural societies. The effect was strong in the Midwest because societies were well-established rural institutions in many settlers' northeastern points of departure. This supposition is supported by Patent Office correspondence and the secondary literature. See (all in RG 16) George Fisher to Patent Office, Sept. 8, 1853, vol. 4 (1853), 103, and George Fisher to Patent Office, Feb. 17, 1855, vol. 6 (1854–55), 1004; Albert C. Ingham to Patent Office, Oct. 28, 1853, vol. 4 (1853), 711; John Harold to Patent Office, Feb. 12, 1855, vol. 6 (1854–55), 984; W.H.L. Smith to Patent Office, Feb. 15, 1855, vol. 6 (1854–55), 998; Fred Kniffen, "The American Agricultural Fair: Time and Place," *Annals of the Association of American Geographers* 41 (Mar. 1951): 44; Merrill E. Jarchow, "Early Minnesota Agricultural Societies and Fairs," *Minnesota History* 22 (Sept. 1941): 25.

In the case of older states, the figures more likely underestimate than overestimate the true totals. The density of settlement and activity in the older states probably meant that even well-informed correspondents, on whom the survey relied, could not have kept abreast of each new organization's founding. Pawley finds that the Patent Office survey counted about two-thirds of New York's official agricultural societies and perhaps only one-third or less of its total number of agricultural and horticultural societies, exclusive of possibly hundreds of smaller "farmers' clubs" (" 'The Balance-Sheet of Nature,' " 50–51). Similar circumstances may have depressed southern totals, but there is no reason to suppose that undercounting for either southern region was worse than for the Northeast. In short, while the absolute figures are somewhat off the mark, the relative difference between North and South is probably about right.

Michigan, Ohio, and even Iowa. To the extent that southerners did organize vibrant agricultural societies, they tended to be concentrated in the Upper South.[93]

The disparity aligns with broader sectional trends in economic development. What allowed the North to develop more rapidly than the South in the antebellum period, several historians have found, was the much higher density of its rural population and consequently the greater size and accessibility of its consumer markets for manufactured goods.[94] A similar dynamic was likely at work in the agricultural reform movement, which depended on well-attended fairs and a large market for agricultural publications. The point can be gener-

TABLE 2.6.
Structure of the Farm Sector by Region in 1860

	Number of farms (1000s)	Average farm size (acres)	Improved acres (%)	Number of farms of 500 or more acres
Midwest	666	128	53	2,348
Northeast	565	108	64	591
Southwest	408	294	2	7,696
Southeast	357	352	33	13,808

Sources: Compiled from census data collected in Study 2896 of the Inter-university Consortium for Political and Social Research (ICPSR) and accessed via IPUMS National Historical Geographic Information System: Version 14.0 [Database] (Minneapolis, MN: 2019), http://doi.org/10.18128/D050.V14.0.

alized. The North's greater rural population density sustained not only deeper consumer markets but thicker associational networks, including those knit together by agricultural societies.

The rural North's more egalitarian social structure also mattered. Northern farms were smaller, more numerous, and more intensively cultivated than their southern counterparts (table 2.6). Their inhabitants were more literate and better educated. Packed together relatively tightly, rural northerners interacted with each other more frequently and multiplied civic associations. For example, the Guilford Farmers' and Mechanics' Society was born of a casual encounter among local farmers in the town store. Similarly, the *Cultivator*'s Oxford agent picked up subscribers who happened to live near his church.[95] One can, of course, imagine similar occurrences in the South, but they must have happened less often. Because the northern countryside was denser and more equal, it compounded encounters among people who could readily collaborate to form new civic organizations.

On the other hand, the South, besides being more sparsely populated, included many more very large farms, that is, plantations. This aspect of southern society raised the barriers to forming agricultural societies and reduced their benefits, because wealthy planters could afford to establish private libraries and conduct costly experiments on their own. Moreover, social hierarchy—and, perhaps, concerns about policing large assemblies of slaves—strongly militated against the kind of popular fairs that were common in the North. In general, southern agricultural reform appears to have been an unapologetically elitist enterprise. A recent study concludes that "one simple explanation for the low subscription rolls of southern agricultural serials, low membership in agricultural societies, and modest agricultural fairs is often ignored—very few people were invited to participate."[96]

The agricultural press also manifested sectional disparity, which should

come as no surprise given the much larger and more literate northern population. By the end of the 1850s, according to one count, thirty agricultural journals were published in the North, excluding the Pacific states, as compared to
eleven in the South. Although these numbers are roughly proportional to sectional free population, the northern journals enjoyed a far larger aggregate circulation. The *Southern Cultivator* and the *American Cotton Planter*, the most
successful southern journals of the 1850s, each claimed a readership of about
ten thousand in 1859. By contrast, the *American Agriculturist* reached as many
as one hundred thousand subscribers, the *New England Farmer* around fifty
thousand, and even relatively small journals such as the *Boston Cultivator* and
Working Farmer more than twenty thousand.[97] Several northern journals enjoyed significant southern readerships, but this ultimately underscores the
North's superiority in the field. If southern subscribers led northern editors to
tiptoe around slavery, they did nothing to change basically northern outlooks,
interests, and loyalties.

For much of the nineteenth century, farmers' majority status allowed agricultural reformers to occupy a unique position in public affairs. They could have
it both ways, calling for specifically agricultural policies while denying any
particularistic class purpose. They could act like a special interest, and a largely
northern one at that, while plausibly claiming to represent the nation. "It is
conceded that money from the State should not be given unless it be to promote
some general object," wrote an advocate of agricultural education in 1850. "But
to what more general object can these grants be applied?"[98] The implication
was that farmers, particularly small-holding northern farmers, constituted society's norm. Few contemporary Americans were prepared to deny that apparent truism. As President Millard Fillmore reminded Congress that same year,
"More than three-fourths of our population are engaged in the cultivation of
the soil. The commercial, manufacturing, and navigating interests are all to a
great extent dependent on the agricultural."[99]

Agricultural reformers also spoke in the voice of scientific expertise. For all
the effort to substitute a democratic vernacular for patrician erudition, the movement was still concerned to establish a set of farming practices grounded in the
empirical study of nature. The obvious tension between majoritarian and expert
modes of knowledge and authority was eased, however, by the circumstance
that both served the needs of nonpartisan anti-politics. If the identification of
farmer with nation tended to render party politics unnecessary or corrupt, the
objectivity of empirical science often did the same.

Since northerners dominated the content of agricultural reform discourse, it
was also possible that the majoritarian and scientific tendencies could be turned

against the southern slave system. In fact, the agricultural reform movement played a critical role in forging the postrevolutionary northern political economy that eventually birthed the Republican Party and brought it to power. The next two chapters show how agricultural reform linked northern farmers' experience of economic development to the emergence of a distinctly northern developmental nationalism.

PART TWO

THE MAKING OF NORTHERN
ECONOMIC NATIONALISM

CHAPTER THREE

Economic Nationalism in the
Greater Rural Northeast

As colonial resistance pitched toward revolution in 1776, Thomas Paine wryly assured Americans that their grain would "always have a market while eating is the custom of Europe." What could be more obvious than the strength of American agricultural exports? In the years before independence, the colonies' ratio of foreign to domestic trade stood as high as four-to-one. If the British refused to take American staples, surely other countries would. Paine simply assumed that American farm surpluses would continue to go abroad regardless of the politics. "Our plan is commerce," he averred, "because, it is the interest of all Europe to have America a *free port*."[1]

But independence did actually change things. Europeans often chose to restrict American access to their imperial trade zones. More important, the internal American economy developed rapidly. Over the next three generations—as territorial conquest enlarged the country, immigrants swelled the population, and the transfer of sovereignty recalibrated government policy—the American foreign-to-domestic trade ratio completely reversed. By the 1840s, exports amounted to only a tenth of nonlocal trade. Everything else flowed through a dynamic internal market that took shape between the poles of Atlantic commerce and neighborly exchange. A robust domestic economy had emerged.[2]

This shift implied not only a new relationship with Europe but new relationships within the United States. The turn from Atlantic to internal trade occurred unevenly. Because the country's leading export, cotton, was confined to the South and its principal northern export, wheat, came increasingly from the Midwest, the domestic economy flourished largely in an area that I call the Greater Northeast. The resulting sectional disparities fueled struggle over national economic policy and conditioned political alliances both within and across the sections. In general, coastal merchants and western farmers invested in traditional export markets stood with southern planters in favor of free trade and aggressive overseas commercial expansion. Conversely, manufacturers clustered in the Greater Northeast tended to seek domestic development through protective tariffs.[3] Despite the conventional wisdom that import substitution amounts to a tax on agriculture, many northern farmers came to support the manufacturers, reasoning that a dependable "home market" was preferable to a contingent foreign one. By acting as a vehicle for repeatedly conveying this message to rural audiences, the agricultural reform movement helped broker a developmental alliance between northern farmers and manufacturers.

Slavery very much complicated the picture because it made for a uniquely nonnegotiable element in American national politics. After independence, the North gradually abolished human bondage at the same time as its economy pivoted inward. Meanwhile, southern planters discovered the secrets of short-staple cotton, leading to a remarkable expansion of slave country and its commodity exports. Yet North and South remained fastened together in a single national polity, so that disagreements over two sets of relatively distinct issues—slavery and trade policy—tended to overlap and get entangled. For a time, the second two-party system of Whigs and Democrats managed to foreground the economic questions while suppressing the matter of slavery. But in a representative democracy demographically dominated by free territory, southern leaders repeatedly insisted on the principle of limited federal powers, even when their own deployments of federal power, such as in the Fugitive Slave Act of 1850, were highly aggressive. Southern leaders were haunted by the thought of an unrestrained national government in the hands of a northern majority at best indifferent to the institution of slavery, at worst openly hostile to it. Slaveholders' anxieties thus tended to implicate the whole range of federal action. To many northerners, economic development came to appear hostage to the security of property rights in human beings.

This entanglement ultimately produced the Republican Party, a political organization that was northern and nationalist with equal militancy. Just as the abolitionist challenge to the Cotton Kingdom fostered southern proslavery ideology, states' rights jurisprudence, and eventual separatism, so too did southern obstruction of development policies foster a northern economic nationalism that Republicans proved best able to capture in the 1850s. The agricultural reform movement mediated this process by channeling the rural North's economic restructuring into a roughly coherent set of ideas that linked agriculture to manufacturing within the emerging domestic economy.

Economic change and ideological construction occurred in tandem. The story is complicated, so some signposting is in order. The shorthand I apply to the two essential developments is the "domestic economy" and the "home market," terms that could be used interchangeably but do better service applied to analytically distinct if historically interwoven patterns of trade and thought. Here, "domestic economy" refers to the period's economic conditions as historians describe them now, while "home market" refers to how contemporaries described those conditions then. Though a somewhat artificial distinction, it illuminates the interaction between material and ideological development. This chapter explains the domestic economy's effects in the countryside and how agricultural reformers cooperated with northern economic nationalists to construe those changes in accordance with the home market idea. It then suggests how politics and contingency gradually bound home market thinking to an implicitly antislavery position. The next chapter delves deeper into the domestic economy to show how leading Republican political economists drew on the discourse of scientific agriculture to interpret the country's developmental trajectory.

Together, these chapters aim to explain why northern farmers would support the Republicans' manifestly developmental vision.[4] The existing scholarship is oddly disjointed on this point. Explanations for the party's formation in the 1850s explicitly downplay questions of economic policy, yet it is well known that Republicans instituted an expansive program of economic legislation the moment they took control of the federal government.[5] Neither has the place of agriculture in Republican thinking been understood. Here, too, there is an odd disjuncture in the scholarship. Historians tend to see the Civil War as a watershed of American industrialization. Yet they have long rejected the so-called economic interpretation of the war by correctly pointing out that the antebellum North was much more agricultural than industrial.[6]

Attending to rural development in the Greater Northeast helps address these disjunctures. The region might seem an unlikely protagonist. Next to the ferocious dynamism of urban growth and western expansion, it appears the site of humdrum stasis or decline. Northeastern farmers did face serious challenges, including deteriorating soils, western competition, worsening parasitic outbreaks, and steady outmigration, each an apparent sign of slowdown. Yet the northeastern countryside was far more vital than typically realized. Alan Olmstead and Paul Rhode have recently demonstrated the huge effect of "biological innovation" in farming regions that economic historians once overlooked because of their relative unsuitability for mechanization. And as David Meyer points out, the spectacular growth of northeastern manufacturing in the last two decades of the antebellum era is simply unintelligible without prosperous nearby farmers to consume the goods.[7] Some rural communities did decline, but the rural Northeast as a whole continued to expand in population and output. Many of its farmers, in accord with agricultural reformers' exhortations, flourished by adopting new practices and technologies while shifting production from grains to a mix of crops that earned the benefit of nearby urban markets. They thereby also laid claim to an ethos every bit as modernizing as the more familiar reformism associated with the urban middle class.

This rural drive to modernity occurred within a developing domestic economy that reoriented northern farmers' commercial ties from an Atlantic to a national framework. Change led to new national policy demands, including protective tariffs to encourage domestic manufactures and, later, new federal agencies to promote agricultural reform. All of this played out in dynamic interaction with the South's quite different developmental trajectory, gradually putting enormous pressure on the established structures of the American state, which can be fairly characterized in this period as a slaveholding republic.[8] The Republican Party's rise to power and the transformative economic program that it implemented once there—including the destruction of slavery—cannot be understood apart from this story.

The Domestic Economy

The domestic economy emerged in what I call the Greater Northeast. Less a neatly bounded space than a set of conditions, the Greater Northeast expanded out of the Northeast proper—New England and the mid-Atlantic states—into the Ohio River Valley and the Great Lakes' region, as well as the upper Chesapeake around Baltimore. The region's economy was defined by the growing presence of cities and manufacturing surrounded by dense hinterlands of free farmers growing a diverse mix of crops. Maps 3.1 and 3.2 show cities, major transport routes, and county population densities after removing urban and enslaved people in order to highlight the enormous disparity between southern and northern hinterlands. Comparatively, the Greater Northeast fostered a much larger and more diverse public sphere of civic associations and print discourse, giving rise to the agricultural reform movement. It also oriented farmers toward domestic rather than transatlantic markets, establishing a complicated reciprocal relationship with cities: a wide range of raw materials and organic energy flowed to town, while consumer goods, new technologies, and fertilizers flowed back to the countryside.

The shaping of this geography had roots in the colonial era. Market exchange in the thirteen colonies largely followed the dictates of transatlantic trade, but whereas this was almost entirely the case in the Chesapeake and Lower South,

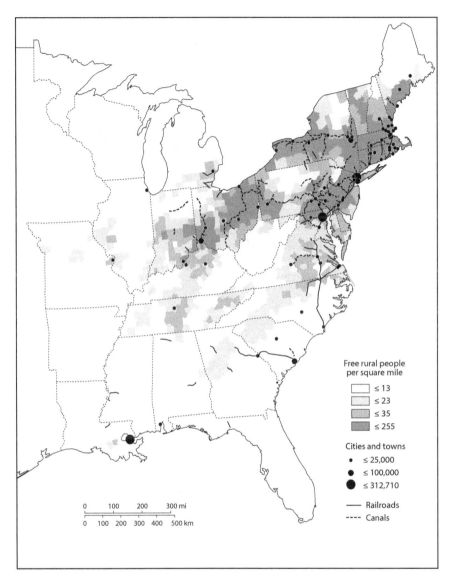

Map 3.1. The Greater Northeast in 1840. Map by Bill Nelson.

it was less so in New England and the mid-Atlantic. New England's signal difficulty—its lack of an agricultural staple that could pay for the manufactured imports it needed—stimulated creative efforts to generate some other basis for effective trade, leading to significant internal development. In the 1640s, for instance, its colonial governments brazenly experimented with import substitution policies directly at odds with British imperial regulations. Lacking cap-

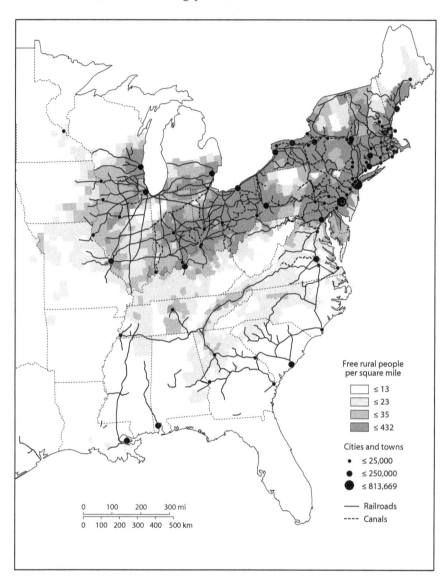

Map 3.2. The Greater Northeast in 1860. Map by Bill Nelson.

ital and technical expertise while facing metropolitan opposition, bootstrap industrialization largely failed. Instead, New England prospered by developing a diversified economy of fisheries, shipbuilding, mixed agriculture, timber and naval stores, and limited manufacturing. The Middle Colonies, which enjoyed the advantage of staple wheat production, also developed significant processing and manufacturing capacities. As in New England, however, these remained "tied, more or less directly, to the export sector," with merchants playing the key intermediary role by establishing northern ports as "hub[s] of intercolonial trade." The upshot was that, by the 1760s, the northern colonies enjoyed the rudiments of a domestic economy. Yet into the 1770s they were still riding an "export-led boom" indicative of continued dependence on the imperial trade system.[9]

The Revolutionary period disrupted this Atlantic orientation without immediately providing a clear alternative. The nonimportation movement, the war itself, and the closure of Caribbean markets underscored calls for a viable domestic manufacturing sector. The idea, in brief, was to use protective tariffs and subsidies to encourage a manufacturing sector that could offer American farmers a reliable domestic trade partner and thereby secure national economic independence. But capital and technical expertise remained in short supply, and the splintering of revolutionary political coalitions prevented a consistent development policy. Farmers made do with an astonishing expansion of household manufactures between 1770 and 1790. Then, the fallout from the French Revolution brought a lengthy period of European warfare and renewed demand for American foodstuffs. Farmers turned toward the Atlantic once more until the belligerents' interference with American shipping and the looming threat of Tecumseh's western Indian alliance led to a second war with Britain, again cutting off overseas markets.[10]

The War of 1812 marked the pivot of a transition phase. The emergence of domestic manufacturers generated new urban populations that offered farmers attractive domestic consumers. Equally important was the war's impact on Native Americans. By devastating tribes in the trans-Appalachian West—the actual point of the war, to a large extent—the army opened the sluices for a torrent of white settlers. Expansion into the Old Northwest, in turn, affected the rural Northeast in two very significant ways: first, by opening a channel of continuous out-migration and, second, by eventually inundating the region with competing grain and other agricultural products. After the 1820s, northeastern farmers experienced urban-industrial growth and western expansion as a carrot-and-stick combination.[11]

None of this could have happened without the antebellum transportation revolution. The importance of turnpikes, canals, steamboats, and railroads may seem obvious given standard depictions of the early Republic's rutted roads and forbidding mountain barriers. But it is worth remembering just what was at stake. Through most of recorded history, large bodies of water have tended to connect diverse groups of people; large bodies of land, to divide even similar ones. Economic development and political integration away from natural waterways inevitably required extensive infrastructure works, from Rome's proverbial road building to medieval China's Grand Canal.[12] So too in the early

United States. Artificial rivers and iron horses converted the northern interior into a fluid trade zone. "No country on earth, ancient or modern, can produce any thing in physical achievements at all comparable to this," boasted one northerner. John Quincy Adams described it as a "a boundless ocean without a shore."[13]

The transportation revolution exposed the northeastern countryside to the full force of western competition and enlarged the hinterland commerce that fueled urban growth. In response, farmers altered their crop mix, specializing in products that benefited from proximity to domestic consumers. The spatial dynamics of this process were described by Johann Heinrich von Thünen, a contemporary German aristocrat and agricultural improver with a penchant for mathematical modeling. Von Thünen posited an "isolated state" composed of a single central city surrounded by a geographically homogenous hinterland. Under these circumstances, agriculture would sort itself into specialized commercial zones based on distance to the urban market, forming a pattern of concentric rings. Similarly, as land value declined in proportion to distance from the urban market, so would the intensity of agricultural production. In reality, variations in geography and transportation warp the rings into odder shapes, but the basic pattern remains one of concentric agricultural zones. Although few contemporary Americans seem to have been aware of Von Thünen's model, many understood that distance from urban markets tended to produce stratified agricultural zones.[14]

The appearance of Von Thünen rings in the antebellum era thus indicates the new centrality of American cities as agricultural markets. Around Philadelphia, the distinctive zones were clearly discernible by 1840, whereas they had not been when Thomas Paine thumbed his nose at the British Empire three generations earlier. A similar pattern developed around Syracuse, New York, in the 1840s and 1850s as the combination of older canal and newer railroad links stimulated urban growth and transformed the surrounding hinterland. By the 1860s, the same process was transforming the agricultural surroundings of Madison, Wisconsin.[15] Thus the immediate hinterlands of first the large coastal cities and then the progressively more western interior canal and railroad towns turned to market gardening, truck farming, and the supply of hay and forest products for rapidly rising urban populations. Proliferating railroad routes expanded these inner rings in the 1850s by, for example, extending urban "milksheds" and the truck farming zone. Improved means of harvesting and packaging reinforced the effect. For instance, mechanical presses and the "revolving" rake significantly enlarged the range of commercial hay production that fueled horse-based urban transport. Further out, farmers tended to specialize in wool, dairy, and wheat.[16]

Nothing more obviously encouraged farmers to link their interests with manufacturers than wool production, which rose rapidly after 1800 thanks in part to the merino mania. After the War of 1812, returning British imports temporarily stymied domestic woolens, but ensuing tariff protection helped bring the industry back to life. As raw wool prices rose in the 1820s and 1830s, a second "sheep mania" took hold in the New England hill country, contributing to rural tariff support. A similar process occurred in the hill towns of the Hudson Valley, in central New York and western Pennsylvania, and throughout the Northeast, encouraging pro-tariff views and, according to one historian, expanding farmers' "mental horizons" as well. As wool growing moved into Ohio and further west, farmers in these areas, too, came around to support tariff protectionism.[17]

Rising western competition and reduced rates on raw wool after the 1846 Walker Tariff pushed marginal eastern producers out of the business. If they could manage it, they moved into dairying or, alternatively, into mutton production, for which they imported entirely different kinds of breeds. Elsewhere, however, wool growers persevered and even thrived thanks to continuous improvement in breeds and care. In Chelsea, Vermont, for instance, labor scarcity impeded a switch to the more lucrative dairy business until the end of the century, but area farmers maintained stable incomes in the intervening decades by upgrading their sheep flocks. Olmstead and Rhode estimate that, nationally, the average clip of raw wool per sheep more than doubled from 1800 to 1860, while the quality of the fiber improved significantly. These advances, they contend, contributed to "a complete redesign of the physical makeup of the sheep" in the two centuries before 1940, just one of the many ways in which "biological innovation" mattered long before genetic hybrids (figure 3.1).[18]

Figure 3.1. American merino sheep in the late nineteenth century. Published in Stephen Powers, *The American Merino: For Wool and Mutton* (New York: O. Judd Co., 1887). Wikimedia Commons.

Over the course of the nineteenth century, dairy farming supplanted not only wool but commercial wheat in much of the Northeast. One reason was declining soil fertility, which farmers addressed by adopting a set of practices known as convertible agriculture. This involved enlarging livestock herds, typically of milch cows, in order to produce soil-restoring manure, as well as more milk, butter, and cheese. If the new farming practices encouraged dairying, however, they did not demand abandonment of wheat. That step was driven by two other factors that impinged with increasing force in the first half of the nineteenth century: destructive pests and western competition.

Appearing first on the seaboard and moving inexorably west, the Hessian fly, the wheat midge, and the "blast" (black stem rust, a type of fungus) were only the worst of a host of infestations that devastated wheat yields. In 1811, the fly wreaked such havoc in eastern New York that John Jay compared wheat growing to "taking a ticket in a Lottery—more blanks than prizes."[19] The midge appeared about a decade later. In 1854, the year it entered the Genesee Valley, the New York State Agricultural Society estimated $15 million in damage. Largely because of the midge, wheat production in New York declined by forty-four percent from 1849 to 1859. To combat such threats, American researchers, farmers, and travelers sought pest-resistant wheat varieties and cultivation methods. "Without significant investments in maintenance operations," Olmstead and Rhode conclude, "grain yields would have plummeted as the plant's enemies evolved," leading to yields perhaps less than half of those actually achieved by 1909. Mediterranean wheat proved particularly important because it was both suitable to the late planting that combated the fly and enjoyed resistance to the midge. Introduced from Europe in 1819, it was the dominant variety by the 1850s. Farmers tried many others. In 1837, for instance, the New Castle County (DE) Agricultural Society heard about "Italian Spring Wheat" and resolved to obtain twelve barrels of seed for distribution among members.[20] Contemporary agricultural surveys identified literally scores of wheat strains in cultivation, many unknown only a few years earlier. This widespread and continuous experimentation indicates just how dynamically innovative American agriculture was in the period.[21]

Nevertheless, competition from high-yielding western farms beyond the pest frontier forced many northeastern farmers to give up wheat. In New York, the opening of the Erie Canal exposed eastern portions of the state to grain imports from Genesee and later from Ohio. In turn, wheat in eastern Ohio suffered in the 1850s in the face of new pests, declining soil fertility, and competition from the rest of the emerging midwestern breadbasket. The shift was far from total. In parts of New York, Pennsylvania, and the Chesapeake, wheat production continued with more intensive methods. This involved greater capital investment as farmers purchased new machinery and the horses to operate them, in addition to seed and fertilizer. The new tools included the much-studied mechanical reaper but also improved plows, seed drills, manure spreaders, fanning mills, cultivators, harrows, and horse-powered threshers, not to mention improved breeds of horses. Economic competition and ecological constraint thus required significant adjustment.[22] When northeastern farmers continued growing wheat commercially, a higher proportion of their crop went to domestic consumers than did the wheat of the Midwest.[23]

Wheat's decline helped make dairying an increasingly important source of northeastern farm earnings. Indicative of the region's scholarly neglect, economic historians have paid far more attention to grains and cotton, but because women typically took charge of the dairy, rural gender historians have done revealing work on the subject.[24] Dairy products included butter, cheese, and milk, with butter by far the most important. Exports, especially to the West Indies, were significant throughout the early Republic, but these declined to almost nothing during the War of 1812 and never really recovered.[25] Thereafter, domestic city dwellers and workers in newly founded manufacturing villages became the primary consumers. Cheese production, which centered in the St. Lawrence and Mohawk River Valleys of New York and in the Western Reserve of Ohio, followed a somewhat different path, enjoying growing European markets throughout the antebellum period. Still, the vast majority of saleable American cheese went to domestic consumers.[26] Milk remained an entirely domestic trade.

Serious dairy production required farmers to intensify inputs of both capital and labor relative to land. A substantial dairy required new buildings, including redesigned barns and specialized sheds fitted with stanchions to confine cows during milking, as well as smaller outbuildings such as an ice house. "A pervasive concern with system informed the arrangement" of these structures because the constant care of dairy cows raised labor demands, fostering attention to efficiency. Other capital costs went to new tools such as box churns, improved butter-working tables, butter prints and pails, cheese vats, multi-blade steel dairy knives, and "self-acting" cheese presses. Among these items, even those that could be made locally were increasingly factory produced. The Patent Office issued 244 patents for butter-related machinery in the years between 1802 and 1849; from 1850 to 1873 that number leapt to 1,360. Farmers also enlarged cattle stocks and, to a lesser extent, upgraded breeds. To feed their herds they planted higher-yielding grasses and acquired more land for fodder production, which then necessitated additional fertilizers and investment in planting and harvesting machinery. These multiple needs hint at the complex interdependencies of farm operations and, increasingly, of the reciprocal relationship between the agricultural and manufacturing sectors. Steadily rising milk yields accompanied the changes. "In just a generation," concludes Sally McMurry, "a dynamic innovativeness had replaced conservatism" in the economic strategies of dairy farming families.[27]

Observing the constant outflow of migrants, some contemporaries and historians have thought that the northeastern countryside was suffering economic devastation. Yet rising land values tell a different story. Soil depletion, pest infestation, western competition, and outmigration—the whole range of rural problems—were not so great, given proximity to urban markets, to make farming untenable. In fact, at midcentury northeastern farms appear to have been slightly more profitable than midwestern ones on average.[28]

Rather than overall decline, land pressure structured a process of social differentiation. High land values gave smaller landowners a double incentive to migrate: on the one hand, they could not expect to settle their children nearby; on the other, they would earn a tidy sum from selling land they did possess, money that would go further in the West where lands recently expropriated from Indians were relatively cheap. Those who remained tended to fall into one of two categories. At the upper end were the farmers most committed to reform and improvement, generally older and wealthier than those who left. These "persisters" enjoyed the prosperity to engage in the more capital-intensive farming that could thrive in the region and to expand operations by buying their departing neighbors' land. They also married later and practiced birth control to reduce fertility—both signs of middle-class formation. At the lower end, impoverished farmers and immigrants who lacked the resources to set up in the West were increasingly drawn into tenancy, outwork and wage labor, or held on to marginal farms where access to forested uplands provided supplementary resources outside the market. What was happening, then, was not absolute decline, but social stratification.[29]

In comparative perspective, however, the rural Northeast remained quite egalitarian. The northern countryside enjoyed greater wealth equality than contemporary urban areas, the South, and the United States as a whole. Within the North, rural wealth distribution differed little between the Northeast and Midwest once age is accounted for. Most middling northern farm families worked with their own hands, and any additional hired labor often came from relatives and neighbors. Hence, one agricultural editor urged farmers to educate their children so that they "would no longer complain of the difficulty of obtaining *good help.*"[30] Celebrations of what historians call the "agricultural ladder," in which wage labor during youth leads to propertied independence by middle age, made a good deal of sense. There is evidence that rising wages actually made it easier to acquire a farm in the 1850s and 1860s than beforehand. For many farmers, then, economic development offered a middle-class competence, what agricultural reformers extolled as the virtues of "that just medium which affords the truest sources of man's happiness, 'neither poverty nor riches.'"[31]

Many of the agricultural developments described above are manifest in the experience of the Squires family, as documented in the diary of one of its sons, Francis. In 1840, the family were living fifty miles north of Utica, New York, and specializing successfully in dairying. We do not know if they subscribed to an agricultural journal, but we do know that they practiced up-to-date techniques such as rotating crops, augmenting soil with plaster, and stabling cattle in winter, and that the father won a premium for his cheese at the 1844 county fair. Despite their large and modern operation, the family depended mostly on their own labor and exchanging work with neighbors. Only during the bottleneck of the haying season did they hire extra hands. In 1846, the family relocated to Oswego County, where they shifted production in a number of ways. Francis and his brother engaged in full-time coopering for neighboring manufacturers, while their parents handled a reduced dairy business directed toward fresh butter, which was more profitable than cheese given the nearby urban markets. The family changed course again in the 1850s, moving into commercial apple production and stock raising. In 1853, Francis observed that his father could still "do a good days [*sic*] work" at sixty-eight years old. Members of the rural middle class responding dynamically to economic change, the Squires family remained laboring people.[32]

Similar examples are easily multiplied.[33] None, perhaps, are really representative, but that is part of the point. Northeastern farming was diverse and dynamic. It resists easy generalization. "Any observant American," wrote one well-traveled southerner in the 1850s, "will be utterly astonished at the variety and quantity of Northern agricultural productions kept for sale."[34] Besides wool, wheat, and dairy, there were fodder crops to supply energy for urban horses; truck farms and market gardens that provided urban consumers with fresh fruits, vegetables, and eggs; and various niche economies such as cut flowers for the homes of the wealthy and hops for workingmen's beer.

The significance of the domestic economy hinges on this variety. Ramifying development created a relatively autonomous economic space in the American interior that challenged the colonial-era dominance of the Atlantic world. Foreign trade expanded after independence thanks to cotton and other exports, and some northeastern farmers, such as Connecticut's tobacco growers, fully participated in this expansion.[35] But, in general, farmers in the Greater Northeast experienced capitalism as a national phenomenon, extending well beyond local communities yet significantly bounded by a market structure oriented to domestic towns and cities. Aided by new transportation links and partially freed from the spoilage constraints of very long-distance trade—but also pushed by new competitors and environmental challenges—middle-class farmers followed the dictates of agricultural reform to intensify labor and capital inputs, experiment with new techniques and technologies, and shift production toward an eclectic crop mix bound for domestic consumption.

In doing so, they gradually reimagined their world. Once understood by reference to the polarities of locality and empire, it now became framed by the categories of the North and the nation. And this, in turn, involved new ideological and political commitments. Thomas Paine's vision of America as a coastal free port gave way to a new vision of a gargantuan home market. Southerners, meanwhile, conceived of the United States as basically an expansive trade federation within the larger global market. A politics pitting domestic development against international commerce characterized many countries during the nineteenth century. But the United States was unusual in one very important regard: its trade politics overlapped the geography of slavery.

The Home Market

Slavery caused the Civil War. The North's part in this event was determined by the emergence of the Republican Party, which reflected genuine repugnance at human bondage, fears of slaveholding's antidemocratic entailments, and the manifold resistance of enslaved people. But American history from Reconstruction to the modern carceral state shows plainly that white northerners' commitment to black liberation has been lukewarm at best. On the other hand, the ambition of Republican economic policy remained consistent. Neither abolitionism nor free labor ideology can explain the full form and scope of this program, which from 1862 until past the turn of the century shaped America's ascent to global industrial power. For that, we need a story about northern economic nationalism. That story centers on the idea of the home market.

Since at least the 1600s, close European observers of political economy had understood that manufactures were what made countries rich and powerful.[36] Technological advances upped the stakes by the time the colonial crisis unfolded in the late 1700s. Despite losing much of its empire, Britain emerged from that crisis more powerful than ever as the "workshop of the world." It was clear to many American nationalists, particularly in the states of the Northeast that had colonial experience with limited manufacturing and economic diversification, that the United States would need an industrial policy to catch up. Most economists remain skeptical about protectionism, but it is a matter of historical record that industrialization has almost universally occurred under one form or another of protectionist regime. As one early American tariff advocate observed, "Every nation that follows that same policy is rich, every nation which neglects that policy is poor. The idea of free trade is utopian."[37] Recent literature on the East Asian "developmental state" underscores the importance for late developers of industrial policy in some form or other.[38]

But in a predominantly agricultural society, not everyone necessarily wanted industrial development. Thomas Jefferson and James Madison famously hated the idea until the humiliations of the War of 1812 convinced them that at least some domestic industrial capacity was necessary.[39] There were obvious reasons for deploring factory conditions that repeatedly led observers to visions of damnation. Recalling William Blake's "dark satanic mills," Rebecca Harding Davis described a fictionalized ironmaking district in Appalachia as a "street in Hell."[40] Back in the 1780s, ordinary craftsmen could clamor for tariff protection because they believed that republican political institutions would empower them to control their own labor. Yet urban craftsmen remained a tiny minority of the population, and after the Constitution shifted the locus of trade policy from the states to the national level, their influence dwindled rapidly.[41] Farmers, the vast majority of the electorate, were the crucial constituency. They were the ones who had to be convinced of the benefits of protectionism if a nationalist economic program was ever to achieve sustained expression. Mathew Carey, the leading protectionist of the 1820s, stated the situation plainly: "As the agriculturists are now, and are likely to be for a century at least, the predominating interest in this country, and have a decided influence in its legislation, it is of immense importance that they should form correct views on the system best calculated to promote the general welfare."[42]

This was where the home market thesis came in. Carey and other economic nationalists repeated the same simple argument: American farmers would benefit from the growth of domestic industry because it would provide a reliable home market for their goods. There was "an identity of interests between agriculture and manufactures," they insisted. This principle formed the foundation of protectionist appeals to farmers for the rest of the nineteenth century. "The more manufacturers you have the more consumers there will be," explained Thomas H. Dudley to the New Jersey Agricultural Society in 1882, "and the more extended and better the farmer's market." As early as the 1810s and increasingly from the 1860s, protectionists were trumpeting the same message throughout the Midwest. Home market rhetoric was one of the Greater Northeast's defining conditions, and by midcentury, the domestic economy's emergence was turning it from merely a plausible projection of the country's future into an apparently accurate description of what was actually happening.[43]

In 1819, the home market idea simultaneously received a major impetus and a major challenge when a serious financial panic and Missouri's application for statehood sparked parallel crises that fractured the nationalist coalition and exposed diverging sectional trajectories. In the North, the post-panic depression fostered support for a protected home market. In the South, the rancorous debates over slavery in Missouri led to a renewal of states' rights rhetoric and constitutional arguments against protectionism, positions that dovetailed with cotton exporters' free trade interests. The overlapping of these fault lines helped consolidate the emerging categories of North and South.

The financial crisis and subsequent economic depression followed a collapse in European demand for American farm commodities. With agricultural prices in steep decline, many northern commentators argued that only an enlarged domestic manufacturing sector could reconstitute the market.[44] In a series of 1821 pamphlets whose title, "The Farmer's and Planter's Friend," indicates their target audience, Mathew Carey maintained that the era of high European demand for American farm products had ended permanently and that commodity prices would remain depressed unless the domestic economy was rebalanced by expanding the manufacturing sector. The same point was made before the New York Board of Agriculture in George Tibbits's precisely titled *Memoir on the Expediency and Practicability of Improving or Creating Home Markets for the Sale of Agricultural Productions and Raw Materials, by the Introduction or Growth of Artizans and Manufacturers*.[45] Nicholas Biddle, the future president of the Second Bank of the United States, similarly thought that by supporting tariffs farmers could "by their own efforts retrieve the loss of the foreign markets."[46]

Some coastal merchants fought to prevent this domestic reorientation. Members of the Massachusetts Society for Promoting Agriculture, who were closely connected to Boston's mercantile interests, bitterly opposed protective tariffs as "unnatural and morbid."[47] But most agricultural organizations explicitly aligned themselves with manufacturers. In 1820, for instance, a petition from a subsidiary of the New York Board of Agriculture reminded Congress that the board "embraces the encouragement of domestic manufactures, as well as the cultivation of the soil."[48] A year later, the Berkshire County (MA) Agricultural Society petitioned Congress for a second time to raise tariff rates so that "a home market for the farmer will be provided."[49] Agricultural societies in Connecticut, Ohio, Maryland, and Pennsylvania made similar cases for a turn to protectionism.[50]

The wool industry occupied a special place in the home market vision. Americans knew that it had been a key to economic power in Europe since the Middle Ages, but perhaps even more important in the American context was the nexus that it formed between wool growers and manufacturers. The Panic of 1819 led to renewed arguments that, with proper government care, wool offered a promising avenue back to prosperity for both groups. In 1820, for instance, John Skinner's *American Farmer* ran a series of essays arguing that farmers would derive great benefit from a tariff-protected domestic woolens industry. "Let not the American Farmer think these are matters, with which he has no concern," the author warned. "He is as deeply interested in them, as any other in the community."[51] Two years later, a committee of the Bucks County (PA) Agricultural Society encouraged farmers to expand sheep flocks now that "our manufacturing establishments are increasing with stability."[52] Agricultural society members in Berkshire argued the same thing, and, as it turned out, woolens mills powered local development for the next half century.[53] Over the next decade or so, similar statements appeared in a mass of petitions, speeches, editorials, and resolutions.

Agricultural reform at this time still tended to reflect the views and interests of the rural patriciate, including mega-landlords such as Robert R. Livingston and Stephen Van Rensselaer, for whom domestic manufacturing, internal improvements, and scientific agriculture were all parts of an expansive developmental outlook aimed at establishing American nationhood while raising the value and income of their land holdings. But that is not to say that developmentalism had no popular appeal or support. Less exalted farmers did, in fact, expand wool production and express belief in the home market idea. As the American interior continued to fill up with settlers, ordinary rural northerners attained a critical stake in economic development. By midcentury, the home market idea appeared to accord with what farmers in the Greater Northeast had actually experienced: a shift toward production for domestic towns and cities. While cotton planters and merchant princes still looked to export markets, northeastern farmers literally lived the home market as the American countryside transformed around them. Ralph Waldo Emerson channeled the prevailing view when he observed, in an 1858 address at his county agricultural fair, that the northeastern farmer enjoyed "the advantage of a market at his own door, the manufactory in the same town."[54]

Agricultural reformers had been saying this for years. Protectionist sympathies remained largely unchanged with reform's shift from elite project to popular movement. Virtually all northern farm journal editors "insisted that agriculture profited from the growth of manufactures" and historians have again and again found evidence that farmers responded positively to the message.[55] The fairs provided opportunities to reiterate the point and, perhaps more important, to stage the domestic economy and mark its annual progress. The fairs modeled the connection of agriculture and manufacturing by "embracing the entire circle of the industrial pursuits of our citizens."[56] Editors and orators expressly highlighted the implications of this side-by-side arrangement of goods, praising the "nice adjustment and harmonious grouping of the varied productions of the husbandmen, the artisan, the manufacturer, and the artist."[57] As one of Wisconsin's first agricultural implement manufacturers explained, "Agricultural Associations are every where founded upon the principle of the intimate relations of all the industrial pursuits."[58] It seems reasonable to surmise, then, that a significant number of northern farmers viewed a tariff-protected home market as a good bet.

The home market thesis held appeal in the Upper South, too.[59] With a significant urban-manufacturing base, relatively dense hinterlands, and a mixed agriculture not necessarily committed to foreign markets, the Upper South resembled the Greater Northeast, most obviously around the cities of Baltimore, Cincinnati, Louisville, and St. Louis. Many leading protectionists hailed from these areas. Hezekiah Niles, who published a popular digest of national events and official communications out of Baltimore, was probably the country's most important tariff advocate after Mathew Carey. John Skinner, another Marylander, established a tradition of home market advocacy in the pages of the *American Farmer* that lasted into the McKinley era.[60] Undoubtedly the most important Upper South exponent of the home market thesis was Kentucky's Henry Clay. "It is most desirable that there should be both a home and a foreign market," Clay argued in Congress, "but with respect to their relative superiority, I cannot entertain a doubt. The home market is first in order." This was because it offered strategic security in case of war, steadier demand than foreign markets, and the "creation of reciprocal interests" linking Americans together. "A genuine American System," he concluded, "is only to be accomplished by the establishment of a tariff."[61]

This reasoning won few converts further South. Although in 1816 many southerners had somewhat reluctantly accepted temporary protectionism as a strategic measure, by 1820 they began to change their minds.[62] In shifting position, they moved the tariff and the American System's broader vision from the realm of policy, a space for negotiation, to the realm of principle, a ground for unyielding resistance. The South's export economy put its interests on the side of free trade, but the tariff would never have proved so divisive if not for slavery. For at the same moment that the Panic of 1819 led northern farmers to welcome a protected home market, the acrimony of the Missouri Crisis severely undercut the idea among southerners, who grew alarmed that federal power might be turned against slavery. Clay thoroughly repudiated federal intervention on "that delicate subject." He himself owned dozens of people. Yet many of his peers regarded his assurances as insufficient, indeed as "insulting to the understandings of every . . . slave holder."[63]

In 1820, Virginia's United Agricultural Societies expressed slaveholder understandings in a series of petitions to Congress. The first simply averred that "bounties, monopolies, or protective duties" were useless to alleviate economic "calamities in their nature as inevitable as they are incurable, by legislative interposition." This foreshadowed growing southern invocations of laissez-faire principles in national economic policy debates. The second petition was considerably more strident. The tariff bill before Congress, it argued, "contemplates nothing less than a radical change in our political institutions." The new policy aimed to destroy the country's international commerce by provoking a trade war. Once customs receipts plummeted, farmers would end up saddled with internal taxes while "another party, less attached to the soil, and completely dependent on the bounty of government, is to be raised to opulence and power." Moreover, the home market argument for expanding the manufacturing sector amounted to a program for converting farmers into an industrial proletariat. "In plain English, the hardy, independent sons of our forests and our fields are called on to consent to be starved into weavers and button-makers." Here the petition previewed proslavery ideologists' later critique of northern wage labor.[64]

Rejecting a government-sponsored alliance between farmers and domestic manufacturers, Virginia's leading agricultural reformers stuck by the Old Republicans' "marriage" of "agriculture and foreign commerce."[65] That union had been proposed by James Madison in the 1790s as the basis of national economic policy, and it had been codified with strong southern support in the Navigation Act of 1817, which aimed to bolster American shipping. Although many southerners disapproved of discriminating against foreign shippers, they rarely attacked the policy with the rancor and high constitutional principle they reserved for the tariff.[66] Thus, when the House Agriculture Committee's veteran Jeffersonians took up the Virginia petitions in 1821, they quickly moved past questions of expedience to argue that the tariff was an illegal encroachment on "state sovereignties."[67]

Recourse to states' rights offered a defense of slavery without saying so. The logic was this: by locating sovereignty in the states and limiting national powers to their narrowest constitutional span, slavery could be shielded from federal interference. North Carolina's Nathaniel Macon spelled it out in an 1818 letter—republished portentously in 1857—urging a colleague to oppose federally funded transportation projects as unconstitutional. "If Congress can make canals they can with more propriety emancipate," he warned.[68] Northerners' push to exclude slavery from Missouri and the entire Louisiana Purchase drove that warning home, leading one South Carolinian to stress the overriding importance of "keeping the hands of Congress from touching the question of slavery."[69] As another writer put it unceremoniously, "the blacks constitute either absolutely, or instrumentally, the wealth of our southern states."[70]

While Carey and Clay argued the home market thesis, Virginia's Old Republicans revived the "Spirit of 98" with its "interposition" doctrine sanctioning the states to declare federal law unconstitutional. Taking up the banner of states' rights and strict constructionism, the so-called Richmond Junto rehabilitated once outcast radical opponents of federal power. It now mended fences with John Randolph and gave a public platform to John Taylor of Caroline.[71] Randolph was by this time legendary for his intemperate defense of slaveholder sovereignty. In 1807 he had famously declared, "If union and the manumission of slaves are to be put into the scale, let union kick the beam!" Taylor, in the wake of Missouri, feared that any consolidation of the federal government would inevitably lead to conflict over slavery and so developed an influential theory of the union as a compact of severally sovereign states. He was also a kind of godfather to Virginia's agricultural reformers. Not only did his arguments inform the United Agricultural Societies' anti-tariff petitions, but the organization's secretary, Edmund Ruffin, would soon emerge as his heir: the South's preeminent agricultural reformer, an opponent of federal power, an aggressive defender of slavery, and, finally, a passionate secessionist. Legend has it that Ruffin fired the first shot of the Civil War.[72]

Strict constructionism gradually gained influence in the wider South, if not right away and never completely. In 1820, even South Carolinians voiced their tariff opposition primarily in practical rather than constitutional terms.[73] Yet within less than a decade—after they blamed Denmark Vesey's aborted slave rebellion on loose northern talk about natural rights and after David Walker worked to put his *Appeal* for immediate emancipation into slaves' own hands— South Carolina's planter elite would lead a new movement to "nullify" the so-called Tariff of Abominations in order to protect their particular interests and peculiar institutions from outside meddling. When South Carolina finally seceded a generation later, the states' rights doctrine once brandished against tariffs was explicitly harnessed to the defense of slavery.[74] In 1859 and 1860, John Calhoun's son, a prominent agricultural reformer and soon-to-be secession commissioner, addressed the state agricultural society in order to rail against "unjust and outrageous" tariffs, the "ignorant and stupid nature of the negro," and the intolerable menace of the "Black Republicans." Edmund Ruffin attended the second of these talks and found it much to the point.[75] In the two southern bellwether states of Virginia and South Carolina, agricultural reformers tracked a politics that linked free trade, strict limits on federal power, and the defense of slavery.

The tariff proved especially susceptible to these sectionalizing linkages for several reasons. To begin with, pro- and anti-tariff interests plausibly mapped onto the geographic division between free and slave states. The correspondence was far from perfect, especially in the West and Upper South, but it was close enough to become a vehicle for expressing antagonistic sectional interests.[76] Institutional features of American federalism amplified this tendency. From the Constitutional Convention until the late 1800s, everyone agreed that customs duties would provide the lion's share of federal revenues.[77] This meant that negotiations over rates were institutionally hardwired. Facing an increasingly strident and sophisticated northern protectionist lobby, southerners grounded their opposition in the principles of states' rights, strict constructionism and laissez-faire.[78] As Andrew Calhoun put it, "To represent the South, or cotton country, requires a thorough knowledge of its great and commanding interest, and as a minority section, the uncompromising advocates [*sic*] of its rights."[79] The tariff also implicated national governing power more than any other major issue except for the disposition of western territory. To be sure, clashing views on federal banking and transportation policies provoked major political battles through the 1830s and 1840s. But these issues could be addressed at the state level, whereas states could not engage in protectionism. The tariff, as one southern opponent pointed out, "necessarily involves complete unqualified jurisdiction over a territory."[80] Not only did this mean that tariff debates *had* to take place at the national level, it meant that, unlike banking and internal improvements, the tariff was poorly adapted to the Jacksonian two-party system's characteristic mode of connecting state with national politics.

The party system kept sectionalism effectively at bay between the Missouri Compromise and the US-Mexico War. By identifying political divisions that were meaningful within both states and the nation, the parties linked political leaders across sectional lines.[81] This worked especially well when it came to banking, which mobilized competing interests everywhere and could be grafted onto existing intrastate political divisions. Nullification failed in 1832 because most southern politicians embraced the emerging partisan alignment annealed by Andrew Jackson's bank veto and its cascading financial ramifications in the states. For strict constructionists like the Richmond Junto's Thomas Ritchie and New York's Van Burenites, an ideology of limited government and Jackson's charismatic appeal made a suitable basis for tying the "planters of the South and the plain republicans of the north" within the Democratic Party. Other southerners opted for the Whigs, the party of government-sponsored economic development. Yet in the cotton states, many Whigs were actually states' righters opposed to Jackson's dictatorial style, while those who embraced the developmental platform were more interested in banks and internal improvements than in protectionism.[82]

Among the slave states, the full scope of Clay's American System held consistent appeal only in the border states. With trade patterns similar to the Greater Northeast's, the home market idea suited this area. But this was also slave country. Clay always found himself caught between the two commitments. Perhaps his most characteristic move was to embrace the American Colonization Society, a contradictory and ineffective compromise on slavery that promoted the expulsion of freed blacks and that could be assimilated to the American System's vision of a proactive national government.[83] By the 1850s, however, precisely these twinned commitments—too obligated to slavery for the North, too invested in federal power for the South—had rendered Clay's legacy and the remaining Upper South Whigs irrelevant as a political force. Squeezed in the middle, the Upper South's agency was reduced to picking sides in the Civil War.

It might have turned out differently. Had Clay won the vanishingly close presidential race of 1844, perhaps he could have kept the United States from conquering half of Mexico.[84] Then the question of slavery's status in the territories may not have reemerged with such vehemence, southerners may not have converted the Democratic Party into a mechanism for obstructing federal development policies demanded in the North, and the economic controversies that fueled the Jacksonian era may have continued to run orthogonally to the slavery issue. Instead, those things did happen, and the result was that divisions over slavery and economic development lined up with one another in the 1850s as they had when the Panic of 1819 coincided with the Missouri Crisis. A run of binaries now stacked up in ordered columns: national versus state sovereignty, active versus limited government, domestic versus overseas markets, sectoral diversification versus concentration, free versus slave labor, and, finally, North versus South.

The concatenation of factors that gradually linked the agricultural reform movement's dominant northern wing to the Republican Party's antislavery politics had both structural and contingent determinants. When independence broke the grip of the British imperial trade system, northern domestic economic development quickly led to policy demands on the national government, which slaveholders opposed as inimical to their export interests and portentous of future moves against slavery. Yet the construction of a northern identity cannot be taken for granted, and domestic development cannot be read simply as industrialization. Because farmers remained a majority of the northern electorate, their stake in development was critical. The home market thesis did essential ideological work, reducing the complexity of the domestic economy to the figure of the nation. Understood as a mutuality of agriculture and manufacturing, this was an easy-to-grasp nationalist vision that was plausibly grounded in farmers' day-to-day experience.

The agricultural reform movement delivered the message over and over again. It first provided a forum for economic nationalists such as Mathew Carey and then took up the cause itself with gusto. John Skinner's ideological trajectory is illustrative. Initially he lacked strong feelings about the tariff, but the 1819 financial crisis that struck only a few months after he began publishing the *American Farmer* led him to turn the journal into a home market advocate. As he grew more confident in the idea, he drifted northward from Baltimore. In 1845, he started a new agricultural journal with the financial backing of Horace Greeley, the influential New York newspaperman who advocated both agricultural reform and tariff protectionism. Three years later, he moved the journal to Philadelphia, renamed it *The Plough, the Loom and the Anvil*, and dedicated its pages to disseminating the elaborate protectionist theorizing of Mathew Carey's son, Henry.[85]

It was Henry Carey who did the most in the 1840s and 1850s to deepen the agro-industrial linkage at the heart of the home market thesis, moving beyond the simple reciprocity of interests that his father's generation of economic nationalists tended to stress. Drawing heavily on the discourse of agricultural reform, Henry described a more complex set of interdependencies associated with the progress of science and technology. The next chapter tackles this intellectual program and its place in the ideological orientation of the early Republican Party.

CHAPTER FOUR

Henry C. Carey and the Republican Developmental Synthesis

During the 1840s and 1850s, Henry Charles Carey emerged as the central figure of the American school of political economy and a key theorist for the nascent Republican Party. In copious writings theoretical and popular, he expanded on the home market idea of his father's generation with an original theory of agro-technological development. His big point was that manufacturing provided agriculture not only with markets for its output, but with technological inputs to enhance its productivity—everything from steel plows to chemical fertilizers. "Improvements in agriculture always accompany manufactures," he maintained.[1] Industrialization was thus what made agriculture scientific. For Carey, this clearly implied that farmers should support a protective tariff. Southern planters were characteristically hostile to the idea. "Sheer nonsense," jeered a letter in the *Southern Cultivator*, while a proslavery ideologist mocked Carey as "the great doctor of nations" with "the remedy in his pocket."[2]

The dispute, on the surface, pitted free trade against protectionism. But beneath the policy question yawned a deeper chasm over conceptions of how the economy worked. Southerners tended to equate national wealth with staple exports.[3] Northerners like Carey, on the other hand, believed that economic development depended on complex regional integration. In their view, mere growth became development when town and country meshed into dense exchange networks that offered scope and opportunity for transformative innovation. The home market was therefore more than a way to balance supply and demand between agriculture and manufacturing, it was a cauldron of technological progress.

I call this vision the Republican developmental synthesis. It was a set of ideas that reconciled urban and rural interests within a single framework, providing a common rationale for industrial protectionism and for the agricultural policy instantiated by the land-grant colleges and the Department of Agriculture. It is no accident that Republican Senator Justin Morrill lent his name to both the Morrill Tariff of 1861 and the Morrill Land-Grant Act of 1862. The Republican developmental synthesis helps explain how a party that very quickly became associated with industrialization maintained a social base in the rural and small-town North.

It also brings into focus a neglected aspect of the antislavery imagination. Historians have detailed how Republicans, following the precepts of liberal economic theory, contrasted slavery's vicious incentives with free labor's virtuous ones. But they have paid less attention to how Republicans, following a distinct genealogy of developmental economic theory, contrasted slavery's malignant exploitation of people with technology's ostensibly benign utilization of nature. Leading Republican ideologues saw the coercion of labor as wasted effort better applied to harnessing nature's abundant "forces." This was the essence of economic development. When proslavery theorists argued that white liberty required black bondage, these Republicans answered not only with paeans to free labor but with arguments that science and technology promised rising living standards for all—indeed, that they promised more freedom *from* labor or, at least, a transformed kind of labor that was as much mental as physical. Republicans presented technology as history's underlying engine of emancipation.

These positions were grounded in how northerners thought about nature and its relationship to labor, topics that were richly explored in the discourse of scientific agriculture. As Horace Mann put it, farmers' "pecuniary returns" derived from their coming into "perpetual contact with the forces of nature."[4] The agricultural reform movement thus proved a crucial forum for working out ideas that came to define Republican ideology and policy. Moreover, just as farmers' experience with the domestic economy imparted credence to the home market thesis, their growing awareness of the ways that scientific and technological novelty were transforming agricultural practice lent the Republican developmental synthesis a powerful verisimilitude. Technological progress, in turn, gave evidence of the superiority of free labor. That was what made slavery seem *backward* as well as unjust and undemocratic.

Carey, more than anyone else, attempted to provide an encompassing theoretical framework for the nexus of agricultural reform and industrial development. Echoes and parallels of his thinking, often articulated at agricultural fairs, show how scientific agriculture could be made to ground a technological repudiation of slavery. Agricultural reform thus became central to the intellectual rationale for the Republicans' antislavery stance and economic policy program from the late 1850s onward.

On Manure

Like his father, Henry Carey wrote an endless stream of articles, pamphlets, and books that always came back to protectionism as the one essential policy for national prosperity. For this reason, he is typically understood as a herald of industrialization.[5] But he wrote so extensively about agriculture that he cannot be pigeonholed so easily. Carey's characteristic intellectual move was to resolve oppositions by conceiving a deeper harmony uniting them. He did so with particular originality and effectiveness when it came to the traditional distinction between agriculture and manufacturing. Both, he came to think, were simply ways of turning natural processes toward human ends.

Carey matured his developmental theory in the late 1840s and spent the next two decades elaborating it ad nauseam. It can be boiled down to the following propositions. Economic progress depends on rising agricultural productivity, which can only happen if fields remain near enough to factories to return soil nutrients contained in human and industrial waste back to the land. A tariff barrier permits this by expanding the home market and precluding the need to export agricultural staples, which alienate the nation's soil nutrients. Moreover, the home market creates tightly bound regional economies that foster intellectual exchange and scientific inquiry, leading to new discoveries and technical capacities for efficient utilization of natural resources. By stressing an ecological interrelationship between farming and manufacturing, Carey's theory synthesized the existing tradition of American protectionism with the contemporary discourse of scientific agriculture. It proposed an original model of intensive economic development premised on a collective, hence political, structuring of the natural environment.

Because the manner in which soil produced crops was decisive, Carey devoted a lot of space to the subject of fertilizers. His whole model has been called the "manure theory," an apt designation given the word's field of meaning during the 1800s.[6] "Manure" derives from the Latin *manu*, or hand. It is related to words such as "manipulate," "manage" and, "manufacture," which have to do with literal and figurative handling. Referring to an action, it entered English as a verb that denoted working the land. It meant simply to cultivate the soil. As a noun, it indicated any substance that facilitated this action. Over time,

usage of the verb declined while the noun came to signify the principal traditional fertilizer, animal dung. This narrowing of meaning began in the nineteenth century even as older usages persisted. Hence, when Carey wrote of
manure, he invoked both a substance at the center of northern agriculture and
the more general sense of human manipulation of the land. An analysis of his
developmental imagination therefore has to consider the very prosaic practices
by which manure sustained the northern economy.

A crop on its way to market carries both energy and nutrients away from the
farm. The sun resupplies the energy for photosynthesis, but the ground cannot
keep up the same pace of nutrient production. Many traditional agricultural
systems therefore provide for periods of fallow when the land can replenish itself. At higher population densities, however, fallowing ties up too much acre-
age and must give way to continuous cropping systems that require an intensification of labor to maintain soil fertility. The need to adopt such methods
was perhaps the single most important driver of antebellum agricultural reform.
The first principle of Jesse Buel's "new husbandry" was that "our lands will not
wear out, or become exhausted of their fertility, if they are judiciously managed." He could as well have said, judiciously manured.[7]

The conquest of territory allowed Euro-American settlers, for a time, to substitute landed abundance for intensive soil restoration. Frontier farmers continued this trade-off through much of the nineteenth century, economizing labor
by expending land. Yet those who chose to remain in their communities beyond the pioneer stage eventually had to come to terms with soil depletion. By
the final decades of the eighteenth century, sharply reduced crop yields characterized the entire Atlantic Coast. In the vicinity of Philadelphia, for example,
farms that had once produced twenty-five to thirty bushels of wheat per acre
were down to ten bushels per acre or fewer. Soil acidity, poor drainage, and
erosion from plowing and deforestation aggravated the underlying problem of
uncompensated nutrient extraction.[8]

To remedy this, agricultural reformers began adapting European soil con-
serving techniques. The practices they introduced centered on crop rotations
and the assiduous application of fertilizers. The new rotation schemes alter-
nated grains with fodder crops and introduced two critical advances. First, they
featured nutritious nonnative grasses that allowed farmers to enlarge their livestock herds by providing winter feed. Farmers carefully conserved the manure
to raise grain yields, taking advantage of the fact that animal digestive systems
break down nutrients locked up as organic compounds to speed their availability for plant growth. Second, legumes such as clover and lucerne (alfalfa) not
only fed livestock, they also aided the soil directly because their roots host bac-
teria that fix atmospheric nitrogen in a form that plants can use. This process
was not fully understood until much later, but its practical effects had been

known in the ancient world and increasingly by American seaboard farmers from the late 1700s. Farmers also began experimenting with soil amendments such as lime, marl, and gypsum. As Sally McMurry points out, "numerous diaries show that farmers . . . were spending long hours procuring and hauling fertilizers." By the 1820s, these methods—together known as convertible husbandry or convertible agriculture—were firmly established in the farming districts surrounding Boston, New York, Philadelphia, and other cities.[9]

During this period, Americans reasoned that organic matter extracted from the ground by plant growth had to be replaced with similar organic matter, leading to a "recycling mentality." In its simplest application, this meant convertible agriculture's cycling of nutrients from field to barn and back again. But on a larger scale, the recycling mentality accommodated regional patterns of urban-rural nutrient exchange that developed around major coastal cities after the turn of the century and gradually spread inland as urbanites accounted for an increasing share of the population. Long Island farmers, for instance, grew hay for New York City's horses, then carted the resulting dung back to their fields. Cities provided other fertilizers, too. Farmers purchased spent bone black from sugar manufactories, the by-products of tanneries and glue makers, restaurants' refuse food and offal, ground bonemeal from urban abattoirs, deodorized night soil from vaults and privies, and miscellaneous street sweepings.[10]

By the 1840s, urban-industrial by-products were being chemically processed to render their nutrients concentrated and more easily transportable. One of the first of these artificial fertilizers was "poudrette." Introduced from France and manufactured commercially in the United States from the late 1830s, poudrette was made from night soil, which was collected in cities and mixed with an odor-neutralizing absorbent.[11] The resulting compound was reputed to be a powerful fertilizer, more economical than barnyard manure and transportable at "trifling" cost.[12] Buel termed it a "species of concentrated manure . . . the most efficient, in its immediate effects, of any manure we have tried."[13] Other commercial fertilizers made from night soil were branded with names such as "urate," "pablette," "tafeu," "chemical manure," "chemical compost," and "excrementum" (figure 4.1). Citing such internationally eminent chemists as Justus von Liebig and Jöns Jacob Berzelius, advertisements and catalogs depicted these products as the latest discoveries in agricultural chemistry.[14] Farmers readily adopted them because they had grown accustomed to purchasing the "raw material of crops."[15]

This was a heady period for the mundane but essential subject of soil building with fertilizers. Around this time the commercial exploitation of Peruvian guano—desiccated bird droppings rich in nitrogen—initiated a revolution in global agriculture.[16] Americans participated enthusiastically in this development, but the high price exacted by Peru's state monopoly also led them to seek

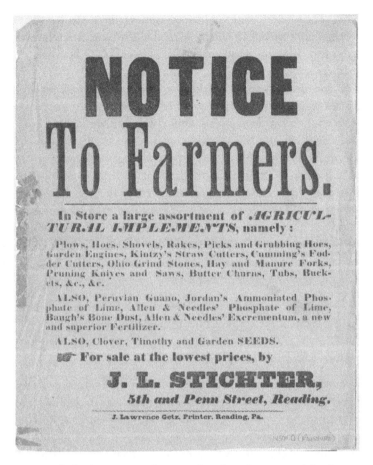

Figure 4.1. Handbill advertisement for agricultural implements and fertilizers, circa the 1850s. Courtesy of the Library Company of Philadelphia.

alternatives. Many agricultural reformers proposed manufacturing a concentrated fertilizer from fish, which had long been applied directly to soils on the coast. In 1851, the famed Philadelphia chemist Robert Hare patented a process for doing just that, and later other patented production methods appeared.[17] None of these, however, proved adequate. More promising was the search for new guano supplies. After 1856, American merchants benefited from the protection of the United States Navy, which was enjoined by the Guano Islands Act to back their claims to uninhabited guano islands. But new deposits were typically smaller than those on Peru's Chincha Islands and tended to derive their value from phosphorous rather than nitrogen. Peruvian guano therefore remained important.

The arrival of the phosphatic guanos did, however, pave the way for superphosphates. The modern world's first important artificial fertilizer, superphosphates became commercially available in the United States from the early 1850s. By decade's end, as many as forty-seven factories existed. These and other artificial fertilizer makers clustered in major northeastern cities because they depended on supplies of industrial chemicals. The growth of manufactures thus created what economists call "spillover effects," changes in one economic activity that benefit another by reducing input costs or enlarging markets. As early industrialization spun off new soil technologies, farmers provided new markets for by-products. Fish oil makers, for instance, began selling their desiccated scrap as "fish guano" from the late 1840s or so.[18]

Within a few years, agricultural reformers noted the "rapid extension of the use of concentrated fertilizers" and began arguing that "chemical manures" would soon occupy a central place in American farming.[19] Total production of artificial fertilizers roughly tripled during the decade, even as guano imports continued to pour in.[20] The novelty of these substances is captured in the orthography of a ten-year-old farm boy's diary:

> Sep 24: Father went to Middlefield and got a load of Fosfate [*sic*]
> Sep 25: To day we soed the 825 pounds of Super Phosate [*sic*]
> Sep 29: Deacon Leete helped us all day and we put 625 pounds of Phosphate and 14 quarts of grass seed.[21]

We can imagine the parents looking over the boy's diary each evening, pointing out spelling mistakes and, in this case perhaps, explaining how superphosphates were made and what they were for. In countless conversations like these, farmers began to reimagine the place of agriculture in the national political economy. Although the really widespread use of commercial fertilizers did not occur until the postbellum period, the 1850s were years of brisk expansion and intense discussion. Even in areas where these newer fertilizers did not immediately enter common practice, extensive experimentation occurred before the Civil War. By the end of the 1850s, agricultural reformers spoke of "the thousand and one fertilizers of the day," remarked that "we are all buying what one of our neighbors comprehensively calls 'bag manure,'" and observed that "every town, almost, has its manure manufactories."[22]

Significantly, the regional recycling paradigm in which nutrients traveled an eternal circuit between farm and city easily contained this phase of fertilizer development. Before the Civil War, the manufacture of superphosphates amounted to mixing a pile of ground bones in a tub of sulfuric acid. While reformers marveled at the use of an industrial chemical in agriculture, they paid as much attention to the animal products containing the critical phosphorous. Later in the century, nonrenewable rock phosphates would replace the bones once collected from urban abattoirs. The Progressive Era agricultural scientist Liberty

Hyde Bailey came to rue overreliance on such "mined fertilizers" that entailed "the exploitation of one place for the benefit of another." But during the 1850s, the full extent of the shift to nonrenewable nutrient extraction remained off in the future. The centrality of organic by-products to the manufacture of superphosphates, fish guanos, poudrette, and other fertilizers supported the basic framework of the recycling mentality. Indeed, one of the major reasons that Peruvian guano's high price riled southern planters more than northern farmers was that the latter had plentiful nearby sources of urban fertilizers. Yet even guano was shoehorned into the recycling paradigm by reasoning that guano birds fed on fish that fed on algae that were ultimately nourished by continental runoff.[23]

The persistence of the recycling mentality undoubtedly had something to do with its moral appeal. In its ordered circuit of nutrients, it seemed to harmonize material advancement with moral rectitude, economic development with ecological stewardship, the city with the country. It allowed agricultural reformers to speak of doing "justice" to the soil instead of "robbing" it.[24] But the recycling mentality also offered American economic nationalists like Henry Carey a compelling new argument in favor of the home market. If commercial agriculture carried vital nutrients from farm to market, overseas exports alienated those nutrients dangerously far away. For Carey, this realization helped provoke a creative and revealing effort to rethink the science of political economy.

Carey's Theory of Development

Carey began from a tradition of economic nationalism that focused on the concept of "productive powers." The term encompassed a country's current capacities and also its future prospects. In the United States and elsewhere, developmental nationalists argued that, given Britain's surpassing industrial lead, the only way to raise national productive powers was to provide a protected market space for domestic infant industries. Their main theoretical beef was with the principle of comparative advantage and the international division of labor, according to which some countries were fitted to manufacturing finished goods while others were suited to producing raw materials. Protectionists regarded this doctrine—and, indeed, the whole fabric of classical liberal political economy—as mere ideological dressing for naked British industrial interests. "English Authors write Free Trade doctrines for other Nations," they cried.[25]

Dissent from liberal political economy led the nationalists also to reject the population and rent theories of Thomas Malthus and David Ricardo, which implied that abject poverty was the natural lot of the masses. For developmental nationalists who were trying to build political coalitions behind ambitious economic programs, this was simply inadmissible. They therefore sought to refute the ineluctable scarcity that Malthus and Ricardo held to govern the world.

In the United States—where popular politics especially mattered—these efforts took on the characteristic features of American exceptionalism, but the basic impulse was common to economic nationalists everywhere and, indeed, to socialists or any other heterodox economic writer who looked to a brighter future.[26]

Importantly, the Malthusian-Ricardian view began from a constrained sense of natural limits that appeared most concretely as a technological bottleneck in agriculture. Malthus accepted that farming productivity could rise somewhat but argued that population rose at a much faster rate, leading to famines, epidemics, and wars as "checks" on population growth. Ricardo added a troubling distributional analysis. Agricultural productivity, he assumed, was largely determined by "the original and indestructible powers of the soil." Although improved implements and fertilizers might raise output, additional applications would bring diminishing returns. As population grew, people would be driven to ever-more marginal lands, steadily raising the cost of subsistence. The logical upshot was that owners of the most fertile lands would accrue unearned rents—the difference between the high costs of producing on marginal lands and the low costs attendant to fertile soils—so that gradually society's wealth would be swallowed up by landlords who contributed nothing but legal ownership.[27]

The limits of agricultural improvement seemed self-evident to Malthus and Ricardo, but not to everyone. An early rebuttal came from Friedrich List, an important German economic nationalist who spent several years in Pennsylvania during the 1820s closely associated with Mathew Carey's milieu. List stressed the unbounded promise of technological progress. Recent improvements had already "increased tenfold the productive powers of the human race for the creation of the means of subsistence," he observed. "Who will venture to set further limits?" His response to Ricardo followed easily from his confidence in the future of agricultural technology. The logical corollary of stressing human artifice was that natural conditions mattered little, so Ricardo's "original powers of the soil" were "unimportant." Instead, rent "rose everywhere with the progress of civilisation, of population, and with the increase of mental and material capital."[28]

Carey began along similar lines. "What are indestructible powers?" he asked. "The most fertile soil, if not renewed, will have its powers destroyed."[29] Since all land required regenerative maintenance, as agricultural reformers reiterated time and again, Ricardo's sharp distinction between the natural environment and human cultivation was arbitrary. But Ricardo never denied that improvements in agricultural technology could slow the rise of rents; he only insisted that improvements faced diminishing returns—that they must run into natural limits fairly quickly—making the shift to marginal soils ultimately certain.[30] Carey crafted an ingenious historical refutation of this argument in *The*

Past, the Present, and the Future (1848), his pathbreaking work. His purpose was to show that increasing returns from technological progress constituted a general phenomenon with no discernible maximum and, in particular, that this was as true of agriculture as of anything else. He aimed to show, in other words, that there was no bottleneck, and he anchored his thesis in the optimistic rhetoric of scientific agriculture.

According to Carey, Ricardo had gotten things backward. People did not begin on the best soils, proceeding to worse when population pressures forced them to. Instead, they first settled "the high and thin lands requiring little clearing and no drainage" because this was all that their primitive science, technology, and organization allowed. Only when their societies advanced could they manage the difficult task of clearing and draining "lower and richer lands." With further progress they would be able to tap fecund subsoils and otherwise command nature to their benefit. Citing endless historical examples spanning the globe, Carey concluded that "everywhere" population growth resulted in an "increased power over land."[31]

The key to this forward movement was what Carey termed "association" or "combination of action." The phrase recalls List's claim that the division of labor requires reintegration, or "union of labor." But whereas List, coming from northern Europe's cameralist tradition, probably had in mind a coordinating role for the state, Carey was getting at something different, which he illustrates with his own version of the conventional economic parable:

> The first cultivator can neither roll nor raise a log, with which to build himself a house. . . . He is in hourly danger of starvation. At length, however, his sons grow up. They combine their exertions with his, and now obtain something like an axe and a spade. They can sink deeper into the soil; and can cut logs, and build something like a house. . . . With the growth of the family new soils are cultivated, each in succession yielding a larger return to labour . . . and thus with every increase in the return to their labour the power of combining their exertions is increased.[32]

What Carey depicts here goes beyond first-order efficiency gains from the division of labor, sometimes known as Smithian growth. He is instead pointing to the power of technological spillover effects. In the parable, it is not the case that some of the family go to farming while the rest go to somehow knocking down trees. Instead, a few make the implements by which all can do more of everything, compounding productivity gains as the effects of new tools cascade through the entire range of economic activities. This was closer to Schumpeterian development—deep, structural transformation that follows from new technology and organization. "Carey's was a great vision," judged Schumpeter himself.[33]

Though dubious as history, Carey's settlement theory was inspired as allegory. It suggested that any static conception of resource endowments, including soil fertility, missed the nature of technological advancement. "All soils have qualities tending to render them useful," he insisted, it was just a matter of learning what those were. Malthus's dire forecast was "absurd" given "our present limited knowledge." The future would certainly bring "better machinery applied to better soils." The proposition that agricultural technology would save the day clearly echoed List and others. But Carey's view was simultaneously more sweeping and more detailed, peppered with references to marl, lime, acidulated bones, under-drainage, and deep plowing that showed off his agricultural literacy and gave his pronouncements the appearance of a firm grounding in modern science. When he asserted that "the whole business of the farmer consists in making and improving soils," he simply repeated an admonition that utterly pervaded the discourse of agricultural reform.[34]

According to Carey, then, no one could say when science and invention would hit some bedrock of natural necessity. It was unlikely to be soon. And it was no more likely in agriculture than in any other sector. But that did not mean that environmental constraints were nothing to worry about. Nature could only be manipulated in accordance with certain regularities that had to be respected. Britain's industrial dominance did the opposite, calamitously distorting the world economy by sucking up soil nutrients in the form of agricultural imports. Carey thus made farmers' prevailing recycling mentality a pillar of his protectionism, arguing that agricultural production must remain in close geographic proximity to urban manufacturing so that "all the manure produced by the land will go back again to the great giver of these supplies."[35]

Carey in Context

Carey's influence was broad in the 1850s. His theories could be heard in addresses at agricultural fairs and read at length in John Skinner's farm journal, *The Plough, the Loom and the Anvil* (figure 4.2). He wrote regularly for Horace Greeley's *New-York Tribune*, one of the country's most important dailies and the newspaper favored by farmers in New York City's vast agricultural hinterland. His major works were repeatedly translated and published abroad, adding to his renown. In Republican Party circles, he was an acknowledged authority and is known to have influenced Ralph Waldo Emerson, Abraham Lincoln, and many others.[36]

The appeal of Carey's ideas derived from the originality and realism with which they addressed a broad range of developmental issues. For northerners, in particular, his depiction of the national economy as a multitude of closely integrated agricultural-industrial zones corresponded quite plausibly with actual development patterns in the Greater Northeast. They also implicitly natural-

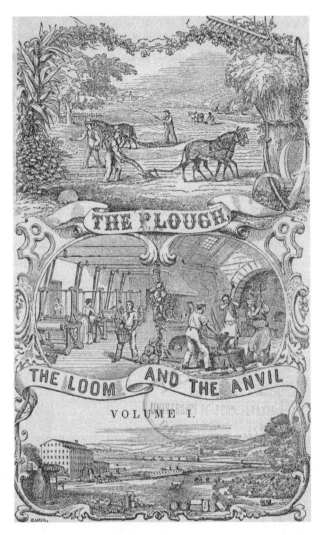

Figure 4.2. Frontispiece to John Skinner's Careyite agricultural journal, *The Plough, the Loom and the Anvil.* The image diagrams the national economy as an interdependence of agriculture and manufactures, with the lower portion highlighting their physical proximity. Wikimedia Commons.

ized Euro-American settlement and boosterism further west. One economic writer observed that Carey's theory "that the inferior lands are first occupied by pioneers, is a fact that strikes one throughout the whole West."[37]

Many contemporaries paralleled Carey's developmental synthesis. One was George Perkins Marsh, remembered today as the author of *Man and Nature* (1864), a monumental study of how human societies alter the environment.

Unlike Henry David Thoreau, with whom he is sometimes paired as a founder of American environmentalism, Marsh did not deplore economic development. Instead, he aimed at rational resource management in the face of nature's complex ecological interdependencies. Steeped in the Scottish Enlightenment's stadial theory of social development and in his own commitments to rural Vermont, he sought a way for modern civilization to promote sustainable material progress. Both he and Carey exemplified a quest shared by many in the nineteenth century, a period of heady technological change coupled with disturbing social and environmental harms.[38]

Marsh first delineated his views in an address at the 1847 Rutland County agricultural fair. There he argued that the "savage . . . desolates the region he inhabits," but that "social man repays to the earth all that he reaps from her bosom, and her fruitfulness increases with the numbers of civilized beings." For Marsh, civilization meant the use of science to domesticate nature and develop its capacities. In *Man and Nature*, he proved more circumspect about the prospects for achieving this while sustaining ecological balance, but he continued to hold that "ingenuity" and "wise economy" would make nature a "plenteous and perennial" source of material well-being.[39]

Marsh shared with Carey the perception that people modify the natural order to a very great extent. For both men, the crucial backdrop to this view was the rapid development of the American economy, which was transforming the landscape in ways too obvious to ignore. Marsh had noticed this as early as the merino mania, in which he personally participated, when the conversion of forested hills into sheep runs led to new patterns of erosion. In *Man and Nature*, he assembled mountains of evidence to show that not only did environments shape human society as Enlightenment thinkers had stressed, but humans could dramatically reshape their environments. Carey's development theory, with its notion of continuing technological transformation, stood in just the same relationship to Ricardian naturalism, which posited a given distribution of factor endowments rigidly determining economic fate. Marsh was more tempered than Carey, but he, too, believed that diminishing returns could be superseded through scientific improvement. Much as Carey maintained that all soils could be made useful through study, Marsh distinguished between the Earth's "spontaneous" growths and its "latent" capacities yet to be developed.[40] Again, like Carey, he argued that manufacturing benefited farmers as much by its technological advances as its markets for agricultural produce. The "mechanic arts," he explained, "are at once the most profitable customers of the agriculturalist, and the most munificent patrons of the investigator of nature's laws."[41]

That Carey and Marsh do not seem to have influenced each other evidences a broader contemporary developmental discourse particularly concerned with soil maintenance. Both certainly read the influential German agricultural chemist, Justus von Liebig, who pointedly asked, "Can it be imagined that any country . . . which, for centuries, exports its produce in the shape of grain and cattle, will maintain its fertility, if the same commerce does not restore in some form of manure, those elements which have been removed from the soil?"[42] Such worries engaged the attention of many nineteenth-century economists. After studying Liebig intensely during the 1860s, for instance, Karl Marx concluded that capitalist agriculture's "progress in increasing the fertility of the soil for a given time is a progress towards ruining the more long-lasting sources of that fertility."[43] By that time, indeed, fertilizer manufacturers had largely shifted to sourcing their raw materials from nonrenewable mineral deposits.

Agricultural reformers, of course, would hardly condemn capitalism out of hand, but they certainly expressed concerns. It was precisely because agriculture had "made wonderful progress" in the preceding years, explained the farm editor, Daniel Lee, that soil depletion was actually accelerating. "Productiveness of crops and destructiveness of soil are the two most prominent features of American agriculture," he observed ruefully.[44] Because Lee's views appeared in the Patent Office's annual reports, which Congress distributed in editions running to the hundreds of thousands, they achieved widespread circulation. Other reformers soon echoed his fears.[45] Even the usually optimistic Horace Greeley suddenly found the prospects for improved agricultural machinery "absolutely baleful."[46] An especially alarming report came from a young assistant agricultural editor named George Waring Jr. Inspired by Lee's calls for making policy on the basis of detailed agricultural statistics, Waring extrapolated from the 1850 census—the first with a separate agricultural schedule—to estimate an annual national nutrient deficit equivalent to no less than 1.5 billion bushels of corn. "To suppose that this state of things can continue, and we as a nation remain prosperous, is simply ridiculous," he concluded. Waring's figures were soon being cited by both Liebig and Carey.[47] By 1858, congressional Republicans were declaring that the threat of soil depletion was "patent to every one paying the slightest attention to the subject."[48]

The recycling mentality linked this threat to the problem of urban public health.[49] As early as 1826, Philadelphia's Board of Health called on the Philadelphia Society for Promoting Agriculture to investigate poudrette as a means for disposing of city wastes.[50] Around this time, too, the French organic chemist Jean-Baptiste Dumas began stressing the need to conserve the nitrogen content of urban sewage for agricultural use, and he later worked to reform the Parisian sewer system accordingly.[51] In Britain, Edwin Chadwick's sewage reforms also leaned on the rhetoric of nutrient recycling. Similarly, George Waring turned from his early work as an agricultural reformer to a career in urban sanitation.[52] By rendering city wastes into profitable fertilizers, sewage reforms promised to solve two of the nineteenth century's most vexing problems: the maintenance of rural soil fertility and urban public health. In 1850, for example, a French sanitary engineer arrived in Philadelphia with a plan to erect "an establishment for the transmutation of feculent matter into inoderous and chemical manure."[53] Other plans soon appeared for shifting city refuse onto farmers' fields.[54]

The topic elicited widespread interest throughout the second half of the nineteenth century. In *Les Misérables* (1862), Victor Hugo made the Parisian sewer into a manifold figure for contemporary social pathologies, one of which was the wanton waste of food-making capacity. "A great city is the most powerful of dung producers," he wrote, "an incalculable element of wealth . . . [that] if restored to the land instead of being thrown into the water, would suffice to nourish the world."[55] A story that begins with the desperate theft of bread thus turns on ecological disjuncture in addition to social injustice. A few years later, the American zoologist Edward S. Morse touched on the topic in his travelogue of early Meiji Japan: "With us sewage is allowed to flow into our coves and harbors . . . to the misery of all. In Japan this material is scrupulously saved and goes to enrich the soil."[56] As it turns out, nutrient recycling was not so simple. Although attempts to realize the vision persist to this day, reformers have always struggled with the problem of cost effectiveness, given the availability of nonrenewable alternatives.[57] In the 1850s, however, exploitation of mineral nutrient deposits was just getting started, and the recycling mentality still reigned.

It was in this context that Carey's vision proved compelling. His theory contributed a rich body of arguments and images that vindicated the home market thesis for a self-consciously scientific age, providing theoretical underpinning for the Republicans' broad developmental program. In linking scientific agriculture with protectionism, he rebutted classical free trade doctrine in a manner that could appeal to the rural voting majority. Carey deepened the home market vision of reciprocal exchange by stressing that manufacturers supplied farmers with essential technological inputs. At the same time, his emphasis on soil fertility paid its due to so humble a chore as manuring. The manure theory, moreover, went beyond trade and mechanization to depict the rural-urban relationship at a chemical level, envisioning a political economy that corresponded with the right circulation of physical matter. In stressing the essential similarity of all forms of production and the complicated interdependencies that bound them together, this view also tended to collapse the distinctions between agriculture and manufacturing in favor a single vision of national productive enterprise. To manure and to manufacture turned out to be one and the same.

"New Slaves"

In addition to countering British political economy and appealing to American farmers, Carey's project undercut the southern case for slave-based agricultural exports. The measure of social progress, Carey believed, was human technical capacity and productive power. Society was really a vast technological system whose structure was co-determined with its developmental trajectory. From this perspective, the South's wasteful export orientation reflected the fact that slavery was an inherently backward mode of social organization.

There was more to this view than the well-known logic of free labor incentives, which had been articulated by Adam Smith in *The Wealth of Nations* (1776) and by others before him. For Carey, the causation ran both ways: not only did slavery retard progress, but technical decline brought slavery. When people lost the ability to make natural forces work for them, they inevitably turned to coercing the labor of one another. Carey thus set up a double binary that extended the existing matrix of distinctions between North and South. On one side was technology and freedom, on the other nature and slavery. Put differently, he posited an inverse relationship between the mastery of nature and the mastery of human beings. In some places, he explained, people tended to become "from year to year more and more the masters, and in others, the slaves of nature."[58]

The best exposition of this view came not from Carey himself, but from his leading disciple, Erasmus Peshine Smith. An attorney and antislavery politico from western New York, Smith was closely associated with William Henry Seward, the leading Republican politician of the 1850s. His lone major work, *A Manual of Political Economy* (1853), went through multiple American editions and was translated into several languages. Carey himself borrowed from it heavily. But Smith was later forgotten and would have remained so if not for the work of the heterodox development economist Michael Hudson. He is worth remembering because his restatement of Carey's ideas in terms of an unmistakable if still inchoate conception of energy brought technology and labor into a single frame, clarifying how Carey's developmental vision could be joined to an antislavery politics.[59]

Smith attempted a project of visionary ambition: "to construct a skeleton of Political Economy upon the basis of purely physical laws, and thus to obtain for its conclusions that absolute certainty which belongs to the positive sciences."[60] By this he meant an account of "the laws of human progress in respect to its material basis, the increased command over matter."[61] He treated economics not as the study of wealth or of labor as conventionally understood but of how humans modified and appropriated the natural environment over time. Only after chapters on "matter and force," "the formation of soils," and the "co-operation of the natural agents with human labour," did his *Manual* turn to such traditional topics as rent, wages, and profit. For Smith, political economy was the science of society's technological mastery of nature.[62] Concerned, like Carey, to refute any notion of insurmountable agricultural limits, he drew heavily on Liebig and the reports of the New York State Agricultural Society to show that scientific agriculture could meet the needs of a growing population.

But Smith went further by situating all human technical capacities within the framework of the newly enunciated principle of energy conservation—what we now call the first law of thermodynamics—which he learned not only from Liebig but from the physicists James Joule and Alessandro Volta.[63] During the 1840s, scientists approached the idea of energy conservation from disparate angles.[64] They did not yet agree on a technical meaning for the word "energy" and instead tended to speak of "force," a word of greater semantic breadth. But each was converging on the idea that all-natural forces were interconvertible, that they were simply different forms of the same underlying phenomenon. Smith applied this concept to economic production under the heading of "The Law of Endless Circulation of Matter and Force." The key point in his formulation was that, as one force became another, it necessarily acted on and altered some material substance. That substance was thus consumed but not destroyed. Rather, it changed into a new form appropriate for some other kind of conversion. The essence of progress, then, was the intentional manipulation of these conversion processes.[65]

Since matter and force were locked in an endless chain of reciprocal events, it is perhaps not surprising that Smith occasionally conflated the terms, as when he wrote to Carey that "every product becomes in consumption a material—or a force, if you please."[66] Still, he was feeling his way toward the idea that "the natural forces are . . . all interchangeable"—that they were all energy.[67] By the late 1850s, his grasp was surer. He now spoke of "potential energy-motive force latent or in action." The concept of conversion linked a variety of seemingly disparate natural phenomena—heat and motion, for instance, or the labor of people, animals, and machines—within a single framework. "The entire universe then is motion," he continued, "and the only point is how much of the universal and ceaseless motion shall we utilize, and how much shall we permit to be working against us."[68] Economic development became simply the harnessing of energy to do humanity's labors.[69]

Theorizing production as a kind of conversion allowed Smith to express Carey's approach in general rather than historical terms. The Malthusian-Ricardian error thus flowed from the misperception "that man's consumption of food is its destruction," when, actually, "in the natural course of things it is returned to the earth, to be again formed into food." Since every product had to "go through a certain orbit" before it could be reused, "the question whether the path be short and direct or whether it be curved and long . . . is the question between home exchanges and foreign exchanges." The fundamental problem now appeared similar to how an economic ecologist would think of it, as a question of energy efficiency. Proximity of agriculture and manufacturing saved energy, which was expressed in cost, and this gave a general material explanation for Carey's oft-repeated argument that regional integration economized transportation charges. For Smith, this meant that it could be no part of the natural order "that the agriculturist of any nation should be 'an exporting interest.' "[70] The recycling mentality was reimagined as a loop of energy conversions powering all of economic development.

Resolving the totality of worldly action into energetic conversions also illuminated technology's relationship to labor and thus to slavery. Smith treated labor as a variable quantity susceptible to improvement. It was the employer's interest to pay laborers above subsistence wages because better food, clothing, and shelter yielded more physical exertion. This had nothing to do with the will and therefore nothing to do with free labor incentives. It was instead an objective fact that could be measured in calories. On this point, Smith ranged freely over physiological and mechanical analogies, in one case discussing "that most wonderful of laboratories, the human stomach," in another case comparing low wages to "precisely the same kind of economy which would keep the steam engines of a nation at half their working power." Chemical, mechanical, and physiological "forces" came into single focus as interconvertible aspects of the same thing. Precisely because people could never compete with machines for power, Smith concluded that their energies were best directed to intellectual work with the help of education. "Man's office in the world is that of engineer," he insisted. "All his real power is mental." Better that the natural forces should substitute for muscle entirely through what he referred to as "the gratuitous concert of natural agents, newly discovered, and made available by tools and machinery." Such technologic channeling of the energy coursing through nature amounted to a multiplication of virtual slaves. Smith calculated that "for every inhabitant of the British Isles there are forces that . . . do the work of twenty-two slaves, without even the slaves' pittance of food."[71]

It meant something to invoke slavery in antebellum America. When Smith instructed his readers to "regard man as the lord, not the slave of nature," the familiar idiom of freedom and enslavement passed down from classical republicanism acquired a new sense in relation to the discourses of popular science and proslavery zealotry.[72] Carey recognized the rhetorical power immediately, incorporating Smith's perspective into his magnum opus, the three-volume *Principles of Social Science* (1858–60). Whereas Carey had written of slavery as a concomitant of underdevelopment before, he had not connected the word to nature with any regularity. In the *Principles*, the linkage appeared repeatedly: "to pass from being the slave, to becoming the master of nature"; "to have everywhere been the slave of nature"; "not only the slave of nature, but also of his neighbor man"; "the ultimate enslavement of man by nature, and by his fellow-man"; and so on. Human slavery was thus an epiphenomenon of the deeper enslavement to natural necessity.[73]

The power of seeing the problem in this way is illustrated by Ralph Waldo Emerson's conversion to Careyism in the late 1850s.[74] "Mr. Carey is the greatest political economist of our country," Emerson informed a foreign visitor.[75] He explained why in an 1858 address to the Middlesex (MA) Agricultural Society: "The theory is that the best land is cultivated first. This is not so, as Henry Carey, of Philadelphia, has shown, for the poorest land is the first cultivated, and the last lands are the best lands. It needs science to cultivate the best lands in the best manner. . . . Thus political economy is not mean, but liberal, and on the pattern of the sun and sky; it is coincident with love and hope."[76] Emerson attempted to capture that hopeful pattern in the lyric epigraph to his essay "Wealth." The poem tells a story of human progress through "Heaven's enormous year," the "deep time" recently discovered by geologists. It begins with a lengthy set of speculations about what might now be called the Earth's biogeochemical processes before turning to human history on the cusp of technological emancipation. At this point Emerson writes: "New slaves fulfilled the poet's dream, / Galvanic wire, strong-shouldered steam." The couplet juxtaposes nature with technology and, in parallel, slavery with liberation. Steam's personification as "strong-shouldered" underscores the substitution of "new slaves," technology, for old ones, humans, now emancipated from want and drudgery.[77] Here slavery acts as a foil against which the world-historical meaning of capitalism's technological revolution can be grasped.

Scientific agriculture, as much as steam or electricity, was at the heart of this revolution. In an essay that expanded on his Middlesex agricultural address and remained indebted to Carey, Emerson wrote that "in the great household of Nature, the farmer stands at the door of the bread-room," controlling "the health and power, moral and intellectual, of the cities." Progress depended on rising agricultural productivity, which, in turn, depended on the substitution of science and technology for human labor. "Who are the farmer's servants?" Emerson asked. "Not the Irish, nor the coolies, but Geology and Chemistry," for "the earth is a machine which yields almost gratuitous service to every application of intellect." By this reasoning, then, "the true abolitionist is the farmer."[78]

Abraham Lincoln, who was also influenced by Carey, similarly contrasted slavery with scientific agriculture.[79] Speaking at the Wisconsin state fair nearly simultaneously with Emerson's Middlesex address, Lincoln began by recapitulating conventional agricultural reformist homilies and assessing the prospects for steam plowing. This was prologue to the better-known second half of the address in which he refuted James Henry Hammond's proslavery "mudsill theory." Nearly the opposite of the manure theory, the mudsill theory was that natural necessity bound the majority of humanity to perpetual physical drudgery. In the North, Hammond argued, menial roles were filled by wage laborers. Against this, Lincoln insisted that upward mobility was the norm in northern society. To deepen the contrast with slavery, he turned to education.[80] "By the '*mud-sill*' theory, it is assumed that labor and education are incompatible," but, he continued drolly, "as the Author of man makes every individual with one head and one pair of hands, it was probably intended that heads and hands should co-operate as friends." Averring that "Free Labor insists on universal education," he then returned to agriculture.[81] "No other human occupation opens so wide a field for the profitable and agreeable combination of labor with cultivated thought," he declared, echoing a claim that agricultural reformers had been advancing for years.[82] Lincoln's reiteration of this view circled back to his earlier, equally conventional suggestion that farmers raise production by "deeper plowing, analysis of soils, experiments with manures, and varieties of seeds, observance of seasons, and the like."[83] Thus, to contrast southern slavery with northern free labor, Lincoln turned to agricultural reform's vision of farmers empowered by science and technology.

The political value of this combination was that it was antislavery without saying much of anything about enslaved people, a line that many Republicans, including Carey, tried to hew to. Indeed, the rhetoric of technological emancipation potentially implied that science would not so much alleviate labor exploitation as dispense with the exploited laborers. This was hinted in Emerson's suggestion that the "farmer's servants" were "Chemistry and Geology," not immigrant workers. Lincoln betrayed a similar ambiguity. In a popular lecture on "Inventions and Discoveries"—contemporaneous with his and Emerson's agricultural addresses—Lincoln offhandedly juxtaposed the invention of printing with "the invention of negroes, or, of the present mode of using them."[84] This peculiar comparison could be read as calling attention to the social construction of exploitation.[85] But another possible reading—suggested by what might have been the remark's humorous wink toward the audience's anti-black sentiment—construes African Americans instrumentally, like Emerson's Irish and Chinese workers, as tools that might be replaced with other "inventions." Crucially, the replaceable people are typed as ethnically or racially other, saving technological emancipation for the nation.

The ambiguity remained twenty years after the Civil War in the imagery adorning an 1885 "diploma" from the Pennsylvania State Agricultural Society (figure 4.3). At the top of the certificate, the figure of Ceres presides over a scene of cornucopia and technology, the social basis of which is suggested by the human figures at the bottom. There, to the left, a depiction of ancient Egypt shows an apparently white overseer looking on as dark-skinned workers use sickles to harvest wheat. To the right, a single white farmer harvests a similar

Figure 4.3. "Diploma" from the Pennsylvania State Agricultural Society, awarded to a premium winner at the 1885 annual fair. Note the repeated technological themes and the way that the lower left- and right-hand images associate slavery with technical backwardness. Courtesy of the Historical Society of Pennsylvania.

field with the aid of a mechanical reaper. The message is clear: freedom and technical progress go together. In the same move from left to right, however, people of color simply disappear from view, eliding the crucial question of whether machinery has displaced the institution of slavery or the people whom it enslaved.

In a country dominated by both farmers and slavery, Republicans drew on the discourse of scientific agriculture to present science and technology as fundamentally emancipatory forces. Their understanding of scientific agriculture promised a new kind of labor that challenged farmers' minds more than it taxed their muscles. This was distinct from free labor ideology as historians typically understand it. The issue here was not how to render wage work compatible with independence in an industrial society but rather how to reimagine farm labor as the progressive management of nature—educated, scientific, and technologically augmented. It was about freedom and national power through productivity.

Despite the agricultural reform movement's many affinities with the Republicans, the fit between the two was nevertheless contingent on a particular historical trajectory. There was certainly nothing in the phrase "scientific agriculture" that inherently linked it to an antislavery agenda, much less a racially egalitarian one. A bi-sectional alliance of farmers on the basis of whiteness was always possible. It was the key to the Jeffersonian-Jacksonian program of territorial expansion and again central in the rapid rise of the Patrons of Husbandry during the period of Reconstruction.[86] In the 1850s, however, Republicans broke the old party ties and forged a new link between northern farmers and manufacturers against the slaveocracy.

Agricultural reformers' arrival in Washington, DC, during the 1850s made this alliance all but inevitable. Their strident calls for new federal agricultural agencies exposed the hostility of slaveholder interests to a national agricultural reform program. The next chapters therefore show how reformers developed a national policy agenda and with what consequences.

PART THREE

TOWARD A NATIONAL
AGRICULTURAL POLICY AGENDA

CHAPTER FIVE

A Crisis of Agricultural Expertise

Sometime in 1856, James Jay Mapes, a well-known figure among American agricultural reformers, began to expound a peculiar new theory he called the "progression of primaries." By "primary" Mapes meant a chemical element, and the ones he had particularly in mind were the dozen or so then known to be essential to plant life. Mapes contended that the primaries could take on different forms and "functions." He speculated that the variations succeeded one another in a progressive sequence and that these differences proved decisive for plant growth. The lowest forms of plant life, the lichens and mosses, took up the primaries as disintegrated rocks and assimilated them in the process of growth. This somehow transformed the primaries into the proper nutrients for the next, higher order of being. Any given element thus climbed up a vital ladder that culminated in humans, converted at each stage into a food suitable for more advanced life. In Mapes's words, "every substance in nature is *progressed* each time it enters into organic life, and is again rendered up for reappropriations to new growths."[1] Mapes could not explain how such transformations occurred. Indeed, he claimed that the physical workings of the process were beyond the scrutiny of contemporary chemical science. Instead, he seemed to rest his case on the blanket assertion that "God's eternal law is progression."[2]

The theory sounds absurd today. It did to many contemporaries, too. The

Genesee Farmer dismissed the "strange doctrine" as "unworthy of serious consideration." Samuel W. Johnson, soon to emerge as the don of American agricultural science, regarded its basic premise as "simply ridiculous."[3] But Mapes enjoyed significant support. In an admiring obituary from 1866, the *Horticulturalist* termed Mapes's progression hypothesis "the most striking" of his "many important theories and discoveries," and as late as 1886, the theory was presented as unproblematically true.[4] At least one article in a professional chemistry journal backed Mapes's ideas "at great length."[5] Meanwhile, the theory took on a life of its own. A member of the American Pharmaceutical Association suggested it as a framework for a comparative study of medicines, while a writer on spiritual health also found the idea fruitful.[6]

The theory had evident appeal. Pursuing the story of why this should have been so reveals much more than just the fate of a quixotic scientific speculation. Mapes's views and their reception reveal a dilemma at the heart of American agricultural reform in the 1850s: how could farmers judge the efficacy of new chemical fertilizers and other novel technologies that were presented as essential to achieving scientific agriculture? The episode exemplifies a general problem of trust in expertise that seems to arise when science is put to commercial use in an unregulated market. It also indicates that Americans sought government-based solutions to such problems long before the state expansions of the Progressive Era. Mapes therefore points to an important rationale for the creation of the land-grant universities and the US Department of Agriculture (USDA) in 1862: a federal guarantee of authoritative knowledge in the service of orderly technological progress. Public expertise would be made to check the claims of private expertise.

The simultaneously promotional and regulatory functions of this kind of governance was characteristic of the American developmental state that emerged out of the Civil War. For agricultural reformers, the free exchange of information was an essential engine of scientific knowledge and its practical application. The comparison of varied experience through public discussion, they believed, produced and diffused true knowledge. During the 1850s, however, they came to realize that open public debate could also generate confusion, that this could impede sustained commercial growth, and that institutions were needed to adjudicate competing truth claims. The story of the Mapes progression thesis illustrates how reformers arrived at this position. Though Mapes's ideas proved a scientific dead end, in some respects they represented a logical response to a crisis in American agricultural science that set in after 1852. That crisis had profound effects for how reformers thought about public policy and, ultimately, about the scope of the American state.

In the years leading up to the crisis, American agricultural reformers had become entranced by visions of a farmers' millennium in which science—

chemistry in particular—played the role of messiah. Development-minded Americans thought of science and technology as the motive force of economic progress. During the 1840s, scientific advances associated with the "mineral theory" of the German chemist Justus von Liebig suggested that a new kind of chemical soil analysis would do for agriculture what steam power was doing for manufacturing. A vigorous campaign to promote soil analyses ensued. But when the procedure's efficacy came into question after 1852, agricultural reformers were caught out on a limb. Mapes found himself especially exposed because not only had he very vocally encouraged farmers to hire chemists such as himself to perform soil analyses, he had also begun to market an artificial fertilizer that was closely identified with Liebig's mineralist views. It was imperative, therefore, that Mapes rectify his reputation and provide a new explanation for the value of his commercial fertilizer. The progression of primaries served that need.

Mapes's predicament epitomizes the general crisis of agricultural expertise that followed the discrediting of soil analysis and the implications the crisis held for a growing marketplace of fertilizers, implements, and other "improvements" predicated on often hazy scientific claims advanced by the purveyors of new-fangled farming technologies. The collapse of the soil analysis craze occasioned criticism of Mapes but also the atmosphere of uncertainty in which his views, speculative as they were, could appear plausible. Mapes capitalized by positioning himself as a "practical" farmer rather than as a cloistered expert and by invoking widely held beliefs in a natural law of progress. These moves earned him support even as they further exposed the challenges of agricultural reform. Entrusting their future to the practices of "scientific agriculture," farmers and reformers alike were troubled by the doubtful state of the science and the simultaneous proliferation of commercial products presenting themselves as improvements. For their part, purveyors of new technologies recognized that uncertainty could hinder commercial growth. In this context, long-standing calls for government provision and supervision of research acquired new urgency, leading reformers to a program of institution building that dominated much of their efforts in the following decades.

The Promise of Agricultural Chemistry

By the late 1840s, the notion that agricultural chemistry furnished the most promising avenue of agricultural reform was well established in the United States.[7] Chemical soil analysis, it was thought, would lay bare the relationship between soil composition and fertility. A naive sense that the major obstacles to rational farming would soon be removed fueled immense enthusiasm. In an 1846 agricultural address, John Skinner suggested that "within a few years, a farmer will make out his prescription for specific manures, according to the crop he wishes to cultivate, and send it to an agricultural chemist to be compounded to order." Five years later, the president of the Massachusetts Board of Agriculture summarized the prevailing wisdom in an official report to the state legislature: "The investigations of scientific men have proved, beyond the possibility of a doubt, that, by the analysis of the soil . . . we are as competent to adapt food to the different species of vegetables, as to the various kinds of animals."[8]

Such views trickled down to the local level of agricultural reform, percolated up into higher intellectual circles, and seeped out into the popular press. A former president of the Lamoille County (VT) Agricultural Society asserted that "knowledge of chemistry is indispensable to the farmer."[9] About the same time, an aspiring planter in southern Maryland confided to his diary that "the analysis of soils . . . is necessary and certain in its effects. I certainly intend to use it."[10] At the crest of the soil analysis wave, one newspaper opined that "the introduction of labor-saving machines created a new era in the history of agriculture, but the application of chemical science to the soil was a grander step."[11] The enthusiasm comes across most strikingly in the frontispiece of the popular textbook *Scientific Agriculture* (figure 5.1). At the center of the engraving is a heavenly hand offering a scroll emblazoned with a list of scientific terms that begins with "chemistry" and ends with "agriculture." No image could better capture the combination of faith in science and divine purpose that animated the agricultural reform movement at midcentury.

Testing soils for their constituent parts was nothing new, having been a mainstay of the geological surveys undertaken by many states in the 1830s.[12] But after 1843, the practice of soil analysis received a new focus from Justus von Liebig's mineral theory. In that year, Liebig's *Familiar Letters on Chemistry and Its Relations to Commerce, Physiology, and Agriculture*, a collection of wide-ranging newspaper articles on the practical applications of chemical science, was published in the United States in at least three separate editions.[13] Liebig was already a recognized authority on agricultural chemistry, but his views had changed subtly from the 1840 publication of his *Organic Chemistry in Its Applications to Agriculture and Physiology*, the work that had established his reputation in English-speaking circles. Whereas he had initially emphasized the role of nitrogen in plant nutrition, he now called attention to phosphates and other inorganic minerals. He argued that such nutrients, where they were not already present in the soil in sufficient quantity and appropriate form, had to be supplied by outside fertilizers. Chemical analysis was therefore required to determine soil composition. Importantly, while earlier soil testing was simple enough for some farmers to undertake themselves, it was now necessary to ascertain mineral proportions with a minute precision only possible for trained professionals.[14]

Liebig looked "to the united efforts of the chemists of all countries" to solve "the most urgent problem" of his time, the specter of Malthusian checks on the

Figure 5.1. Frontispiece to M. M. Rodgers's *Scientific Agriculture* (1848). Courtesy of the Library Company of Philadelphia.

world's rapidly growing population.[15] The chemists' first task was to catalog the chemical composition of every crop. This done, analysis of a given soil would yield a nutrient profile that, when compared with the profile of the desired crop, would determine a precise fertilizer prescription. Employing the accounting discourse that had become standard practice among agricultural reformers on both sides of the Atlantic, Liebig predicted confidently that "the farmer will be able to keep an exact record of the products of his fields in harvest, like the account-book of a well-regulated manufactory; and then by simple calculation he can determine precisely the substances he must supply to each field, and the quantity of these, in order to restore their fertility."[16] It turned out not to be so simple. The soil's relationship to plant growth is more intricate than was imagined, involving, for example, the activities of microorganisms that Liebig knew nothing about. For several years, however, the promise of chemical soil analysis beguiled agricultural reformers.

The growing importance attributed to agricultural chemistry is evidenced by more than just enthusiastic pronouncements. The 1840s witnessed the first attempts to establish modern, European-style agricultural research institutions. The Lawrence Scientific School at Harvard and the Sheffield Scientific School at Yale trace their origins, to a large degree, to agricultural chemistry. Central figures in both institutions obtained doctorates in Europe and returned to the United States with ambitions to institutionalize basic scientific research in agriculture. Eben Horsford at Harvard and Samuel W. Johnson at Yale both studied with Liebig, while John Pitkin Norton, also of Yale, studied with two of Liebig's rivals, the Scottish chemist James F. W. Johnston and the Dutch chemist Gerrit Jan Mulder. These and other pedigreed scientists found it difficult to conduct basic research in an American environment that demanded utility. Hoping to advance agriculture by long-term careful investigation, they tended to justify the funding of new research institutions by exciting farmers' hopes for practical applications. Not until the 1880s did well-funded, reasonably independent agricultural research institutions begin to come into their own. Even then, the pressure to focus on practical applications remained intense.[17]

No one worked more assiduously to popularize the cause of soil analysis than John Pitkin Norton. Norton genuinely believed that soil analysis was the key to a new scientific farming, but he also saw it as a way to interest farmers in the importance of agricultural research.[18] Ironically, Norton identified himself publicly with Liebig's opponents. Where Liebig emphasized inorganic minerals, a second school of agricultural chemistry developed a version of soil analysis in the 1830s and 1840s that stressed the soil's organic acids. But the role that complex organic compounds played in plant growth was poorly understood at the time. Liebig's approach was the more useful in light of contemporary knowledge, so even those who criticized him often ended up adopting it in practice. Hence Norton, too, came to discuss soils and fertilizers in terms of their mineral constituents rather than their organic content as he worked to spread the "gospel of soil analysis." In this way, he and other leading scientific voices helped forge the close popular association between soil analysis and Liebig's mineralism.[19]

The American enthusiasm for soil analysis registered itself not only on the high plane of pure science but on the more practical terrain of the agricultural societies. Increasingly, professional chemists appeared on the scene as lecturers, writers, and consultants. In December 1843, for example, Dr. D. Pereira Gardner, formerly professor of chemistry and botany at Hampden Sidney College in Virginia, advertised a series of lectures on agricultural science, several of which were to focus on soil analysis. Success in this initial effort led to an appointment as "consulting chemist" to the American Institute's Farmers' Club. Gardner subsequently advertised for a second course of lectures, this time promising "full instruction in the analysis of soils," including hands-on practice. Around the same time, he began offering inexpensive commercial soil analyses. Farmers were thereby invited to send in their soil samples for professional testing at a fee.[20]

In later years such "$5 analyses" were criticized as quackery and charlatanism, but in the mid- to late 1840s perfectly reputable figures did the same as Gardner.[21] In 1850, for instance, a New York state assistant agricultural surveyor charged $5 for "complete quantitative analysis of a soil," the sample and fee to be forwarded through the secretary of the state agricultural society.[22] In the same year, Dr. Thomas Antisell advertised $5 analyses, yet it would have been difficult to challenge his credentials. A member of the Royal Dublin Society and the Royal College of Surgeons, he was a longtime Patent Office chemical examiner. In 1849, the American Agricultural Association of New York employed him to succeed Gardner as its consulting chemist.[23] A year later, the respected *American Agriculturist* hired him to give "analyses of soils, and an occasional article on Agricultural Chemistry and Geology," and in the 1860s he joined the Division of Chemistry in the newly created Department of Agriculture.[24]

If the appearance of "consulting chemists" gives one index of the boom in agricultural chemistry, another was the movement in several states to hire official state chemists. As early as 1839, Massachusetts state geologist Edward Hitchcock called for the establishment of a state chemist under the direction of a Board of Agriculture. Shortly thereafter, the Agricultural Committee of the General Court's Senate submitted a majority report recommending the creation of just such a board with powers to appoint a salaried chemist.[25] It seems that nothing much followed because no board was organized until 1851. In January 1853, board member John Adams Nash, an instructor of agriculture at Amherst College, again raised the matter of a state chemist. A committee consisting of Nash, Hitchcock, and several others reported a few months later that while it was "fully impressed with the importance" of soil analyses, it was not yet prepared to recommend "any distinct action."[26] By this time it was becoming apparent that a much larger and better funded institutional structure was needed in order to further agricultural knowledge.

In Maryland, too, legislative attempts to enact the position of state chemist predated the impetus of Liebig's mineral theory. In 1840, D. W. Niall, chairman of the House of Delegates' Committee on Agriculture, submitted an "An Act to Provide for the Appointment of an Agricultural Chemist for the State of Maryland." As in Massachusetts, the idea for such an office was essentially an extension of the state geological survey. According to Niall, Maryland was suffering an "appalling" drain of population and capital that could be forestalled if farmers only understood how to utilize available marl and lime deposits to renovate "exhausted lands," a statement that precisely mirrored Hitchcock's prescription of a state chemist to help "check the tide of emigration that sets so strongly to the great West." Niall's bill therefore required Maryland's official chemist not only to analyze soils from around the state but also to lecture widely to farmers. Although apparently no action was taken at the time, a very similar law passed in 1848.[27] That move is indicative of the revived interest in agricultural chemistry that followed the spread of Liebig's mineral views. The years roughly from 1848 to 1851 witnessed calls for official agricultural chemists in several states, including Ohio, Virginia, and Mississippi.[28]

The collapse of soil analysis fervor, anticipated by an always present undercurrent of skepticism, came in 1852 thanks to a study commissioned by the Ohio Board of Agriculture. At the board's behest, David A. Wells of the Lawrence Scientific School analyzed Scioto Valley soils known for their fertility. To his surprise, their mineral profile was all but identical to that of New England soils known for their barrenness. Wells therefore concluded that mineral content could not in and of itself explain a soil's agricultural potential. Instead, the ground's physical condition, the solubility of mineral nutrients, and other factors affecting uptake were more important. These conclusions punctured the inflated promise of mineral soil analysis.[29] Those who had doubted all along seized on the results to confirm their views. Over the next two or three years, the once muted voices of isolated skeptics grew into a blaring chorus of general disgruntlement. In 1853, for instance, a letter-writer to the *New England Farmer* averred, "I have little confidence in the analyses of soils *in the present state of the science.*" Most soon came to agree that soil analyses' utility to farmers had "been altogether over-estimated."[30]

Samuel W. Johnson helped build the new consensus with his influential 1854 essay, "On the Practical Value of the Analyses of Soils."[31] Johnson rehearsed a litany of damning reasons why recommendations based on analyses of particular soil samples were bound to fail. To begin with, any farm was likely to comprise many types of soil, often intermixed within a small area. In addition, soil that had been plowed repeatedly might vary at every few inches of depth. But even assuming uniformity, he continued, any accidental discrepancy in the sample, such as the presence of bird droppings, would invalidate the results. Moreover, contemporary chemical analysis was not sensitive enough to accurately measure the very minute quantities involved. Still further, even if analysis could perfectly gauge the quantity of a mineral, it could not determine its solubility and readiness for plant uptake. Johnson then referred to Wells in asserting that "so much depends upon the *physical* condition of the soil, that analysis alone, can form no safe basis for judgment." He therefore concluded that "*soil analysis, at best, is a chance game.*" Yet he did not mean to disparage agricultural chemistry as a science, only to point out that, at present, farmers could not expect immediate practical benefit. Instead, a program of sustained institutional research was necessary in order to slowly build up understanding of complex natural processes. The assessment was echoed by an agricultural press that, increasingly critical of soil analysis, was quick to deny that science itself was at fault.

Yet much blame was hurled at the experts. The ties among farmers, reformers, and scientists had always had their tensions. One view was that farming practice was the necessary basis of scientific agriculture. "Great things can be accomplished by each member making observations on his own farm, and reporting the result," maintained the president of one early agricultural society, while the geologist and agricultural surveyor Amos Eaton wrote that he intended "merely to collect, digest and systematize the opinions of those of our own practical farmers, who have been successful."[32] Reformers frequently voiced some variation on the sentiment that science and practice "must endeavor to cooperate for the elucidation of truth."[33] Another view, however, was that science was basically independent of and superior to ordinary practice. Farmers were really "indebted to science and scientific men," who issued instructions from "the retiracy of their studies."[34]

It was not entirely obvious who could lay claim to being a man of science and what that really meant. The experts themselves disagreed about the relative merits of basic research and technological application. Supporters of the former hoped to build institutions insulated from public pressures for quick results. But others—agricultural supply dealers, farm journal editors, and commercial consultants—had to contend directly with a marketplace of ordinary farmers whom they hoped to educate but not alienate. After 1852, the inherent differences came to the surface as agricultural reformers tried to extricate themselves from the soil analysis mess. "*The professors of chemistry are at fault,*" the editor of the *Ohio Cultivator* charged, "*in that they do not as yet sufficiently understand the science they attempt to teach, in its application to practical agriculture.*" The *Cultivator* condemned as a fool "the chemist who shall undertake to sit in his laboratory, and without practice to direct the labors of the field." Fee-charging "consulting chemists" came in for particular resentment. "Sad though it be," the *New England Farmer* noted, "we must believe that learned men will still be found, base enough to deceive their fellow-men."[35] Thus fissures began to appear in the once tight-knit agricultural reform community. The *Prairie Farmer* aptly characterized the new situation when it weighed in on the developing controversy surrounding James Mapes under the headline, "Trouble among the Fraternity."[36]

James J. Mapes Embattled

Because of his public stature, inveterate self-promotion, and frequent endorsement of soil analysis, James Mapes became a prime target for attack.[37] In 1851, for example, Mapes claimed to have produced an excellent crop on his own farm by following the fertilizer prescriptions of a soil analysis. "*In no instance*," he boasted, "has the experiment failed to produce desired crops, of superior quality, where manuring has been founded on the chemical constituents of the soil."[38] Such obvious exaggeration was ripe for criticism after 1852—and precisely because Mapes had been such a respected and widely renowned spokesman for soil analysis beforehand.[39]

Born in 1806, Mapes was the son of a prominent Long Island merchant and banker (figure 5.2).[40] He developed an interest in chemistry at an early age and learned the science largely on his own. Never shy of self-promotion, in the 1830s he went into business as one of the country's first technical consultants and became a frequent expert witness in patent cases. He was also an inventor, developing a long-utilized sugar-refining system and contributing improvements in dyeing, distilling, color making, steel tempering, and various tools and machine processes. These efforts gained him significant recognition by the 1840s. He received an honorary degree from Williams College, an appointment as lecturer at the National Academy of Design, and the title of professor from the American Institute of the City of New York. He held active and honorary memberships in several scientific societies, including the Royal Society of St. Petersburg and the Geographical Society of Paris. In addition, he was an accomplished miniaturist whose portraits were hung at exhibitions of the National Academy. On top of all this, he promoted the cause of technical education. In 1844, he became president of the Mechanics' Institute of New York, where he organized night classes for ambitious mechanics. Around the same time, he founded the New York Farmers' Club, an influential discussion group whose proceedings were reported widely in the agricultural press and the city's daily papers.

In 1847, Mapes left New York City to settle on a farm near Newark, New Jersey. There he established a nursery business, grew fruits and vegetables for the urban market, conducted experiments, and tried out new implements, including several of his own invention. Two years later, he issued the first volume of the *Working Farmer*, a monthly agricultural journal that he continued to edit for the next fifteen years. Mapes also took in students, several of whom later achieved considerable renown. Patrick T. Quinn, Mapes's farm manager for most of the 1850s, became a fixture of New Jersey's agricultural institutions from the 1870s to the 1890s; George E. Waring, who authored the statistical study of soil depletion that so impressed Liebig and Henry Carey, later won

Figure 5.2. John Sartain's engraving, after his own portrait drawing, of James Jay Mapes. Note the listing of Mapes's many honors and titles. Courtesy of the Smithsonian Libraries.

national fame as perhaps the country's leading urban sewage engineer; and Henry Steel Olcott, like Waring an assistant editor of the *Working Farmer*, would go on to co-found the international Theosophist movement.[41]

Mapes was clearly a man of many talents and considerable ability who also enjoyed the support of influential friends such as Samuel F. B. Morse and Horace Greeley. When he died in 1866, Greeley's *Tribune* published a lengthy obituary that summed up his legacy in fulsome terms: "Prof. Mapes was essentially a genius, and was not without the errors of genius; but now that he is dead, we believe it will be generally felt and acknowledged that American agriculture owes as much to him as to any man who lives or has ever lived."[42] In other words, however bizarre the theory of the progression of primaries appears today, we must acknowledge that Mapes was no ordinary crackpot.

Mapes was strongly and very publicly devoted to Liebig, whom he took every opportunity to cite as authority for his own views.[43] It is not surprising, then, to find Mapes on the front lines of the campaign to convince farmers that in soil analysis lay their salvation. "Have you had an analysis made of your soil?" was, in one way or another, the constant refrain of the *Working Farmer*'s first three volumes.[44] Himself a chemist, Mapes offered his own services and, through his advertisements section, those of others. Characteristic of his exuberant entrepreneurialism, Mapes charged the going rate of $5 for the analysis itself but offered a detailed letter of advice for an additional $25. Sometimes he published these letters in a bid, it would seem, both to enlighten his readers and to solicit new clients. In one case he counseled a client in Illinois to augment his soil with chlorine.[45]

But Mapes went further. Drawing on Liebig's mineral theory and his strong emphasis on plants' phosphatic content, Mapes pioneered the commercial manufacture of superphosphates in the United States. Superphosphates were destined to become the world's foremost artificial fertilizer for decades to come, but they were quite new in the 1850s. Reports of their use in Britain began to appear regularly in the American agricultural press from the mid-1840s, typically followed by calls for Americans to do similarly. By decade's end, many farmers had experimented with producing their own superphosphates, and at least two Baltimore firms had offered them for limited sale. But not until Mapes and a newly arrived Englishman, Charles B. DeBurg, introduced their products almost simultaneously in 1852 did a bona fide American superphosphate industry come into existence. Mapes used bones and bone black leftover from slaughterhouses and sugar refineries as his primary source of phosphatic material, whereas by this time the leading British firm of John Bennet Lawes was already shifting toward coprolites, apatite, and other nonrenewable mineral sources.[46] This fact would acquire great significance for Mapes when he introduced his progression of primaries theory several years later.

Equally significant was the fact that superphosphates, or bi-phosphates, as they were also called, were closely identified with Liebig's mineral theory and consequently with the soil analysis craze. Liebig had argued that plants' nitrogen needs were fully supplied by the atmosphere, which was effectively inexhaustible, whereas their equally important phosphatic requirements came only from the ground, which was quickly "worn out." Liebig's endorsement of the manufacture of superphosphate by the acidulation of bones was widely known.[47] Thus, when a Baltimore firm began marketing a limited quantity of its "Renovator" fertilizer in 1850, its advertisement explained that "recently, science has shown the far greater advantage of bone dust (bi-phosphates) dissolved in sulfuric acid."[48] The theoretical underpinnings of superphosphates mattered because the consuming public needed to be educated to appreciate the value of a brand new (and brand name) artificial fertilizer. Indeed, many fertilizer makers sought to associate their products with scientific discoveries. The Lodi Manufacturing Company promoted its "New and Improved Poudrette" by reference to leading European chemists.[49] The George Bommer New York Manure Company advertised a patented "Chemical Manure." Another fertilizer maker simply called itself the Liebig Manufacturing Company.[50] Having cultivated these associations, superphosphate manufacturers had some explaining to do when the currency of mineral soil analysis collapsed.

The storm of withering criticism that descended on Mapes over the next several years centered on the quality of his fertilizer but often touched on his advocacy and solicitation of soil analyses.[51] No one questioned the basic value of superphosphates when properly manufactured, yet the controversy sometimes turned on arcane details of fertilizer application. In one riposte, for instance, the *Genesee Farmer* argued that superphosphates worked best when drilled with the seed, whereas Mapes's advertised additions of Peruvian guano would prove "injurious to the germination of the seed when drilled with it."[52] Such matters could hardly have been considered settled under the prevailing circumstances of uncertainty. Only a few years earlier, a fertilizer dealer noted that "in reference to the application of Guano, there appears to be so much diversity of opinion, that it is difficult to offer any particular method to be adopted as an invariable rule."[53] More damning for Mapes were the well-publicized analyses of commercial superphosphates made by Samuel W. Johnson in 1853 and again in the late 1850s. Johnson pulled no punches. "Of all the many fraudulent and poor manures that have been from time to time imposed upon our farmers during the last four years," he railed, "there is none so deserving of complete exposure, and sharp rebuke, as that series of trashy mixtures known as 'Mapes' Superphosphates of Lime.'"[54] But, again, since the status of agricultural chemistry remained very much up in the air among the farming public, such assertions might be brushed aside as self-interested or premature. With so much disenchantment, accusation, and hand-wringing going around, and no institutional authority to appeal to, the field was wide open for any number of competing theories. "From all quarters comes the cry," wrote one frustrated observer, "we want a systematic theory of agriculture."[55] Agricultural writers often cited the very prevalence of competing views among acknowledged experts as a prime reason why no stock could be put in soil analysis.[56] The same doubts might easily be extended to agricultural chemistry in general.

And indeed, this is precisely what Mapes did. Responding in 1859 to a correspondent's question as to "whether the quality of a fertilizer can be ascertained by the analysis as usually made," Mapes answered, "distinctly, No. Analysis as now made, merely records the constituents of a manure without the slightest note of condition."[57] Mapes thus appropriated the vocabulary of "condition" that Wells and Johnson had applied to a soil's physical attributes. But in accordance with the theory of the progression of primaries, Mapes now referred to the form of plant nutrients' constitutive elements. Crucially, this move allowed Mapes to defend the quality of his "Improved Super-phosphate of Lime." Because that product's primary raw material was animal bones, all of its phosphates came in the most "progressed" possible form, the form they could only have acquired after moving steadily up the food chain.

The progression of primaries thesis remained forever short of evidence, but in the aftermath of an exploded paradigm, speculative thought enjoyed free play. Mapes thus illustrated his point by reference to the phenomenon of isomerism, or cases in which two or more compounds of the same elements in the same proportions possess dissimilar properties. Liebig had discussed such occurrences in his *Familiar Letters on Chemistry*, positing differences in compound structure as the explanation.[58] Mapes took this as his point of departure. Frequently, he gave as an example the apparent fact that "one pound of potash taken from the ashes of a burned haystack will fertilize more plants than will one hundred pounds of potash taken freshly from the feldspar rock."[59] Similarly, he argued, superphosphates manufactured from phosphatic rock would prove practically useless for higher-order plants, whereas those produced from bones were excellent.[60]

Examples of chemistry's apparent failure to explain observed phenomena served a dual rhetorical purpose for Mapes. They cleared the field for his own views and allowed him to present himself as a "practical farmer." The agricultural press was now in the habit of repudiating the "time when it was actually believed that science was to do everything, and practical ability nothing."[61] Mapes therefore boldly arrayed himself on the side of the farmer while eliding his own role in the soil analysis craze. "If the chemists don't look out," he chided, "they will find that those practical farmers will send them back to their laboratories, to re-investigate some of the dogmas." His next move was to preempt his skeptics with a meditation on the contingent nature of scientific knowledge. It was "deference to admitted conventionalities" that made "new observation so difficult of dissemination," he averred, because scientists objected "to every novelty exactly in proportion" as it seemed to contravene their existing conceptual frameworks. Yet the natural world constantly offered up phenomena that could not be subsumed by known scientific rubrics. Researchers ought therefore to "chasten their chemistry by the truths observed, instead of defining the truths by their chemical knowledge."[62]

Striking a populist note, Mapes reaffirmed his conviction that farmers must carefully observe their own operations.[63] In common with virtually all agricultural reformers, Mapes had always advocated formal technical education. But he was also a leading exponent of a more democratic mode of self-education. Since his time at the Mechanics' Institute in the early 1840s, he had advocated for "conversational meetings" structured to facilitate the exchange of technical knowledge by, crucially, avoiding debate. Each speaker was to deliver only the facts of the case as they were known to him, allowing the audience to draw its own inferences. In this manner, Mapes argued, meetings could be kept orderly and informative, and members would benefit by sharing the experiences of others. Mapes organized the New York Farmers' Club in precisely this way. "No means can be so well devised," he insisted, to "enable practical and scientific men to compare notes, and thus to arrive at the truth."[64] Such a forum explicitly called on participants to be the ultimate judges of truth claims, a structure that suited Mapes nicely in his controversy with Johnson, who implicitly claimed the authority of European training. Majoritarian and expert modes of knowledge both served agricultural reformers' efforts to transcend mere politics, but here was a clear case of conflict that threatened the movement's internal coherence. Importantly, Mapes was not so much questioning scientific expertise as its legitimizing warrant. In different ways, both he and Johnson were suggesting that scientific legitimacy ultimately depended on some kind of public accountability. The question, of course, was what kind.

If Mapes had no intention of renouncing science altogether, he did seek to exploit the space between working farmers and research scientists to make room for his own views—and, not incidentally, his own products. The progression hypothesis, he argued, "shows truths in nature which both the laboratory and the microscope have failed to perceive," allowing the "practical agriculturist" to make a better decision regarding which fertilizers to use.[65] Johnson responded sarcastically that the theory was useful only "to account for the great value of Mapes' superphosphates!"[66] In later years Johnson would continue his crusade against fertilizer frauds and help initiate the wave of state fertilizer inspection laws that began in the late 1860s.[67] For his part, Mapes fought back even from the grave (figure 5.3). According to a 1927 advertisement for the fertilizer company built by his son, "the good farmer of today knows, as Prof. Mapes did eighty years ago, that the crop is the best judge of fertilizer values. He knows that two fertilizers of the same analysis may give widely different results because of the different materials from which they are formulated."[68]

"Progress Is a Law of Nature"

The survival of the Mapes brand for so long suggests that it may not have been such a bad product after all.[69] Mapes certainly had his supporters. One of the

What Prof. Mapes Did in 1847
The Good Farmer Does in 1927

"I'll go to the crop", said Prof. James J. Mapes, originator of Mapes Manures. "I'll ask the crop to tell me what fertilizer it needs". Although famous as an expert chemist, Prof. Mapes knew that he could not depend on chemical analysis alone. So, in 1847, he bought a farm to check up, in the field, what he had learned in the laboratory.

The good farmer of today knows, as Prof. Mapes did eighty years ago, that the crop is the best judge of fertilizer values. He knows that two fertilizers of the same analysis may give widely different results because of the different materials from which they are formulated. So he buys his fertilizer on the basis of crop results, not on analysis alone.

That is why Mapes users are so loyal to Mapes Manures. And that is why more good farmers every year are becoming Mapes users. We go to the crop; we ask it what materials it likes best; we put these materials into Mapes Manures. Mapes Manures are made to grow good crops—not to sell at a price. They are first made right, then priced as low as possible.

If you are not a Mapes user, try Mapes this year. Compare the crop *yield*; compare the crop *quality*; compare the crop *profits* with the result from any other fertilizer you can buy. Mapes "costs little more—worth much more".

Just Mail This Coupon Today

Write today for a list of the crop brands and prices of Mapes Manures. You'll be surprised at the little difference in cost between Mapes brands and other brands. Mapes "costs little more—worth much more". Please tell us what crops you plan to fertilize so that we can be of the greatest possible service to you in selecting the right brand to suit your special needs.

The Mapes Formula and Peruvian Guano Co., Dept. 13,
270 Madison Ave., New York, N.Y.

Without obligating me in any way, please send me your list of crop brands and prices.

I use............tons of fertilizer on the following crops: ....

....

My name is.......................................

P. O...............................State.......

MAPES
Manures

Figure 5.3. A 1927 advertisement for Mapes Manures obliquely referencing the antebellum controversy over James Mapes's superphosphates and his theory of the progression of primaries. Published in Williams Haynes, *Chemical Pioneers: The Founders of the American Chemical Industry* (New York: D. Van Nostrand Co., 1939). HathiTrust Digital Library.

most prominent was Henry Flagg French, a man of some importance in agricultural reform circles and beyond. A New England lawyer and future assistant secretary of the Treasury, he served at various times as an officer of the New Hampshire State Agricultural Society, assistant editor of the *New England Farmer*, and president of the Massachusetts Agricultural College.[70] French never endorsed the progression of primaries unequivocally, but he gave it a sympathetic hearing. As late as 1876—ten years after Mapes's death, when his reputation needed no defense—he still referred to the progression hypothesis as "certainly plausible."[71] Like Mapes himself, French put the theory in the context of disappointed hopes for chemical soil analysis. "A few years ago," he wrote in 1859, "all the world was talking of soil analysis. The theory was beautifully simple." Alas, it turned out that "the plant knows more than the chemist! There *are* differences which the chemist cannot detect."[72] French noted that hay fed to cows and returned to the land as manure performed admirably as a fertilizer, whereas simply spreading out the hay and plowing it under did no such service. "It is not enough, then," he concluded, "that we apply to the soil merely the elements of which the required crops are composed. There must be reference always *to the form* in which those elements exist."[73] From the perspective of an educated and engaged, but ultimately lay farming public, Mapes's reference to "isomeric" substances that seemed chemically identical but were in fact decisively different did appear to explain some of the failures of soil analysis.

Yet the crisis in agricultural chemistry was not enough to make the Mapes hypothesis "plausible." For this, the mechanism Mapes proposed had to accord with prevalent notions of the ordering of nature. To the extent that Mapes described such a mechanism, it resolved into the "eternal law" of "progression." French found this highly appealing. "We all believe in *progress*," he affirmed, "and that nature usually walks onward to higher and higher results."[74] The notion that a progressive tendency inhered in nature itself was remarkably common in the nineteenth century.[75] Speaking before the Plymouth Agricultural Society in 1855, for example, the physician, chemist, and geologist Charles T. Jackson stated flatly that "progress is a law of nature." He continued, "Geology reveals that the lower order of sensitive beings gave way to those of a higher grade, until the last term of physical creation was attained in the creation of man, whose improvement, as a rational creature, and an immortal soul, is still destined to be onward and upward."[76] Mapes appropriated this reasoning to suggest that the megafauna of past ages had been "formed as mere machines for the progression of primaries," and, having served this purpose "by the mastication and digestion of food, its assimilation and their decay, have gradually become extinct."[77] This view seems to parallel the trope of the "vanishing Indian": dinosaurs and indigenous peoples had each played their part in the divine plan and then melted away. French, too, framed Mapes's theory within geological deep time. "Every little shell of the seashore is composed of matter in a condition somewhat different from that in which it before existed. It was before part of a rock; it has advanced to be part of an animal. It is chiefly lime now, as it was before; but lime of somewhat different properties."[78]

Belief in progress stirred many of Mapes's backers. One editor drew the connection explicitly when he reprinted one of Mapes's articles because of its "bearing on the great law of Progress."[79] Similarly, a member of the Farmer's Club commented after a Mapes disquisition that "we are all familiar with the doctrine of progression in all things." He then added, revealingly if somewhat absurdly, "our common potato is from a very little tuber, not fit to eat . . . yet it has progressed so much in my time as to be, to me, one of the most delicious and wholesome articles of food."[80] Such statements imbued the natural world with anthropocentric purpose that legitimized pursuit of its mastery, whether by agricultural reformers or Careyite economic nationalists. Precisely this made the progression of primaries appealing and "certainly plausible" to contemporaries.

Despite the failures of soil analysis, then, agricultural reformers continued to express great confidence, buoyed by a pervasive faith in the immanence of progress. A full three years after Wells's study, a rank-and-file member of the agricultural reform community urged farmers to "summon chemistry, geology, philosophy, mathematics, to our aid, and press onward to develop new resources and principles."[81] Yet vague invocations of science and the spirit of progress were not really enough anymore. As Johnson put it in tellingly gendered terms that evoked the need both to protect and to discipline a dependent, "science should carry herself modestly, as befits her youth, and not talk too loudly on all occasions of old-foggyism vs. progress."[82] Hence, the *Maine Farmer* called for a thorough course of experiments to evaluate Mapes's claims. The editor explained that "the subject of fertilizers and their particular action, wise as we think we are in regard to them, is yet in its infancy and need[s] the most patient scrutiny and investigation."[83] Agnosticism concerning both Mapes and his critics was the order of the day.

Seeking Institutional Authority

By the late 1850s, then, everyone seemed to agree that agricultural science remained in "her" "infancy." Uncertainty would remain for many years. In the preface to the 1868 edition of his textbook *The Elements of Agriculture*—first published in 1853 just as the controversy over soil analysis began—Mapes's student George Waring noted that in "the intervening years . . . the veil which hangs about the true theories of agriculture has grown harder to penetrate."[84] Decades later, Liberty Hyde Bailey noted that "the principles of chemistry as applied to farming afforded a central idea around which all other agricultural questions could be crystallized."[85] This was a research agenda, not a program of practical applications. Hence in 1858, Horace Greeley could not deny the proposition "that what is termed Agricultural Science—Soil Analysis, Special Fertilizers, and all that—is quackery and humbug." Yet he insisted that "the more urgent your proofs that no Science of Agriculture now exists, the more obvious the truth that one is urgently needed."[86]

How to move forward? Agricultural reformers had long advocated for government sponsorship of agricultural education and research. In the prevailing atmosphere of uncertain knowledge, the creation of institutions with the where-withal and authority to settle basic questions appeared all the more urgent. In an article advocating a federal department of agriculture to supervise a system of experimental institutions, Freeman Cary of the Farmers' College in Ohio argued that until rigorous research was introduced, the proliferation of the agricultural press would only add "to the already labyrinthian modes and per-plexities." Elsewhere, Cary argued that general farming practices could not progress until "science herself is divested of many of her crudities." The existing institutions of agricultural reform, he continued, had taken farmers about as far as they could go. Genuine agricultural science "can not be done by farmers, nor societies, nor clubs, nor lyceums, without proper teachers, without appara-tus, without text books, where problems long and complicated, and extending to numerous and varied experiments, and often through a series of years, are to be demonstrated."[87]

The status of agricultural technology was at the center of the problem. Farmers found themselves adrift in a rapidly expanding market for agricultural "improvements" that included everything from artificial fertilizers to mechan-ical reapers to drainage systems. As French put it, "the market is full of scien-tific *manures*, as well as of scientific principles."[88] It was imperative to establish criteria for evaluating such technologies. Thus when Justin Morrill spoke in 1858 in favor of his land-grant bill to create a new class of agricultural and mechanical colleges, he inveighed against "unsustained speculations" of "the laboratory" before arguing that Americans needed "a careful, exact, and systematized reg-istration of experiments—such as can be made at thoroughly scientific institu-tions, and such as will not be made elsewhere."[89]

The creation of the USDA and the land-grant university system followed a long campaign of advocacy, one that drew as much momentum from the en-thusiasm for agricultural chemistry and soil analysis as from the subsequent disappointments. But the crisis of expertise in the mid-1850s demonstrated that institutions of agricultural education and research should serve not only as founts of *new* knowledge, but also as centers of *authoritative* knowledge able to discipline a potentially unruly market of scientific and technological claims. In congressional debates over the creation of the USDA, for instance, one senator argued for a powerful agency precisely so that it could ensure that agricultural knowledge was "indorsed [*sic*] from the national Government."[90] A decade later, the USDA's chief clerk endeavored to show that the department was living up to this standard. The Chemical Division, he explained, "embraces a thor-ough inquiry into the constituent elements of superphosphates and other com-mercial manures, and it is intended to furnish the farmer with a measure of their value which will serve him as a guide."[91] The federal government was to regulate the market by the provision of reliable information.

Agricultural scientists aligned themselves with this civic mission, anticipating that the exposure of commercial fertilizer frauds would lead the public to fund basic research.[92] This was clearly what Evan Pugh envisioned during his tenure as the first president of the Pennsylvania Agricultural College. Pugh's ideas were strongly influenced by his visit in 1854 to the agricultural experiment station at Möckern, Germany, which proved attractive to him because it followed a course of experimentation directed by local farmers' wants.[93] The station was "remarkable for its practical bearing," he noted in an article for the *Pennsylvania Farm Journal*, before explaining the need for new experimental institutions to "grind out original facts from uninvestigated nature, and shape them into science that they can be brought before the agriculturist and the student of the agricultural school." The basic problem was an absence of "known facts in the agricultural world sufficient to found a rational answer" to pressing questions.[94] Accordingly, under Pugh's leadership from 1859 until his death in 1864, the Agricultural College of Pennsylvania defined itself as an "educational," "practical," and "experimental" institution, but also as an institution for "protecting the industrial interests of the State, and most especially the agricultural interest, from the sale of bad or worthless or too high priced material (as manures, seeds, plants, and implements used in agricultural practice)."[95]

The basic problem of evaluating new agricultural technologies went well beyond fertilizers. This is clear from agricultural reformers' calls for more rigorous trials of new farming implements and machines from the 1840s onward. Field trials of plows, reapers, and other gadgets grew increasingly elaborate, evolving from a kind of popular sporting event into highly technical affairs. By the early 1860s, expectations had changed enough for at least one agricultural society to refuse to award premiums for mowers and reapers unless tested in the field.[96] The movement to provide impartial analyses of machinery paralleled the trend toward fertilizer testing but also differed in significant ways. Agricultural societies proved capable of organizing occasional field trials, but fertilizer testing had to be done on a more regular basis in specialized institutions. In part, this was because the mechanical principles involved in agricultural machinery were better understood and more readily visible than the chemistry behind plant fertilizers.

In 1852, the New York State Agricultural Society noted that "the great and increasing variety of machines evidences the urgent necessity . . . for a complete and satisfactory trial."[97] According to another observer, farmers were in "quite an excitement . . . as regards labor-saving implements, in regard to which is the cheapest, most durable, and the best worker."[98] A proposal for a uniform point scale by which to judge reapers and mowers was soon in circulation, and although it appears that it was never used, the basic idea of greater rigor and uniformity in implement testing was widely approved.[99] For instance, after the

1856 implement competition at the annual exhibition of United States Agricultural Society (USAS), the Committee on Discretionary Premiums complained that it could not make proper decisions without systematic trials. The committee, which included Mapes protégés George Waring and Henry Olcott, proposed a "Great National Trial in the Field" of agricultural implements and machines.[100] With this plan the committee responded to a common grievance, voiced by farmers, reformers, and manufacturers alike, against awarding premiums on the basis of visual examination alone.[101]

Systematic implement testing was a major undertaking. The actual organization in 1857 of the "Great National Trial of Machinery and Implements of Every Description Pertaining to Agriculture" shows why. Because different implements were designed for different tasks and different crops, they could not all be tested at the same time and place. While most were to be assessed at the September USAS fair in Louisville, Kentucky, the agricultural press focused much of its attention on the "Great National Trial of Mowers and Reapers" to be held at Syracuse during the July harvest. The organizers promised to provide each machine with "at least four acres of grain and three acres of grass" in measured plots.[102] With over ninety entrants reported at one point, several hundred acres of private wheat and hay fields had to be allotted, all within reasonable proximity for the judging committee to be able to visit. Ultimately about forty distinct machines arrived, several contending in both categories, making for an event of unprecedented scale that one farm journal characterized as "the most important trial ever held in this country."[103] It would not be repeated until after the Civil War, when the New York state legislature appropriated $45,000 for a competition featuring nineteen distinct implement and machine classes. The report of that "Second Great National Field Trial," replete with charts, illustrations, and figures, ran to over two hundred pages.[104]

The challenge of establishing institutions of authoritative knowledge to structure emerging markets for new-fangled agricultural technologies recurred again and again. Fruit tree nomenclature and the descent lines of improved livestock breeds exhibited some similar problems to those afflicting fertilizers, implements, and machines, though the inherent instability of biological reproduction made things even more complicated, and the institutional solutions differed.[105] The fertilizer market proved the hardest to tame and the most in need of government intervention. "Extensive fraudulent practices and the widespread suspicion of these practices poisoned" the industry until effective state inspection regimes took shape in the 1870s and 1880s.[106] Among the problems endemic to the fertilizer trade was the potential variability of any given product over time and the impossibility of assessing a product's value without elaborate chemical tests. Implements were less prone to these difficulties, but the difference was a matter of degree rather than kind. The quality of specific implements could vary significantly, especially as a result of the licensing system in which patents were farmed out to regional manufacturers. And while a purchaser might readily assess a mower's capabilities with a simple field trial, its long-term durability, ease of repair, and performance under changing field conditions remained open to question. In the cases of livestock and fruit-tree cuttings, marketing problems arose from the mutability of living organisms, which might take years to become fully manifest.

If purchasers thus tempered their enthusiasm for novel technologies, businessmen recognized the impediment to sales. As a group, therefore, businessmen supported the structure provided by public field tests, fertilizer inspection laws, and authoritative agricultural research. In the 1870s, for instance, one fertilizer manufacturer argued that it was the "bounden duty of government" to make sure everyone was playing by the same rules.[107] On the other hand, as individual operations, purveyors of new farming technologies lashed out against adverse assessments of their own products. For example, a Pennsylvania maker of Kirby's American Harvester devoted eleven pages of its 1859 catalog to a careful explication of the Kirby's strong performance at the Great National Field Trial, while it simultaneously disputed in the local press the fairness of another field trial in which its product had fared poorly.[108]

Although product trials and agricultural research institutions were framed as protections for wary farmers, they were part and parcel of a deeper reform effort to encourage adoption of new technologies. That is, such institutions were meant to structure the agricultural tech market for orderly growth. That commercial purveyors of novel technologies were integral members of the reform movement is evidenced by their contributions to the establishment of agricultural colleges. In New York, for example, the Allen brothers, who operated a large agricultural supply warehouse and manufactory, were centrally involved in efforts to found an agricultural college from the 1830s onward.[109] Levi Stockbridge was not only a fertilizer maker but an early professor at the Massachusetts Agricultural College.[110] The founding of the Maryland Agricultural College in 1856 was made possible in part by the stock subscriptions from various agricultural supply companies, including the guano import firm F. Barreda & Brother, the farm machine manufacturer George Page & Co., and the famous reaper makers Obed Hussey and C. H. McCormick.[111] When the college opened its doors in 1859, it immediately began analyzing fertilizers offered for sale in Baltimore and Washington, DC.[112]

In short, the expansion in commercial agricultural technologies and the simultaneous crisis of agricultural expertise of the 1850s drove reformers, scientists, businessmen, and farmers all to seek authoritative institutions able to bring structure to an inchoate market. Although the form such institutions ought to take was not always obvious, in many cases reformers gravitated toward government, which boasted unparalleled resources and public legitimacy. It was in this context that they began to plan large-scale agricultural institutions able to conduct original research, test products, and educate farmers. This effort drew on both a longer heritage of agricultural schooling advocacy and a broader movement for technical training known as "industrial education." The concrete development of this institutional agenda forms the subject of the next chapter.

CHAPTER SIX

From *"Private Enterprise"* to *"Governmental Action"*

Agricultural reformers strove to establish specialized institutions of agricultural education throughout the antebellum period. Their efforts yielded mostly frustration. Time and again, they underestimated the costs of realizing their ambitions. Things only got harder in the 1850s when the discrediting of commercial soil analysis brought a general reassessment of the state of agricultural science, leading reformers to the conviction that education could not move forward without a parallel program of credible scientific investigation. Consequently, the small-scale private initiatives of the 1840s gave way to state-level lobbying for public funding in the early to mid-1850s and, when state funding proved unreliable, to a federal campaign that eventuated in the Morrill Land-Grant Act and the creation of the Department of Agriculture.

Efforts to found specialized institutions of agricultural education and research took may forms from the early 1800s to the Civil War. The difficulties encountered were complex and require working through in some detail, but there are two broad themes. The first is the challenge of securing adequate funding. The second concerns the form of the proposed educational institutions, particularly the relationship between curriculum and employment. The solution to the funding problem was straightforward and well-adapted to the capacities of the agricultural reform movement. After numerous failed private efforts, reformers concluded that government support was essential and mobilized politically to secure it. The question of the fit between education and work proved trickier. It arose in multiple ways and complicated the politics of state involvement. Without public funding, agricultural schools could not prove themselves, but until they proved themselves, they could not reliably count on public funding. Only the federal government had the resources to sustain a prolonged period of experimentation that was ultimately as much about institutional mission and design as about science.

Scholars have sometimes wondered whether farmers themselves cared about agricultural education, but a lot of evidence shows that many of them did.[1] Northern farmers displayed a remarkable commitment to schooling in general and a growing focus on the natural sciences in particular. Moreover, numerous rural academies, whose financial model effectively required them to respond to student demand, taught subjects such as agricultural chemistry. Finally, farmers manifestly *did* care about the few agricultural colleges that got started during the antebellum period and continued to care after the Civil War, when the Grangers and the Populists subjected fledgling land-grant colleges to intense scrutiny.[2] A significant number of farmers were obviously invested in these institutions. The well-known problem of low agricultural enrollments during the early years of the land-grant schools did not reflect farmers' apathy but rather the difficulty of settling on the appropriate design, curriculum, and culture for a new kind of educational institution.

Middling northern farmers pursued literacy and numeracy as never before during the antebellum period.[3] Before 1850, according to one study, "the rural North led the world in the building of schools, the hiring of teachers, and overall enrollments."[4] According to another, farmers within the rural North "seem to have invested much more in the education of their children" than did non-farmers, and northeastern rates of school attendance appear to have been higher than midwestern rates.[5] Rising interest in schooling beyond the elementary level further attests to these trends. Enrollment increases in New York Regents academies, mostly located in small country towns, outpaced new school capacity in every decade between 1820 and 1860. This demand for education, several scholars have found, "was rooted in rural life and the commercial farming economy."[6]

Education was valued for many reasons, but economic goals were increasingly prominent among them. Agricultural reformers relentlessly insisted that economic development required a new degree of scientific and technological literacy. "The farmer is no longer a mere laborer," argued James Mapes. "To succeed in competition with the improvements of the day, he must be educated to a fair extent."[7] Though some rural youth viewed schooling as a way to get "beyond the farm," this was far from universal.[8] The first dean of Cornell University's College of Agriculture, Isaac Roberts, recalled that ambitious farm families in the 1850s "laid almost as much stress upon 'schooling' as upon manual dexterity and willingness to work."[9] Education could thus be seen as an essential complement to physical labor, not an escape from it.

Economic priorities appeared as a new emphasis on the natural sciences. In 1843, the Cortland Academy reported to the New York Regents that courses in "Algebra, and Natural Philosophy" were "required" by many of the area's common schools, while another rural academy noted that such subjects "seem to be regarded of much importance."[10] Around the same time, petitioners called on the Pennsylvania legislature to "enable all classes of the community in every section of the State, to collect, examine, and understand the natural productions of their respective vicinities."[11] Such demands led the New York Regents to observe in 1857 that "science is greatly popularized," for "it is a conceded principle of political economy, that science and knowledge constitute the most productive capital."[12] Horace Mann, the era's leading education reformer, situated the natural sciences' popularity squarely in the context of agricultural reform. "Agriculture requires knowledge for its successful operation," he explained. "This brings into requisition all that chemical and experimental knowledge which pertains to the rotation of crops, and the enrichment of soils."[13] As Mapes put it, "Chemistry, Natural Philosophy and Natural History constitute the *grammar* of Agriculture."[14]

These were not merely the pronouncements of reformers from on high. The tenant farmers Levi and John Weeks, who made their children's shoes themselves, subscribed to farm journals, adopted improvements, and attended lectures on electricity, magnetism, physiology, and chemistry.[15] In tiny Fayettesville, Vermont, fairgoers marched under a banner emblazoned with the Baconian slogan, "Knowledge is power."[16] Members of Pennsylvania's Octorara Farmers' Club met monthly for decades to discuss how scientific agriculture might serve practical needs, publishing over three hundred original essays in the local newspaper between 1856 and 1887.[17] Although scientific learning might serve as little more than a badge of middle-class respectability, the evidence for agricultural reform's impact was all over the land itself: in redesigned barns and outbuildings, new implements and machines, fields of crops in rotation spread with artificial fertilizers, improved livestock of every description, and countless experiments with new crop varieties imported from every part of the world.

In short, rural interest in natural science as a source of agricultural improvement was real and widespread. This provided a social basis for building a new institutional apparatus of specialized agricultural education and research. But effectively assembling the nuts and bolts proved far more difficult than imagined.

False Starts

Proposals for agricultural education appeared as early as the postrevolutionary period. They tended to fall into two categories. On the one hand, patrician reformers envisioned agricultural instruction alongside the classical college curriculum for the sons of the elite. On the other hand, they embraced the model of manual labor schools for youth of moderate means. By the late 1830s, both ideas were losing ground. State support for patrician agricultural colleges failed the test of democratic politics, while the manual labor concept proved ineffective and fell out of favor.

The earliest efforts at formal agricultural education aimed to establish professorships at existing colleges. These rarely amounted to much, so by the 1810s reformers were more likely to call for separate agricultural institutions. At a time when college education was restricted to the elite, these calls, too, retained a distinctively elite flavor. Frequently their leading theme was that too many young men were attempting to enter the legal, medical, and clerical professions. In 1811, for example, "A Farmer" contended that the professions had become "overstocked," but that state-funded agricultural schools might convert the "idlers" into "good practical farmers."[18] As late as 1845, Horace Greeley could still write that because "the Country is greatly overstocked with Lawyers, Doctors, etc. . . . the soil is the only sure recourse." This vision of agricultural education as preparation for a profession akin to the law reflected the social standing of leading reformers in the early Republic, some of whom believed that "many wealthy merchants" would gladly have their sons trained as scientific farmers.[19] Even the plainspoken Greeley thought at first of agricultural graduates as a vanguard to set an example for "the less informed many."[20] Such elitist rhetoric contrasted with the later push that presented agricultural schooling in the idiom of democratic access and public service.

In 1819, Simeon De Witt gave a full exposition of the patrician reformers' vision in his *Considerations on the Necessity of Establishing an Agricultural College, and Having More of the Children of Wealthy Citizens, Educated for the Profession of Farming.*[21] De Witt, who as president of the New York Society for the Promotion of the Useful Arts was connected to New York's reform-minded landlords, argued that the sons of the rich too often sunk into lives of urban dissipation. Since no gentleman's scion would abide apprenticeship to a common farmer, De Witt proposed a grand state college to teach modern agriculture at the appropriately elevated level. Knowledge would then trickle down to the rural masses. This seemed like a plea for the state to sustain upper-class ne'er-do-wells against the children of "industrious mechanics" and "those extraordinary geniuses, that not unfrequently rise from the mansions of obscurity."[22] In a political climate that increasingly claimed to favor democracy over privilege, this was an easy target, and reformers soon found themselves branded as arrogant aristocrats.

The New York legislature declined to consider De Witt's plan, but it did establish the well-funded state Board of Agriculture. In 1822, the board brought on Jesse Buel as recording secretary. Though Buel was the son of "unassuming" New England farmers and once published a newspaper called the *Plebian*, he initially perpetuated an elite vision of "polite education, combined with a practical knowledge of agriculture."[23] In 1833, he authored the New York State Agricultural Society's proposal for a college with a suggested tuition of $150 a year, a figure comparable to the costs of attending Harvard or Yale.[24] "If it should be said that this would be a school only for the children of the opulent," a sympathetic committee of the state assembly explained, "the unanswerable argument is, that it is the same in regard to our colleges, and must be so of necessity."[25] Others, however, did not perceive the necessity. Labor leader George Henry Evans called the report "an aristocratic production," adding that he favored a state agricultural and mechanical school, but not "for the exclusive benefit of the rich."[26] Several years later, the legislature chartered an agricultural college, providing no funding but naming Buel and others to solicit $100,000 in stock subscriptions. The effort was quickly doomed by the Panic of 1837, which quashed all hope of raising the funds.[27]

Other reformers, meanwhile, pursued a very different kind of institution: the manual labor school, based on the model established by Philipp Emanuel von Fellenberg, a wealthy Swiss educational reformer, on his Hofwyl estate. Fellenberg combined academic instruction with agricultural and mechanical labor in a way that aimed to provide students with technical training and a means of their own support.[28] In the 1820s and 1830s, the Fellenberg system appealed to a broad range of American educational reformers. Evangelical abolitionists were particularly drawn to the idea. The abolitionist preacher Theodore Dwight Weld became a leading exponent of manual labor schooling after spending time at the Oneida Institute, a multiracial evangelical seminary in Whitesboro, New York, where students labored three hours a day in exchange for room, board, and tuition. He subsequently helped found Oberlin College as a manual labor institution.[29] Surprisingly, perhaps, many manual labor institutions were also founded in the South.[30] Another champion was Robert Dale Owen, who had himself been educated at Hofwyl and who based his "state guardianship" plan of universal free education on his experiences there. Evans and other workingmen's advocates backed this and similar proposals.[31]

For agricultural reformers, who in common with labor leaders sought to develop new forms of vocational training, the manual labor idea appealed as a means for poor students to finance their own practical farming education.[32]

After visiting Fellenberg's school in the 1820s, for example, the Pennsylvania gentleman farmer Anthony Morris determined to found a similar institution near Philadelphia, where he hoped to provide the sons of "moderate farmers and mechanics" with instruction in "theoretical and practical agriculture, the sciences connected with it, and the mechanic arts." Morris quickly obtained the endorsement of leading agricultural figures, but his school seems to have lasted only a single term.[33] Numerous difficulties beset the plan, including trouble finding qualified teachers. More fundamentally, Morris's goals were grounded in an incongruous conservatism caught between social control and self-interest. One of the school's "great objects," he wrote to a friend, was "a reform of that unbridled licenciousness [*sic*] of manners and habits which belong to the boys of America." But another object, according to a prospective backer, was to generate "profits" and "private advantages" from the erection of an extensive industrial village.[34]

Similar efforts also ran into problems, and by the mid-1840s, manual labor schools had largely fallen out of favor. The system's self-financing promise proved elusive. Some reformers had always understood the need for serious financial backing. One American visitor to Hofwyl argued that for a similar institution to succeed "in this country it must be undertaken either by an able founder and zealous capitalist, like Fellenburgh, or by a company with ample funds."[35] Moreover, in at least one case the host community opposed the very idea of a self-financing institution because it vitiated the benefit of having students as paying customers for local goods and services.[36] The same logic seems to have been at work in Easton, Pennsylvania, when town voters petitioned the state legislature to deny public funds to Lafayette College, at that time operated on manual labor principles. Such an appropriation, they argued, would amount to a taxpayer subsidy for "a private manufacturing establishment."[37]

Equally damaging to the manual labor idea was its growing association with charity for the lower classes.[38] One historian argues for a cultural mismatch of class values at the very heart of the concept, for it aimed to dignify manual labor while providing the educational means out of it.[39] Just as patrician agricultural colleges were pitched too high, then, manual labor schools were pitched too low. Physical farm work remained an integral part of future proposals, but reformers soon realized that agricultural education in the United States could not gain public support on a two-tiered class plan.

New Directions

Reformers turned to new options in the 1840s. The most obvious was simply to expand existing agricultural institutions. The whole reform movement, after all, had always been a didactic enterprise centered on the concept of "emulation"— friendly rivalry in pursuit of improvement—which formed an essential principle of pedagogical reform in the early Republic. Fairs, in particular, were lauded as sites where farmers met to observe each other and learn best practices. "The Fair is eminently an occasion of *thought*," asserted one farm journal. "It is not simply the husbandman's fruits and cattle and machinery that we see at the Exhibition," but "the *very process* by which he succeeded."[40] As Greeley put it, "the great end of all such exhibitions is an improvement of the breed of farmers— of men."[41]

Most reformers nevertheless believed in the need for formal agricultural education. During the 1840s and early 1850s, they commonly argued that small-scale private efforts had to show positive results before state legislatures would agree to public aid. Because "such schools are here an experiment," argued one, "it now seems obvious that if any early progress is made in their establishment in our State, it must be effected by private enterprise."[42] Almost a decade later, Samuel W. Johnson still believed that "while appeals to Legislatures have been made in vain for the endowment of agricultural schools . . . it remains to private or corporate enterprise to open the way."[43] The *Country Gentleman* summed up this line of thinking when it argued that "it is by gradual steps, and not by any miraculous providence or superhuman legislative effort, that agricultural education is to be secured for the farmers of our country."[44]

The well-known agricultural editor Daniel Lee exemplifies both the legislative disappointments that drove reformers down the path of "private enterprise" and the substantial barriers to success. As a member of the New York Assembly in 1844 and 1845, Lee pushed vigorously for agricultural schooling. At first, he introduced a bill for a "State Agricultural School" capitalized at up to $100,000, accompanying it with a lengthy committee report in which he drew attention to the state's declining wheat yields.[45] When the bill failed, he offered a more economical proposal to subsidize the conversion of his alma mater, the Fairfield Medical College in Herkimer County, into an agricultural institution.[46] Again the legislature demurred, so after finishing his term in the Assembly, Lee opened the private Western New York Agricultural School on a friend's estate near Rochester. By the fall of 1846, he was reporting that a dozen or so students "work daily in the Laboratory at the analysis of soils, fertilizers, and other substances."[47] But only a year later, the endeavor was defunct.

Reflecting on the experience, Lee wrote that "an Agricultural School, to be perfect in all its details, requires the expenditure of more money than any one or two men of ordinary means can afford." The problem was not a shortage of interested students but a lack of accommodations. "It is idle to suppose that men of literary and scientific attainments will throw away their time on a school where only 15 or 16 students can be furnished with rooms and other necessaries."[48] Future efforts would prove Lee correct that buildings, laboratories, and experimental grounds required more capital than reformers could likely gather from private sources. His analysis notwithstanding, many reformers continued to insist that "we must commence in a small way at first, with a few students."[49] In a typical pattern that mirrored his effort, a reformer established an "institute" on the property of a substantial local farmer, where students could board with the family while the reformer conducted courses and demonstrations.[50] These ventures were necessarily limited to a handful of students and rarely succeeded in getting off the ground.

The Orange County Scientific and Practical Agricultural Institute demonstrated the final inadequacy of such efforts. Established by Dr. James Darrach in the spring of 1846, the institute was conceived as a collective effort by several farmers in and around Walden, New York. Darrach explained that after careful study of Fellenberg's plans and those of others, he had concluded that existing agricultural schools suffered from two defects. First, they concentrated on teaching agricultural theory and manual skills but not how to manage the complicated ordering and planning of farm operations. Second, "a single farm was . . . insufficient to afford necessary opportunities for practical education." Instead, "in districts where farms were of moderate size and the farmers generally of superior character and practicing a mixed husbandry, they might unite in an association under proper regulations to receive, and become practical instructors, each to a few young men." The idea was for youth to live and work on area farms while taking courses from Darrach in the afternoons and evenings.[51] In contrast to most other ventures of this kind, the Orange County Institute actually operated for several years, but it endured a precarious existence. Within two years of its founding, Darrach was casting about for other work, and when an opportunity appeared in 1854, he jumped at it.[52] As Lee had suggested, independent ventures in agricultural instruction were not likely to attract "men of literary and scientific attainments" for long.

Darrach's experience highlights something else, too. The relatively egalitarian social structure of the northeastern countryside did well for the sprawling agricultural reform movement, but it was ill suited to endeavors that required large concentrations of funds. Over the course of the nineteenth century, businessmen who made fortunes in commerce and manufacturing endowed numerous successful colleges. But outside of the plantation South, few farmers amassed enough wealth to do likewise for agricultural institutions. Government was the obvious next step.

In the meantime, a limited but successful form of agricultural education occurred when rural academies added courses on agricultural chemistry and other relevant subjects. The agricultural press reported favorably on several such schools, but many took similar steps without attracting much notice. For example, the Clermont Boarding Academy for Boys in Frankford, Pennsylvania, gave notice of a winter course on "the application of Chemistry to Agriculture"

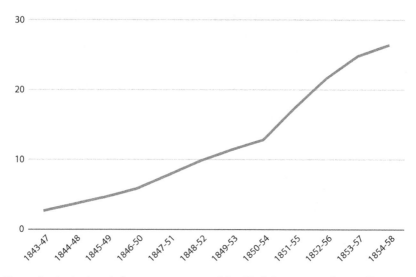

Figure 6.1. Agricultural chemistry courses in New York Regents academies (five-year moving averages). Annual reports of the Regents of the University of the State of New York for the years 1843 to 1858.

as early as 1844 and as late as 1895.[53] A few established colleges did similarly.[54] Noting the trend in 1851, a Maine newspaper commented "that the demand for greater enlightenment among farmers, induces the Academies and Colleges of our country to furnish the requisite facilities."[55]

The New York Board of Regents tracked instruction in agricultural chemistry among incorporated academies under its supervision from 1843 to 1858.[56] At the start of the period, only the Lowville Academy in Lewis County offered such a course, but over the next fifteen years, scores of academies did so. The rate of increase far outpaced the growth in the total number of academies over the same fifteen-year span. Figure 6.1 tracks five-year moving averages of Regents academies that taught agricultural chemistry, showing a steady climb and pronounced uptick in the early 1850s, right around the time of the soil analysis craze. By the middle of the decade, students interested in the topic could choose from more than thirty academies statewide in any given year. While many academies claimed to offer these classes only once, several did so in most years. The completeness of the data is suspect but suggests, if anything, underreporting. For example, the East Bloomfield Academy appears on the list of agricultural chemistry providers in every year from 1846 to 1856 except for 1853 and 1854, and similarly anomalous gaps occur in other cases as well. The data take no account of schools that did not report to the Regents. Nor is it clear why the Regents stopped recording courses in agricultural chemistry after 1858. Since they continued to tally offerings in less common subjects such as zoology and

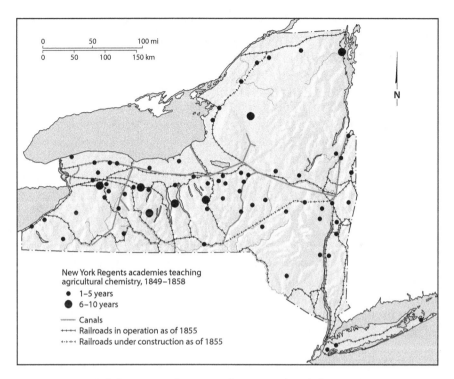

Map 6.1. New York Regents academies teaching agricultural chemistry, 1849–58. Map by Bill Nelson.

mineralogy, it seems likely that many academies were simply folding agricultural topics into general chemistry instruction. In advertisements, academies throughout the Northeast continued to highlight offerings in the subject.

Map 6.1 shows the locations of Regents academies teaching agricultural chemistry in the decade from 1849 to 1858. It should be immediately apparent that interest in the subject was geographically widespread. Closer inspection suggests that the relevant academies served commercial farming districts within range of major transportation routes. Revealingly, few of the academies appeared in the large cities along the Erie Canal, but rather in secondary hinterland towns such as Homer and Prattsburgh. Clusters are discernible around the railroad junction of Batavia in the Genesee wheat country, in the dairy region south of the Erie Canal between Syracuse and Rome, and along the planned Watertown and Potsdam Railroad in far upstate St. Lawrence County, another dairy region.

Agricultural reformers were often closely connected to such rural schools. In the winter of 1845–46, the principal of the Cortland Academy in Homer, Samuel Woolworth, initiated a "regular course of instruction on Agricultural

Chemistry and Geology." The topic was almost certainly influenced by the academy's board of trustees, which included several farmers, each of whom served as an officer of the Cortland County Agricultural Society at one point or another.[57] As was common among academies of the period, Woolworth's winter lecture series was open not only to students but to the general public. Two years later it was reported that the talks were packing the academy lecture hall. Local farmers were so gratified that they presented Woolworth with a silver cup in commendation of his "willing[ness] to become a laborious pioneer in the noble enterprise of imparting chemical and geological science to farmers."[58] Woolworth may have particularly excelled as a speaker, but many others gave similar agricultural lecture series. In 1852, for instance, Emily Dickinson wrote to her brother about the lecture offerings at the local lyceum, noting that John Adams Nash was "giving a course of Agricultural ones, twelve in all." Nash, who taught farming at Amherst College, published an agricultural textbook the following year, one of at least thirteen to appear in American publication between 1842 and 1861.[59] The links between rural academies and agricultural reform were varied and many.

But the academies also partially preempted reformers' goal of independent agricultural institutions. The era's "schools for every purpose," they offered broad curricula to attract students. This dictated flexibility in admitting students of widely varying ages for brief and discontinuous periods. Farm youth tended to intersperse study with work, typically attending school in the winter while laboring the rest of the year.[60] In December 1847, for instance, Benjamin Gue noted that "after husking corn and threshing most of the buckwheat I finished my work for this year and went to Canandaigua to school for the winter." Four months later he found himself "back again on the farm ready to begin work for the summer."[61] This was why agricultural reformers scheduled lecture series in the winter months. For the same reason, rural youth who might want to study agricultural subjects did not necessarily have the luxury of completing a formal curriculum. Gue did not return to school for another two years, this time to the East Bloomfield Academy.[62]

Rural students who attended school in this way often continued their studies at home.[63] In the winter between his stints at Canandaigua and East Bloomfield, Gue attended lectures, participated in debating societies, and read "Todds [*sic*] Student Manual."[64] Although he rarely discussed the particulars of his studies, he did mention instruction in chemistry at the Canandaigua Academy. Perhaps he continued this study at East Bloomfield, which reported teaching agricultural chemistry in the same year that he attended.[65] Whatever the case, he did not go on to college. Yet he clearly valued higher education, for after migrating west in the 1850s, he came to play a central role in the founding of Iowa State Agricultural College.[66]

Besides the financial challenges and the seasonal labor factor, the relationship between college-level education and employment presented additional difficulties.[67] A formal agricultural degree mostly likely led to a career as a specialist, yet few such jobs existed.[68] Even after the creation of new government agricultural agencies in the 1860s, "a period of limited opportunities" meant that the USDA easily attracted experts "in spite of low salaries and unfavorable conditions."[69] Unlike engineers and chemists, agricultural graduates did not enjoy robust demand from private industry. They also faced obstacles as entrepreneurs because many of the period's biological innovations, such as pest-resistant crop varieties, could not be patented.[70] By century's end, this situation had begun to change, in part because developing food industries and fertilizer manufacturers found increasing use for agricultural experts. Equally important was the proliferation of government institutions such as land-grant universities, federally funded experiment stations, and other agencies. The USDA expanded rapidly, particularly in scientific research, after its elevation to cabinet status in 1889. At century's end, advanced agricultural studies suddenly became a viable career option.

The Rensselaer School, which one historian calls the country's "first college of agriculture," is exemplary in this regard.[71] Founded in 1824, Rensselaer's original mission was to teach "the application of science to the common purposes of life," which perforce included farming.[72] Over the years, it produced a steady flow of uniquely qualified graduates in a period when few schools offered advanced scientific training. Several of its alumni would become important agricultural reformers, including the geologist George Hammell Cook, the entomologist Asa Fitch, and the chemist Eben Norton Horsford.[73] Nevertheless, from 1835, agricultural science began to decline at Rensselaer as civil engineering and industrial chemistry took precedence. After 1850, it emerged almost wholly as an engineering school. Rapid economic development in the antebellum period generated demand for engineers to build roads, bridges, steam engines, and so forth, while industries from tanning to textiles required chemists. Neither the public nor the private sectors, however, were prepared to employ graduates in the inchoate field of agricultural science.

Despite the generally acknowledged need for agricultural research, even the best-trained agricultural scientists struggled to find employment before the Civil War. Horsford, the first American to study with Justus von Liebig, found so little support at Harvard in his ambition to replicate Liebig's agricultural research laboratory in the United States that he eventually moved entirely into industrial chemistry.[74] Such leading postbellum agricultural scientists as Samuel W. Johnson and William H. Brewer bounced around throughout the 1850s.[75] Johnson attempted to invent employment out of whole cloth when he proposed "county agricultural institutes" that would fund laboratories staffed by salaried agricultural chemists. He noted that "there are certain manufacturing establishments in our country, that pay competent men $2,500 annual salary, and even more."[76] But his plan shows precisely why farming differed from manufacturing. Individual farmers, unlike industrial enterprises, were not in a position to hire their own expert researchers—at least not in the North, where plantation-style megafarms were virtually nonexistent. Hence, Johnson urged farmers to associate together. But as experience would show, the government was a much more likely form of associative action in this instance.

The slow emergence of university-level agricultural education exhibits the classic developmental problem of "linkages," in this case between schooling and employment. Without agricultural schools there would be a dearth of qualified agricultural experts, but without adequate career prospects for the experts, enrollments would lag, undermining the rationale for specialized institutions of agricultural education. The problem was basically similar to the one faced by Robert R. Livingston and James Mease back in the 1810s in trying to get up a wool industry: no high-quality wool without advanced manufacturing, no advanced manufacturing without high-quality wool. Reformers solved that one with state-funded premiums and carefully constructed tariff schedules leavened with a heavy dose of developmental ideology. Agricultural education, too, would require state intervention and a developmental ethos.

The Rise and Fall of Farmers' College

One rural academy did attempt to expand its agricultural offerings in the antebellum period, resulting in the formation of Farmers' College in southern Ohio. For a brief moment in the 1850s, it appeared as if Farmers' College had indeed established the country's first bona fide collegiate department of agriculture, complete with laboratory, experimental farm, botanical garden, and even a monthly farm journal. Within a very short time, however, the school's finances foundered. As operating expenses exceeded income from tuition and investments, the trustees were forced to cannibalize the school's endowment, leading to a downward spiral of budget cuts and property sales that left the college struggling to keep its doors open after 1858. The rise and fall of Farmers' illustrates the financial obstacles to institutionalizing agricultural education after the crisis of expertise of the 1850s led to greater emphasis on original research. Even with able leadership and community support, the demands of scientific investigation proved too costly for a small private college to sustain. Reformers then concluded to again seek government aid.

The moving force behind Farmers' College was the educator and agricultural reformer Freeman G. Cary, by all accounts a man of unusual energy and charisma. The son of New England migrants to the Cincinnati area, Cary grew up in a farming family that was also active in a variety of reformist causes, including temperance and abolitionism.[77] In 1827, he entered Miami University, where he came under the influence of Robert Hamilton Bishop, the school's president who two years later opened a short-lived agricultural department.[78] Cary returned home after graduating and became an advocate of agricultural schooling as well as an active member of the Hamilton County Agricultural Society. He soon opened the Pleasant Hill Academy on the family farm, and by the early 1840s, it was enrolling 120 students annually. When Bishop was eased out of Miami University over a religious dispute, Cary invited him to Pleasant Hill to help turn the academy into a college. According to an alumnus, Cary's charisma "carried the farmers by storm," and within the year four hundred stockholders, mostly farmers and mechanics from the surrounding counties, had raised $13,000. In 1851, Cary led a second fundraising campaign that secured $100,000 in scholarship stock subscriptions for a permanent endowment fund.[79]

The expanded school was renamed Farmers' College of Hamilton County for the composition of its student body and its avowed focus on agriculture. From its inception, Farmers' endeavored to provide a "business education" with a "direct relation to the practical duties of life" and especially to "agricultural pursuits."[80] While there does not appear to have been much positive instruction in practical agriculture to begin with, the faculty did include a professor of "Chemistry and its application to Agriculture and the Arts."[81] A flexible curriculum and the granting of diplomas for abridged periods of study reflected Farmers' origins as a multipurpose academy and supported the boast that "no Institution of learning in the West has a firmer hold upon the workingmen than Farmers' College."[82] By the early 1850s, the college enrolled as many as eighty students a year while a preparatory department continued the work of the original academy. If Murat Halstead's memoir from nearly fifty years later can be trusted, three-quarters of the student body came from farm families. Among several distinguished alumni from this period was none less than a future United States president, Benjamin Harrison.[83]

In 1853, Cary and the board of trustees determined to establish a full-scale agricultural department, planning for a laboratory, experimental farm, and botanical garden. The energetic Cary resigned his position as president of the college to oversee the development of the new division. For a third time, it seems, Cary was able to "carry the farmers by storm," quickly securing another $100,000 in scholarship stock subscriptions. An 1853 map of the proposed new grounds shows the locations of separate experimental fields for grasses and grains, a "Fruit Department," vegetable patch, nursery, park, and botanical garden. It is not clear how much of the plan was realized, but a laboratory building known as "Polytechnic Hall" was definitely completed.[84]

The agricultural department accepted its first class of students in the fall of

1856. The college catalog proudly heralded the event, boasting that the department constituted "The First Complete Institution of the Kind Organized on the Continent of America!" It then enumerated the department's educational goals. Besides focusing on soil fertility, crop varieties appropriate to local conditions, and ways to combat pest infestations, it indicated that Farmers' intended to conduct original scientific research of utility to the public. The experimental farm would thus constitute a testing ground and "theater" of observable improvements.[85]

That Farmers' College intended its agricultural department to play a broad social role was in keeping with its stated mission. Cary, Bishop, and the trustees had always understood it in the context of American developmental aspirations. An 1850 report to the board of trustees situated curricular innovation within the context of "a country teeming with *undeveloped* resources, inexhaustible in its *latent* wealth." Existing American colleges, the report continued, focused only on "Greek and Latin verbs,—as though Homer and Demosthenes, Virgil and Horace, were the substratum of republican government, and lay at the foundation for developing the resources of this new and vast continent."[86] The committee charged with planning the agricultural department likewise premised the venture on the goal of "developing the resources of the country."[87] Positioning itself as an agent of progress, Farmers' College claimed a role in the grand project of American nation building.

Cary elaborated on the development theme in the pages of *Cincinnatus*, a monthly agricultural journal published by the faculty of Farmers' College beginning in 1856. "From the very nature of our soil," he assumed, the United States would remain an agricultural nation for generations to come. He therefore reasoned that "a correct and intelligent system of agriculture lies at the very foundation of our individual, social, and national prosperity."[88] What exactly did this mean? Owing to the crisis of scientific agriculture that followed the discrediting of soil analysis in the early 1850s, reformers were revising their understanding of agricultural education to put greater stress on research. "It is difficult for agricultural education to go further," argued one, "for agriculture has not yet become a fixed science."[89] Daniel Lee similarly believed that the "occult phenomena of tillage and husbandry cannot be successfully investigated by common farmers with their present advantages, and therefore they need institutions designed expressly to develop new truths."[90] Such institutions, another contended, had to be "founded on the most liberal scale" in order to undertake the "Herculean" task of careful and sustained experimentation.[91] Freeman Cary fully concurred with these views. Not just individual farmers, but even the existing institutions of agricultural reform—the societies, fairs, and journals—could not be expected "to investigate understandingly the laws, numerous and complicated as they are, involved in agricultural science."[92] Farmers' College, he hoped, could take on such a role and ultimately "settle many important inquiries."[93]

But it turned out that the costs exceeded even Cary's formidable fundraising abilities. As early as 1854, Farmers' began running an annual deficit that could only be met by dipping into its capital stock. The school's impressive endowment was not as large as it appeared. Agent fees and unredeemed pledges cut into receipts. Moreover, each stock share guaranteed its holder a perpetual scholarship, which detracted from tuition income. There was nothing unusual about these difficulties, which typified the contemporary practice of raising capital from surrounding communities by means of scholarship stocks. Genesee College, which, like Farmers', had its origins in an academy, faced the same kinds of problems and overcame them only through belt-tightening measures and outside help.[94] As a Methodist institution, it could subject delinquent coreligionists to disciplinary measures within the church organization. Only when these failed, did it resort to court proceedings that, in at least one case, required Farmers' to wait nearly twenty-five years for a favorable judgment.[95] Methodist channels were essential also to winning a series of legislative subsidies.[96] Farmers' College could only fall back on a loose network of agricultural societies, which did not enjoy centralized leadership and general funds in the way of a religious body. Moreover, Farmers' had committed itself to erecting research facilities that could not be scaled back easily.

What remained of Farmers' endowment proved insufficient to cover the capital outlays and operational costs of a research university on a "liberal scale." As a result, the trustees were forced to reduce expenditures, dismiss faculty, and sell college property.[97] The school's fate was finally sealed when the Ohio legislature rebuffed its bid to become the beneficiary of the state's Morrill Land-Grant Act allotment.[98] It appears that the Board of Agriculture, fearing that the state's existing colleges would carve up the Morrill endowment if any were allowed to press its claims, interpreted the terms of the grant to require a new, state-run institution. For Farmers', the ambition to build a modern research facility had destroyed a thriving local institution and, with it, the idea that "private enterprise" was likely to build a successful agricultural college.

The Trouble with State-Level Funding

Even before the final demise of Farmers' College clinched the case, most reformers had resolved to again lobby state legislatures. During the 1850s, their efforts yielded notable if still partial successes, especially in Michigan, Pennsylvania, and Maryland, all of which founded lasting public agricultural colleges during the decade. These victories, however, were tempered by some embarrassing defeats. Ironically, on the eve of the Civil War, the states with the strongest agricultural organizations—Massachusetts, New York, and Ohio—had achieved the least. Furthermore, even the successful cases were characterized by deep financial instabilities in their early years. As a result, reformers would ultimately turn from the states to the federal government.

Some reformers had never been convinced to abandon the campaign for public funding. The American Institute, an important pro-development organization that served as New York City's agricultural society, petitioned the state legislature throughout the 1840s for up to $50,000 to establish an agricultural and mechanical college. Its corresponding secretary explicitly protested against a strategy of private funding. "This has been already tried and has utterly failed," he observed.[99] Others increasingly agreed.[100] The perceived need for authoritative scientific research on a large scale was a major factor. One New York assemblyman cited exactly this for his view that "private enterprise" was insufficient.[101] Of course, Albany was never going to fund a state agricultural college in New York City.

The shift back to public funding was also fueled by Americans' growing awareness of state-sponsored agricultural schools in Europe. During the 1840s, the minister and prominent agricultural reformer Henry Colman reported at length on such institutions in Ireland, England, and France as part of a broader survey of European agriculture. Having left America before the wave of failed private institutes, he did not emphasize the prevalence of government funding in Europe, but later accounts drew frequent attention to this fact.[102] James Mapes, for example, reprinted articles from European journals detailing the continent's burgeoning farm school system and other state agricultural development policies. The situation at home was "very humiliating" by comparison, he grumbled.[103] In 1851, Edward Hitchcock prepared a second major report on European agricultural education for the Massachusetts Board of Agriculture. Unlike Colman, he stressed the critical importance of state sponsorship, arguing that the "schools usually fail, if they do not receive efficient aid from the government."[104] The common school advocate Henry Barnard reiterated the point in the second edition of his massive survey of European educational institutions.[105]

The Hitchcock report enjoyed widespread influence among agricultural and educational reformers.[106] Reading it alongside the accounts by Colman, Mapes, Barnard, and others, Americans gained a new awareness that Europeans were forging ahead with agricultural education, a realization that both gave assurance of the project's feasibility and raised anxiety that the United States was falling behind. A *New York Times* article that clearly bore the imprint of the Hitchcock report complained that whereas American "state legislatures are deaf, and Congress will not hear," in Europe "the subject is better appreciated."[107] Hitchcock's findings were also summarized in the 1851 Patent Office agricultural report, of which more than 140,000 copies were printed. "Is it not possible for the United States to have one school worthy of the republic?" editorialized Daniel Lee, who authored the report.[108] The future secretary of state, William H. Seward, soon warned that "if we should continue to neglect agricultural improvement, England, Ireland, France, Spain, Italy, Germany, and Russia, would not."[109]

Even as reformers insisted that state backing was essential, they assumed that planning and operation would be left to them. Hitchcock argued that "those agricultural institutions succeed best which are started and sustained by the mutual efforts and contributions of individuals, or societies, and of the government."[110] At a time when the tradition of mixed public-private enterprise in banking and transportation had been largely repudiated, the legal structure of early state agricultural schools institutionalized a partnership between state and society.[111] For example, Maryland chartered an agricultural college in 1856 (now the University of Maryland, College Park) as a private joint stock company but tethered it to the state in several ways. The board of trustees was to be composed of a representative from each county so that every political jurisdiction in the state would enjoy a voice in its direction. The charter also provided that an annual state appropriation would kick in once $50,000 in stock subscriptions had been raised. Finally, the charter required that the professor of chemistry "carefully analyze all specimens of soil that may be submitted to him by any citizen of this State, free of charge."[112]

The 1855 charter of Farmers' High School, soon renamed the Pennsylvania Agricultural College (now Pennsylvania State University, State College), went further toward intertwining state and society. Control of the board of trustees was vested in the state's official agricultural societies, and the college was required to submit an annual financial report to the state agricultural society for inclusion in its own legally mandated report to the legislature. Since the county societies were bound by a similar reporting requirement, the college charter helped establish an interconnected system of semipublic agricultural institutions under the direct control of a self-selected group of reformers but formally supervised by elected officials. The college's public mission was further reinforced when the legislature coupled funding with new mandates, similar to the ones imposed by Maryland, to chemically test citizens' soil and fertilizer samples without charge. These provisions justified the founders' assertion that "this is not a mere private enterprise or speculation, intended to benefit corporators or stockholders," but rather "a *State Institution*."[113]

The initiative for state involvement in agricultural education, as in the case of the laws governing agricultural societies, came from reformers, not politicians or bureaucrats. Consequently, state supervision was not accompanied by firm financial commitments, and the early agricultural colleges, though identified with state governments, stood on shaky fiscal ground. In Pennsylvania, the legislature provided no funding whatsoever at first. The initial endowment consisted of $10,000 appropriated by the state agricultural society from its own funds and a $5,000 bequest from a wealthy member of the Philadelphia Society for the Promotion of Agriculture. Once the school was located on donated land in Centre County, hometown Republican politico Andrew Curtin helped raise an additional $10,000 from nearby residents. In May 1857, the legislature did provide $25,000 and a promise for another $25,000 the following year if a like amount could be raised from private donations. With $50,000 in hand and solid prospects for another $50,000, the board decided to purchase additional land and approved an ambitious main campus building. Disaster struck almost immediately, however, when the Panic of 1857 killed the fundraising drive and with it the matching state grant. Meanwhile, the contractors had underestimated construction costs and went bankrupt. Additional contributions from trustees and local citizens amounting to over $10,000 could not prevent the need to mortgage the grounds to complete just one wing of the main building. When the college opened its doors in the winter of 1859, basic facilities such as a kitchen and dining room remained unfinished, and the whole venture was near collapse despite significant student enrollment (figure 6.2). A bill to rescue the college with a $50,000 appropriation generated little enthusiasm among legislators and may never have passed if not for the intervention of Andrew Curtin, now governor, who just happened to come from the town where the school was located. By 1865, the college was still struggling under a mountain of debt.[114]

Figure 6.2. Students at Farmers' High School of Pennsylvania (1860). Eberly Family Special Collections Library, Penn State University Libraries.

New York's agricultural college builders fared worse. Confronted with many of the same obstacles that faced their counterparts in Ohio and Pennsylvania, they could not obtain public funding at critical moments and watched one effort after another collapse. The story begins in the late 1840s, when the state's agricultural reformers resumed lobbying the legislature, which responded by commissioning a group of them to study and report on the matter.[115] The commission proposed an annual state subsidy of $10,000 for a college able to pursue "authentic" research in addition to teaching. A special committee of the Assembly concurred, insisting that "the great mass of the agricultural community . . . demands the establishment of an Institution."[116] But legislators ultimately buried the matter by narrowly voting for a second study commission. Greeley found the situation mystifying. "The Assembly," he observed, "seems to have an invincible reluctance to take up the subject."[117]

Part of the problem was the failure to unite on a common project. The American Institute had been petitioning the legislature for support to build an agricultural college downstate since the 1840s. Luther Tucker, the influential farm editor and recording secretary of the state agricultural society, joined a plan to establish a world-class scientific university in Albany. Chartered in 1851, the scheme was already dead the following year.[118] Another project, led by a former president of the state society, John Delafield, developed in the Finger Lakes region. This one received a charter in April 1853 as the New York State Agricultural College (NYSAC).[119] The very same month, however, the legislature also chartered People's College, a planned agricultural and mechanical school that had Horace Greeley's backing. None of these endeavors were awarded public funding.[120]

The NYSAC plan, abandoned when Delafield suddenly died, was given fresh life in the mid-1850s by a dynamic minister and educator named Amos Brown. As principal of Ovid Academy, Brown had instituted courses in agricultural science that proved so popular he was able to convince the NYSAC's trustees to move the agricultural college from Delafield's hometown to nearby Ovid. He then secured an interest-free loan from the legislature and raised a large sum in private subscriptions from area farmers. With the chairman of the board of trustees elected governor in 1856, the future suddenly looked bright for the New York State Agricultural College.[121]

Meanwhile, Greeley's involvement with People's College turned him oddly hostile to state aid. He began to argue, uncharacteristically, that "as to an Agricultural and Mechanical College . . . we are warmly in favor of it, but not of its endowment by the State."[122] This followed from his objection to the monopolization of public funds by sectarian and liberal arts colleges committed to the classical curriculum.[123] They "swarm among us like the frogs of Egypt," he complained, "and State gratuities are the slime wherein they are bred."[124] It was a tactical assault on the educational establishment, not a statement of small-government principles.[125] Only three months after objecting to the use of New York's educational funds "for the special benefit of a limited class," Greeley reasoned that, when it came to *federal* agricultural spending, "great common benefits are judiciously sought, [and] it is but just that they should be sought at the expense of the community."[126] By the end of 1856, he had abandoned all pretense of a principled stand against public subsidies to the "limited class" of farmers. The *Tribune* was now gushing over the Morrill land-grant bill and calling it "The People's College Bill."[127] Still a paper institution at this point, People's was in fact moving aggressively to position itself as the Morrill bill's beneficiary. Leading this charge was none other than Amos Brown, who, after losing the confidence of NYSAC's trustees, became People's president and soon went to Washington to lobby for the land-grant bill.[128]

Brown's dismissal from NYSAC deflated local enthusiasm and hastened the departure of several professors.[129] The institution's problems ran deep. The trustees had used up more than half their funds on a school site and consequently had to scale down their construction plans. Even by focusing on only one wing of the original blueprint, as in Pennsylvania, they could not avoid mortgaging college land.[130] In June 1860, with the first term set to commence in December, the college president reported to the trustees, "We seem to be hanging still in doubt."[131] Desperate for funds as the opening of the first term approached, several trustees advanced $5,000 while a local attorney began serving processes on the delinquent subscribers.[132] Two years later he resigned his post as college legal counsel. "I have already involved myself in personal controversies and quarrels without number by reason of the collections I have already made," he explained. "I cannot endure the thing any longer."[133] Somehow the college succeeded in opening as planned with an adequate enrollment, but finances continued to deteriorate. Only two months later, trustee William Kelly summarized the report of the school's Committee of Finance as "by no means cheerful." By the end of April 1861, operations had been suspended indefinitely, and from there the situation rapidly went downhill as defaults mounted and a local "evil genius"—those are the actual words that Kelly used—bought up remaining mortgages in order to dismember the college's land holdings and turn a profit.[134]

The passage of the Morrill Land-Grant Act provided a final glimmer of hope, but Amos Brown proved a better operator within the legislative sausage factory.[135] In 1863, he helped get the state to allot New York's entire Morrill grant to People's College. Almost immediately, however, he fell out with People's mercurial financial patron, and the whole project crumbled. Forced out, Brown and several erstwhile People's trustees aided Ezra Cornell, who had already secured the agreement of NYSAC's trustees, to transfer New York's Morrill grant to his project in Ithaca. A rare combination of bona fide agricultural reformer, business tycoon, and philanthropist, Cornell assured his university's future by endowing it generously. In the meantime, People's College ceased to exist, and the New York State Agricultural College at Ovid was converted into a mental asylum.[136]

New York's byzantine politics made things especially difficult there, but the problems were basically similar elsewhere. Every agricultural college that managed to get off the ground in the 1850s suffered from serious financial instabilities.[137] Reformers lacked experience as educators, harbored vague and inchoate plans, and consistently underestimated costs. But they were learning by experience and observation. In the fall of 1857, one New Yorker drew on his own fleeting experiment with agricultural education to warn—correctly, as it turned out—that the trustees of Pennsylvania's agricultural school had wildly unrealistic building plans that would leave them insufficient operational funds.[138] The president of Farmers' College similarly cautioned the backers of People's College not to neglect operational costs, for tuition income would prove "but a drop in the ocean."[139] Such hard-won wisdom led a later observer to praise the Morrill Act's requirement that land-grant funds be dedicated to operating expenses only.[140]

Facing insufficient and unreliable funding from private donors and state legislatures, would-be agricultural college builders soon turned to the federal government. In 1854, just as the financial troubles of Farmers' College were becoming evident, Freeman Cary organized a well-attended conference on "Industrial University Education." The participants, who included Supreme Court Justice and perennial presidential hopeful, John McLean, resolved "to direct public attention to the importance of individual and governmental action."[141] Three years later, Cary proposed that the Agricultural Division of the Patent Office be reorganized as an independent federal agency able to contract with Farmers' and similar institutions to conduct experiments.[142] Then, in the winter of 1858–59, Cary traveled to Washington to lobby for the Morrill bill. There he met not only Amos Brown of People's College, but the president of the recently opened Michigan Agricultural College, Joseph R. Williams, and the founder of the Maryland Agricultural College, Charles B. Calvert. Each understood that the federal government could potentially supply a level and consistency of funding that state governments and private donations were unlikely to match. The next chapters consider the consequences of this shift to the national political arena.

PART FOUR

AGRICULTURAL REFORM VERSUS THE SLAVEOCRACY

CHAPTER SEVEN

Movement into Lobby

By the 1850s, most agricultural reformers had concluded that the federal government was essential to their vision. Although ideas about the precise character of the institutions they wished to establish remained inchoate, several concerns stood out. The promise and challenge of agricultural science required sustained research by trained experts in costly facilities; technological novelty required new public authorities to discipline the market; and farmers required specialized education to best utilize science and technology. Reformers therefore focused on two types of institutions. First, they sought a federal agricultural department that could serve as an authoritative source of scientific knowledge and market information. Second, they sought public agricultural colleges to train rural youth and engage in systematic research. Numerous attempts to found such institutions had taught them that only the federal government could guarantee the necessary funding.

At the national level, however, reformers encountered a government racked by sectional conflict over the future of slavery. During the late 1840s, the issue became increasingly unavoidable in Congress. When the federal executive branch was reorganized in 1849 by the creation of the Department of the Interior, reformers saw an opportunity to elevate the Patent Office's de facto "Agricultural Division" into an independent bureau, but powerful southern politicians quietly blocked the move behind the scenes. Reformers responded by organizing the United States Agricultural Society (USAS) to lobby Congress more effectively. The new organization met annually in Washington, DC, working to build influence much as the state societies had done during the 1830s and 1840s. Besides seeking a national agricultural agency, the USAS also supported Republican Justin Morrill's bill to provide federal land grants for agricultural colleges. This time southern opponents were unable to stifle discussion and had to assail the bill publicly in congressional debate. Although they cast their denunciations in the language of constitutional strict construction, what really concerned them was the prospect of creating a new federal bureaucracy with a mandate to reform agriculture at just the moment when antislavery Republicans appeared poised to gain control of the national government. Determined to kill the Morrill bill, southern members of Congress signaled that agricultural reform policy had become sectionalized, with only shrinking factions of southern Know Nothings and northern Democrats defying a long-suppressed politics of slavery that was about to shear the country in two.

The campaign for federal agricultural institutions shows that slavery engulfed all other issues over the 1850s. But it also indicates that those other issues independently amplified the upsurge of slavery politics. The Second Party System of Whigs and Democrats had effectively segregated slavery from other policy questions, especially those connected to economic development, at the national level. By the 1850s, however, sophisticated and well-organized advocacy groups were putting tremendous pressure on that system by mounting powerful demands from outside the received party structures, making it more difficult for party managers to control the public agenda. As political abolitionism succeeded in making slavery the one inescapable issue, other movements were driven into sectional alignment. The combined action of these forces then pulverized the hard but thin protective shell that party politicians had constructed around the explosive force of slavery during the 1830s and 1840s.

The agricultural reform movement contributed powerfully to this dynamic because it was large and influential and pushed for policies at odds with what the master class saw as its core interest. Reformers were proposing a basic reorientation of national agricultural policy. In the Jeffersonian-Jacksonian dispensation, the federal government promoted an ostensibly yeoman farming vision by means of territorial expansion, Indian dispossession, land surveying, and liberal land distribution policies. Simultaneously, it sought to open overseas markets for staple exports. None of this was abandoned after the Civil War, but an entirely new form of agricultural governance emerged alongside it. A thicket of new agencies—land-grant colleges, experiment stations, and the USDA's ever-growing roster of specialized bureaus—sought to modernize farmers' operations much more directly than ever before. Federal agents might then be coming onto the farm or plantation, looking around and suggesting changes. It was inevitable, given the agricultural reform movement's heavy northern tilt and deepening ties to the antislavery Republican Party, that southerners would regard this as a major change in the federal compact and a deep threat to plantation slavery.

Origins of the Agricultural Division of the Patent Office

Attempts to enlist the federal government in the cause of agricultural reform went back to George Washington.[1] Urging Congress to follow Britain's lead and create a national Board of Agriculture, he argued that "advance in population and other circumstances of maturity . . . renders the cultivation of the soil more and more an object of public patronage." A federal agricultural board would act as a clearinghouse of information and award premiums to encourage "a spirit of discovery and improvement."[2] The proposal went nowhere legislatively, but it did make for a useful rhetorical weapon in the arsenal of later agricultural reformers, who were more than happy to invoke the "illustrious farmer of Mount Vernon." Contrasting Americans' pursuit of prosperity with the intrigue of European geopolitics, reformers took up Washington's image as a modern Cincinnatus who preferred agriculture to power. The first president's stated belief that he knew "of no pursuit in which more real and important service can be rendered to any country, than by improving its agriculture," corroborated the reformist view that government's very purpose was economic development.[3]

The first serious push for national agricultural institutions had to wait until the late 1830s. It comprised a flurry of petitions advocating various plans, an effort to secure the Smithsonian fund for agricultural purposes, and the creation of a kind of backdoor agricultural agency within the Patent Office. The results of these efforts were inconclusive but nonetheless significant. Although reformers achieved few of their proposals, the Patent Office's ad hoc agricultural mission took root and fed into the burgeoning agricultural reform movement of the 1840s.

The bureaucratic entrepreneur behind the Patent Office's role was Henry Leavitt Ellsworth, the son of a former Supreme Court Chief Justice and a "man of large ideas" interested in more than just the routine registration of patents. Ellsworth had helped establish a county agricultural society in his native Connecticut during the reform wave that followed the War of 1812. Later, he bought large tracts of land in the West, settled in Indiana, and began to report on various experiments to increase crop yields. As a result of these activities, he was already "one of the best-known figures in agriculture" when he became patent commissioner in 1835. He soon convinced Congress to expand and professionalize the agency, making it better able to handle the steady stream of patent applications and allowing him to indulge his interest in scientific agriculture.[4]

In his new position, Ellsworth started to collect and distribute seeds of potentially valuable plant varieties. Most of these he obtained from returning consuls and naval officers, who had been directed by the Treasury Department to look out for additions to American agriculture. The Patent Office, he suggested to Congress, should be made the central repository for these collections.[5] The agency was constantly "crowded with men of enterprise, who, when they bring their models of their improvements in such [agricultural] implements, are eager to communicate a knowledge of every other kind of improvement in agriculture, and especially new and valuable varieties of seeds and plants." Rural businessmen who came to Washington to patent their inventions seemed an ideal conduit for carrying foreign seeds and plants back to their farming communities. Ellsworth cited cases in which new varieties of wheat and corn increased yields by as much as twenty percent. A concerted seed distribution program might therefore significantly raise national agricultural productivity.[6]

The House Committee on Agriculture took up the recommendation in March 1838 and quickly returned a favorable report along with a bill appropriating the $5,000 Ellsworth had requested. Although the bill failed, the following year Congress granted $1,000 from the Patent Office fund for the collection of agricultural statistics and other purposes. Most of this went to seed distribution, which reached thirty thousand packages in 1840 and twice that amount seven years later.[7] Where exactly all these packages went is not entirely clear, but many of them were channeled through state and local agricultural organizations.[8] The program proved important in at least two regards. Economically, it helped to sustain American agricultural yields in the face of mounting pest infestations and also to acclimate staple crops to new environmental conditions.[9] Politically, it began to link agricultural societies to the federal government.

Ellsworth simultaneously moved to fill the annual Patent Office reports with agricultural information. Of special significance was his attempt to compile national farming statistics by corresponding with prominent reformers around the country. As with the seed program, this effort both relied on and strengthened the country's existing network of agricultural societies. Communications, sometimes directed through members of Congress, linked local organizations to the national government, increasing the relevance of both. By the mid-1840s, agricultural matters accounted for over eighty percent of the Patent Office report, which ran to several hundred pages each year. John Quincy Adams remarked that Ellsworth had produced "a calendar of mechanical and agricultural inventions and discoveries more sought after than any other annual document published by Congress." The report was in such demand that Ellsworth could not keep up with requests.[10]

In 1838, an opportunity arose to expand the federal government's agricultural mission when the United States took possession of a $500,000 bequest left

by the wealthy English chemist, James Smithson, "to found at Washington . . .
an Establishment for the increase and diffusion of knowledge among men."[11]
The Patent Office's Charles Lewis Fleischmann quickly recognized the fund's
potential for agriculture. Born in Bavaria, Fleischmann had attended the Royal
Agricultural and Technical School at Schleissheim before coming to the United
States in 1832. In April 1838, he presented Congress with "a tightly constructed
and informative memorial" arguing for government action to bring American
agriculture up to European standards. When Smithson's funds arrived shortly
thereafter, Fleischmann submitted a second memorial calling for their application to the founding of a national agricultural school. This proposal was popular
with reformers. The New York State Agricultural Convention, for instance,
petitioned Congress to adopt a plan similar to Fleischmann's.[12]

Reformers quickened their efforts by attempting to form a national agricultural society. Discussion had been under way for some time when, in April
1841, Solon Robinson issued a call for a meeting in Washington later that year.
According to Robinson, "the object of all state and county societies has been of
a local nature . . . and they have been too weak in numbers to command legislative aid." Reformers therefore needed to establish a national association capable of advocating for a "National Agricultural School" financed by the Smithson fund. "When once organized," Robinson declared, "we will soon stand, a
united force of many thousands, whose voice will be heard in the halls of
Congress."[13]

Ellsworth fully endorsed this movement, serving as an officer in the new
national society and providing facilities for its meetings. Circumstantially, it
seems he might have orchestrated the whole thing. Paul W. Gates points out
that Fleischmann's petitions must have had his approval.[14] Between 1838 and
1840, Congress also received a spate of petitions from local agricultural reformers proposing everything from an expansive "Agricultural and Mechanical Department" to a national museum and repository of agricultural improvements
to a mandate for the inactive House Committee on Agriculture to begin issuing an annual report. Although none mentioned the Smithson fund, the timing
and local provenance suggest an effort to engineer the appearance of a public
groundswell.[15] At any rate, Ellsworth advocated for the new organization and
its aims. "The formation of a National Agricultural Society has enkindled
bright anticipations of improvement," he wrote in the 1841 annual Patent Office report. "A munificent bequest is placed at the disposal of Congress, and a
share of this with private patronage, would enable this association to undertake, and, it is confidently believed, accomplish much good."[16] It would not be
the last time that the Patent Office played a key role in agricultural reformers'
efforts to lobby Congress.

From the beginning, however, several important figures expressed reservations about the feasibility of a national agricultural society. Particularly significant were the objections of Edmund Ruffin, the famous Virginia agricultural reformer and southern separatist. Ruffin argued that although the objects of the national association were noble, the "corrupt political atmosphere of the city of Washington" would inevitably doom the effort. "There would probably be more exertion made by members of the society in using the opportunity for seeking office, or other private benefits to themselves individually from the public purse, than to promote the interest of agriculture and the common weal."[17] Ruffin was careful to express the hope that all would go well, despite his fears, because respected friends were involved in the effort. But his distrust of national politics is noteworthy in light of his later secessionism.

Ruffin need not have worried yet. Agricultural reformers had just begun to achieve their aims at the state level. The attempt to create a national organization was premature and dissipated after only two meetings. The absence of state subsidies and a regional base in which to hold fairs and solicit members help explain this rapid demise, as does the relatively undeveloped national transportation system, which made an annual journey to Washington a real commitment. The Smithsonian fund went to other purposes.[18]

Ellsworth left the Patent Office several years later, but the agency's agricultural initiatives continued to expand. In 1848, Congress voted a special appropriation of $1,000 for chemical analyses of crops. The following year, the transfer of the Patent Office to the newly created Department of the Interior was accompanied by a semiformal recognition of its agricultural work. The respected farm editor, Daniel Lee, was invited to take charge of what was now unofficially designated the "Agricultural Division of the Patent Office," and the "agricultural portion" of the annual report was hived off as its own volume. By 1850, the office's agricultural budget, which came out of the fund generated by patent fees, had risen to $5,000. Congress soon appropriated much larger sums directly from the Treasury, reaching as high as $75,000. By 1860, the Agricultural Division had a dozen or so people on staff and had expanded physically with the creation of a five-acre "propagating garden." Meant to supply the seed and plant distribution program, the garden emulated long-standing European policies of agricultural improvement by the development of commercial crops in imperial botanical gardens.[19]

Additional federal appropriations, as with the major state agricultural organizations, came in the form of separately budgeted printing and binding costs for the annual agricultural report. The disparity between direct and indirect funding, however, was much larger in this case, for by the early 1850s Congress was printing the report in enormous quantities. In 1851, the House and Senate ordered a combined 145,420 copies; in both 1855 and 1856, the number climbed

TABLE 7.1.
Printing and Binding Costs for the Annual Patent Office Agricultural Report, 1851–1860

	Number of pages	Cost per copy (cents)	Total copies	Total printing costs ($)
1851	688	40.6	142,500	57,794
1852	456	26.4	142,500	37,598
1853	456	51.3	150,000	76,910
1854	560	57.8	167,920	96,989
1855	550	61.7	267,920	165,412
1856	600	68.9	267,920	184,695
1857	568	45.3	242,920	110,019
1858	568	44.4	222,940	99,084
1859	604	46.0	326,550	150,129
1860	504	36.1	240,000	86,639
		Annual mean, 1851–54	150,730	67,323
		Annual mean, 1855–60	261,375	132,663
		Totals, 1851–60	2,171,170	955,251

Sources: Compiled from the occasional reports of the Superintendent of Public Printing from the 33rd through the 37th Congresses.

to 267,920; and in 1859, after a slight dip in the intervening years, it peaked at more than 300,000 (table 7.1). Over the ten years from 1851 to 1860, the federal government published nearly 2.2 million copies of the annual agricultural report at an expense exceeding $950,000. To this must be added the costs borne by the post office as members of Congress used their franking privileges to mail these heavy reports to their constituents. One congressman remarked that there was "more call for this document than all others of a public character," so that even "four hundred volumes for each Congressional district" were not enough.[20]

Yet for all its growing prominence, the Patent Office's agricultural work remained makeshift and precarious. The so-called Agricultural Division had no official existence, as hostile southerners frequently pointed out. Reformers and their political friends were also dissatisfied by the division's subsidiary positioning within another agency.[21] "The vast interest of agriculture has only a single desk and a subordinate clerk in the basement of the patent-office," complained William Seward in 1852.[22] The popular annual reports were never meant to "supersede the necessity of an institution on a more liberal scale," argued another member of Congress.[23] As one of Henry C. Carey's congressional allies put it, "We want practical information and scientific investigation, and we have them now in some degree in the agricultural branch of the Patent Office . . . but we can secure them to a much greater extent."[24] Reformers and their supporters, in short, wanted more.

The Campaign for a Federal Bureau of Agriculture, 1849–1852

In 1849, the federal executive branch was reorganized with the creation of the Department of the Interior. Agricultural reformers believed that the new structure for domestic governance would finally mean official attention to their cause. Strengthened in the interval by the rapid growth of agricultural societies, publications, and fairs throughout the country, they now mounted a much broader and more effective lobbying campaign than they had at the beginning of the decade.

Reformers had long supported creation of a "Home Department," hoping that it would include a bureau of agriculture. In 1845, for instance, the National Convention of Farmers, Gardeners and Silk Culturists proposed "that an earnest appeal be made to Congress to adopt the recommendation of our father (Washington) and establish a 'Home Department' for the encouragement and support of the agricultural interests of our country." The following year the convention renewed its call and sent Congress a memorial that quoted from Washington at length.[25] By the end of the decade, reformers had grown increasingly hopeful that creation of an Interior Department would include an agency specifically dedicated to agriculture.[26]

Reformers anticipated success because they thought they had become "of some account in the *commonwealth*."[27] Increasingly emboldened, they articulated their demands with some militancy, enjoining Congress to "listen to the public voice," insisting that "something should be done for agriculture," and urging famers not to "rest until their reasonable demands are complied with." Time and again declaring that farmers constituted the vast majority of voters, they deplored politicians' clichéd praise for agriculture—"so often showered upon us as an opiate to lull us to sleep"—and demanded action instead of rhetoric.[28] "If we prove not recreant to our own best interest," they told themselves, "we shall have all that we require."[29]

One of the most energetic actors was Frederick Holbrook, a member of Vermont's state Senate and later its wartime Republican governor. In the fall of 1849, Holbrook penned an article calling for an agricultural bureau in the new Interior Department. His extensive agricultural reform credentials lent his views weight. Besides writing regularly in the farm press, Holbrook lead several agricultural societies and had designed a plow reportedly known to every farmer in Vermont. He soon convinced his colleagues in the legislature to appoint a committee to study the question. His article then formed the basis of the committee's official report, which the legislature endorsed and forwarded on to Congress.[30]

The Vermont report draped itself in the familiar mantle of Washington's message to Congress and preemptively rebuffed "the bug-bear of 'constitutional objections.'" Unlike earlier petitions to Congress, it predicated its recommendation squarely on the concrete issues of soil fertility and pest control. The nutrient depletion that now plagued the seaboard states would soon come to the West, the repot argued, making the problem a national one of great "magnitude and importance." The report also acknowledged the changing structure of American agriculture by noting the rising importance of fresh fruit, market vegetables, and other crops especially susceptible to destruction by insects and therefore requiring the aid of entomological research. The report concluded with six suggestions, most of which defined the proposed bureau as a source of authoritative information. Apart from conducting its own investigations, it would maintain a constant correspondence with agricultural societies throughout the country and the world.[31]

Many farm journals reprinted the Vermont report, which bore the imprimatur of a state legislature, in whole or in part.[32] Reformers in other states soon began pressing for legislative resolutions instructing members of Congress to work toward establishing an agricultural bureau. In an address of December 1849, for example, Professor E. D. Sanborn urged the New Hampshire legislature to follow Vermont's lead. In March of the following year, Daniel Lee asked the editor of the *Michigan Farmer* to obtain similar resolutions from his state. In short order, both assemblies complied.[33] By May 1852, at least seven additional states had sent Congress resolutions favoring an agricultural bureau, an indication of agricultural reformers' influence in state capitals.[34]

Congress heard directly from the agricultural societies, too, but more impressive is the fact that thousands of ordinary farmers took it upon themselves to call on Washington officials.[35] Significantly, all of them were northern or nearly so, the only exceptions hailing from the future state of West Virginia. In December 1849, Thomas W. Reece of Winchester, Indiana, wrote to his congressman to urge "the organizing of an *agricultural beaureau* [*sic*], in the home department," adding, "ours is a purely an [*sic*] agricultural district."[36] Two months later, Congress received a group of preprinted petitions numbering over two thousand signatories. Most of these came from rural Pennsylvania, but a few came from New York, Massachusetts, Maine, Ohio, and western Virginia. Analysis of one petition suggests that a large majority of the signatories were farmers (see table 2.2).[37] Another group of petitions that arrived in 1852 requested "prompt and efficient action," deeming it unnecessary to "enlarge upon the magnitude of the Agricultural Interest."[38] By that time some were growing impatient. "Will congress *condescend* to give us an agricultural Bureau in the Department of the Interior?" asked a correspondent to the Patent Office.[39]

Reformers' expectations were initially bolstered by the incoming Whig presidential administration. In his first annual report of December 3, 1849, Interior Secretary Thomas Ewing argued that existing appropriations for the Patent

Office's agricultural activities were "wholly inadequate." He recommended a separate agricultural bureau, and President Zachary Taylor reiterated the proposal in his State of the Union message.[40] The agricultural press immediately responded with praise for Ewing's "enlightened" report and Taylor's "sound, common-sense, patriotic" address.[41] After Taylor's death, the Fillmore administration added proposals for an official mineralogist and chemist and for the conversion of Mount Vernon into a national model farm. Fillmore devoted significant space to the matter in his first and second annual messages to Congress, while additional details appeared in the reports of his Interior Secretary, Alexander H. H. Stuart. But stalled progress was evident when Fillmore's final message mentioned the bureau only in passing and Stuart dropped the matter entirely.[42]

Despite the concerted lobbying effort, it became clear that Congress was unlikely to act. Congressional Democrats were hostile to the creation of a new federal agency that would serve as a source of patronage for a Whig president. In July 1850, the House Committee of Agriculture took up the issue and split along strictly partisan lines. Chairman Nathaniel Littlefield (D-ME) and the committee's remaining four Democrats requested to be discharged from further consideration of the numerous petitions on the subject, including one that Littlefield had himself presented. The committee's four Whigs submitted a minority report that included a draft bill prepared by Daniel Lee proposing an agricultural bureau funded at a modest $15,000.[43] Although the Democrats gave no reason for their opposition to the measure, only two months earlier Democratic Senator Daniel Dickinson had fought a budget amendment to rebuild the national greenhouse and botanical garden, which were about to be displaced by the new Patent Office building. The $5,000 appropriation, Dickinson alleged, exemplified "the begetting sin of this Government—patronage."[44]

Yet the failure of the agricultural bureau cannot be assigned entirely to partisanship. In April 1850, two months before Democrats on the House Agriculture Committee decided to bury the issue, Daniel Sturgeon, a Democrat from Pennsylvania and chairman of the Senate Committee on Agriculture, introduced a bill that was very similar to the one prepared by Lee for the House Whigs' minority report. Evidently, then, Lee was in contact with both Democrats and Whigs. The inference is reinforced by the fact that in the next session of Congress, Representative James Duane Doty, a Democrat from Wisconsin, gave notice that he would reintroduce the Sturgeon bill. Two weeks later, New York Whig Henry Bennett announced that he would introduce a different bill for an agricultural bureau. In the next Congress, both the Democrat Doty and the Whig Bennett gave notice of their intentions to again present such bills, although only Doty seems to have actually done so. And Doty apparently conferred not only with Lee and Sturgeon but with Eben Newton, an Ohio Whig and fellow Agriculture Committee member, on the language and extent of the bill.[45] At about the same time, Democratic Party leader Stephen Douglas supported an agricultural bureau in addresses before both the New York and Maryland State Agricultural Societies.[46] Among northern members of Congress, then, both Democrats and Whigs could be found who supported such an agency.

On the other hand, the *Southern Planter* attacked the "perniciousness of this scheme," suggesting that support for the agricultural bureau had sectional determinants. Some southern Whigs favored the proposed agency, but southern Democrats, unlike their northern co-partisans, were almost universally hostile.[47] This opposition appears most clearly in simultaneous debates over the printing of the Patent Office's agricultural report. In March 1850, the House considered whether to print the mechanical and agricultural portions of the report separately and in what quantities. The debate began with the recommendation from the Committee on Printing to issue thirty thousand of the former and seventy thousand of the latter. The year before, the House had ordered ninety thousand copies of the combined report, so there was nothing really new in the amount, only in the proposal to publish the two sections separately.[48] Frederick Stanton (D-TN) saw in this "the germ of the agricultural bureau."[49] Robert McLane (D-MD), Thomas Bayly (D-VA) and Robert Toombs (W-GA) all spoke against a large printing, arguing that the reports were a way for congressmen to bestow patronage on constituents. When other representatives argued that the agricultural report provided valuable information, Abraham Venable (D-NC) asserted that "this Government was never intended to be the great schoolmaster of the people." It was all just "an entering-wedge to an agricultural department."[50] The term, "entering wedge," was by this time a conventional way to critique any proposed expansion of federal functions and was especially favored by southerners when they disapproved of a federal action related to slavery.

Northern representatives responded that farmers demanded the agricultural report. According to John Alsop King (W-NY), a former president of the New York State Agricultural Society, "this practice of printing the Patent Office report, has not originated in this House, but has arisen out of the loud demand made for it by the people." Cullen Sawtelle (D-ME) sought to represent the "agricultural interest" and was "prepared to give his vote for printing the largest number of copies of this report." Joseph Casey (W-PA) added that "I will go with gentlemen for the erection of an Agricultural Bureau." Ultimately the House agreed to John Wentworth's (D-IL) proposal for a larger edition than originally contemplated: one hundred thousand copies of the agricultural portion and fifty thousand of the mechanical portion. At fifty cents per copy, this would have amounted to a $50,000 appropriation for agriculture, far more than the $15,000 proposed for a separate agricultural bureau.[51]

Two months later, when the Senate debated its own proposed printing of thirty thousand additional copies of the report, southern talking points were much the same. Jefferson Davis (D-MS) sought to expose bureaucratic creep in the Patent Office. "An agricultural bureau is growing up in it," he alleged, "and the proposition is in the minds of many that it should have a distinct organization, and be separated from the department. This I hold to be no part of the functions of this Government." Mississippi's other senator, Henry Foote, objected to a large edition of the agricultural report because he distrusted the Patent Commissioner, whom he charged with leaking the mechanical portion of the report for private printing by Horace Greeley, "a philosopher and philanthropist of the strong Abolition stripe." James Murray Mason (D-VA) argued that the Constitution authorized a Patent Office strictly to secure patents and not to publish speculative reports. Only a handful of southern senators, mostly Whigs, seemed untroubled.[52]

An analysis of Congressional voting on the printing of the agricultural report (table 7.2) reveals that northerners supported a large print run by overwhelming majorities in both chambers, regardless of party. A correlate is that, although Democrats split about evenly, that split was accounted for almost entirely by section. The few southern Democratic votes in favor came from the Upper South, whereas Lower South Democrats opposed all but unanimously. Southern Whigs were divided. Finally, southern members of the House were more hostile to the large edition than their Senate colleagues. Since the lower chamber is the more representative, this suggests that the politicians closest to the currents of southern public opinion were especially opposed to the Patent Office's agricultural work.

The debates over the agricultural report help explain why little action was taken on the several bills for an agricultural bureau even after the election of a Democratic president in 1852. More was at stake than patronage. It was rather a question of the acceptable domain of federal governance. Yet editions of the Patent Office's agricultural report continued to grow. It seems that members of Congress were being inundated with requests from constituents. Writing to the Patent Office in 1850, a rural merchant from central New York commented that the "reports that have been distributed in this co. in the last 2 year have been more benefit to us than all that Congress has done for us for the last 10 years besides." He added that "it is the Agricultural part that makes it so valuable with us."[53] When Robert Toombs renounced his allotment of copies in 1854, even southern senators rose to claim his share for themselves. One Mississippi Democrat admitted, "I have much larger applications for this work than I can answer."[54]

Southern Democrats had effectively conceded the printing issue, but they were determined to go no further. Through the mid-1850s, they successfully

TABLE 7.2.
House and Senate Votes on a Large Edition of the Patent Office Agricultural Report

House of Representatives			Senate		
	For	Against		For	Against
Region					
Northeast	67	6	Northeast	13	4
Northwest	30	7	Northwest	9	2
Upper South	13	28	Upper South	4	3
Lower South	2	24	Lower South	9	9
Party					
Democrat	38	48	Democrat	17	13
Whig	70	16	Whig	16	1
Free Soil	4	1	Free Soil	2	0
Democrats					
Northern Democrats	33	11	Northern Democrats	11	2
Southern Democrats	5	37	Southern Democrats	6	11
Whigs					
Northern Whigs	60	1	Northern Whigs	9	0
Upper South Whigs	8	7	Upper South Whigs	3	0
Lower South Whigs	2	8	Lower South Whigs	4	1

Source: Cong. Globe, 31st Cong., 1st Sess., 506, 922.

prevented legislation for an agricultural bureau from ever reaching the floor of either chamber. Each bill that was introduced was immediately referred to committee, never to be heard from again. Northern congressmen made four major speeches in favor of an agricultural bureau in the spring and summer of 1852, all when Congress had resolved itself into Committee of the Whole to discuss other matters.[55] Members of Congress sympathetic to agricultural reform were therefore forced to work indirectly by increasing budgets for the Patent Office's Agricultural Division. The situation only began to change when agricultural reformers strengthened their lobbying powers in the midst of the party system's breakdown and transformation.

The United States Agricultural Society

As the campaign for an agricultural bureau stalled in 1851 and 1852, reformers refused to scale down their demands. On the contrary, they escalated them, calling not just for a bureau but for a full-fledged department headed by a cabinet-level secretary. To lobby Congress more effectively, they worked to build a viable national organization. The result was the United States Agricultural Society (USAS), a body that gradually increased its influence until it disbanded in 1862, when its primary goal was accomplished with the creation of the US Department of Agriculture by the wartime Republican Congress. The USAS tried to project a conciliatory nationalism that largely ignored the deepening sectional rift over slavery. Yet the organization was never truly national. Instead, it was dominated by agricultural reformers from New England and the mid-Atlantic states north of the Potomac. Most of these men began the decade as Whigs and ended it as Republicans. That shift indicated that despite its conservative unionism, the USAS found that its aims alienated southern Democrats while aligning nicely with the Republicans' brand of northern nationalism.

Southern fears of expanding federal powers could not have been allayed by reformers' growing boldness. The charge that reformers sought an "entering-wedge" for still more federal largesse was entirely justified by reformers' own statements. As early as 1848, agricultural reformers were calling for federal land grants to endow state agricultural colleges.[56] Two years later, the editor of the *American Farmer* asserted emphatically, "*The conservation of the agricultural interests, require more than just the establishment of an Agricultural Bureau.* They require also, an appropriation of a portion of the public domain, for the promotion of agricultural education."[57] The states "should be induced" to found agricultural colleges, insisted one correspondent, adding that "the establishment of an Agricultural Bureau will soon awaken attention to and give interest to such schools."[58] By 1851, the *Michigan Farmer* seemed to believe that, if the bureau were created, land-grant colleges would follow as a matter of course. "Why not?"[59] Even when reformers were not dreaming of federally sponsored colleges, they were envisioning the proposed bureau as the keystone of a national system of state and local agricultural organizations. It would form "a nucleus—a central office, or general agency" to which "the State Societies could be rendered valuable adjuncts."[60] It could hardly have been more obvious that reformers imagined a federal bureau as the beginning of something bigger.

By early 1851, however, some reformers had grown frustrated with the lack of congressional action. It had been more than a year since President Taylor publicly threw his administration's support behind an agricultural bureau, yet virtually no progress had been made. Reformers therefore called for a "National Agricultural Congress."[61] That this call grew out of the stalled campaign for a federal agricultural agency is manifest. One of its primary movers was Daniel Lee, who as head of the Patent Office's Agricultural Division was so closely involved in legislative efforts at that very time. In the summer of 1851, Lee circulated a letter proposing to form "a National Board or Bureau of Agriculture."[62] The editor of *The Plough, the Loom, and the Anvil* understood this as an essential step toward lobbying Congress. "The time will never come when a Congress of politicians will do what ought to be done for the great farming interest of this country, unless this interest is organized in some way to give expression to its views."[63] Much the same opinion was articulated by the president of the Kenosha County (WI) Agricultural Society. "If we remain divided and isolated our moral force will be lost," he said. "We must bring the science of combination to bear upon our purpose," for politicians had to "be pressed into it by public sentiment."[64]

There remained some ambiguity as to whether a national agricultural organization was supposed to lobby for a federal agency or operate as a substitute. Lee seemed to contemplate the latter when he argued that "it is a foolish waste of time and of energies, to go to a political Congress for any assistance whatever."[65] Fully committed to his adopted state of Georgia by this time, Lee may have understood the hostility of southern politicians better than his northern counterparts in the agricultural press. The *Cultivator*, on the other hand, hoped that a national convention "might secure the passage of the bill now before Congress, for organizing an Agricultural Bureau at Washington—an object, we believe, very generally desired."[66]

In May 1852, the presidents of leading state agricultural organizations circulated a call for a national agricultural convention the following month in Washington, DC. The only southern organizations to join the call were the Maryland State Agricultural Society and Georgia's South Central Agricultural Society, whereas the North was represented by the state organizations of Massachusetts, New York, Pennsylvania, Ohio, Indiana, Vermont, New Hampshire, and Rhode Island.[67] The decision to meet in Washington reflected the intention to lobby legislators. Agricultural reformers had been employing a similar tactic for years by convening annual meetings in state capitals when legislatures were in session. When the convention commenced on June 24 and formed the United States Agricultural Society, several congressmen were in attendance, including supporters of a federal agricultural bureau such as James Doty, and national party leaders such as Stephen Douglas and John Bell. It could not have been a coincidence that, on the day the convention opened, Representative Jerediah Horsford delivered a major speech in favor of an agricultural bureau. Horsford, a New York Whig, was the father of the noted American agricultural scientist, Eben Newton Horsford.[68]

Although most delegates wanted vigorous lobbying of Congress, the matter generated heated debate at first. Marshall P. Wilder called for "proper Governmental aid" in his presidential address and a Pennsylvania delegate drew applause when he declared the "right" of "the agricultural interests of the nation . . . to demand an agricultural department of this Government." Yet some delegates objected, citing constitutional objections and patronage concerns, both of which were forcefully rejected by leading reformers. Charles B. Calvert, president of the Maryland State Agricultural Society, demanded not just a bureau but a department with a cabinet-level secretary to give farmers institutional representation in the federal executive. John Alsop King, a former president of the New York State Agricultural Society, insisted that a federal department was the "*one thing*" the convention should seek. Wilder, Calvert, and King were all Whigs, leading Democratic Senator Stephen Douglas to charge that the convention was becoming "a partisan political organization." In the end, the delegates adopted a tepid resolution requesting Congress to give "such efficient aid as in their wisdom shall be best calculated to advance the great interests" of agriculture.[69] Some observers were disgusted by the "truckling" weakness of this "mere suggestion."[70]

After the initial meeting, the USAS quickly consolidated itself into an organization pursuing the policy preferences of mostly Whig agricultural reformers in the Greater Northeast. Within a few months, Wilder, Calvert, King, and a few others, including Frederick Holbrook, were firmly in control. Despite its distinct Whiggish tilt, the USAS explicitly disavowed any "sectional or party purpose" for the same reasons that the farm press repeatedly sneered at "politicians."[71] Establishing itself as a credible voice for the agricultural public meant continuing the strategy of nonpartisan anti-politics.

Wilder acted with particular energy and shrewdness as president to make the USAS into a reputable organization. In January 1853, he wrote to King about the inner circle's deliberations on how to strengthen the infant society. "To create an interest as extensive as possible and thus to act in the end on the National Government," he explained, the USAS would employ agents to go about the country soliciting memberships. Wilder made it a point to further promote the USAS in the public eye by having it sponsor "national" agricultural fairs in collaboration with state and local societies (figure 7.1).[72] In the planning of these exhibitions, he told King, it was critical that the "Executive Committee should show a bold front, else we may by and by find the power departing from us."[73] The key was to make sure the USAS got the public credit. Through high-profile events, such as the 1857 "Great National Trial of Mowers and Reapers," the USAS achieved a public reputation that opened doors in Washington.[74]

But the USAS's pretensions to being a truly national organization for agriculture were belied by the composition of its leadership and membership.[75] Of the 152 delegates who made the first convention's initial roll call, only four came from the Lower South. Forty-five delegates represented the Upper South, but almost two-thirds of these came from nearby Maryland and Delaware, whose agricultural sectors were tied to urban development in Baltimore and Philadelphia and whose farm organizations strongly supported new government agricultural initiatives. Virginia's state agricultural society, on the other hand, studiously ignored the USAS. Despite its proximity to the capital, Virginia sent only ten delegates to the convention, none of whom made much of an impression in the official proceedings.[76] Georgia's South Central Agricultural Society, which had signed on to the initial call for the national convention, sent no del-

Figure 7.1. The United States Agricultural Society's 1856 exhibition in Philadelphia. Agricultural reformers often criticized horse races, which attracted fairgoers, as mere entertainment that distracted from the fair's serious aims. The main aim of the USAS, however, was to establish itself as a prominent organization in public consciousness. Races and commemorative prints served this purpose admirably. Note the flag advertising the society's sponsorship to spectators. Courtesy of the Library Company of Philadelphia.

egates at all and instead issued its own call for an "Agricultural Congress of the slave-holding states" to meet in Macon. "Mindful of the calumnies which some of our political brethren of the North have so long been propagating against us," the Georgia organization intended "to establish and fortify a public opinion within our borders in antagonism to that without, in relation to ourselves and our institutions."[77] In subsequent USAS meetings, the militant South entirely disappeared from the picture. No delegate count was recorded for the first annual meeting in January 1853, but a committee comprising a delegate from each state "represented in the minutes" included only one member from the Lower South. The January 1857 meeting included no delegates at all from the Lower South and only two from Virginia. Of the remaining thirty-seven southern delegates that year, thirty hailed from Maryland, six from Kentucky, and one from Delaware. Meanwhile, New England and the mid-Atlantic states continued to dominate both delegate and member counts. In 1857, they accounted for 77 of 142 total delegates and, by 1860, 220 of 297 life members.[78]

Influenced by Maryland's and Delaware's agricultural reformers and led by the conservative Wilder, the USAS took an accommodationist stance toward slavery. Yet it still found itself almost entirely cut off from the Lower South. The USAS strategy of forming ties with agricultural societies around the country pertained, in practice, only to organizations from the border states and northward. From its formation until the outbreak of the Civil War, the USAS held only two of its "national" exhibitions in the South. The first was in Louisville, directly across the Ohio River from Indiana, in conjunction with the South-Western Agricultural and Mechanical Society, whose president endorsed government support for agricultural institutions on the eve of bitter southern resistance to the Morrill land-grant bill. The second took place in Richmond by invitation of the Virginia Central Agricultural Society, an organization of town merchants that broke from the state society when the latter decided to hold its fair in Petersburg that year.[79] Neither group promised durable contacts with southern planters. It is telling that although Edmund Ruffin agreed to participate in the Richmond fair as a judge, he appears neither to have attended a single USAS meeting nor to have published an essay in its journal nor otherwise to have communicated with the organization.[80]

The absence of a truly national member base did not prevent the USAS from attempting to influence federal lawmakers on a range of issues. In February 1854, for example, the USAS adopted a resolution that the federal government purchase Mount Vernon as grounds for a national agricultural college and experimental farm, a proposal that had been floating around within the agricultural reform movement for some time. The society then presented the resolution to Congress. In May, the Senate Committee on Agriculture, headed by Florida Whig Jackson Morton, reported favorably on the resolution, and Senator Thomas Rusk, a maverick Texas Democrat and the lone USAS member from the Lower South, successfully moved to print two thousand extra copies of the report.[81] Yet nothing more came of the effort, and the society remained unable to achieve its primary goal of a federal agricultural agency.

Prospects began to improve only when the Republican Party took shape after 1854. In that year, congressional Democrats passed the Kansas-Nebraska Act, which formally repealed the Missouri Compromise and provoked mass protest across the North. The Whig Party had largely disintegrated by this point, a victim of its inability to manage its members' opposing views on anti-liquor legislation at the state level and on slavery at the national level. In its place now rose a movement to bring together an all-northern party composed of former Whigs, dissident antislavery Democrats, and the nativist Know Nothings. Candidates representing this incipient coalition, soon to be called the Republican Party, swept into office in the 1854–55 midterm elections, gaining control of the House. A bruising fight for the House speakership followed before the Republican candidate was ultimately chosen. The immediate significance of these events for the USAS was that the Speaker of the House had the power of committee appointments, which seasoned lobbyists had long understood as a critical point of control in the legislative process.[82]

The Republicans' adoption of the agricultural reform cause was immediately evident in the composition of the House Committee on Agriculture, which had lain mostly dormant under years of Democratic control. The *New-York Tribune* noted that the committee was "cast more strongly than usual" with the aim of "creating a distinct Agricultural Bureau in the Department of the Interior."[83] It is likely that the USAS had a direct hand in this development. The committee chairman was David Holloway, a prominent Indiana Republican who also published the state's only agricultural journal and had attended the USAS meeting in January 1856 while the House speakership battle raged.[84] In August, he introduced a well-conceived bill for an agricultural department, accompanied by a report declaring that "the people—the *sovereign people*—are now demanding that this great interest shall receive the attention and patronage of government." Registering the influence of reformers' lobbying efforts and of the USAS in particular, the report added that "petition after petition has been received from the people; agricultural societies in the counties, State boards of agriculture, the United States agricultural society, and State legislatures, have passed resolutions recommending the establishment of an agricultural department."[85] Yet in the midst of a tumultuous session that saw the brutal political beating of an antislavery senator, the bill never made it to the House floor, much less a vote.

The USAS continued to work to make its presence felt on Capitol Hill. Members of Congress and the administration were always present at its annual meetings. By 1856, most were Republicans, many of them key party leaders familiar to political historians of this era, including Horace Greeley, Henry Wilson, William Fessenden, Israel Washburn, Schuyler Colfax, and Justin Morrill.[86] At the 1858 annual meeting, for example, Republican Senator James Harlan of Iowa urged "cooperation by Congress with this Society, in aiding the objects of its organization."[87] The USAS's growing ties to the Republican Party were even more clearly embodied in John Alsop King. Tapped by Wilder at one point to succeed him as USAS president, King's election as the Republican governor of New York—in a campaign that heavily stressed King's long-standing opposition to slavery in the western territories—made this impossible. Yet Wilder begged him to remain a nominal member of the executive committee, for his name had "always given character to the Society and will help us more now than ever."[88] Perhaps Wilder understood that the USAS was steadily drawing closer to Republicans.

The USAS meanwhile gained the services of two consummate Washington insiders, Benjamin Brown French and Benjamin Perley Poore. French, a charter

USAS member who became its treasurer in 1855, served as clerk of the House of Representatives and in other official capacities through several succeeding administrations. The brother of a leading New England agricultural reformer and USAS member, French had a strong commitment to the organization's goals and even noted his backing of "*a Department* of Agriculture, not a Bureau," in his diary. His political connections and knowledge of official protocols were invaluable.[89] Poore was a prominent journalist and political writer who worked as the Washington correspondent for the *Boston Journal*. He became USAS secretary in 1857, although, like French, his involvement dated to the organization's founding. In 1858, the society established a permanent Washington office for Poore, taking a step toward maintaining a year-round presence in the capital. Poore then turned the society's annual publication into a quarterly journal and later into a monthly bulletin. In these ways, the USAS increasingly resembled a modern special interest organization, complete with central office and regular printed member communications.[90]

These connections allowed the USAS to repair its relationship with the Patent Office's Agricultural Division, which had grown strained after the departure of Daniel Lee in 1852. Agricultural reformers considered Lee's replacement, Daniel Jay Browne, a party hack and a lightweight. They disparaged his agricultural reports as haphazard anthologies "thrown together for the most part as though they had been put into press with a pitch-fork."[91] Acting on such complaints and hoping to boost its own standing, the USAS made a bid in 1853 to gain control of the Patent Office's annual agricultural appropriation.[92] When this move failed, however, the USAS had to come to grips with the fact that the Patent Office was a key player in the reform movement. It controlled up to fifteen thousand copies of its own annual report in addition to hundreds of thousands of seed packages, both essential tools for building a national constituency in favor of expanding federal agricultural functions. As one congressman explained, "the agricultural part of the Patent Office reports, like leaven, are [*sic*] beginning to move some of the people."[93]

Holloway and Poore each played a crucial role in mending the rift between the USAS and the Patent Office. In 1856, even as he was preparing the bill for an agricultural bureau, Holloway worked behind the scenes to secure a substantial raise to the Patent Office's agricultural budget. In April, he got a $30,000 appropriation into the annual "deficiency" bill, which effectively doubled the Agricultural Division's funding for the year. In August, he pushed through a $75,000 budget for the following year. Separately, he also managed to nearly double the number of copies of the agricultural report. Altogether, he greatly increased the resources at the division's disposal.[94] Poore worked simultaneously to raise the agency's public stature. In a dispatch to the *Boston Journal*, for example, he detailed its activities in order to demonstrate "the value of the

'Agricultural Bureau' to the yeomanry of our land." Division chief Browne, he added, was "admirably qualified for his task." The following year Browne was invited to join the USAS Executive Committee, and when Poore took charge of the USAS's monthly bulletins in 1858, he made sure to report favorably on the Patent Office's doings and to defend its record.[95] These efforts at reconciliation would pay handsome dividends when the USAS threw its support behind the Morrill land-grant bill in 1858 and 1859.

The fight for that law is the next act in this play. The stage was set by the emergence of the Patent Office's Agricultural Division, the campaign for a federal agricultural agency, the creation of the USAS, and the Republican Party's adoption of the agricultural reform cause. By the late 1850s, southern Democrats could see that, despite their sidelining of legislation for an agricultural bureau, in point of fact, the Agricultural Division *was* a federal agricultural bureau, and a growing one at that. Reformers, however, were hardly satisfied with the arrangement and were steadily building up lobbying power. By establishing the USAS in the public eye and making connections with Republican politicians, they positioned themselves to interact directly with federal officials while also aiding the Agricultural Division to continue expanding its purview. They were thus poised to bring to bear at the national level the same kind of influence they had already deployed in the states.

But the USAS, like the agricultural reform movement as a whole, was not as national as it pretended to be. Despite the active presence of Maryland slaveholders such as Charles Calvert, it was largely a northern organization, as its deepening ties to the Republican Party implied. As much as the USAS wished to ignore slavery and act as a force for national unity, it ended up doing the opposite. In its own right and as a coordinating device for the vast network of the agricultural reform movement, it helped channel the influence of the northern agricultural public in support of Justin Morrill's agricultural college bill, a measure that slaveholders deeply opposed, even feared. The fight over the Morrill bill would therefore lay bare the sectionalization of agricultural reform. Any power that the USAS could wield in that context would inevitably also serve the ends of the Republican Party.

CHAPTER EIGHT

The Sectionalization of National Agricultural Policy

A hundred years after the Morrill Land-Grant Act was passed in 1862, Clark Kerr called it "one of the most seminal pieces of legislation ever enacted."[1] The law established a unique system of service- and research-oriented public universities that have played a foundational role in American history ever since. Yet when the Morrill bill first reached the Senate in 1859, Virginia's James Murray Mason called it an "extraordinary engine of mischief," and his southern colleagues voted overwhelmingly against it.[2] On the face of things, this seems odd. Southerners called themselves an "agricultural people."[3] The measure was known as the "agricultural college bill" throughout its legislative history. What was the catch?

The fight over the Morrill bill featured two kinds of political misdirection. On the one hand, southern Democrats insisted that the measure was unconstitutional. Putting this claim in context, however, shows that fear of federal action against slavery, not abstract constitutional principle, was at the root of southern opposition. The concurrent rise of the Republican Party and the Patent Office's Agricultural Division within a political system that ran on patronage alarmed proslavery zealots. A system of federally financed agricultural colleges linked to a federal agricultural agency dispensing favors to farmers' organizations around the country suddenly loomed as a potentially unprecedented fount of national power to shape the operations of farms on the ground. In the South, of course, this would inevitably concern slavery.

On the other hand, because the Morrill bill emerged from the agricultural reform movement, it was subject to the logic of nonpartisan anti-politics. That is, agricultural reformers presented it as if it were a straightforward, common-sense policy demanded by farmers everywhere. "We do not meddle in politics," began one farm editorial urging passage of the law.[4] In fact, the bill was pushed by Republicans because scientific agriculture was central to their economic program and the developmental synthesis on which it was predicated. Yet Republicans denied partisan intentions, instead calling attention to agricultural reformers' vocal support for the measure. Good politicians, they understood that the fiction of a policy somehow outside politics made southern obstructionism seem all the more obnoxious. The agricultural reform movement's lobbying power was thus added to the scale on the side of what was effectively a major piece of Republican legislation.

In one of the classics of the coming-of-the-Civil War genre, David Potter argued that slavery "structured and polarized many random, unoriented points of conflict on which sectional interest diverged."[5] But this way of putting it begs the question by subtly naturalizing what distinguished the sections. Slavery did not "structure" a preexisting set of sectional divergences, it *was* the sectional divergence. The categories of "North" and "South" could not have emerged had gradual emancipation after the American Revolution not created a geographic bloc of free states. Everything else was overlaid on top of this basic division. In the case of scientific agriculture, which the Morrill bill aimed to advance, there was nothing inherently sectional. The whole country farmed, and while environmental conditions and other factors varied, they could differ as much within each section as between the two. What mattered was where slavery was.

Southerners opposed the Morrill bill because it had the potential to alter the federal government's relations to slavery. For years the federal government had upheld slaveholders' prerogatives in myriad ways, effectively constituting the antebellum United States as a "slaveholding republic."[6] The Republican Party threatened to change this, so planters were never going to allow the creation of new national agencies that might reach into the plantation. As the South Carolina firebrand James Henry Hammond put it, "Government is no sooner created than it becomes too strong for society; and shapes and moulds, as well as controls it."[7] Unwilling to be shaped, molded, or controlled by governing institutions grounded in free-state priorities, the master class opened a sectional rift where otherwise none would have been. It was slavery all the way down. No other breach could have required suturing with bayonets.

Origins of the Morrill Land-Grant Bill

Agricultural reformers' struggles to establish colleges for farmers with private and state-level funding finally led them to seek endowments from the federal public domain. The use of public lands for education enjoyed a long-standing precedent in Anglo-American governance. The Northwest Ordinances famously reserved a portion of each township for the support of local common schools. But the Morrill bill was a departure in that it proposed to apply western lands to institutions hundreds or even thousands of miles to the east. It was an odd way to allocate government resources, necessitated by constitutional objections against federal spending of general revenues. Land grants worked around such limitations because the Constitution explicitly empowers the federal government to dispose of the public domain. This option became especially attractive after the US-Mexico War, which greatly increased the stock of federal lands. Suddenly, proposals for using the public domain to finance everything from railroads to insane asylums to veteran pensions flooded Congress. The upshot was that land grants could fund just about any kind of public investment anywhere.[8]

The first widely discussed proposal for land-grant colleges was an Illinois plan for "Industrial Universities," a term that embraced mechanical in addition to agricultural education.[9] The United States Agricultural Society (USAS) took the matter up in January 1856 and appointed a committee to consider it. The two northern members soon returned a majority report expressing "entire and hearty concurrence" with the Illinois plan. J.D.B. DeBow, the committee's lone southerner and the editor of the South's preeminent economic journal, dissented. A confirmed modernizer, DeBow recognized a strategic role for the state in economic development, but he was also a proslavery stalwart wary of empowering a national government that might fall into hostile northern hands. In 1857, he wrote of his long-standing wish for southern states to establish agricultural bureaus. "This is the line of legitimate action," he explained, "and would obviate any dependence upon the National Government."[10] Similarly, he argued that the USAS should not endorse the Illinois plan because "a large number of States represented here do not admit the *constitutional* power of Congress over the public lands, in the manner and to the extent which is claimed."[11] The USAS ultimately ignored DeBow's objection, adopting the majority report in January 1857 and thus lending its name to the cause of public land for agricultural and mechanical higher education.[12]

Significantly, Justin Morrill, who in December would introduce the land-grant bill in the House of Representatives, was present at both the 1856 and 1857 USAS meetings.[13] The Illinois plan must have figured into this thinking, but Morrill had his own established connections to the agricultural reform movement and its aims. In 1847, for instance, he authored a prize-winning essay for the Orange County (VT) Agricultural Society. Morrill entered Congress with the Republican wave that followed the Kansas-Nebraska Act, and he immediately joined the Committee on Agriculture made newly active by Republican appointees. One of his very first actions was to offer a resolution requesting the committee "to inquire into the expediency of establishing a Board of Agriculture under the direction of the Secretary of the Interior; and, also, of establishing one or more national agricultural schools upon the basis of the naval and military schools."[14] The Morrill bill clearly originated with the agricultural reform movement and was generally referred to as the "agricultural college bill."

The legislation that Morrill introduced in 1857 would ultimately undergo several changes, but its basic features were already in place. The law would furnish states with portions of the public domain to found colleges in which the "leading object" would be "such branches of learning as are related to agriculture and the mechanic arts." Each state was entitled to twenty thousand acres (later raised to thirty thousand acres) for each of its members of Congress. The bill thus favored the more populous eastern states. It also favored southern whites, who would benefit from the three-fifths clause. Because an agricultural college in the slave South was almost sure to include instruction on slave management, slaves were to be made to subsidize their own more efficient exploitation. Slaveholders in the cotton states, where the proportions of enslaved African Americans were especially high, would benefit most of all. These points must be kept in mind when considering the intensity of southern hostility to the proposal.

The bill included several additional provisions. An innovative device addressed the conflicts that might arise were one state to own land in another. States in which federal lands remained would have to locate their grants on those lands. Other states would receive land scrip whose location would be determined only upon its sale and transfer by the states to private parties. This stipulation originated with an earlier proposal—known as the Dix bill after the social reformer, Dorothea Dix—that would have provided land grants for states to build asylums for the "indigent insane." Part of the spate of land-grant schemes that followed the conquest of northern Mexico, the Dix bill never became law but left a legacy in its land-scrip provision. Another significant feature of the Morrill bill was that the states' proceeds from land sales, excepting ten percent that could be applied to grounds for an experimental farm, had to be invested in a permanent endowment. In this way, Morrill ensured that states did not use up all of their funds erecting institutions they could not afford to operate, showing that he had observed the overextension that was crippling so many contemporary experiments in agricultural higher education. Several additional conditions bound states further. One, a requirement that each school report annually to the "the agricultural department of the Patent Office," proved especially controversial for reasons to be explained shortly.[15]

Agricultural reformers mobilized quickly to support the bill. In January 1858, Joseph R. Williams, a former Republican newspaper editor who had just been appointed as the first president of the Michigan Agricultural College, circulated a call in the agricultural press for reformers to exert themselves in the bill's behalf.[16] Others responded, working to secure backing from agricultural societies and state legislatures.[17] USAS member John Jones, for example, talked up the bill before Delaware's leading agricultural society.[18] At least two state societies and two state legislatures petitioned Congress on the matter before the bill was even reported back from committee.[19] Altogether, Congress would receive thirteen petitions from state legislatures calling for the Morrill bill's enactment, and thirty-some more from major agricultural organizations.[20] These efforts amply indicated the agricultural reform movement's capacity to mobilize.

Moves in the House

Neither the widespread public support nor the disproportionate benefits for the slave states impressed southern Democrats, who vehemently opposed the bill from the beginning. When Morrill asked that it be referred to his own Committee on Agriculture, John Letcher (D-VA) instead moved its referral to the Committee on Public Lands, chaired by Williamson R. W. Cobb (D-AL). Morrill pleaded not to have the measure "strangled" by a hostile committee, but Letcher's motion succeeded.[21] In April 1858, Cobb submitted the committee's majority report against the bill.[22] The report laid out the rhetorical strategy pursued by southern Democrats and their northern allies throughout the congressional debates that carried into the winter of 1858–59. The main tack was constitutional strict construction against the specter of a federal leviathan that might overwhelm the states' particular—not to say peculiar—institutions. Although neither Cobb nor any other member of Congress referenced slavery directly, the Republican Party press would soon draw the connection.

Most of the southern case against the Morrill bill was actually cribbed from the earlier debate over the Dix bill.[23] That proposal had passed Congress in 1854 only to be vetoed by Democratic President Franklin Pierce, an archetypical "northern man with southern loyalties."[24] Pierce reasoned that if the federal government had the power to provide for the indigent insane, it had the power—the obligation, really—to provide for all needy Americans. Yet he could find no "authority in the Constitution for making the federal government the great almoner of public charity throughout the United States." Such responsibilities for "the social relations [and] internal arrangements of the body politic" lay squarely with the "independent and sovereign States," which had "scrupulously measured such of the functions of their cherished sovereignty as they chose to delegate to the general government."[25] Speaking of "social relations" and "internal arrangements" was an oblique way to refer to slavery and insisting that these were strictly state domains was a way to protect the institution. As one southern senator argued ominously, if the Dix bill opened the door to federal social policy, it would "lead to dangerous projects of sectional advancement."[26]

Supporters of the Dix bill pointed to Article 4, Section 3 of the Constitution, which states that "Congress shall have Power to dispose of and make all needful Rules and Regulations respecting the Territory or other Property belonging to the United States." They argued that this enumerated a blanket federal power over federal land. Pierce replied that the clause applied only to the land cessions made by the states upon entering the Union and not to further territorial acquisitions, an interpretation similar to the one articulated by Chief Justice Roger Taney in the Dred Scott decision a few years later. Invalidating Congress's power to legislate for the territories, Taney contended that the power delegated to Congress in Article 4, Section 3 was confined "to the territory which at that time belonged to, or was claimed by, the United States" and did not apply to subsequent acquisitions. But while denying Congress the power to grant lands for social ends, Democrats like Pierce and Taney acknowledged its authority to exercise "prudent proprietorship." By this criterion, grants for railroads and schools could be justified if they raised the prices of adjoining government tracts. "All such grants of land are, in fact, a disposal of it for value received," Pierce explained, before adding that "they afford no precedent or constitutional reason for giving away the public lands."[27] In effect, Pierce was arguing that the federal government could act like a land developer but not a sovereign.

Opponents of the Morrill bill employed identical reasoning. At one point in the debate, Senator George Ellis Pugh, a Democrat from southern Ohio later to earn notoriety for defending the Confederate sympathizer, Clement Vallandigham, against charges of sedition, read Pierce's veto message aloud word for word.[28] The majority report of the House Public Lands Committee likewise reiterated Pierce's logic. According to the report, the public domain was "a source of revenue" that could not be parceled out "without a consideration," unless the grant raised adjoining land values and thereby maximized government revenues. The majority report conceded that the objects of the Morrill bill were worthy, but the constitutional constraint was paramount, for by denying the federal government "all authority to act in relation to the domestic affairs of the several States," it "established the only solid foundation for the perpetuation of the federal Union." Thus, as long as the Constitution was assiduously adhered to, the "various, and even conflicting, habits, customs, and local interests in the different States will be protected by their legislatures, and are in no danger of being overridden by the federal government."[29] As with

Pierce's veto message, it did not take great acuity to read between the lines an allusion to slavery and a veiled threat of disunion.

Accompanying this was a minority report signed by the committee's only two Republicans, one of whom, Henry Bennett of New York, had introduced legislation for an agricultural bureau in the early 1850s. The Republicans' statement rehashed many of the claims, by now familiar, made by agricultural reformers. Agriculture constituted the "mainspring of national prosperity" yet had not benefited from scientific advancement as much as commerce and manufactures. The threat of soil depletion was "patent to every one paying the slightest attention to the subject." European countries had already established public institutions to address such problems, yet the American government withheld it "fostering care." The constitutional question was immaterial, for "in the opinion of the undersigned, there is no limit to the uses and purposes to which the public domain may be applied but the discretion of Congress."[30]

Morrill's supporters employed a clever parliamentary procedure to outmaneuver southern Democrats and engineer a quick vote.[31] With Morrill delivering a forceful speech and opponents wrong-footed, the House passed the measure by the slim margin of 104 to 102 on April 22, 1858 (table 8.1). A breakdown of the voting in the House alone reveals an almost direct clash between future Unionists and secessionists. Seventy-eight southern representatives voted on the measure, with only thirteen casting yes votes. Of these thirteen, eight were Know Nothings, all of them from Upper South states that fell within the penumbra of the Greater Northeast. That left a mere five southern Democrats in support of the proposition. These included a Marylander, Delaware's lone congressman, and Francis P. Blair, an "Independent Democrat" from Missouri with ties both to Republicans and to Maryland's agricultural organizations. Republicans voted yes almost unanimously, with just six of eighty-four breaking party ranks. Each of these six dissenters represented a state of the Northwest, which overall supported the bill by the small margin of twenty-six to twenty-one, whereas the Northeast went for it sixty-five to sixteen. This reflected western ambivalence about legislation that aided regional development but favored the populous East in its allocation of grants and threatened to facilitate land speculation through the paper scrip provision. Northern Democrats, who mostly opposed, provided the balance of support with thirteen critical yes votes.

Further analysis of the northeastern vote adds evidence that rural support for the bill was broad and deep. Other than Galusha Grow, who may have believed that it would somehow interfere with his pet project of homestead legislation, only Democrats opposed the bill in the Northeast. All of these Democrats came from New York or Pennsylvania. One group clustered in and around New York City and probably represented that area's ties to cotton. The second

TABLE 8.1.
Congressional Voting (House and Senate Combined) on the Morrill Bill, 1858–1862

	Morrill bill (1858–59)		Morrill bill (1862)		USDA bill (1862)	
	For	Against	For	Against	For	Against
Overall	129	124	122	32	150	20
Chambers						
House	104	102	90	25	125	7
Senate	25	22	32	7	25	13
Parties						
Republican	94	6	78	22	27	4
Democrat	23	112	18	7	103	12
American/Unionist	12	6	26	3	20	4
Sections						
North (free)	112	41	98	31	126	16
South (slave)	17	83	24	1	24	4
Union states	123	46	122	32	150	20
Confederate states	6	78	—	—	—	—
Regions						
Northeast	78	16	70	4	78	7
Northwest	34	25	28	27	48	9
Upper South	15	34	24	1	24	4
Lower South	2	49	—	—	—	—
Select combined splits						
Northeastern Democrats	13	15	11	1	14	0
Northwestern Democrats	2	16	7	6	8	3
Northeastern Republicans	65	1	57	2	62	7
Northwestern Republicans	29	5	21	20	39	5

Sources: Cong. Globe, 35th Cong., 1st Sess., 1742; 35th Cong., 2nd Sess., 734; 37th Cong., 2nd Sess., 2017, 2634, 2770; Kenneth A. Martis, *The Historical Atlas of Political Parties in the United States Congress, 1789–1989* (New York: Macmillan, 1989), 110–11, 114–15, 393–95.

group was scattered around Pennsylvania and must have represented the Buchanan administration's special influence in that state. By this time, most dissident Democrats had already joined the Republicans' coalition. Remaining Democrats were therefore hard-core party loyalists. In light of this, the decision of three Pennsylvania Democrats to break ranks with the administration and vote *for* the Morrill bill seems telling. These congressmen represented the fifteenth, sixteenth, and seventeenth congressional districts, which comprised a band of counties that bisected the state, running north to south from Potter County on the New York border, through Centre, and down to Bedford, Fulton, Franklin, Adams, and York counties on the Maryland border. The region, as might be guessed, was overwhelmingly agricultural. Its population was eighty-three percent rural; not a single town surpassed nine thousand residents.[32] It would therefore seem that these Democrats either believed in the Morrill bill as policy or thought that it was popular among their farmer constituents.

Agricultural reformers and Republican editors immediately took notice of the bill's passage in the House. Horace Greeley, who was both, "rejoiced" and assumed that "the concurrence of the Senate is hardly doubtful." The *Chicago Tribune* was less sanguine, noting that "the Slaveocracy of course voted against it." It added that "the farmers can look for nothing from this Congress or its Administration. The only product regarded now as of national importance is cotton—the only live stock, young niggers."[33] Meanwhile, Democratic papers greeted the bill's passage mostly with silence. Thus, in spite of significant northern Democratic support, the measure was largely associated with the Republican Party and, to a lesser extent, with the dying remnants of Upper South Whiggery now organized in the American Party.

The House's action invigorated reformers, who renewed their advocacy. One agricultural editor instructed farmers to tell members of Congress "that there is no subject more important than this. If you speak, they will listen!"[34] Another recommended, "Let the officers of the various Societies, take immediate action upon the subject, and appeal to their Senators in behalf of the measure."[35] Because senators were then chosen by state legislatures rather than directly by voters, this was really a call for agricultural reformers to go to work at the state level, where they were already influential. Especially strong advocacy came from reformers directly connected with nascent agricultural schools.[36]

Joseph R. Williams again led the way. His address closing the New York State Agricultural Society's annual fair in October covered the topic exhaustively. No event provided a better opportunity to spread the message, for this was the largest and most established agricultural fair in the country, attended by tens of thousands and much reported in the press.[37] Williams began by praising the great strides made in agriculture over the previous generation. He quickly turned, however, to a catalog of problems, including soil depletion, pest infestations, unsound veterinary practices, and the lack of education among farmers. On the other hand, hybridized flowers were "an instance where research, purely scientific, has often doubled the value of the earnings of the farmer or gardener." Having established the stakes of scientific agriculture, Williams asked, "Are facilities for sufficient education within reach of the youth of the rural population?" The answer, of course, was no. There were not enough colleges, and the existing ones were inappropriate for farmers because their classical curricula ignored science and ruined students for physical labor. "A new order of institutions has therefore become an absolute necessity," he insisted. Registering the financial lessons of recent years, Williams concluded by stressing that action had to occur at the national level. Only the federal government could supply "more liberal aid than private individuals or capricious State Legislatures would be likely to afford."[38]

Williams's talk contrasted strikingly with one delivered at about the same time by John C. Calhoun's eldest son, Andrew, the president of the South Carolina State Agricultural Society. Calhoun spoke distinctly as a slaveholding planter and an "uncompromising" advocate of southern interests. Whereas Williams's standard of achievement was "an educated people," Calhoun's was "a well fed negro." He railed against federal support for agricultural colleges and pointedly decried calls from fellow agricultural reformers to lobby for the Morrill bill. "In free states," he admitted, "agricultural schools are very important," but "the slaveholder, when well informed, can apply his means to follow the precepts of science, without governmental aid." The clash with Williams could not have been clearer. Unlike northern small holders, Calhoun was saying, wealthy planters could acquire scientific knowledge privately and simply command their slaves to work according to plan. Indeed, a special agricultural education was wrong for planters, because what they really needed were the timeless maxims of classical antiquity, which taught how to defend class interests. The Morrill bill would undermine "manly self-reliance," erode the states' sovereignty, and foster a high tariff by reducing revenue from land sales. Resistance to such "extravagant and unconstitutional" "usurpations" was the only way to prevent the federal government from "assuming powers inconsistent with the peace, security, or prosperity of the South."[39]

The Senate Debate and the Larger Context

The Senate began debate on the Morrill bill in February 1859. Responding to Williams and the better part of the agricultural reform movement, Benjamin Wade (R-OH) reminded his colleagues that the bill "has been favored by almost every agricultural society" and that many senators were under instruction from their state legislatures to pass it.[40] Taking their cues from Calhoun, southern Democrats spared no hyperbole in their denunciations. According to James M. Mason (D-VA), the bill was an "unconstitutional robbing of the Treasury for the purpose of bribing the States." Clement Clay (D-AL) called it "one of the most monstrous, iniquitous, and dangerous measures which have ever been submitted to Congress." Jefferson Davis (D-MS) regarded the agricultural reform movement's entire policy agenda as "fraudulent."[41]

Southerners and their northern Democratic allies were especially troubled by the seemingly innocuous provision that the land-grant schools report to "the agricultural department of the Patent Office." This, opponents insinuated, opened the door to centralized control from Washington. "I know of no such department," Mason railed, "but it is perfectly homogeneous with this bill. . . . The bill has a right to anticipate that, if this sort of policy is commenced under the auspices of the Federal Government, an agricultural department will be necessary to supervise it." Just as southern Democrats had suggested in the early 1850s that a federal agricultural bureau formed an "entering-wedge" for the expansion of domestic federal power, they now saw the same danger in federal land grants for state agricultural colleges. "It requires none peculiarly conversant with the working of any Government, more especially this," Mason warned, "to see that in a very short time the whole agricultural interests of the country will be taken out of the hands of the States and subjected to the action of Congress, by direction or indirection, either for the promotion of it in one section or the depression of it in another.[42]

Several other southern senators asserted much the same. Benjamin Fitzpatrick (D-AL) saw in the Morrill bill an attempt "to establish a new theory in . . . the relations of this Government towards the States." James Green (D-MO) believed it was "the introduction of a swallowing-up system that will conglomerate every power in this Government . . . and every farm will belong to the Federal Government." Clement Clay, who claimed to be an "ambassador from a sovereign State" rather than a United States senator, observed with alarm that the measure would "unlimit all the limitations of the powers of Congress."[43]

Northern Republicans ridiculed these worries and emphasized the substantive benefits of national agricultural improvement and democratized higher education. Jacob Collamer (R-VT) refused to split hairs over the limits of the Constitution's territorial clause "for it clearly has none," a statement praised by the *New-York Tribune*'s Washington correspondent.[44] When Mason decried the possibility of Congress one day "fasten[ing] upon the southern States that peculiar system of free schools in the New England States," James Harlan (R-IA) mocked him. "It may be that it is a blessing to Virginia that she is now more largely represented by adult white people who are unable to read and write, in proportion to her population, than any other State of the Union," said Harlan. "It is a blessing, however, that the people of my State do not covet. . . . They prefer that the mind of the laborer should be developed."[45]

The Senate narrowly approved the measure on February 7 by a margin of 25 to 22 (see table 8.1).[46] Sixteen Republicans cast yes votes, while the remaining three missed the roll call. No Republican senator opposed the bill. It could not have passed, however, without two other voting blocs. The first was composed of old-line Whigs from the Upper South. Back in 1850, when the Senate voted for the first time to print the agricultural portion of the Patent Office report as a separate volume, there were fourteen Whig senators from throughout the South and, of the eight who voted on the measure, only one opposed. In 1858, former southern Whigs now representing the American Party still overwhelmingly supported federal aid to agriculture. But only five remained, all save one from the Upper South. The second bloc of crucial votes came from northern Democrats, who backed the bill five to four. Five more northern Democratic senators missed the roll call but registered their choices, and this group approved the measure four to one. Amos Brown of the People's College of New

York, in Washington to lobby for the bill, observed that "the South . . . are [*sic*] as much as possible working it into a party question."[47] For this reason, Clement Clay called it "a bill which the Democratic party of this country has been committed against for thirty years past."[48] In fact, many northern Democrats supported the policy and, as later developments would show, more would have done so if not for the influence of their southern co-partisans.

Southern Democrats' view of federal agricultural policy can be better understood by examining their wholehearted approval for the Guano Islands Act of 1856, only two years before digging in their heels against the Morrill bill. Guano was the miracle fertilizer of the nineteenth century. The stuff formed when rare environmental conditions turned eons of compacted bird droppings into a nutrient-rich stratum of rock. The best deposits occurred on the Chincha Islands off the coast of Peru and had been utilized sustainably by indigenous peoples for centuries. Thanks to the emergence of agricultural chemistry in the early 1800s, Europeans began to take notice, and large-scale commercial exploitation soon followed, with the first transatlantic shipments in 1840. Two years later, Peru nationalized the Chincha deposits and leased commercial rights to a British firm. Almost overnight, guano had become a major item of world trade.[49]

Stories of guano's "incredible fertilizing properties" spurred its popularity in the United States.[50] It entered the American market easily because farmers had already grown accustomed to commercial soil amendments. In 1854, the peak year of importation, retail sales approached $9 million.[51] By that time, according to one historian, "fervent testimonials of farmers operating holdings of all sizes indicate the existence of a literal guano crusade."[52] But Peru's government monopoly meant high prices and short supplies. Successive administrations negotiated to no avail and more aggressive efforts nearly provoked a war. In 1852, a group backed by the New York merchant Alfred Benson convinced Secretary of State Daniel Webster that a second guano-rich archipelago off the Peruvian coast, the Lobos Islands, remained unclaimed. Webster ordered naval protection, and Benson fitted out a large fleet of ships. It soon turned out, however, that Peru actually did own the islands and had ruled them off limits. With the American merchant fleet armed and under way, an international clash appeared inevitable. Last minute talks averted the crisis but left American demands no better satisfied.[53]

The affair proved only an opening scuffle in a developing inter-imperial guano rush. In 1855, Benson formed the American Guano Company, reportedly capitalized at $10 million, to mine the remote Pacific islands of Baker and Jarvis.[54] He then got the Pierce administration to send two naval vessels to inspect the sites and, acting through William Seward, petitioned Congress to have his company's claims to the islands confirmed. Meanwhile, he ginned up publicity, sending samples to the Patent Office for chemical analysis and talking up his discoveries to agricultural reformers.[55] In June 1855, the influential New York Farmers' Club resolved that "it is the duty of the American Government to assert its sovereignty over any and all barren and uninhabitable guano islands of the ocean which have been or hereafter may be discovered by citizens of the United States."[56] Agricultural reformers also mobilized "a powerful organized effort . . . in Washington." In 1854, a USAS committee met with the assistant secretary of state, who assured them that the government would arrange cheaper guano imports. No such thing occurred, so in 1856, some sixty incensed farmers and planters attended a "Guano Convention" in the capital. By then Congress had delved into the "guano question" no less than nine times, and two presidents had addressed the matter in their annual messages.[57]

Congress shifted focus from negotiation to exploration by passing the Guano Islands Act in 1856. The law, which enjoyed broad northern and southern support, allowed any American citizen to declare an unclaimed guano island as US territory, secured exclusive mining rights to the discoverer, and authorized the US Navy to provide protection. Merchants took advantage immediately, leading to "a vast amount of exploration and discovery." All told, the State Department would come to recognize seventy claims to guano islands throughout the Pacific and Caribbean.[58]

Sponsoring the law was on odd political pairing: the Republican northern champion, William Henry Seward, and the arch–southern Democrat, James Murray Mason. Seward's involvement was in keeping with his long-standing support for agricultural reform, economic development, and commercial expansion, as well as his connections with Benson. Mason's role might at first seem puzzling. His attack on the Morrill bill does not easily square with his statement that guano merchants required "the arm of Government . . . extended over them."[59] But Mason could reconcile these positions by distinguishing between national powers at home and abroad. Speaking against the proposal for a new Department of the Interior in 1849, he asked, "Was not the Government devised, planned, and organized to manage the exterior, the foreign relations of the States?" An Interior Department would bring the "industrial pursuits of our people . . . within the vortex of Federal action."[60] Conversely, when it came to overseas commerce, he favored the vigorous exercise of national power. As chairman of the Senate Foreign Relations Committee, he repeatedly pushed diplomatic efforts to expand foreign markets.[61] Indeed, Mason specialized in state building for the projection of American global power. In the 1850s, he presided over reforms that professionalized and expanded the State Department's diplomatic and consular services. These moves paralleled naval reforms led by other southern militants, such as Abel Upshur and James Dobbin, designed to expand American foreign trade.[62] Global commercial expansion served the southern export economy well. Hence, in opposing a federal agricultural bureau, the *Southern Planter* observed that "the indirect action of Congress in extending our commerce as our expanding enterprise requires has aided us more than its direct action could have done."[63]

The principle of unlimited national powers abroad coupled with strictly limited ones at home could still accommodate the use of federal power domestically to serve slaveholder interests. At the very moment that Mason articulated the distinction, he was drafting one of the most far-reaching expansions of federal domestic powers in American history: the Fugitive Slave Act of 1850, a law that compelled every able-bodied man in the United States to turn slave hunter when the government came calling.[64] The issue was never federal power per se, but the legal basis on which it could be wielded and, ultimately, the uses to which it could be put. For southerners like Mason, the Constitution formed desirable grounds for determining the scope of federal power because it was a document that recognized and protected slavery in myriad ways.[65] It clearly authorized the rendition of runaway slaves, giving Mason all the justification he needed for turning the entire country into a "carceral landscape."[66] Yet precisely this made the objection to land-grant legislation so outrageous to northerners. Article 4, Section 3 sure looked like plenary congressional power over the public domain. When Mason and his ilk argued for constitutional limits even here, under the tortured legal doctrine of "prudent proprietorship," it seemed they were simply asserting the whip hand in national politics to bury popular northern policies for economic development and social welfare.

Republicans saw this as a naked power play that finally exposed the "Slave Power" for what it had always been. They now proposed to fight it at every turn. Although they conceded that the Constitution forbade direct interference with slavery in the states where it already existed, they followed abolitionists in arguing that the federal government could take many actions to hem in and gradually eradicate the institution.[67] Mason gestured to this when he alleged that the Morrill bill formed just one part of a "*general* system of bringing the domestic affairs of the States within the range of congressional legislation."[68] The issue at stake was not a principled reading of the Constitution but the actual uses of the national state.

An Antislavery Iron Triangle?

It was in this context that the Patent Office's Agricultural Division appeared threatening to proslavery politicians. By the mid-1850s, it had "somewhat suddenly arisen in the public view," as one newspaper correspondent remarked. At the same time, agricultural reformers' lobbying and the Republican electoral wave indicated that, were it made an independent agency, the scope of federal agricultural reform policy would only continue to grow.[69] It therefore seemed that the creation of a national agricultural bureaucracy could hand Republicans a new instrument for advancing their antislavery agenda.

Political scientists sometimes speak of a power structure they call the "iron triangle," which is thought particularly to characterize agricultural policy. The term refers to a mutually supporting arrangement of legislators, bureaucrats, and special interests. In the United States, it is associated with the emergence of the congressional "farm bloc" and the American Farm Bureau Federation during the early twentieth century. Already in the 1850s, however, the rise of the Agricultural Division and the creation of the USAS foreshadowed this kind of politics. For southern members of Congress, the addition of Republican legislators made this a threat to slaveholder sovereignty.

Essential clues are to be found among the arcana of federal budgeting and administrative procedure. In 1856, as Republicans augmented the annual deficiency bill with agricultural appropriations for the Patent Office, a few southern Democrats sniped that the Agricultural Division was unconstitutional. But more important is what they revealed about the division's growing network of influence. Thomas Clingman (D-NC), for instance, complained that the annual agricultural report was so popular that "to satisfy the wants of the community," he would have to "give one copy to each voter."[70] He added that the constant mailing of reports and seed packages had become onerous. Clingman opposed increasing the division's budget, but he wanted to be unburdened and agreed with others that if the distribution of reports and seeds were to be made at all, it ought to occur through the country's agricultural societies. Lewis D. Campbell, the powerful Ohio Republican who chaired the Ways and Means Committee, added that this would have the benefit of encouraging agricultural societies to form wherever they did not already exist.[71]

But opponents of a federal agricultural agency could hardly have been happy to see the division extending ties to farmers' organizations, especially in the South. Consider a letter from the Kentucky State Agricultural Society's corresponding secretary expressing thanks for twenty-five seed packages. "It is by such acts that a government wins the sympathy and maintains the loyalty of her citizens," he wrote.[72] The division's surviving records are filled with letters like these.[73] They demonstrate that many people already viewed it as a national "agricultural bureau" and that they well understood the benefits of a channel to the federal government.[74] Any southerner who opposed the growth of a federal agricultural bureaucracy must have been wary of the reciprocal empowerment this relationship implied. Local agricultural societies gained popular support, the better to lobby for expanding federal agricultural policy. Moreover, as a Mississippi congressman remarked, "not only the wealthy planters, but the poor men are taking an interest in it," potentially undermining planter hegemony.[75]

The division's avenues for influence were many. The simple privilege of sending mail for free was a major asset.[76] This allowed the division to form a partnership with the nation's premier scientific institution when the Smithsonian wanted to compile national meteorological data by circulating blank sheets throughout the country.[77] Meanwhile, American diplomats, consular officials, and naval officers all over the world were pressed into service to procure seeds and cuttings.[78] The division expanded this aspect of its operations when its appropriation increased in 1856. Its major initiative that year was the acquisition of sugar cane cuttings from South America for planters in Florida, Louisiana, and Texas. It was easy to see in this a deliberate effort to cultivate a southern constituency.[79] The press provided another possible lever of influence and prestige. In 1856, the editor of the *American Agriculturist* wrote to acknowledge receipt of several seed packages, some of which he intended to test for reporting in his paper, while a general interest magazine solicited the division's help in filling its columns. The huge circulation of the annual report was yet another boon. One well-known agricultural writer noted his preference "to publish through the immense edition of the Patent Office Report." Even Edmund Ruffin, who was typically hostile to any kind of federal involvement in agriculture, could not resist submitting a few articles for publication when he wrote to acknowledge receipt of Japanese seeds brought back by the Perry Mission.[80] Nothing better illustrated the power of a federal agency to do what Ruffin feared most: use its resources to "corrupt" even such an unbending states-righter as Ruffin himself.

The Agricultural Division's rise helped propel the Patent Office and its commissioner, Charles Mason, to sudden prominence. Mason was generally regarded as an exceptional administrator. He had graduated first in his class at West Point in the same year that Robert E. Lee finished second and had later become chief justice of the Iowa territory. Appointed head of the Patent Office in 1853, he was astonished to learn only two years later that "the farmers and mechanics of the country were beginning to use my name in connection with the Presidency." As one historian explains, the seed packages and agricultural reports were reaching literally hundreds of thousands of people, and "the name of Charles Mason was firmly and favorably associated with each of these transactions." Mason was himself amazed by the range of operations he oversaw, noting in his diary that "the Patent Office with the National Gallery and Agricultural Branch is more extensive in its scope and scale of importance than the whole of the Navy or War Department." A West Pointer, he could not have made the comparison idly.[81]

What made all this potentially ominous to proslavery southerners was that, at the same time as Mason and the Agricultural Division suddenly rose, Republicans were talking about using federal patronage to weaken slavery.[82] Southern militants feared that a Republican administration would open the mails to abolitionist pamphlets—banned from the South since the presidency of Andrew Jackson—which might incite slaves to rebellion.[83] If this were even remotely realistic, it does not require much imagination to envision a Patent Office agricultural report filled with articles and statistics designed to show the benefits of free-soil agriculture and directed at non-slaveholding southern white farmers, the "poor men" who were taking such an interest in the annual report even in Mississippi. Indeed, the North Carolina dissident, Hinton Rowan Helper, had already used figures from the "Bureau of Agriculture in Washington" to argue exactly this in his fiery antislavery manifesto, *The Impending Crisis of the South*.[84] Leading Republicans endorsed the book. What would stop them from publishing more politic versions of his argument in future Patent Office reports? Indeed, as early as 1851, the report was praising an openly antislavery effort to introduce free labor agriculture to Virginia.[85] Whoever came to head a federal department of agriculture, observed the *Southern Planter*, would inevitably engender "some sectional feeling."[86]

But the real danger of federal patronage was subtler. It could be used to strengthen slavery-skeptical politicians in the border states, where the peculiar institution was relatively weak. Slavery excepted, large parts of the border states resembled the Greater Northeast's domestic rural-urban trade patterns. This was why the agricultural reformers of Delaware, Maryland, Kentucky, and Missouri often aligned with their northern rather than their southern colleagues. Abolitionists sought to take advantage of this by extending a "cordon of freedom" around the slave states that would successively weaken and kill the institution wherever it came close to free soil. Maryland was a prime candidate for the policy. If Republicans could abolish slavery in Washington, DC, where Congress had clear constitutional authority to do so, and bolster Maryland's antislavery politicians with patronage, they might bring slavery to an end in a state where it was already in partial decline. Virginia would be next. With "Lincoln at the helm," predicted one agricultural reformer and Republican activist in 1860, "emancipation in the border states . . . will soon be upon us."[87]

Maryland's agricultural reformers did not, by and large, oppose slavery. In fact, their leading figure, Charles Calvert, was a substantial slaveholder. But even Calvert's commitment to the institution was nowhere near what proslavery southerners would have deemed reliable. When he established the Maryland Agricultural College on one of his plantations just outside the national capital in 1856, Calvert invited an antislavery Quaker, Benjamin Hallowell, to serve as president. Hallowell, who had designed his own Maryland farm to showcase free labor, was willing to take the job only on the condition that no slaves be put to work at the college. Amazingly, Calvert and the trustees agreed. The point bears emphasis: an institution designed to train plantation owners was to operate without slavery. The implausibility of this arrangement is undoubtedly what led to Hallowell's rapid departure, but the fact that it was even considered, much less implemented, speaks to the distance between Maryland's agricultural reformers and a Calhounite like James Mason. The latter had every reason to believe that Calvert and his ilk would do business with a Republican administration. And indeed they did. Although Calvert opposed emancipation until the very last minute, he remained a staunch Unionist throughout the secession crisis.[88]

A crafty maneuver by the Agricultural Division in collaboration with the USAS and key Republicans suggested the way things were trending in the winter of 1858–59. The House had recently passed the Morrill bill, and the Senate was about to discuss it. The patent commissioner now convened an "Advisory Board of Agriculture" in aid of the congressional mandate to gather farm statistics. This allowed the division to bring leading agricultural reformers to Washington at government expense. Only three of the twenty-two invitees represented slave states, and none was from the Lower South.[89] Ten had close ties to the USAS. Among them were Freeman Cary, the abolitionist leader of Farmers' College, and David Holloway, the Republican former chairman of the House Agriculture Committee. Others included the USAS president and secretary, the head of the Smithsonian, Amos Brown of People's College, and Charles Calvert, as well as Justin Morrill and several members of Congress.[90] "All . . . were in favor of donations of lands . . . for the establishment of Agricultural Colleges."[91]

Meeting on January 3–11, the better part of the group immediately reconvened as the annual USAS meeting and assembled for an additional three days. Delegates then heard Freeman Cary deliver a powerful address supporting the Morrill bill.[92] Cary later wrote to Morrill with a list of politicians he had contacted, promising "to leave nothing undone that is in my power to accomplish the passage of your bill."[93] Thus, just two weeks before the Senate took up the matter, the capital was practically swarming with leading advocates of agricultural education. Southern Democrats were not amused and called for an investigation.[94] The chair of the House Agriculture Committee duly requested and accepted an explanation from the patent commissioner. The same congressman had only six months earlier told the same commissioner that American farmers "universally" approved "of what the General Government has done and is doing in their behalf."[95] Perhaps this was what James Mason had in mind when he contended that "it requires none peculiarly conversant with the working of any Government, *more especially this*," to imagine what, from his perspective, would have been an unholy alliance of agricultural reformers, federal bureaucrats, and Republican politicians.[96]

Southern Democrats took the matter seriously enough to prevail on President

James Buchanan for a veto. Republican newspapers commented on the likelihood of the move almost immediately after the Morrill bill passed the Senate. "There is no interest so deserving, no measure so needful or just," the *Chicago Tribune* opined, "but they must go to the wall if they conflict with the remorseless purpose of slavery."[97] Some observers close to the action had been expecting a veto for months. Amos Brown predicted the outcome shortly after the House vote in May 1858. "The South are [*sic*] very hostile to the measure," he explained to a colleague.[98] Sure enough, Buchanan struck down the bill as "both inexpedient and unconstitutional." In a move sure to infuriate Republicans, he justified his position by citing Taney's interpretation of Article 4, Section 3 in the Dred Scott case.[99]

Republican editors roundly condemned the president. "The simple truth," charged Horace Greeley, "is that he is a tool of the Slave Power, its creature, its instrument, and the Slave Power is radically hostile to educated labor."[100] According to the *Chicago Tribune*, nothing but "the remorseless negative of slavery" could explain the president's decision.[101] The *Philadelphia Press* highlighted a pattern of southern obstructionism. "Here was a farmer's bill, pure and simple," its Washington correspondent exclaimed, "but it has met the same fate which is threatened upon the interests of the manufacturers!"[102] Similar complaints pervaded the Republican Party press. "This thing must have an end," demanded an irate letter to the abolitionist *National Era*.[103]

Agricultural Policy in a Republican Congress

The end came when secession left Congress in northern hands. In December 1861, nine months after the firing on Fort Sumter, President Lincoln suggested the propriety of establishing a federal agricultural agency.[104] The following month, several members of Congress heard USAS president William B. Hubbard again pronounce the "absolute necessity" of a federal department of agriculture. The USAS subsequently appointed committees to lobby Congress for both the department and the land-grant bill.[105] It helped that Charles Calvert was now in the House and on the Agriculture Committee. In February 1862, that committee reported unanimously in favor of a bill that proposed, in essence, to take the Agricultural Division and redesignate it as an independent department headed by a commissioner who, though not a member of the Cabinet, would report directly to the president. A brief discussion followed before the House passed the bill with minor amendments by an overwhelming majority of 125 to 7 (see table 8.1).[106]

A good deal more debate occurred in the Senate, even if no one doubted that some kind of official federal agricultural agency would ultimately result. The bill under consideration differed from the House version only in tightening up language designed to ensure that any future expansion of the department would require congressional approval.[107] Senator James Simmons (R-RI) took charge of shepherding it into law. A conscientious if lukewarm supporter of the measure himself, Simmons was determined to satisfy agricultural reformers' claims, repeatedly noting that they had been demanding a federal agricultural department for years.[108] He drew special attention to the USAS. "The president of the society was before us this morning," he noted at one point, "urging us to pass the bill."[109]

Debate centered on how extensive to make the new agency. One senator insisted that, among other things, it ought to collect reliable statistics on internal trade. Lincoln had gestured in this direction by speaking of "an agricultural and statistical bureau."[110] The report of the House Committee on Agriculture argued similarly that the entire Census Bureau might ultimately "be transferred to the agricultural department."[111] In fact, the census had already begun moving in this direction. Under Superintendent Joseph C. G. Kennedy, who was also connected to the USAS, the 1860 census featured the first separate volume on agriculture.[112] These points underscore the growth of the domestic economy and agriculture's centrality within it. Whereas customs houses provided a convenient way to measure foreign trade, the domestic economy required an entirely different kind of information-gathering apparatus, one that only a robust modern state could implement.

Several senators objected to the more ambitious proposals, especially since paying for the war seemed the higher immediate priority. The most trenchant criticisms came from William Pitt Fessenden, a fiscal hawk who chaired the Finance Committee. Fessenden vindicated reformers when he admitted that the Agricultural Division's introduction of new crops, though only occasionally successful, easily repaid its budget by raising the national product. He also acknowledged that the division was overdue for some kind of official status. But he advised parsimony, for he was certain that patronage politics, bureaucratic entrepreneurship, and the agricultural lobby would quickly expand the agency's size and budget. The division's brief history suggested the inevitability of this process. The Senate barely rejected Fessenden's preference to downgrade the proposed agency to a bureau within the Interior Department, but then easily passed the original bill, twenty-five to thirteen (see table 8.1). The House quickly concurred, and President Lincoln signed it into law on May 20, creating the US Department of Agriculture (USDA).[113]

The Morrill Land-Grant Act soon followed. The only material changes from the original bill were an increase in the land allotted to each state from twenty thousand to thirty thousand acres per member of Congress and the addition of military training requirements. Though passage was never in doubt, a small band of western senators concerned about land speculation succeeded in winning some concessions, the most important of which limited the amount of land scrip that could be located in any single state to one million acres. Unlike their erstwhile southern Democratic colleagues, who had attacked the agricultural reform movement's basic aims, these western senators were careful to get on record that "the establishment of agricultural colleges in our country must meet the approval of all thinking men." Agricultural reformers' political arrival was further underscored when Benjamin Wade noted that "most of the free States" had passed legislative resolutions instructing their senators to support the bill. The Senate easily passed the law on June 10, and the House did likewise a week later.[114]

Analysis of these combined roll call votes confirms that sectionalism had driven a close, but potentially temporary, alignment of Republicans and agricultural reformers. The land scrip provision led members from public domain states in both parties to divide on the bill. This is clearly evident in 1862, when northwestern Republicans provided a bare majority of twenty-one to twenty. In 1858–59, however, sectional pressures pushed Republicans from the same states to close ranks behind the bill, twenty-nine to five. At that time, the land speculation issue had also provided cover for northwestern Democrats to oppose the bill in order to satisfy the Buchanan administration and the southern wing of the party. With that influence gone in 1862, northwestern Democrats divided about evenly, seven to six. Meanwhile, the few remaining northeastern Democrats went for the measure eleven to one, with all but one of the New York and Pennsylvania delegations voting yes.

Shortly afterward, the USAS disbanded, its goals accomplished. Its members had regarded the society as a way to establish federal agencies that, they assumed, would be headed by agricultural reformers such as themselves. Through the 1860s and 1870s, every commissioner of agriculture was both a prominent agricultural reformer and a Republican Party loyalist.[115]

Back in 1818, North Carolina's Nathaniel Macon asked a southern colleague "to examine the Constitution . . . and then tell me, if Congress can establish banks, make roads and canals, whether they cannot free all the slaves in the United States?" Macon already had an inkling of where the antislavery political drive would come from. "We have abolition, colonization and peace societies," he explained, "and if the general government shall continue to stretch its powers, these societies will undoubtedly push it to try the question of emancipation." Yet he hoped that "under a fair and honest construction of the Constitution, the negro property is safe and secure." Two years earlier, Virginia's John Randolph had marveled at a sudden awakening of "the great Leviathan." He did not mean the Hobbesian beast that stood over and above society but the more elusive sovereign power immanent within it, "the people." *That* leviathan was a sleeping giant, mighty but lethargic. The conservative constitutional theorist, A. V. Dicey, later noted that it had been "roused to serious action but once during the course of more than a century"—meaning the Civil War. Macon and Randolph undoubtedly would have preferred for it never to have been roused at all.[116]

The dilemma of antebellum slaveholders was embedded in these statements. They were a minority regional elite committed to a fundamentally hierarchical social structure in a polity pledged to some idea of popular sovereignty. If the antislavery voice could not be silenced directly, its power must be constrained within strict constitutional limits. The formula was useful but always too confining, cast aside by slaveholders themselves whenever they wished to call on federal power for their own purposes. For a generation, the Whigs and Democrats did the work that Macon and Randolph assigned to the Constitution by providing slaveholders with failsafe veto points. No ambitious northern politician could hope to get far at the national level without conciliating his party's southern wing. The party system thereby suppressed national debate over slavery.

But this presupposed that the parties could control the field of public discourse. That capacity, never complete to begin with, continuously eroded owing to trends in technology and culture that historians sometimes call the antebellum communications revolution, which opened channels for new public actors. The South was not immune to these changes, but the North was far more affected because of its larger, denser, better educated, and more egalitarian social structure. The situation dramatically altered the nature of northern politics as the parties were buffeted by the demands of new social movements and increasingly organized trade and advocacy associations. Southern elites were often baffled and revolted by all this. The North appeared to them as a society roiled by disordering "-isms."

By the 1850s, constitutional limits and the party system no longer functioned as they used to. This was why the question of territorial slavery raised by the US-Mexico War could not be resolved in the same way that the Missouri Compromise had resolved essentially the same question in the era of Macon and Randolph. Then, political elites came to a deal and soon coalesced into rival parties that tacitly cooperated to bury slavery in the national discourse. Now, in the 1850s, the parties were in no position to dictate terms in the public sphere. Proslavery militants saw two options: either slavery must be nationalized—through, for instance, a tough fugitive slave law and a federal slave code for the territories—or they must secede to reestablish the slaveholding republic on more secure foundations.

As the events of the 1850s unfolded, the agricultural reform movement made substantial, concrete demands on the federal government from a mass base over which the slaveholders had no leverage. This was, in a sense, the cost of the southern export orientation. It left slaveholders with few organic links to the interior. In their own state legislatures, they simply rigged the districting to cut the backcountry out of power. Among coastal bankers, merchants, and textile manufacturers, they retained some sway. Everywhere else their influence was exercised indirectly through the parties that were being pressured and displaced from every quarter.

In this context, agricultural reform developed tangible policy impact at the national level by eschewing the third-party route and instead building a mutually reinforcing assemblage of farmer organizations, print publications, and government agencies. This was bad enough on its own, truly dangerous in cahoots with the Republicans, who were "wide awake" and ready to rouse the people's leviathan in more ways than one.[117] That was what James Murray Mason meant when he spoke of "this" government involving itself with agriculture "for the promotion of it in one section or the depression of it in another"; what the *Southern Planter* meant when it warned that new federal agricultural agencies would generate "a wider battle ground, and more numerous weapons"; and what the roll call votes suggest that most southern members of Congress meant when they said no to new federal agricultural agencies.[118]

Epilogue

"What has government done for agriculture?" The question was such a common refrain in the farm press that even supporters of public funding for agricultural interests were sometimes moved to reply that the army, the rectangular
survey, and the property system—the whole settler-colonial apparatus—were
what government had done.[1] But "scientific agriculture" called for something
else: the intensive reform and improvement of the extensive farming practices
that had hitherto characterized Euro-American settlement. From the patrician
promoting societies to the breakup of the Union and after, the politics of agricultural reform concerned how to approach this undertaking and what institutional forms to give it.

The Robert Livingstons and Elkanah Watsons of the early national period
tried to engineer their desired changes from the top down with only limited
success. Powerful as they were, they were not British aristocrats. Southern planters like Andrew Calhoun and Edmund Ruffin came closer. For them, science
was to be deployed at the plantation level with the aid of agricultural organizations and state governments fully controlled by fellow slaveholders. In keeping
with the "mudsill theory," a few would think and command while most did hard
labor.

The agricultural reform movement that emerged in the Greater Northeast

had distinctive social foundations and mechanics. It followed a governmental-
izing path because its constituency of small-holding, middle-class farmers read
journals, formed associations, and learned to put great faith in science yet
lacked huge pools of private capital. Modest public funding obtained through
quasi-democratic lobbying served some of their goals directly. More important,
it strengthened the movement's capacity to demand additional aid, leading to
another cycle of civic organizing and state building. Agricultural reformers
continued to shimmy upward, pushing with one foot on the opinion-forming
power of civil society, with the other on the resource-providing power of the
state. Gradually, they established agricultural reform as a permanent object of
government administration, building out domains of relative institutional autonomy insulated from party politics by the seemingly paradoxical pairing
of majoritarian nationalism and scientific expertise. At the federal level, this
involved a repudiation of strict constructionism, which, whatever else it might
have been, was the final bulwark of the slaveholding republic.

The struggle against the slaveocracy proved the occasion for the erection of
a new developmental state on top of the old settler-colonial one. The creation
of the USDA and the land-grant university system epitomized the shift. Western settlement continued and even accelerated, but simultaneously a new kind
of national governing apparatus emerged to intensify economic development
in older regions. It took some time for this to become apparent, but an early indication came from the rapid expansion of federal statistics collection. Census
reports grew larger even as various federal agencies began gathering and publishing more data more frequently, casting their statistical gazes over a wider
range of objects and moving from decennial to annual and even monthly reporting.[2] To know the domestic economy required new kinds of state cogni-
zance of the national territory, because internal trade is harder to observe than
foreign trade, which passes through the choke points of customs houses. The
rise in federal data collection thus signaled the decisive turn toward domestic
development. The USDA was exemplary. In the 1860s, the department refined
the procedures initiated by Henry Ellsworth two decades earlier to generate the
country's first annual series of crop statistics.[3] As usual, new data were prelude
to new action.

By the 1880s, the scope of that action was astonishing. Most dramatic were
the campaigns of the Bureau of Animal Industry (BAI). The BAI's creation
within the USDA in 1884—three years before the better-known railroad regu-
lator, the Interstate Commerce Commission (ICC)—was a landmark expansion
of federal functions. The agency was charged with investigating and containing
potentially devastating livestock epizootics such as bovine pleuropneumonia
and, later, Texas fever. "The stakes were huge," write Alan Olmstead and Paul
Rhode, because "the capital stock (valued at current dollars) invested in live-

stock and accoutrements exceeded that invested in railroads."[4] The agency developed the world's first area eradication program of an epidemic disease, which involved quarantining and destroying the property of powerful interests and rewriting state laws to allow federal exercise of local police powers. In rapid order, new legislation fully brought forward the power of the federal agricultural state. In 1887, Congress passed the Hatch Act, creating a system of agricultural experiment stations that became nodes for linking the land-grant universities with the USDA. Two years later, it elevated the department to cabinet-level status. By the end of the century, the USDA was generally regarded as the most competent and effective arm of the federal government.[5]

That an American developmental state arose first and most decisively in *agriculture* is the surprising fact that requires rethinking some basic categories. It is almost bracing to read Frederick Jackson Turner, the preeminent theorist of settler individualism, writing approvingly in 1911 that the USDA "tells the farmer when and how and what to plant."[6] Three years later, the creation of the Cooperative Extension Service formalized the tutelary state envisioned a century earlier by patrician reformers and, it seems, endorsed by Turner. Under this program, which the USDA directed but the land-grant universities administered, county agents were placed in rural communities to demonstrate the latest in scientific agriculture. Through the associated youth group, 4-H, the USDA did more than regulate, promote, or instruct; it reached deep into the household to shape a new generation of farmers according to official designs.[7]

The obvious significance of these later developments has obscured their roots. If there has been little scholarly appreciation for the origins of the USDA, there has been even less for the first two decades of its existence. Administrative histories from the early twentieth century spend much time on George Washington's portentous correspondence with the founders of the British Board of Agriculture during the 1790s before hastening to the department's creation in 1862 and then leaping gracefully over the next twenty years to get to the dramatic growth of the 1880s.[8] More recently, the political science subfield known as American Political Development has produced several illuminating comparative studies that consider why the USDA proved so successful, but these, too, effectively begin in the 1880s or later.[9]

The lacuna is unfortunate and indicative of larger historiographical patterns that bear scrutiny. The birth of the new agricultural state must have been, as a simple matter of timing, interwoven with the contemporary transformations of the Civil War and Reconstruction. Yet because the USDA and Morrill bills do not fit neatly within the model of a party state, they rarely find a place in histories of this era. Neither appeared in the 1860 Republican Party platform, nor did Republicans use the new agencies to further their Reconstruction program. The USDA *could* have tried to help the freedpeople become independent farmers as part of a broader mandate to repattern southern agriculture. It *could* have sought out the freedpeople for their expert knowledge of important crops. That it did neither of these things is patent from standard accounts of Reconstruction, which barely mention the department—with one exception: they cite its reports and statistics.[10] Data, however, do not collect themselves. The mere existence of crop figures is evidence that the USDA was present in the postbellum South through its correspondent network and that it was doing important epistemic work.

It is not every day that a new department of the federal government is created, nor a national system of higher education launched. Major policy shifts like these are invariably connected to bigger changes. A political history of the era must at least be able to account for them. While there is little point to exaggerating what might have been had congressional Republicans given the USDA a prominent role in Reconstruction, it is still worth asking why nothing was tried, why this lack should seem so self-evident, and why the federal agricultural state took a giant leap forward only a few short years after Reconstruction's demise.

Agricultural Reform and the Free Labor Synthesis

A full answer is well beyond the scope of this study, but some hypotheses can be ventured based on a critical, if necessarily selective, look at the historiography of American politics during the Civil War era. My sense is that the figure of the Jeffersonian yeoman continues to ground the historical imagination in unacknowledged ways, making it difficult to recognize farmers as political agents central to the construction of a powerful national state. A succession of historical paradigms has, in particular, treated northern agriculture in characteristically partial ways that have obscured its history of independent mobilization.

The Progressive Era historians understood the Republican Party as a grand bargain between East and West. The party's linkage of manufacturing with agriculture expressed this geographical alliance. In Charles and Mary Beard's influential "economic interpretation" of the Civil War, the 1860 party platform provides the obvious evidence: a tariff for eastern manufacturers, homesteads for western farmers, a transcontinental railroad to connect them.[11] Like the Prussian "marriage of iron and rye," the Beardian thesis made for a pithy digest of a complicated political realignment. Its somewhat Faustian quality probably added to its narrative appeal, and it was subsequently reinforced by Barrington Moore's epic study of comparative political development, *Social Origins of Dictatorship and Democracy*.[12] The relevant categories in this story were class and geography, which generated "social forces" whose political expressions were more or less ineluctable.

Importantly, the grand bargain was readily legible in Jeffersonian terms, according to which a well-defined temporal sequence of social development—pastoral, agricultural, commercial, industrial—could be mapped east to west as a stratification of settler space. This, of course, was Frederick Jackson Turner's "frontier thesis," the post hoc Jeffersonian apologia for American settler colonialism.[13] There was no room in the grand bargain for the USDA and the Morrill Act, policies that manifested an agricultural developmentalism closely aligned with industrialization and rooted as much in the rural Northeast as in the Midwest. Only twenty years *after* the official closing of the frontier could Turner look to the USDA as a force for reconstituting farmer independence in a markedly industrial society—by telling them what to do. The picture was convincing if one understood the great break in American history to be not the destruction of slavery in a cataclysmic midcentury war but rather the transformation of an expanding rural-agricultural society into a consolidating urban-industrial one at century's end. How the USDA came to exist in the first place seemed neither here nor there.

Subsequent analyses shifted away from the Progressives' social determinism toward a greater attention to the mechanics of political mobilization and institutionalization, which largely meant the parties. One cluster of historians and social scientists developed an elegant account of the structural resilience of the nineteenth-century two-party system.[14] Generative of many insights about the operational demands of American politics, this view explained the timing of the Civil War as a function of the rise of the Republican Party at the expense of the Whig-Democratic configuration, which had previously managed sectional tensions effectively enough.[15] It did not, however, have much to say about how specific issues arose or why parties chose one policy over another. It either reverted to highly contingent accounts of elite political maneuvering or, alternatively, to an evolutionary theory of modernization in which social change was basically exogenous to political institutions. Thus, the party system effectively substituted for a national state until the growing complexity of industrial civilization forced "adjustment" toward the end of the century in the form of new administrative bodies insulated from partisan meddling.

What the Republican Party was actually about has been better explained by Eric Foner's immensely influential free labor synthesis. Foner's central analytic framework, a supple conception of ideology, bridges the socioeconomic determinism of the Progressive historians and the structural essentialism of the party system scholars. Ideology for Foner is a means of political coalition building, cementing disparate social groups together by formulating a common understanding of the world that party leaders can render into an actionable political program. Ideology is therefore a method of mobilization. In describing the Republican Party's formation, Foner draws on a range of partisan sources to identify a central core of ideas whose "lowest common denominator" was "free labor."[16] Since this is the opposite of slavery, and slavery was at the heart of the era's political crisis, the idea makes intuitive sense. Although it is not always obvious why free labor should be regarded as logically antecedent to certain other core commitments, such as Unionism (read: nationalism), the overall picture is illuminating and convincing.[17]

The explanatory power of this view derives in part from explorations of what Foner calls free labor's "ambiguities."[18] Juxtaposed with slavery, the Republican vision appeared sharply delineated, but it became fuzzy with slavery's destruction. After the war, the problem of how to reconcile free labor liberalism with workers' economic security appeared increasingly intractable, as the labor historian David Montgomery observed in an influential monograph that informed Foner's approach.[19] The rise of industrial labor strife was thus key to Reconstruction's unraveling because, by exposing the inadequacies of free labor ideology in the face of a deepening divide between workers and capitalists, it weakened Republicans' commitment to remaking the South in their own free labor image.[20] The underlying social development here was a bifurcated process of class formation by which master craftsmen became industrial manufacturers at the same time as journeymen became industrial wage laborers. The account is therefore basically urban and worker-centered.[21] Influential studies subsequently elaborated on the interplay of *urban* social and ideational dynamics.[22] These scholars regarded "free labor" from the perspective of the industrial labor movement and echoed Karl Marx's famous characterization of workers under capitalism "as free in the double sense"—free to sell their labor and free from any other way to make a living.[23]

It has always been known, however, that the Republicans' voting base was in the country, not the city. A rich body of literature on the rural "transition to capitalism" explains a lot about the emergence of the middle-class farmers who composed this base.[24] But the Fonerian approach to ideology—as a complex of ideas whose fundamental significance is the political coalition it enables—was not an analytic category in this work. Instead, the history of American rural capitalism began with a search for a collective *mentalité* that determined farmers' stance toward market norms without respect to the political commitments that this might entail.[25] The advent of agricultural societies, fairs, and periodicals was noticed, of course, but these were regarded as signs of commercial values, not as institutions that could produce a distinct agricultural public with the potential for independent political mobilization. Small-holding northern farmers not yet enmeshed in the market implicitly appeared as a kind of free peasantry—that is, a yeomanry—who practiced "composite" or "safety first" agriculture to secure themselves a "competency" in a manner essentially consonant with freedpeople's aspirations for their own land. A corollary was that yeomen remained oriented to their local communities so long as they held out against the atomizing forces of the market. The emergence of new, *super-local but sub-universal* categories was rarely considered. There was therefore nothing here to disturb the labor-movement conception of free labor as a mobilization device. Marx's shadow again seems in evidence, illustrated in this case by his description of the French peasantry as a collection of structurally similar but disconnected local communities that could not mobilize "in their own name."[26] Similarly lacking an independent ideological and organizational history, American farmers were given no particular part to play in the great political upheaval of the Civil War era. They simply waited in place to be swept up by one party or the other.

The ideology of agricultural reform has, however, received attention from rural gender historians. Their work is not usually engaged with the causes or outcomes of the Civil War, but it does have important things to say about political change. Particularly in studies by the social historians Sally McMurry and Paula Baker and the historical sociologist Elisabeth Clemens, farm women are shown to have pursued innovative rhetorical and organizational strategies that gradually established entirely new models of political influence toward the end of the nineteenth century.[27] Other feminist historians have explored the inadequacies of "free labor" for describing the condition of women, who were typically under the formal control of a male head of household.[28] In general, too, feminist scholars have stretched the category of "labor" to embrace reproductive and affective work, significantly altering the meaning of the term. This shows, for instance, that the category of labor need not hinge on a sharp distinction with capital.

The shift in the historiography of slavery toward a greater focus on the "chattel principle" has also subtly undercut the utility of the free labor framework. If slavery is understood primarily as a *property* system rather than a *labor* system, the distinction with northern free labor becomes less apposite. Indeed, one of the reasons for viewing slavery in terms of property rights is that it exposes connections to global capitalism, including financial linkages to the North that go beyond textile merchants and manufacturers directly implicated in the cotton economy to the entire range of northern institutional investors—commercial banks, insurance companies, and savings funds—that effectively owned shares of enslaved people.[29] Sectional differences fade in this work and, as some critics have suggested, need to be reinscribed by reference to politics and the state.[30] Recognizing northern complicity in the vitality of slave capitalism, we need new explanations for why the Civil War happened, why the North won, and why reunion took the course that it did.

Many of these historiographical strands tend to converge on the Homestead Act as the Republicans' crucial policy proposal. The measure was a lightning rod for proslavery hostility during the 1850s because it would promote free settlement of western territory. It "played a key role in the Republicans' free labor outlook," Foner observes, because it promised an avenue of social mobility to address urban poverty and labor unrest, the glaring flaw in northern society.[31] Although seemingly a farmers' policy, its intellectual origins can be traced in part to radical workingmen's circles. Moreover, its specific provisions were designed to reproduce the patriarchal household and its internal gender hierarchy as the basic unit of American society. It also accelerated western settlement and the war on the Plains Indians that some historians have folded into a "Greater Reconstruction."[32] Finally, it foreshadowed one of the central dilemmas of Reconstruction as traditionally understood: how far to push land reform and for whom. Its resonance was obvious in the Southern Homestead Act of 1866, a last-ditch effort to secure landed independence for the freedpeople after Andrew Johnson clipped the Freedmen Bureau's mandate over confiscated lands. For all these reasons, the Homestead Act was obviously very important. Yet there was more to the postbellum developmental state than federal land policy.

The USDA and the Morrill bills evidence a major social mobilization that has gone largely unnamed and unexamined. These policies were not about securing land but about what to do with it in hand. If labor was crucially at stake, it was not in a manner categorically distinct from capital. According to agricultural reformers, big concentrations of capital in land and slaves were suspect, but productivity-enhancing technology was seen as a means to empower and liberate labor in its toilsome struggle with untamed nature. Edward Everett, the secretary of an Illinois agricultural society and namesake of a famous New England economic nationalist, made the point explicitly, arguing that "agricultural machinery . . . may be looked forward to as one of the most likely means by which the emancipation of the slave may be brought about."[33] Scientific agriculture's technological vision thus evoked an alternative freedom narrative, one that imagined substituting natural "forces" for difficult or coerced human labor. That was why Horace Greeley marveled at the display of labor-saving implements and machines at the 1849 Syracuse fair and why Abraham Lincoln—a man who certainly regarded agriculture as toilsome and was deeply fascinated by invention—spent a good portion of his Wisconsin fair address discussing the prospects of steam plowing. Yet for Everett, Greeley, and Lincoln to have been in a position to contemplate these things, and for the USDA and Morrill bills to have made it through Congress, it was first necessary to represent and mobilize farmers as a distinct interest that was somehow also the nation. That was what the agricultural reform movement achieved.

Farmers' Organizations and the Reconstruction of the Party System

Although Republicans like Greeley and Lincoln made use of the ideology of scientific agriculture, the institutions of the agricultural reform movement developed separately from party structures and continued to retain significant organizational independence as the postwar national agricultural state began to emerge. This helps explain why the USDA seems to have formed no part of Republicans' Reconstruction agenda and might even have worked against it. The end of slavery and the creation of federal agricultural agencies drastically changed the calculus of mobilizing farmers for politics "in their own name" and almost immediately began shifting their organizations away from a tight Republican orbit.

Contrary to the view that the party system survived the realignment of the 1850s structurally intact, the persistence of the two-party configuration masked important changes. As early as the 1840s, the party system was being reshaped by the proliferation of new civic and business organizations bearing their own internal structures and logics. Among the factors fueling the shift were technical improvements in communications, laws of general incorporation, a culture of joint action through association, and the emergence of distinctive publics around new print genres. These conditions fostered the rise of organized influence networks unbound by partisan disciplinary mechanisms. For instance, temperance advocates played a key role in the collapse of the Whigs by rendering it impossible for the party either to avoid or to take a coherent stand on contentious anti-liquor legislation.[34] Sophisticated business lobbying was also on the rise, evidenced by a wave of political scandals that concerned the line between legitimate and corrupt ways of swaying lawmakers.[35] As the range and influence of associations continued to grow after the Civil War, party leaders began to refashion policymaking as a process of brokering deals among the representatives of corporate and public interest organizations. New conduits between state and society took shape, and the paths to governing power were reconfigured. Although the parties remained central, they had in fact been changed and partly displaced.

Yet partisanship still defined "politics." Today it is common to speak about "the politics of [X or Y]" with the understanding that various organizations and "stakeholders" might be involved. But in the 1800s, it was rare to identify discrete political domains with their own distinctive power arrangements. Thus, when I write about "agricultural politics," I mean a broad but nevertheless delimited *field of contestation*, whereas antebellum agricultural reformers rarely used the term at all, and, when they did, they meant *a set of principles or positions* to take within a basically unitary political realm. Given the continuing equation of politics with partisanship, the organized influence networks that arose at midcentury tended to deploy various modalities of nonpartisan antipolitics as rhetorical strategies for policy advocacy. For instance, women's groups entered the public sphere speaking the language of domesticity, religiosity, and moral reform, in the process fashioning new "organizational repertoires" that significantly bypassed the parties.[36] Agricultural societies used a similar trick in claiming to represent the country's rural majority and the largest sector of the economy. "Nominally nonpartisan," observes the historian, Charles Postel, these organizations were actually "profoundly political."[37]

After the Civil War, the agricultural reform movement split into three distinct but interconnected organizational patterns. The first, already evident in the 1850s, encompassed a rising number of crop-specific associations—the Western New York Dairymen's Association, the National Wool Growers' Association, etc.—that pursued technical problems and narrow special interests. The second, composed of new government agencies such as the USDA, the land-grant universities, the experiment stations, and the cooperative extension service (together with state-level analogs), successively redefined governmental involvement in the day-to-day practices of ordinary farmers. The third was made up of politicized farmers' organizations such as the Patrons of Husbandry and later the Farmers' Alliance, which went beyond the old agricultural societies to engage in sweeping efforts at reform of the American political economy. A party-centric view of politics is insufficient for understanding how these groups interacted or what they accomplished. We might instead turn to the agricultural reform movement's two modalities of nonpartisan anti-politics: scientific expertise and majoritarian nationalism.

Expertise was clearly central to the making of a federal developmental state. The agricultural reform movement's policy aims entailed building up administrative capacities in the executive branch. The new agencies then became focal points for the crop-specific associations and also for manufacturers' groups with backward and forward linkages to agriculture. Despite important differences, government bureaucrats and the representatives of particularistic interests could come together around a language of expertise grounded in shared commitments to specific knowledge about biological processes, production statistics, market conditions, and the like. Over time, the land-grant colleges contributed to this nexus by providing a common educational background for both public- and private-sector agricultural scientists.

Although expertise offered partial insulation from partisan legislators and the higher echelons of the executive bureaucracy, it was not enough on its own to create and sustain these conditions. Agricultural reformers always insisted that appointees to the new federal agricultural posts be "above political contamination" and that "no changes should be made with a change in the presidency."[38] Yet there was little institutional space for such a vision in the patronage-based party system of the mid-nineteenth century. Reformers therefore fashioned a majoritarian modality of nonpartisan anti-politics that helped them assemble a popular base of farmers with which to force their way into partisan legislatures, reaching the federal level during the uniquely volatile decade of the 1850s. Ideological affinities, institutional momentum, and slaveholder intransigence then brought them into close alliance with the Republican Party. But reformers retained significant organizational independence and a growing stronghold in the new developmental state that came out of the war. They could and would come to cultivate other political allies.

Through the 1860s and 1870s, every commissioner of agriculture was *both* a Republican patronage appointee *and* a prominent agricultural reformer with a distinct set of organizational connections and allegiances. The latter stretched across the agricultural public called into existence by the farm press.[39] That this public could figure itself as both a specific interest and as the great American demos distinguished bureaucratic development in agriculture from other sectors. Counterintuitively, majoritarian nationalism could be made into a pillar of scientific expertise. The USDA was "peculiarly the people's Department," as Lincoln described it in his final State of the Union message.[40] Logically, then, its scientists and officials were the people's experts. Almost as soon as it was created, the USDA was seeking to mobilize constituent support, arguing that "the general good is promoted by the fostering of the agricultural interest . . . which lies at the foundation of our national greatness," and calling on farmers "to press as an argument upon their representatives" the need to expand the USDA's budget and purview.[41]

The USDA quickly became a massive fulcrum for reciprocally expanding the scope of farmers' organizations and the national agricultural state, much in the same way as antebellum agricultural reformers had obtained state-level public funding to build up agricultural societies and then used the societies to gain more funding. In its early years, the USDA carried on the Patent Office's work of distributing seeds and reports in order to enlarge the network of agricultural organizations and thereby to give it a political base independent of the parties. Government patronage enhanced the standing of local organizations and worked as a de facto national subsidy for agricultural societies and farmers' clubs.[42] For example, the Agricultural and Horticultural Society of Grundy County (IL) seems to have been founded in 1854 specifically to receive seeds and reports from the Patent Office.[43] The USDA formalized the policy of working through established agricultural organizations and published directories to encourage the founding of more.[44] The network not only strengthened the USDA's hand in Congress; it was also essential to compiling national crop statistics—perhaps the department's signal early achievement—which depended on regularly canvassing a vast network of local correspondents.[45]

The USDA's outreach, networking, and information gathering gave birth to the most innovative and important farmer organization of the Reconstruction era: the Patrons of Husbandry. The Grange, as it was commonly known, was founded in 1867 by a handful of federal bureaucrats, three of whom worked for the USDA. The idea originated in 1866 when the department dispatched Oliver Kelley to reestablish channels for obtaining "the usual statistical and other information from . . . the States lately in hostility against the Government."[46] Kelley used his credentials as a freemason to gain entry to elite planter circles otherwise hostile to federal agents. This was the spark for the Grangers' characteristic melding of masonic-style ritual with farmer solidarity.[47]

Significantly, Kelley had been an agricultural reformer and serial experimenter with farmers' organizations long before he went South. His plan for the Grange owed many debts to his prior involvement in the agricultural reform movement, including his embrace of scientific agriculture and technology.[48] Like Elkanah Watson in the 1810s, Kelley's significance is that his exuberance, imagination, and promotional skill led him to hit upon a formula for realizing a widespread impulse to organize farmers in new ways. The trend to go beyond the agricultural societies was already evident in the 1840s when James Mapes established the model of the farmers' club and, in the 1850s, when the crop associations began to proliferate. Kelley recapitulated each of these moves, taking a hand in founding the Benton County Agricultural Society (1852), the Northwood Farmers' Club (1855), and the Minnesota Fruit Growers' Association (1866). At each step, he connected his organizations with the emerging federal agricultural agencies in Washington.[49]

Kelley's vision for the Patrons was an ambitious bid to establish a federal-farmer nexus on a vast scale. As Charles Postel shows, "from its earliest planning stages, the Grange was to be a farmers' political lobby, focusing on Washington and with the immediate goal of enhancing the power of the Department of Agriculture."[50] The organizers sought a million members and came close to achieving this within less than a decade. Yet in keeping with agricultural reform's nonpartisan strategy, Kelley insisted that Grange meetings "must avoid politics" to better "exert a quiet influence."[51] One way to engage farmers' attention and forge durable ties with the USDA was to make local Granges into agencies for collecting crop statistics, a role Kelley had once reserved for agricultural societies. His correspondence with the Patent Office along these lines in the 1850s led to his hire as a "statistician" at the USDA in 1862 and, subsequently, to his southern assignment.[52] This aspect of Kelley's story suggests the way that the social conditions of statistics collection, which required forming relationships on the ground, could generate new networks that converged on federal policy in Washington, DC.

Kelley's mission to the South did more than inspire a distinctive set of Granger rituals as a means of farmer organization. It advanced a program of sectional reconciliation on the basis of white supremacy. Kelley and other Grange officers encouraged planters to lead the organization in the South, looked the other way when black farmers were excluded, and argued for an end to congressional Republicans' policy of military protection for freedpeople's rights. Former slaveholders quickly recognized that an organized national community of self-consciously white farmers could serve as an effective vehicle to combat Reconstruction. By the early 1870s, they had turned the Grange into "a refuge for rural white power across the former Confederacy."[53]

Exemplary in this respect was David Wyatt Aiken, a South Carolina planter and politician who rose to prominence by orchestrating the assassination of the black congressman Benjamin Franklin Randolph. Invited by Kelley to join the Patrons in 1872, Aiken launched himself into the work enthusiastically and sat on the National Grange's executive committee as the organization reached the peak of its power in 1875 with 860,000 members in more than 21,000 local granges, nearly 8,000 of which were in the South. Individual Patrons differed in their partisan affiliations, and some local and state Granges contributed to cross-racial farmer coalitions. But the national office encouraged "disaffection" with the Reconstruction regime and, "in key [northern] states . . . provided an ideological way station for Republicans moving to the Democratic position" of outright opposition to federal intervention in behalf of the freedpeople.[54]

To what extent USDA officials shared the Patrons' antagonism to congressional Reconstruction remains an open question. The department benefited from the organization's advocacy, but its move toward scientific professionalization also made it wary of the Patrons' sometimes amateurish and chaotic style. Still, it could hardly ignore the Grange's explosive growth in the 1870s, and it may have been particularly interested in piggybacking on the organization's southern ties to gain support in Congress and build its network of southern crop reporters, which it described in part as "planters distinguished in their vocation."[55] The eminent mid-twentieth-century agricultural historian Theodore Saloutos suggested that Kelley was only one of several USDA emissaries to the South and that the department's earnest concern "with helping the farmers make the postwar adjustments" was an essential precondition to the Grangers' success in the region.[56] Whether the USDA saw African Americans as "farmers" Saloutos does not say, but it seems doubtful that the department would have confronted southern Grangers on this point while they were lobbying to bring the USDA into the president's cabinet and, simultaneously, to enact state laws to restrict black labor. It is telling that, upon entering Congress in 1876, the same year that Democratic "redeemers" took control of South Carolina, Aiken emerged as a vocal champion of the USDA's elevation to cabinet rank.[57] The contrast with Andrew Calhoun's vehement opposition to a federal role in agricultural development could not have been drawn more sharply. Having lost the fight against the creation of a new kind of national agricultural state, redeemed South Carolina would endorse its expansion the better to make it unequivocally white.

The irony of the Civil War is that, by destroying slavery, it removed a basic obstacle to white solidarity. Alongside growing industrial cities teeming with labor militants and foreigners of doubtful racial classification, emancipation opened a path to refigure the mythic Jeffersonian yeoman as the beleaguered white norm of American nationality. As farmers North and South came together in fraternal union, sentimental evocations of a supposedly simpler past were in abundance. But this should not be mistaken for mere nostalgia or traditionalism. It instead signaled a revisioning of scientific agriculture and the agricultural state. With the rise of scientific racism, the new imperialism, and Jim Crow segregation, technological mastery was increasingly attributed to uniquely white capacities. In 1898, for instance, the USDA's chief chemist, H. W. Wiley, testified to Congress that Caribbean cane sugar was "the great *natural* source of sugar" and "an industry of a less advanced and *less developed race*," whereas beet sugar, made with a German process transplanted to the upper Midwest, was "an industry of the advanced and *most developed human race*" that demonstrated what "intelligence, *science* and agricultural skill can do."[58] In this account, technological backwardness indexed racial inferiority instead of labor exploitation, while science became a distinguishing property of whiteness.[59] It seems at least possible that the new centering of racism that followed Reconstruction's demise and accompanied the USDA's emergence as an exemplar of the federal administrative state was predicated on the shifting composition and geographical center of agricultural organizations made possible by the Civil War's undoing of the master class. Significantly, by the early twentieth century, the USDA may have had more influence on the conditions of southern rural black labor than the Freedmen's Bureau ever did.[60]

What all this shows is that there was never one traditional past and one modern future for American agriculture. The nineteenth century cannot be narrated as a series of moments, from the Louisiana Purchase to the Civil War to the defeat of the Populists, that marked the gradual decline of the Jeffersonian agrarian republic and, conversely, the ascendance of a Hamiltonian industrial capitalism. Uniquely, the United States emerged at century's end as *both* an industrial *and* an agricultural global power.[61] Although the proportional predominance of farmers in the population was bound to decrease, the terms on which this could occur were multiple and varied. Politics and policy were determinative from the level of the village to the nation, and this, in turn, shaped American history more generally—in the first place, because rural people remained the majority of the electorate and agriculture the largest sector of the economy throughout the period, and, in the second place, because the struggle to shape the course of agricultural modernization centered on state institutions, much more so than was true of industrial labor and capital, which never produced anything comparable to the USDA and the land-grant university system. Indeed, farmers' movements were responsible for basic features of the twentieth-century American state, from the structure of the Federal Reserve to the distinctively American penchant for delivering social welfare by the provision of low-interest credit.[62]

Yet agriculture has been repeatedly constructed as somehow antecedent to politics and farmers as anything but the agents of state development. Perhaps there is a clue here to the abiding mystery of American governance. The state has become something like the dark matter of American history: research shows it to be there but cannot say what it is or even how to see it directly.[63] It has been described as "hidden," "submerged," and "out of sight," as a kind of visual "effect" whose "boundaries" remain to be established, even as akin to a Rube Goldberg contraption or an M. C. Escher–like optical paradox.[64] Some of the murkiness might be dissipated if the nineteenth-century countryside were understood as a space of independent political organization attuned to the complex and changing conditions of agriculture within a broader historical trajectory that, for a formative moment, hitched an agenda for domestic economic development to the destruction of slavery.

Manuscript Collections

AI-NYHS   American Institute of the City of New York for the Encouragement of Science and Invention. Records, 1808–1983 (MS 17). New-York Historical Society.

ASBS-MMSL   Agricultural Society of Bucks County. Communications, 1820–1823 (BM-B-428). Mercer Museum and Spruance Library, Doylestown, PA.

ASNC-HSD   Agricultural Society of New Castle County. Records, 1836–1872 (Ms. Book Box 92). Historical Society of Delaware, Wilmington.

Brewer-YU   Brewer, William Henry. Papers, 1852–1909 (MS 100). Yale University. Microfilm.

Carey-HSP   Carey, Henry Charles. Papers. Edward Carey Gardiner Collection. Historical Society of Pennsylvania, Philadelphia.

CCAS-CCHS   Chester County Agricultural Association and Chester County Agricultural Society. Records (MG 2.2). Chester County Historical Society, West Chester, PA.

Darrach-YU   Darrach Family Papers (MS 167). Manuscripts and Archives, Yale University.

DCIS-APS   Delaware County Institute of Science. Minutes and Papers, 1833–1873. American Philosophical Society, Philadelphia.

Everett-HML   Everett, Edward. Papers, 1849–1909. Hagley Museum and Library, Wilmington, DE.

FCAS-FMHC   Fairfield County Agricultural Society. Records, 1840–1851 (MS B90). Fairfield Museum and History Center, Fairfield, CT.

Haines-APS   Haines III, Reuben. Correspondence. Series 2. Wyck Association Collection, 1663–1972. American Philosophical Society, Philadelphia.

Hare-APS   Hare, Robert. Papers, 1751–1858. American Philosophical Society, Philadelphia.

King-NYHS   King, John Alsop. Papers, 1834–1866 (MS 351). New-York Historical Society.

MAS-CFL   Middlesex Agricultural Society. Records, 1803–1892. Concord Free Library, Concord, MA.

McAllister-LCP   John A. McAllister Collection of Civil War Era Printed Ephemera, Graphics and Manuscripts. McA MSS 017: Commonwealth of Pennsylvania, General Assembly Records, 1783–1859. Series 2: Petitions, Remonstrance and Memorials. Library Company of Philadelphia.

Morris-HSP   Morris, Anthony. Family Papers, box 3. Historical Society of Pennsylvania, Philadelphia.

MPP-HSP   Miscellaneous Professional and Personal Business Papers, 1732–1945. Historical Society of Pennsylvania, Philadelphia.

O'Reilly-NYHS   O'Reilly, Henry. Papers, 1832–1873 (MS 464). Series 6: New York State Agricultural Society, 1841–1856. New-York Historical Society.

PSPA-UP   Pennsylvania Society for Promoting Agriculture. Records. Kislak Center for Special Collections, Rare Books and Manuscripts, University of Pennsylvania.

RG 16   Record Group 16. Records of the Agricultural Division, 1839–1860. Records of the Office of the Secretary of Agriculture. National Archives and Records Administration II. College Park, MD.

RG 233   Record Group 233. Records of the United States House of Representatives. Center for Legislative Archives. National Archives and Records Administration I. Washington, DC.

Seward-UR   Seward, William Henry. Papers. Rare Books, Special Collections, and Preservation, University of Rochester. Microfilm.

Reference Works

ANB   *American National Biography*. Online ed., https://www.anb.org.

APP   The American Presidency Project. https://www.presidency.ucsb.edu.

DAB   *Dictionary of American Biography*. 20 vols. New York: Charles Scribner's Sons, 1928–36.

HSUS   Carter, Susan B., Scott Sigmund Gartner, Michael R. Haines, Alan L. Olmstead, Richard Sutch, and Gavin Wright, eds. *Historical Statistics of the United States*. Millennial Edition Online. https://hsus.cambridge.org.

Introduction

1. Jesse Buel, *The Farmer's Companion, or, Essays on the Principles and Practice of American Husbandry* (Boston: Marsh, Capen, Lyon, and Webb, 1839), 9; Michael R. Haines, series Aa36-92, *HSUS*; *Historical Statistics of the United States: Colonial Times to 1970* Bicentennial ed. (Washington, DC: US Dept. of Commerce, 1975), 1:134 (series D75-84); Robert A. Margo, "The Labor Force in the Nineteenth Century," in *The Cambridge Economic History of the United States*, vol. 2, *The Long Nineteenth Century*, ed. Stanley L. Engerman and Robert E. Gallman (Cambridge: Cambridge University Press, 2000), 214. Employment in manufacturing was derived by multiplying the proportion of manufacturing labor to nonfarm labor (37%), as given in Margo, by the proportion of the nonfarm labor to total labor (41%), as given in *HSUS*.

2. Abraham Lincoln, *The Collected Works of Abraham Lincoln* (Springfield, IL: Abraham Lincoln Association, 1953), 3:472, http://quod.lib.umich.edu/l/lincoln.

3. The literature is immense and growing every day. For exemplary studies, see Gavin Wright, *The Political Economy of the Cotton South: Households, Markets, and Wealth in the Nineteenth Century* (New York: Norton, 1978); James Oakes, *The Ruling Race: A History of American Slaveholders* (New York: Knopf, 1982); Walter Johnson, *Soul by Soul: Life inside the Antebellum Slave Market* (Cambridge, MA: Harvard University Press, 1999); James L. Huston, *Calculating the Value of the Union: Slavery, Property Rights, and the Economic Origins of the Civil War* (Chapel Hill: University of North Carolina Press, 2003); Adam Rothman, *Slave Country: American Expansion and the Origins of the Deep South* (Cambridge, MA: Harvard University Press, 2005); John Majewski, *Modernizing a Slave Economy: The Economic Vision of the Confederate Nation* (Chapel Hill: University of North Carolina Press, 2009); Brian Schoen, *The Fragile Fabric of Union: Cotton, Federal Politics, and the Global Origins of the Civil War* (Baltimore, MD: Johns Hopkins University Press, 2009); Sven Beckert, *Empire of Cotton: A Global History* (New York: Knopf, 2014); Edward E. Baptist, *The Half Has Never Been Told: Slavery and the Making of American Capitalism* (New York: Basic Books, 2014); Sven Beckert and Seth Rockman, eds., *Slavery's Capitalism: A New History of American Economic Development* (Philadelphia: University of Pennsylvania Press, 2016); Matthew Karp, *This Vast Southern Empire: Slaveholders at the Helm of American Foreign Policy* (Cambridge, MA: Harvard University Press, 2016); Caitlin Rosenthal, *Accounting for Slavery: Masters and Management* (Cambridge, MA: Harvard University Press, 2018). The classic statement of planter premoder-

nity is Eugene D. Genovese, *The Political Economy of Slavery: Studies in the Economy and Society of the Slave South* (Middletown, CT: Wesleyan University Press, 1989).

4. Edwin C. Hagenstein, Sara M. Gregg, and Brian Donahue, eds., *American Georgics: Writings on Farming, Culture, and the Land* (New Haven, CT: Yale University Press, 2011), 1, 15–27. For exceptions to the general reluctance to look at northern farmers' relationship to sectional politics, see James L. Huston, *The British Gentry, the Southern Planter, and the Northern Family Farmer: Agriculture and Sectional Antagonism in North America* (Baton Rouge: Louisiana State University Press, 2015); Adam Wesley Dean, *An Agrarian Republic: Farming, Antislavery Politics, and Nature Parks in the Civil War Era* (Chapel Hill: University of North Carolina Press, 2015). Each of these, however, tends to regard northern farmers within the traditional framework of the independent yeoman. For a critique of historians' use of that framework, see Joyce Appleby, "Commercial Farming and the 'Agrarian Myth' in the Early Republic," *Journal of American History* 68 (Mar. 1982): 833–49.

5. Frederick Jackson Turner, "The Significance of the Frontier in American History," in *Annual Report of the American Historical Association for the Year 1893* (Washington, DC: GPO, 1894), 197–227.

6. Richard Hofstadter, "The Myth of the Happy Yeoman," *American Heritage* 7 (Apr. 1956): http://www.americanheritage.com/content/myth-happy-yeoman.

7. The literature on the market revolution is large; for an introduction, see John Lauritz Larson, *The Market Revolution in America: Liberty, Ambition, and the Eclipse of the Common Good* (Cambridge: Cambridge University Press, 2010). For agriculture, see especially Christopher Clark, *The Roots of Rural Capitalism: Western Massachusetts, 1780–1860* (Ithaca, NY: Cornell University Press, 1990); Sally McMurry, *Transforming Rural Life: Dairying Families and Agricultural Change, 1820–1885* (Baltimore, MD: Johns Hopkins University Press, 1995); Donald Hugh Parkerson, *The Agricultural Transition in New York State: Markets and Migration in Mid-Nineteenth-Century America* (Ames: Iowa State University Press, 1995); Martin Bruegel, *Farm, Shop, Landing: The Rise of a Market Society in the Hudson Valley, 1780–1860* (Durham, NC: Duke University Press, 2002); Thomas Summerhill, *Harvest of Dissent: Agrarianism in Nineteenth-Century New York* (Urbana: University of Illinois Press, 2005); Mary Babson Fuhrer, *A Crisis of Community: The Trials and Transformation of a New England Town, 1815–1848* (Chapel Hill: University of North Carolina Press, 2014).

8. For important exceptions, see Emily Pawley, *The Nature of the Future: Agriculture, Science, and Capitalism in the Antebellum North* (Chicago: University of Chicago Press, 2020); Courtney Fullilove, *The Profit of the Earth: The Global Seeds of American Agriculture* (Chicago: University of Chicago Press, 2017); Alan L. Olmstead and Paul Webb Rhode, *Creating Abundance: Biological Innovation and American Agricultural Development* (Cambridge: Cambridge University Press, 2008); Kate Wersan, "Between the Calendar and the Clock: An Environmental History of American Timekeeping, 1660–1920" (PhD diss., University of Wisconsin–Madison, 2019). For environmental historians, development *is* declension. For good elucidation of this perspective, see Steven Stoll, *Larding the Lean Earth: Soil and Society in Nineteenth-Century America* (New York: Hill and Wang, 2002).

9. Deborah Fink, *Agrarian Women: Wives and Mothers in Rural Nebraska, 1880–1940* (Chapel Hill: University of North Carolina Press, 1992), 11, 28; Kristin L. Hoganson, *The Heartland: An American History* (New York: Penguin Press, 2019), xv–xvii.

10. Abe Kōbō, *The Frontier Within: Essays by Abe Kōbō,* ed. and trans. Richard F. Calichman (New York: Columbia University Press, 2016), 147 (emphasis in original). For an elaboration of this idea, see Yuri Slezkine, *The Jewish Century* (Princeton, NJ: Princeton University Press, 2004), 4–39.

11. For the late 1800s and early 1900s, see Gabriel N. Rosenberg, *The 4-H Harvest: Sexuality and the State in Rural America* (Philadelphia: University of Pennsylvania Press, 2015); Alan L. Olmstead and Paul W. Rhode, *Arresting Contagion: Science, Policy, and Conflicts over Animal Disease Control* (Cambridge, MA: Harvard University Press, 2015); Monica Prasad, *The Land of Too Much: American Abundance and the Paradox of Poverty* (Cambridge, MA: Harvard University Press, 2012); Jess Carr Gilbert, *Planning Democracy: Agrarian Intellectuals and the Intended New Deal* (New Haven, CT: Yale University Press, 2015); Charles Postel, *The Populist Vision* (Oxford: Oxford University Press, 2007); Elisabeth S. Clemens, *The People's Lobby: Organizational Innovation and the Rise of Interest Group Politics in the United States, 1890–1925* (Chicago: University of Chicago Press, 1997); M. Elizabeth Sanders, *Roots of Reform: Farmers, Workers, and the American State, 1877–1917* (Chicago: University of Chicago Press, 1999); Adam D. Sheingate, *The Rise of the Agricultural Welfare State: Institutions and Interest Group Power in the United States, France, and Japan* (Princeton, NJ: Princeton University Press, 2001); Daniel P. Carpenter, *The Forging of Bureaucratic Autonomy: Reputations, Networks, and Policy Innovation in Executive Agencies, 1862–1928* (Princeton, NJ: Princeton University Press, 2001); Kenneth Finegold and Theda Skocpol, *State and Party in America's New Deal* (Madison: University of Wisconsin Press, 1995).

12. For representative works, see Richard L. McCormick, *The Party Period and Public Policy: American Politics from the Age of Jackson to the Progressive Era* (New York: Oxford University Press, 1986); Joel H. Silbey, *The Partisan Imperative: The Dynamics of American Politics before the Civil War* (New York: Oxford University Press, 1985); Stephen Skowronek, *Building a New American State: The Expansion of National Administrative Capacities, 1877–1920* (Cambridge: Cambridge University Press, 1982); Michael F. Holt, *The Political Crisis of the 1850s* (New York: Norton, 1983); Harry L. Watson, *Liberty and Power: The Politics of Jacksonian America* (New York: Hill and Wang, 1990); Michael F. Holt, "The Primacy of Party Reasserted," *Journal of American History* 86 (June 1999): 151–57.

13. For important examples, see Richard R. John, *Spreading the News: The American Postal System from Franklin to Morse* (Cambridge, MA: Harvard University Press, 1995); Mark Wilson, *The Business of Civil War: Military Mobilization and the State, 1861–1865* (Baltimore, MD: Johns Hopkins University Press, 2006); Jerry L. Mashaw, *Creating the Administrative Constitution: The Lost One Hundred Years of American Administrative Law* (New Haven, CT: Yale University Press, 2012); Max M. Edling, *A Hercules in the Cradle: War, Money, and the American State, 1783–1867* (Chicago: University of Chicago Press, 2014); Gautham Rao, *National Duties: Custom Houses and the Making of the American State* (Chicago: University of Chicago Press, 2016).

14. William J. Novak, "The Myth of the 'Weak' American State," *American Historical Review* 113 (June 2008): 752–72; Brian Balogh, *A Government Out of Sight: The Mystery of National Authority in Nineteenth-Century America* (Cambridge: Cambridge University Press, 2009); James T. Sparrow, William J. Novak, and Stephen W. Sawyer, eds., *Boundaries of the State in U.S. History* (Chicago: University of Chicago Press, 2015).

15. Don E. Fehrenbacher, *The Slaveholding Republic: An Account of the United States Government's Relations to Slavery* (Oxford: Oxford University Press, 2002); Robin L. Einhorn, *American Taxation, American Slavery* (Chicago: University of Chicago Press, 2006); Gautham Rao, "The Federal *Posse Comitatus* Doctrine: Slavery, Compulsion, and Statecraft in Mid-Nineteenth-Century America," *Law and History Review* 26 (Spring 2008): 1–56; Ryan A. Quintana, *Making a Slave State: Political Development in Early South Carolina* (Chapel Hill: University of North Carolina Press, 2018); Aaron Hall, "Slaves of the State: Infrastructure and Governance through Slavery in the Antebellum South," *Journal of American History* 106 (June 2019): 19–46.

16. For instance, see James Oakes, "Capitalism and Slavery and the Civil War," *International Labor and Working-Class History*, no. 89 (Spring 2016): 195–220.

17. For the twentieth century, see Nick Cullather, *The Hungry World: America's Cold War Battle against Poverty in Asia* (Cambridge, MA: Harvard University Press, 2010); Daniel Immerwahr, *Thinking Small: The United States and the Lure of Community Development* (Cambridge, MA: Harvard University Press, 2015).

18. Eric Foner, *Free Soil, Free Labor, Free Men: The Ideology of the Republican Party before the Civil War* (Oxford: Oxford University Press, 1995); Eric Foner, *Reconstruction: America's Unfinished Revolution, 1863–1877* (New York: Harper and Row, 1988); David Montgomery, *Beyond Equality: Labor and the Radical Republicans, 1862–1872* (New York: Knopf, 1967); Sean Wilentz, *Chants Democratic: New York City and the Rise of the American Working Class, 1788–1850* (New York: Oxford University Press, 1984); Sven Beckert, *The Monied Metropolis: New York City and the Consolidation of the American Bourgeoisie, 1850–1896* (Cambridge: Cambridge University Press, 2001); Heather Cox Richardson, *The Death of Reconstruction: Race, Labor, and Politics in the Post–Civil War North, 1865–1901* (Cambridge, MA: Harvard University Press, 2001). For an interpretation of Foner's work in line with mine above, see Kate Masur et al., "Eric Foner's 'Reconstruction' at Twenty-Five," *Journal of the Gilded Age and Progressive Era* 14 (Jan. 2015): 15. For a recent corrective, see Charles Postel, *Equality: An American Dilemma, 1866–1896* (New York: Farrar, Straus and Giroux, 2019), chaps. 1–3.

19. *Federalist Papers*, no. 10, The Avalon Project, https://avalon.law.yale.edu/subject_menus/fed.asp.

20. I borrow "anti-politics" and a measure of inspiration from James Ferguson, *The Anti-Politics Machine: "Development," Depoliticization, and Bureaucratic Power in Lesotho* (Cambridge: Cambridge University Press, 1990).

21. Buel, *Farmer's Companion*, 15.

22. Buel, *Farmer's Companion*, 28.

23. Philip Mills Herrington, "The Exceptional Plantation: Slavery, Agricultural Reform, and the Creation of an American Landscape" (PhD diss., University of Virginia, 2012), chap. 1.

24. William Henry Seward, *The Works of William H. Seward*, ed. George E. Baker (Boston: Houghton, Mifflin, 1884), 3:178.

25. See, especially, Sarah T. Phillips, "Antebellum Agricultural Reform, Republican Ideology, and Sectional Tension," *Agricultural History* 74 (Autumn 2000): 799–822. For the important concept of the "Slave Power," see Corey M. Brooks, *Liberty Power: Anti-slavery Third Parties and the Transformation of American Politics* (Chicago: University of

Chicago Press, 2016); Leonard L. Richards, *The Slave Power: The Free North and Southern Domination, 1780–1860* (Baton Rouge: Louisiana State University Press, 2000).

26. Leonard P. Curry, *Blueprint for Modern America: Non-Military Legislation of the First Civil War Congress* (Nashville, TN: Vanderbilt University Press, 1968); Heather Cox Richardson, *The Greatest Nation of the Earth: Republican Economic Policies during the Civil War* (Cambridge, MA: Harvard University Press, 1997); Richard Franklin Bensel, *Yankee Leviathan: The Origins of Central State Authority in America, 1859–1877* (Cambridge: Cambridge University Press, 1990).

27. See, for instance, Foner, *Free Soil, Free Labor, Free Men*, 29–30; James M. McPherson, *Battle Cry of Freedom: The Civil War Era* (New York: Oxford University Press, 1988), 28; Gary W. Gallagher and Joan Waugh, *The American War: A History of the Civil War Era* (State College, PA: Spielvogel, 2015), 9.

28. Lincoln, *Collected Works of Abraham Lincoln*, 3:473–76 (quotations on 473 and 476).

29. Buel, *Farmer's Companion*, 21.

30. Lincoln, *Collected Works of Abraham Lincoln*, 3:474.

31. Lincoln, *Collected Works of Abraham Lincoln*, 3:473.

32. Buel to Seward, Dec. 26, 1838, Seward-UR, reel 7.

33. For apposite reflections on this point, see the discussions in Pawley, *Nature of the Future*; Hoganson, *Heartland*; Rosenberg, *4-H Harvest*; Postel, *Populist Vision*.

In Medias Res

1. "State Fair at Syracuse," *Hudson River Chronicle*, Sept. 18, 1849, 2; "The State Fair," *New-York Daily Tribune*, Sept. 13, 1849, 1.

2. "The State Fair," *Literary Union*, Sept. 22, 1849, 394.

3. "Ninth Annual Show and Fair of the N.Y. State Agricultural Society," *American Agriculturist* 8 (Oct. 1849): 300.

4. Benjamin Gue, *Diary of Benjamin F. Gue in Rural New York and Pioneer Iowa, 1847–1856*, ed. Earle D. Ross (Ames: Iowa State University Press, 1962), 51–52.

5. Letter to the editor, *Robert Merry's Museum* 18 (1849): 187; "Increasing Public Interest in Agriculture," *Working Farmer* 1 (Oct. 1849): 129–30.

6. *Transactions of the New York State Agricultural Society* 9 (Albany: Weed, Parsons & Co., 1850): 12–17, 157; "Close of the Farmers' Fair," *New-York Daily Tribune*, Sept. 17, 1849, 2; "New York State Fair," *Pittsfield (MA) Sun*, Sept. 20, 1849, 2; "The Fair at Syracuse," *Farmer's Cabinet* (Amherst, NH), Sept. 20, 1849, 2; "New-York State Agricultural Society," *Cultivator* 6 (Oct. 1849): 304.

7. *Transactions of the New York State Agricultural Society* 9 (1850): 12.

8. Letter to the editor, *Robert Merry's Museum*, 187.

9. *Transactions of the New York State Agricultural Society* 10 (Albany: Charles Van Benthuysen, 1851): 20.

10. Gue, *Diary of Benjamin F. Gue*, 51–53.

11. "The Farmer's State Fair," *New-York Daily Tribune*, Sept. 14, 1849, 1.

12. Gue, *Diary of Benjamin F. Gue*, 52.

13. "State Fair at Syracuse," 2.

14. "Cattle Show and Fair," *New England Farmer* 1 (Oct. 13, 1849): 340.

15. "Increasing Public Interest in Agriculture," 129–30; "New-York State Agricultural Society," 304–6; "Ninth Annual Show and Fair of the N.Y. State Agricultural Society," 300–302.

16. Letter to the editor, *Robert Merry's Museum*, 187.

17. Alan L. Olmstead and Paul W. Rhode, *Creating Abundance: Biological Innovation and American Agricultural Development* (Cambridge: Cambridge University Press, 2008), 302.

18. "Cattle Show and Fair," 340.

19. "The New York State Fair," *Ohio Cultivator* 5 (Oct. 1, 1849): 291 (emphasis in original).

20. "The Farmer's State Fair," 3 (emphasis in original).

21. Gue, *Diary of Benjamin F. Gue*, 29, 31, 33, 41, 48.

22. "Fair of the State Agricultural Society," *Genesee Farmer* 10 (Oct. 1849): 228.

23. Gue, *Diary of Benjamin F. Gue*, 53; "The State Fair," *New-York Daily Tribune*, 1; *Transactions of the New York State Agricultural Society* 9 (1850): 14.

24. "The New York State Fair," 291; "New-York State Agricultural Society," 304.

25. "Close of the Farmers' Fair," 2.

26. "The State Fair," *New-York Daily Tribune*, 1; "State Fair at Syracuse," 2; "Domestic Notices," *Magazine of Horticulture* 15 (Oct. 1849): 465–68.

27. "Ninth Annual Show and Fair of the N.Y. State Agricultural Society," 300.

28. *Albany Evening Journal*, Sept. 14, 1849, 2; "The State Fair," *Literary Union*, 394.

29. William M. Reser, "Indiana's Second State Fair," *Indiana Magazine of History* 32 (March 1936): 30–31.

30. *Annual Report of the Transactions of the Pennsylvania State Agricultural Society* 1 (1851–54): 36.

31. David P. Jackson, ed., *The Colonel's Diary: Journals Kept before and during the Civil War by the Late Colonel Oscar L. Jackson, Sometime Commander of the 63rd Regiment O. V. I.* (1922), Internet Archive, https://archive.org/details/colonelsdiaryjouoojack, 11.

32. Albert Lowther Demaree, *The American Agricultural Press, 1819–1860* (New York: Columbia University Press, 1941), 202.

33. Ariel Ron, "Developing the Country: 'Scientific Agriculture' and the Roots of the Republican Party" (PhD diss., University of California, Berkeley, 2012), 238–40.

34. "New-York State Agricultural Society," 304.

Chapter 1 · The Limits of Patrician Agricultural Reform

1. "Communication," *Connecticut Journal*, July 12, 1810, 3.

2. Kariann Akemi Yokota, *Unbecoming British: How Revolutionary America Became a Postcolonial Nation* (New York: Oxford University Press, 2010).

3. George Washington to Alfred Young, Aug. 6, 1786, in Franklin Knight, ed., *Letters on Agriculture from His Excellency, George Washington, President of the United States, to Arthur Young, Esq., F.R.S., and Sir John Sinclair, Bart., M.P.* (Washington, DC: Published by the Editor, 1847), 16; "Another Sheep Shearing," *Poulson's American Daily Advertiser* (Philadelphia), Nov. 23, 1810, 2. See also Tamara Plakins Thornton, *Cultivating Gentlemen: The Meaning of Country Life among the Boston Elite, 1785–1860* (New Haven, CT: Yale University Press, 1989), 27–29.

4. *Memoirs of the Philadelphia Society for Promoting Agriculture, Containing Communi-*

cations on Various Subjects in Husbandry & Rural Affairs, to Which Is Added, a Statistical Account of the Schuylkill Permanent Bridge, vol. 1 (Philadelphia: Jane Aitken, 1808), xxvi.

5. Samuel Miller, *A Brief Retrospect of the Eighteenth Century: Part First*, vol. 2 (New York: T. and J. Swords, 1803), 262; Simon Baatz, *"Venerate the Plough": A History of the Philadelphia Society for Promoting Agriculture, 1785–1985* (Philadelphia: Philadelphia Society for Promoting Agriculture, 1985), 5–6; Ulysses Prentiss Hedrick, *A History of Agriculture in the State of New York* (Albany: New York State Agriculture Society, 1933), 113–15.

6. Joseph F. Kett, *The Pursuit of Knowledge under Difficulties: From Self-Improvement to Adult Education in America, 1750–1990* (Stanford, CA: Stanford University Press, 1994), 105.

7. Fredrik Albritton Jonsson, *Enlightenment's Frontier: The Scottish Highlands and the Origins of Environmentalism* (New Haven, CT: Yale University Press, 2013), 44.

8. David Hackett Fischer, "John Beale Bordley, Daniel Boorstin, and the American Enlightenment," *Journal of Southern History* 28 (Aug. 1962): 339; Olive Moore Gambrill, "John Beale Bordley and the Early Years of the Philadelphia Agricultural Society," *Pennsylvania Magazine of History and Biography* 66 (Oct. 1942): 410–39; Elizabeth Bordley Gibson, *Biographical Sketches of the Bordley Family, of Maryland* (Philadelphia: Henry B. Ashmead, 1865), 82–87; J. B. Bordley, *Essays and Notes on Husbandry and Rural Affairs* (Philadelphia: Budd and Bartram, 1801), 387–96.

9. Baatz, *"Venerate the Plough,"* 12; Joseph Whitla Stinson, "Opinions of Richard Peters (1781–1817)," *University of Pennsylvania Law Review and American Law Register* 70 (Mar. 1922): 185–97; Carol E. Brier, "Tending Our Vines: From the Correspondence and Writings of Richard Peters and John Jay," *Pennsylvania History* 80 (Jan. 2013): 85–111.

10. Donald Benedict Marti, "Agrarian Thought and Agricultural Progress: The Endeavor for Agricultural Improvement in New England and New York, 1815–1840" (PhD diss., University of Wisconsin, 1966), 12; Stanley Elkins and Eric McKitrick, *The Age of Federalism* (New York: Oxford University Press, 1993), 623–26.

11. R. O. Bausman, J. A. Munroe, and James Tilton, "James Tilton's Notes on the Agriculture of Delaware in 1788," *Agricultural History* 20 (July 1946): 177.

12. Baatz, *"Venerate the Plough,"* 13–15; Lucius F. Ellsworth, "The Philadelphia Society for the Promotion of Agriculture and Agricultural Reform, 1785–1793," *Agricultural History* 42 (June 1968): 192–93; Frederick B. Tolles, "George Logan and the Agricultural Revolution," *Proceedings of the American Philosophical Society* 95 (Dec. 1951): 591; Frederick B. Tolles, "George Logan, Agrarian Democrat: A Survey of His Writings," *Pennsylvania Magazine of History and Biography* 75 (July 1951): 267–74.

13. Quoted in Tolles, "George Logan, Agrarian Democrat," 265.

14. "Constitution of the Philadelphia County Society for the Promotion of Agriculture and Domestic Manufactures," *American Museum* 5 (Feb. 1789): 161.

15. *Memoirs of the Philadelphia Society for Promoting Agriculture*, 1:xxi–xxx.

16. Baatz, *"Venerate the Plough,"* 1–20; Ellsworth, "The Philadelphia Society for the Promotion of Agriculture and Agricultural Reform, 1785–1793," 192–94.

17. Robert H. Wiebe, *The Opening of American Society: From the Adoption of the Constitution to the Eve of Disunion* (New York: Vintage Books, 1985), 197; Jeffrey L. Pasley, *"The Tyranny of Printers": Newspaper Politics in the Early American Republic* (Charlottesville: University Press of Virginia, 2001), 302; Andrew Shankman, *Crucible of American*

Democracy: The Struggle to Fuse Egalitarianism and Capitalism in Jeffersonian Pennsylvania (Lawrence: University Press of Kansas, 2004), 97, 143. See also the aims and officers of the proposed American Board of Agriculture in "Address from the American Board of Agriculture," *National Intelligencer*, Mar. 2, 1803, 1; "American Board of Agriculture," *Farmer's Cabinet*, Mar. 17, 1803, 2.

18. Carroll W. Pursell, "E. I. Du Pont, Don Pedro, and the Introduction of Merino Sheep into the United States, 1801: A Document," *Agricultural History* 33 (Apr. 1959): 86–88; Carroll W. Pursell, "E. I. Du Pont and the Merino Mania in Delaware, 1805–1815," *Agricultural History* 36 (Apr. 1962): 91–100.

19. David Humphreys, "Dissertation on the Merino Breed of Sheep," in *The Miscellaneous Works of David Humphreys* (New York: T. and J. Swords, 1804), 353.

20. *Daily Advertiser* (New York) Sept. 11, 1802, 3; *Columbian Advertiser* (Alexandria, VA), Sept. 17, 1802, 2; *New-Jersey Journal*, Sept. 21, 1802, 1; *Massachusetts Spy*, Sept. 22, 1802, 4; *Republican Gazetteer* (Boston), Sept. 22, 1802, 1; *Eastern Herald* (Portland, ME), Sept. 27, 1802, 2; *Otsego Herald* (Otsego, NY), Nov. 18, 1802, 1.

21. Quoted in Mark Mastromarino, "Fair Visions: Elkanah Watson (1758–1842) and the Modern American Agricultural Fair" (PhD diss., College of William and Mary, 2002), 170.

22. Haines to Richard Hartshorne, Oct. 21, 1810, Haines-APS, box 15, folder 137.

23. Ezra Ayers Carman, Hubert A. Heath, and John Minto, *Special Report on the History and Present Condition of the Sheep Industry of the United States* (Washington, DC: GPO, 1892), 350–51.

24. Haines to John Smith Haines, Aug. 31, 1813, Haines-APS, box 15, folder 136.

25. "Comments on Farmer's Register—No. 11," *Farmer's Register* 3 (June 1835): 116.

26. Mastromarino, "Fair Visions," 289. See also, George Steuart Mackenzie, *A Treatise on the Diseases and Management of Sheep* (Edinburgh: A. Constable, 1809), which appeared in an American edition the following year; Caleb Hillier Parry, *An Essay on the Nature, Produce, Origin, and Extension of the Merino Breed of Sheep* (London: William Bulmer and Co., 1807), a copy of which, now part of Loganian Library housed at the Library Company of Philadelphia, bears the inscription, "Dr. Logan from the author"; and for an American compilation of Parry essays, see *Antidote to the Merino-Mania Now Progressing through the United States: Or, the Value of the Merino Breed, Placed by Observation and Experience, upon a Proper Basis* (Philadelphia: J. & A. Y. Humphreys, 1810).

27. Robert R. Livingston, *Essay on Sheep* (New York: T. and J. Swords, 1809), 3–4, 9.

28. Livingston, *Essay on Sheep*, 9, 138.

29. *The Constitution of the Merino Society of the Middle States of North America* (Philadelphia: Printed for the Merino Society, 1811), 4, 7.

30. "Sheep-Shearing," *Connecticut Mirror* (Hartford), July 2, 1810, 3. See also Arthur H. Cole, "Agricultural Crazes: A Neglected Chapter in American Economic History," *American Economic Review* 16 (Dec. 1926): 625–26.

31. Alan L. Olmstead and Paul Webb Rhode, *Creating Abundance: Biological Innovation and American Agricultural Development* (Cambridge: Cambridge University Press, 2008), 297.

32. "Dogs," Monticello, accessed Dec. 9, 2016, https://www.monticello.org/site/house-and-gardens/dogs.

33. For examples of petitions, see McAllister-LCP, boxes 17 and 19, item nos. 7351 F

65, 7351 F 95, and 7361 F 44; draft petition, CCAS-CCHS, Jan. 13, 1820, box 2; constitution and minutes, ASNC-HSD, Jan. 14, 1836, and June 2, 1838; *Ohio Cultivator* 4
(Feb. 1, 1848): 19. For changing laws, see George M. Stroud, *A Digest of the Laws Pennsylvania: From the Year One Thousand Seven Hundred, to the Thirteenth Day of October,
One Thousand Eight Hundred and Forty,* 6th ed. (Philadelphia: M'Carty & Davis, 1841),
295–300. For the issue's persistence, see "Dogs and Dog Laws," *Report of the U.S. Commissioner of Agriculture* (Washington, DC: GPO, 1863), 450–63; J. F. Wilson, *The Sheep-
Killing Dog,* Farmer's Bulletin 935 (Washington, DC: USDA Division of Publication,
1918).

34. "No Dog Tax—Poetic Remonstrance," *Ohio Cultivator* (Apr. 1, 1849): 101. For
comments on dog taxes, see *Reporter* (Washington, PA), Jan. 15, 1821, 3 and Feb. 19,
1821, 1; *Genesee Farmer* 9 (Mar. 2, 1839): 67; *Ohio Cultivator* 5 (Apr. 1, 1849): 101, and 7
(Jan. 1, 1851): 6; *Maine Farmer* 28 (Aug. 23, 1860): 2. The issue has been studied in the
context of Georgian England: see Lynn Festa, "Person, Animal, Thing: The 1796 Dog
Tax and the Right to Superfluous Things," *Eighteenth-Century Life* 33 (Mar. 20, 2009):
1–44; Ingrid H. Tague, "Eighteenth-Century English Debates on a Dog Tax," *Historical
Journal* 51 (2008): 901–20.

35. Mark Mastromarino, "Fair-Weather Friends: Merino Sheep and the Origins of the
Modern American Agricultural Fair," in *New England's Creatures: 1400–1900,* ed. Peter
Benes, Dublin Seminar for New England Folklife Annual Proceedings (Boston: Boston
University Press, 1993), 99–101; Thornton, *Cultivating Gentlemen,* 29; Rodney C. Loehr,
"The Influence of English Agriculture on American Agriculture, 1775–1825," *Agricultural
History* 11 (Jan. 1937): 5.

36. "Clermont Sheep-Shearing," *American Citizen* (New York), July 3, 1809, 2.

37. Quoted in Mastromarino, "Fair Visions," 189.

38. "Clermont Merion Sheep Shearing," *Columbian* (New York), June 20, 1810, 2;
"Arlington Sheep Shearing," *American Watchman and Delaware Republican* (Wilmington), May 15, 1811, 4.

39. Donald Ratcliffe, "The Right to Vote and the Rise of Democracy, 1787–1828,"
Journal of the Early Republic 33 (2013): 224, 230, 239. See also the characterization of
Livingston's meetings with Thomas Jefferson as a kind of "diplomacy" between "two
great powers," in Elkins and McKitrick, *Age of Federalism,* 241.

40. "Arlington Sheep Shearing," *Farmer's Repository* (Charles Town, [West] Virginia),
May 18, 1810, 2.

41. "On the Encouragement Given to the Manufactory of Fine Cloth," *Archives of
Useful Knowledge* 1 (July 1, 1809): 17–20. For the text of the relevant laws and the premium winners, see *Transactions of the Society for the Promotion of Useful Arts, in the State
of New-York* (Albany, NY: Websters and Skinners, 1814), 3:225–50. For the yearly expenditures entailed by the premiums, which exceeded $20,000 in the period from 1809 to
1815, see Henry S. Randall, *Fine Wool Sheep Husbandry* (Albany, NY: C. Van Benthuysen, 1862), 31.

42. John Lauritz Larson, *Internal Improvement: National Public Works and the Promise
of Popular Government in the Early United States* (Chapel Hill: University of North Carolina Press, 2001), chap. 1.

43. Elkanah Watson, *History of Agricultural Societies, on the Modern Berkshire System:
From the Year 1807, to the Establishment of the State Board of Agriculture in Albany, January*

10, 1820 (Albany, NY: D. Steele, 1820), 119–20; Donald B. Marti, *To Improve the Soil and the Mind: Agricultural Societies, Journals, and Schools in the Northeastern States, 1791–1865* (Ann Arbor, MI: Published for the Agricultural History Society and the Dept. of Communication Arts, New York State College of Agriculture and Life Sciences, Cornell University, by University Microfilms International, 1979), 26; Mastromarino, "Fair Visions," 71–72; John L. Brooke, *Columbia Rising: Civil Life on the Upper Hudson from the Revolution to the Age of Jackson* (Chapel Hill: University of North Carolina Press, 2010), 243, 250; Lawrence A. Peskin, *Manufacturing Revolution: The Intellectual Origins of Early American Industry* (Baltimore, MD: Johns Hopkins University Press, 2003), 128–29.

44. Mastromarino, "Fair-Weather Friends," 95.

45. Letter to the editor by "A Friend to Textiles," *Sun* (Pittsfield, MA), Jan. 30, 1808, 4.

46. Mastromarino, "Fair Visions," 158–90.

47. Mastromarino, "Fair Visions," 291.

48. Edward Roberts Barnsley, *Agricultural Societies of Bucks County, Pa.* (Doylestown, PA: Edward W. Schlechter, 1940), 5–13; Baatz, *"Venerate the Plough,"* 39.

49. *Agricultural Museum* 1 (1811): 172, 353, 366; *Agricultural Museum* 2 (1812): 328, 335; "Columbian Agricultural Society," *National Intelligencer*, Nov. 22, 1810, 3; "Columbian Agricultural Society," *Berkshire Reporter*, July 4, 1810, 3; Claribel R. Barnett, "'The Agricultural Museum': An Early American Agricultural Periodical," *Agricultural History* 2 (Apr. 1928): 99–102.

50. Mastromarino, "Fair Visions," chap. 5, especially 182–87.

51. Quoted in Marti, "Agrarian Thought and Agricultural Progress," 29.

52. Donald B. Marti, "Early Agricultural Societies in New York: The Foundations of Improvement," *New York History* 48 (Oct. 1967): 318–19; David Gary, "Mundane Radicalism: Enlightenment Thinking and Free Labor Politics on Rufus King's Long Island Farm" (unpublished manuscript in author's possession), 40.

53. MSPA, *Centennial Year*, 31–32; Thornton, *Cultivating Gentlemen*, 95–103; Baatz, *"Venerate the Plough,"* 39–40; Mastromarino, "Fair Visions," 296.

54. Barnsley, *Agricultural Societies of Bucks County, Pa.*, 18; Robert Leslie Jones, *History of Agriculture in Ohio to 1880* (Kent, OH: Kent State University Press, 1983), 274–80; Marti, "Agrarian Thought and Agricultural Progress," 108, 120–21.

55. Charles P. Daly, "Anniversary Address before the American Institute, 'on the Origin and History of Institutions for the Promotion of the Useful Arts,' Delivered at the Hall of the New York Historical Society, on the 11th of November, 1863," in *Report of the American Institute of the City of New York for the Years 1863, '64* (Albany: Comstock & Cassidy, 1864), 68; Baatz, *"Venerate the Plough,"* 44.

56. W. H. Brewer, "Agricultural Societies, What They Are and What They Have Done," in *Annual Report of the Secretary of the Connecticut Board of Agriculture* 14 (Hartford, 1881), 107.

57. "Cattle Show and Fair," *Connecticut Courant*, Sept. 18, 1821, 3.

58. Wayne Caldwell Neely, *The Agricultural Fair* (New York: Columbia University Press, 1935), 3–23, 155–84.

59. John Iverson, "Introduction to Forum on Emulation in France, 1750–1800," *Eighteenth-Century Studies* 36 (Winter 2003): 218.

60. John Shovelin, "Emulation in Eighteenth-Century French Economic Thought," *Eighteenth-Century Studies* 36 (Winter 2003): 224–30.

61. Quoted in Jay Fliegelman, *Declaring Independence: Jefferson, Natural Language, and the Culture of Performance* (Stanford, CA: Stanford University Press, 1993), 180.

62. J. M. Opal, "Exciting Emulation: Academies and the Transformation of the Rural North, 1780s–1820s," *Journal of American History* 91 (Sept. 2004): 445–70.

63. "Address, &c.," *American Farmer* 1 (Jan. 14, 1820): 329.

64. Quoted in Marti, "Agrarian Thought and Agricultural Progress," 98.

65. *Centennial Year, 1792–1892, of the Massachusetts Society for Promoting Agriculture* (Salem, MA: Salem Observer Office, 1892), 82.

66. *Centennial Year,* 34–35.

67. *Transactions of the New Hampshire State Agricultural Society* 1 (Concord, NH: Butterfield and Hill, 1853): 14–20; Marti, *To Improve the Soil and the Mind,* 28–30; Marti, "Early Agricultural Societies in New York," 314–21.

68. Baatz, *"Venerate the Plough,"* 38, 40.

69. Marti, "Agrarian Thought and Agricultural Progress," 138–39; Marti, "Early Agricultural Societies in New York," 321–22; Marti, *To Improve the Soil and the Mind,* 28–30.

70. *Memoirs of the Board of Agriculture of the State of New York,* vol. 2 (Albany: Packard & Van Benthuysen, 1823), preface with unnumbered pages.

71. Marti, "Agrarian Thought and Agricultural Progress," 146–48; Marti, "Early Agricultural Societies in New York," 323–24; Thomas Summerhill, *Harvest of Dissent: Agrarianism in Nineteenth-Century New York* (Urbana: University of Illinois Press, 2005), 34.

72. Pennsylvania Agricultural Society, *Memoirs of the Pennsylvania Agricultural Society* (Philadelphia: J. S. Skinner, 1824), preface with unnumbered pages.

73. Baatz, *"Venerate the Plough,"* 42–46.

74. Marti, "Agrarian Thought and Agricultural Progress," 108–17 (quotation on 112); *Transactions of the New Hampshire State Agricultural Society* 1 (1853): 29.

75. Marti, "Agrarian Thought and Agricultural Progress," 101–2. See also Thornton, *Cultivating Gentlemen,* 70, 99–104.

76. Volume recording premiums planned and awarded for each fair, MAS-CFL, series 2, item 3.

77. Mary Summers, "Conflicting Visions" (unpublished doctoral dissertation manuscript in author's possession), chap. 2.

78. Marti, *To Improve the Soil and the Mind,* 14. See also Neely, *Agricultural Fair,* 69–71; Jones, *History of Agriculture in Ohio,* 274–80.

Chapter 2 · Agricultural Reform as a State-Building Social Movement

1. Lewis F. Allen, *Address Delivered before the New-York State Agricultural Society; at the Capitol, in the City of Albany, on the Evening of the 18th January, 1849* (Albany: Weed, Parsons and Company, 1849), 5, 7, 12.

2. Cong. Globe, 32nd Cong., 1st Sess., appendix, 494; Albert Lowther Demaree, *The American Agricultural Press, 1819–1860* (New York: Columbia University Press, 1941), 18; Donald B. Marti, *To Improve the Soil and the Mind: Agricultural Societies, Journals, and Schools in the Northeastern States, 1791–1865* (Ann Arbor, MI: University Microfilms International, 1979), 162; Clarence H. Danhof, *Change in Agriculture: The Northern United States, 1820–1870* (Cambridge, MA: Harvard University Press, 1969), 56–57; Emily Pawley, "'The Balance-Sheet of Nature': Calculating the New York Farm, 1820–1860"

(PhD diss., University of Pennsylvania, 2009), 62–63; Jeremy Fisher, "Improving the Soil and Mind: The Geography of *The Cultivator*" (MA thesis, Pennsylvania State University, 2008), 37; Gilbert M. Tucker, *American Agricultural Journals: An Historical Sketch* (Albany, NY: Privately printed, 1909). For examples of journal mergers, see *Cultivator* 7 (Jan. 1840): 5; *Farm Journal and Progressive Farmer* 6 (Jan. 1856): 29.

3. Solon Robinson, *Solon Robinson, Pioneer and Agriculturist: Selected Writings*, ed. Herbert Anthony Kellar (Indianapolis: Indiana Historical Bureau, 1936), 1:31; Danhof, *Change in Agriculture*, 58; *DAB*, 10:231.

4. See, for example, *Semi-Weekly Eagle* (Brattleboro, VT), Oct. 12, 1847, 2.

5. *Germantown (PA) Telegraph*, Jan. 30, 1850, 4.

6. "Our Agricultural Department," *Puritan Recorder* 34 (Sept. 27, 1849): 154.

7. Danhof, *Change in Agriculture*, 55; Pawley, "'The Balance-Sheet of Nature,'" 58–61; James Green, "Henry Carey Baird and Company, America's First Technical Publishers," *PASCAL News* 1 (Sept. 1991): 7–9.

8. Claribel R. Barnett, "'The Agricultural Museum': An Early American Agricultural Periodical," *Agricultural History* 2 (Apr. 1928): 99–102.

9. *Centennial Year, 1792–1892, of the Massachusetts Society for Promoting Agriculture* (Salem: Salem Observer Office, 1892), 7, 28–32; *Inquiries by the Agricultural Society* (Boston: Young & Minns, 1800); Marti, *To Improve the Soil and the Mind*, 11; "Preface," *Massachusetts Agricultural Journal* 3 (Nov. 1813): iii–v.

10. Quoted in Tamara Plakins Thornton, *Cultivating Gentlemen: The Meaning of Country Life among the Boston Elite, 1785–1860* (New Haven, CT: Yale University Press, 1989), 137 (emphasis in original).

11. I here use a contracted version of the editor-biography method employed in Jeffrey L. Pasley, *"The Tyranny of Printers": Newspaper Politics in the Early American Republic* (Charlottesville: University Press of Virginia, 2001), 13, 320, and throughout. The accounts of individual agricultural editors in the succeeding paragraphs are based on the following sources: *ANB, DAB*; Demaree, *American Agricultural Press, 1819–1860*; Marti, *To Improve the Soil and the Mind*; Donald Benedict Marti, "Agrarian Thought and Agricultural Progress: The Endeavor for Agricultural Improvement in New England and New York, 1815–1840" (PhD diss., University of Wisconsin, 1966); Donald B. Marti, "Agricultural Journalism and the Diffusion of Knowledge: The First Half-Century in America," *Agricultural History* 54 (Jan. 1980): 28–37; George F. Lemmer, "Early Agricultural Editors and Their Farm Philosophies," *Agricultural History* 31 (Oct. 1957): 3–22; Tucker, *American Agricultural Journals*. Additional sources are noted where relevant.

12. Allen, *Address Delivered before the New-York State Agricultural Society*, 7. For Southwick's libel suit, see Pasley, *"The Tyranny of Printers,"* 279.

13. In addition to sources cited above, see Jesse Buel, *Jesse Buel, Agricultural Reformer: Selections from His Writings*, ed. Harry J. Carman (New York: Columbia University Press, 1947).

14. There are few secondary sources on Tucker besides his entry in *DAB*; for obituaries, see *Maine Farmer* 41 (Feb. 8, 1873): 1; *Massachusetts Ploughman* 32 (Feb. 8, 1873): 1; for an early biographical sketch, see "Luther Tucker, Esq.," *New England Farmer* 7 (Jan. 1855): 28.

15. *Farmer's Monthly Visitor* 1 (Dec. 20, 1839): 184; "Death of Samuel Sands," *American Farmer* 10 (1891): 175; for Brown, see *DAB*.

16. *New York Farmer* 1 (Jan. 1828): 1; *Ohio Cultivator* 1 (Jan. 1, 1845): 1; *Cultivator* 2 (Mar. 1845): 86.

17. Thornton, *Cultivating Gentlemen*, 43–55; Mark Mastromarino, "Fair Visions: Elkanah Watson (1758–1842) and the Modern American Agricultural Fair" (PhD diss., College of William and Mary, 2002), 82–89; Marti, "Agrarian Thought and Agricultural Progress," vi–viii, 15–16; Demaree, *American Agricultural Press, 1819–1860*, 78–79.

18. C. A. Bayly, *Imperial Meridian: The British Empire and the World, 1780–1830* (London: Longman, 1989), 121–26, 155–60.

19. *American Farmer* 1 (May 1819): 64; *Farmer's Monthly Visitor* 1 (Jan. 15, 1839): 1.

20. Harold T. Pinkett, "The 'American Farmer,' a Pioneer Agricultural Journal, 1819–1834," *Agricultural History* 24 (July 1950): 146–51; Demaree, *American Agricultural Press, 1819–1860*, 23–38.

21. Marti, *To Improve the Soil and the Mind*, 128, 148; Demaree, *American Agricultural Press, 1819–1860*, 46–47, 57, 143; Richard A. Wines, *Fertilizer in America: From Waste Recycling to Resource Exploitation* (Philadelphia: Temple University Press, 1985), 99–102.

22. *Cultivator* 4 (Mar. 1837): 28; *Practical Farmer* (Mechanicsburg, PA) 1 (Sept. 1838): 266; Fisher, "Improving the Soil and Mind," 51–60.

23. I draw here on Benedict R. Anderson, *Imagined Communities: Reflections on the Origin and Spread of Nationalism* (London: Verso, 1991); Michael Warner, *The Letters of the Republic: Publication and the Public Sphere in Eighteenth-Century America* (Cambridge, MA: Harvard University Press, 1990); Michael Warner, *Publics and Counterpublics* (Cambridge, MA: MIT Press, 2002); David M. Henkin, *City Reading: Written Words and Public Spaces in Antebellum New York* (New York: Columbia University Press, 1998); David M. Henkin, *The Postal Age: The Emergence of Modern Communications in Nineteenth-Century America* (Chicago: University of Chicago Press, 2006).

24. *Practical Farmer* (Mechanicsburg, PA) 1 (Nov. 1837): 27. Members of the publishing committee were identified in the 1840 and 1850 manuscript census schedules for Silver Springs Township, Cumberland County, PA.

25. Pawley, "'The Balance-Sheet of Nature,'" 59.

26. Sally McMurry, "Who Read the Agricultural Journals? Evidence from Chenango County, New York, 1839–1865," *Agricultural History* 63 (Autumn 1989): 1–18; Fisher, "Improving the Soil and Mind," 66–127.

27. Similar practices are documented in Pawley, "'The Balance-Sheet of Nature,'" 64.

28. Thomas J. Aldred Papers, MPP-HSP. Jefferson's article appears in *Transactions of the American Philosophical Society* 4 (1799): 313–22. For similar practices, see "John G. Edge Daybook and Ledger, 1832–1883" (Ms.76704), Chester County Historical Society, West Chester, PA.

29. Lawrence M. Colfelt, "Autobiography by Rev. L. M. Colfelt," *Gazette* (Bedford, PA), Nov. 5, 1926; Charles Colfelt ledger and miscellaneous accounts, 1844–57, MPP-HSP.

30. *Cultivator* 1 (Feb. 1844): 41; 2 (Mar. 1845): 89; 4 (Mar. 1847): 91; 6 (Dec. 1849): 381; *Pittsfield Sun*, Feb. 8, 1844, 4; *Annual Report of the Commissioner of Patents, Agriculture* (1846): 186.

31. "Commerce of Knowledge," *Farmer's Monthly Visitor* 1 (Aug. 20, 1839): 124.

32. Donald B. Marti, "Early Agricultural Societies in New York: The Foundations of Improvement," *New York History* 48 (Oct. 1967): 324–27 (quotation on 326); *Journal of*

the Assembly of the State of New-York, 64th sess. (Albany: Thurlow Weed, 1841), 740; Marti, *To Improve the Soil and the Mind*, 49–58; *Transactions of the New York State Agricultural Society* 1 (Albany: T. Weed, 1842): 5–15.

33. *Journal of the Assembly of the State of New-York*, 64th sess. (1841), 740; *Transactions of the New York State Agricultural Society* 1 (1842): 5–15; Marti, *To Improve the Soil and the Mind*, 49–58; Allen, *Address Delivered before the New-York State Agricultural Society*, 7–12.

34. Marti, "Early Agricultural Societies in New York," 324, 326–27.

35. On this point, see Ronald P. Formisano, *The Transformation of Political Culture: Massachusetts Parties, 1790s–1840s* (New York: Oxford University Press, 1983), 271.

36. Marti, "Early Agricultural Societies in New York," 324–28 (quotation on 327); Marti, *To Improve the Soil and the Mind*, 49–58, 142–43. For the Whig leanings of reformers in general, see Pawley, "'The Balance-Sheet of Nature,'" 42; Mary Summers, "Conflicting Visions" (unpublished doctoral dissertation manuscript in author's possession), chap. 3.

37. Allen to Seward, Nov. 16, 1838, Seward-UR, reel 6. For Allen as "Ulmus," see Marti, *To Improve the Soil and the Mind*, 50.

38. *Documents of the Assembly of the State of New-York, Sixty-First Session* (Albany: E. Croswell, 1838), 4:1 (doc. no. 161, Feb. 10, 1838). For Allen's favoring of internal improvements, see the letter cited above and Allen to King, Nov. 10, 1860, King-NYHS, box 2. Allen's vision for the west is laid out in "Letter from Ulmus," *Genesee Farmer* 7 (Jan. 14, 1837): 12.

39. Allen to Seward, Nov. 16, 1838, Seward-UR, reel 6.

40. It is worth noting that in 1836 Buel had been the Whig candidate for governor in a campaign all had understood to be doomed. With Martin Van Buren heading the presidential ticket, the Democrats swept New York easily.

41. Charles Strong, "Patronage to Agriculture," *Cultivator* 5 (Oct. 1838): 141; Buel to Seward, Dec. 26, 1838, Seward-UR, reel 7 (emphasis in original).

42. Anderson, *Imagined Communities*, 35.

43. "Serious Suggestions Addressed to the Interests and Honor of Farmers," *Cultivator* 5 (Dec. 1838): 169; Allen to Seward, Nov. 16, 1838, Seward-UR, reel 6; "Letter from Ulmus," *Genesee Farmer* 7 (Jan. 14, 1837): 12 (emphasis in original).

44. William Henry Seward, *The Works of William H. Seward*, ed. George E. Baker (Boston: Houghton, Mifflin, 1884), 3:185–86.

45. "Ohio State Agricultural Convention," *Ohio State Journal and Register*, Jan. 8, 1839, 1.

46. Robert Leslie Jones, *History of Agriculture in Ohio to 1880* (Kent, OH: Kent State University Press, 1983), 280–88; *Journal of the House of Representatives of the State of Ohio* 44 (Columbus: C. Scott and Co., 1846): 40, 46, 57, 64–65, 82, 90, 103–4, 112, 117, 123, 129–30, 141, 148–49, 159, 167, 176, 183–84, 192, 208, 218–19, 227, 240, 245, 267, 280, 292, 302, 326, 341, 351, 359, 383, 514.

47. "Bill for the Encouragement of Agriculture," *Weekly Ohio State Journal*, Jan. 24, 1846, 2.

48. *Annual Report of the Ohio State Board of Agriculture* 21 (Columbus: Richard Nevins, 1867): 476–77; *Acts of a General Nature and Local Laws and Joint Resolutions Passed by the General Assembly of the State of Ohio* 53 (Columbus: Statesman Steam Press, 1856): 208; Jones, *Agriculture in Ohio*, 288–290.

49. *Ohio Cultivator* 7 (Apr. 1, 1845): 53.

50. For general accounts, see Demaree, *American Agricultural Press, 1819–1860,* 199–200; Fred Kniffen, "The American Agricultural Fair: The Pattern," *Annals of the Association of American Geographers* 39 (Dec. 1949): 264–82.

51. "List of Committees and Premiums for the Cattle Show and Exhibition of the Middlesex Agricultural Society, at Concord, on Wednesday, September 28th, 1859" (Concord, MA: Benjamin Tolman, 1859), MAS-CFL, series 5, folder 4; for the number of members, see the handwritten report of May 27, 1857, series 2, item 5.

52. Eli T. Hoyt to Rufus Hoyt, May 24, 1841 and Oct. 7, 1841, FCAS-FMHC, folder 5, series A; *Public Acts Passed by the General Assembly of the State of Connecticut in the Years 1839, 1840, 1841, 1842 and 1843* (Hartford: John L. Boswell, 1845), 6–8.

53. "The County Fair," *Semi-Weekly Eagle* (Brattleboro, VT), Oct. 6, 1851, 2; "Our County Fair," Oct. 7, 1852, 2; 1850 federal population census, 36.

54. Catherine E. Kelly, "'The Consummation of Rural Prosperity and Happiness': New England Agricultural Fairs and the Construction of Class and Gender, 1810–1860," *American Quarterly* 49 (Sept. 1997): 582.

55. William Joseph Buck, *History of Montgomery County within the Schuylkill Valley* (Norristown, PA: E. L. Acker, 1859), 93–94. For other examples, see *A History of Jefferson County in the State of New York, from the Earliest Period to the Present Time* (Albany: Joel Munsell, 1854), 401–8; William T. Martin, *History of Franklin County* (Columbus, OH: Follett, Forster & Co., 1858), 96–104.

56. Jean M. O'Brien, *Firsting and Lasting: Writing Indians out of Existence in New England* (Minneapolis: University of Minnesota Press, 2010).

57. Haines to Jane [Haines], Oct. 17, 1830, Haines-APS, box 15.

58. Jochen Welsch, "'If the Worcester Boys Want to See Cattle Haul, They Must Come to Kennebec': The Trial of Working Oxen as an Expression of Regional Agricultural Values, 1818–1860," in *New England's Creatures: 1400–1900,* ed. Peter Benes (Boston: Boston University, 1993), 85–94.

59. Volume of manuscript records, mostly reports of fairs, MAS-CFL, series 2, item 5.

60. Kelly, "'The Consummation of Rural Prosperity and Happiness,'" 580; Gabriel Rosenberg, "Fetishizing Family Farms," *Boston Globe,* Apr. 10, 2016, https://www.boston globe.com/ideas/2016/04/09/fetishizing-family-farms/NJszoKdCSQWaq2XBw7kvIL /story.html.

61. "Ninth Annual Show and Fair of the New N.Y. State Agricultural Society," *American Agriculturist* 8 (Oct. 1849): 300.

62. Quoted in Edward Roberts Barnsley, *Agricultural Societies of Bucks County, Pa.* (Doylestown, PA: Edward W. Schlechter, 1940).

63. Nancy Grey Osterud, *Bonds of Community: The Lives of Farm Women in Nineteenth-Century New York* (Ithaca, NY: Cornell University Press, 1991).

64. Sally McMurry, *Transforming Rural Life: Dairying Families and Agricultural Change, 1820–1885* (Baltimore, MD: Johns Hopkins University Press, 1995).

65. "State Fair at Syracuse," *Cultivator* 6 (Oct. 1849): 304.

66. Mastromarino, "Fair Vision," 246, 251. On the persistence of the consensual style in northern rural communities, see Michael Zuckerman, *Peaceable Kingdoms: New England Towns in the Eighteenth Century* (New York: Knopf, 1970); Hal S. Barron, *Those Who Stayed Behind: Rural Society in Nineteenth-Century New England* (Cambridge:

Cambridge University Press, 1984), chap. 6; Paula Baker, *The Moral Frameworks of Public Life: Gender, Politics, and the State in Rural New York, 1870–1930* (New York: Oxford University Press, 1991), 21–23, chap. 4.

67. Paula Baker, "The Domestication of Politics: Women and American Political Society, 1780–1920," *American Historical Review* 89 (June 1984): 620–47.

68. Allen, *Address Delivered before the New-York State Agricultural Society*, 14–15; "Letter from Ulmus," *Genesee Farmer* 7 (Jan. 14, 1837): 12 (emphasis in original).

69. Marti, *To Improve the Soil and the Mind*, 45–123. For examples of tax exemptions, see *Laws of the General Assembly of the Commonwealth of Pennsylvania* (Harrisburg: J.M.G. Lescure, 1849), 327; ibid. (Harrisburg: Theo. Fenn and Co., 1851), 557–58; ibid. (Harrisburg: Theo. Fenn and Co., 1853), 712–13; ibid. (Harrisburg: A. Boyd Hamilton, 1857), 196–97; ibid. (Harrisburg: A. Boyd Hamilton, 1861), 265–67.

70. *Annual Report of the Secretary of the State Board of Agriculture of Massachusetts* 1 (Boston: William White, 1854): 16.

71. "An Act to Facilitate the Forming of Agricultural and Horticultural Societies," *Laws of the State of New York*, 76th sess. (Albany: Weed, Parsons and Co., 1853), 716–18 (chap. 339); "An Act to Facilitate the Forming of Agricultural and Horticultural Societies," 78th sess. (Albany: Van Benthuysen, 1855), 777–80 (chap. 425).

72. *Transactions of the New York State Agricultural Society* 16 (Albany: C. Van Benthuysen, 1856): 493–94; "An Act to Exempt Lands Held by Agricultural Societies from Taxation," *Laws of the State of New York*, 79th sess. (Albany: J. Munsell, 1856), 205–6 (chap. 133), 304 (chap. 183). See also the ledger and register in ASNC-HSD.

73. *Journal of the House of Representatives of the State of Ohio* 53 (Columbus: Richard Nevins, 1857), 511–12; *Acts of a General Nature and Local Laws and Joint Resolutions Passed by General Assembly of the State of Ohio* 53 (Columbus: Statesman Steam Press, 1856), 171–78, 248–49; *Ohio Cultivator* 14 (Apr. 1, 1858): 104.

74. *Journal of the Assembly of the State of New York* (Albany: Charles Van Benthuysen, 1858), 768–69.

75. Cong. Globe, 31st Cong., 1st Sess., 1642.

76. *Transactions of the Illinois State Agricultural Society* 2 (Springfield: Lanphier and Walker, 1857), xi; *Acts and Resolves Passed by the General Court of Massachusetts* (Boston: William White, 1856), 268.

77. For figures on the Patent Office Agricultural Report, see table 7.1; for *Uncle Tom's Cabin*, see Ronald D. Patkus and Mary C. Schlosser, "Aspects of the Publishing History of *Uncle Tom's Cabin*, 1851–1900," Vassar College Libraries, Archives and Special Collections, http://specialcollections.vassar.edu/exhibits/stowe/essay2.html.

78. Cong. Globe, 32nd Cong., 1st Sess., appendix, 746.

79. Marti, "Agrarian Thought and Agricultural Progress," 285–86.

80. Emily Pawley, "Accounting with the Fields: Chemistry and Value in Nutriment in American Agricultural Improvement, 1835–1860," *Science as Culture* 19 (Dec. 2010): 461–62; Pawley, "'The Balance-Sheet of Nature,'" 141–42.

81. "Agriculture in Common Schools," *New-York Daily Tribune*, Jan. 23, 1855, 4.

82. See, for example, "Resolves for Reprinting a Report on the Insects of New England, Which Are Injurious to Vegetation," *Acts and Resolves Passed by the General Court of Massachusetts* (Boston: William White, 1859), 466–67 (chap. 93).

83. Pawley, "Accounting with the Fields," 463, 468, 471; Benjamin Cohen, *Notes from*

the Ground: Science, Soil, and Society in the American Countryside (New Haven, CT: Yale University Press, 2009), 36–37.

84. Cong. Globe, 34th Cong., 1st Sess., 1697.

85. Oz Frankel, *States of Inquiry: Social Investigations and Print Culture in Nineteenth-Century Britain and the United States* (Baltimore, MD: Johns Hopkins University Press, 2006).

86. O'Reilly-NYHS, item in the folder marked "Printed material: 1844" (emphasis in original). For the agricultural societies' practice of inviting and sending fair delegates from other societies, see DCIS-APS, Algernon S. Roberts to Dr. Geo. Smith, Apr. 8, 1837, and Jeffersonville Agricultural Association to DCIS, Sept. 20, 1849.

87. *Laws of the State of New York*, 77th sess. (Albany: Gould, Banks & Co., 1854), 616 (chap. 283); ibid., 85th sess. (Albany: Wrightson and Co., 1862), 489–91 (chap. 293); *Transactions of the New-York State Agricultural Society* 14 (1855): v–vi; ibid., 15 (1856): v; Marti, *To Improve the Soil and the Mind*, 122; Asa Fitch, *First Report on the Noxious, Beneficial and Other Insects, of the State of New York* (Albany: C. Van Benthuysen, 1855).

88. *Transactions of the New York State Agricultural Society* 9 (1850): 12; [Untitled lead article], *Horticulturist* 4 (Apr. 1850): 441 (emphasis in original); Allen, *Address Delivered before the New-York State Agricultural Society*, 16.

89. O'Reilly-NYHS, "Printed material: 1844."

90. Charles Tilly, *Social Movements, 1768–2004* (Boulder, CO: Paradigm Publishers, 2004); Sidney G. Tarrow, *Power in Movement: Social Movements and Contentious Politics* (New York: Cambridge University Press, 1998); Sidney Tarrow and Charles Tilly, "Contentious Politics and Social Movements," in *The Oxford Handbook of Comparative Politics*, ed. Charles Boix and Susan C. Stokes (Oxford: Oxford University Press, 2009).

91. For recent work on slaveholders and agricultural reform, see Caitlin Rosenthal, "Slavery's Scientific Management: Masters and Managers," in *Slavery's Capitalism: A New History of American Economic Development*, ed. Sven Beckert and Seth Rockman (Philadelphia: University of Pennsylvania Press, 2016), 62–86; Ian W. Beamish, "Saving the South: Agricultural Reform in the Southern United States, 1819–1861" (PhD diss., Johns Hopkins University, 2013); Philip Mills Herrington, "Agricultural and Architectural Reform in the Antebellum South: Fruitland at Augusta, Georgia," *Journal of Southern History* 78 (Nov. 2012): 855–86; Alan L. Olmstead and Paul W. Rhode, "Biological Innovation and Productivity Growth in the Antebellum Cotton Economy," *Journal of Economic History* 68 (Dec. 2008): 1123–71; Steven G. Collins, "System, Organization, and Agricultural Reform in the Antebellum South, 1840–1860," *Agricultural History* 75 (Winter 2001): 1–27; A. Glenn Crothers, "Agricultural Improvement and Technological Innovation in a Slave Society: The Case of Early National Northern Virginia," *Agricultural History* 75 (Spring 2001): 135–67.

92. Quoted in Drew Gilpin Faust, "The Rhetoric and Ritual of Agriculture in Antebellum South Carolina," *Journal of Southern History* 45 (Nov. 1979): 557.

93. Quoted in David R. Francis, "Southern Agricultural Fairs and Expositions," in *The South in the Building of the Nation* (Richmond, VA: Southern Historical Publication Society, 1909), 5:589.

94. John Majewski, *Modernizing a Slave Economy: The Economic Vision of the Confederate Nation* (Chapel Hill: University of North Carolina Press, 2009); John D. Majewski, *A House Dividing: Economic Development in Pennsylvania and Virginia before*

the Civil War (Cambridge: Cambridge University Press, 2000); Brian Page and Richard Walker, "From Settlement to Fordism: The Agro-Industrial Revolution in the American Midwest," *Economic Geography* 67 (Oct. 1991): 281–315; David R. Meyer, *The Roots of American Industrialization* (Baltimore, MD: Johns Hopkins University Press, 2003).

95. "Guilford Fair, 1859–1960s," Guilford Free Library, Guilford, CT, folder G-F-3; Fisher, "Improving the Soil and Mind," 119–21.

96. Beamish, "Saving the South," 13.

97. Tucker, *American Agricultural Journals,* 76; Weymouth T. Jordan, "Noah B. Cloud's Activities on Behalf of Southern Agriculture," *Agricultural History* 25 (Apr. 1951): 58; *New England Farmer* 5 (Jan. 1853), 15; penciled note on front page of the Library Company of Philadelphia's copy of *Boston Cultivator* 13 (Jan. 1851), with thanks to Connie King for bringing this to my attention; *Working Farmer* 13 (Nov. 1861), 241. See also Demaree, *American Agricultural Press, 1819–1860,* 339, 351, 375. Though the accuracy of self-reported subscription figures is supposition, there is no reason to dispute the order of magnitude, because editors monitored each other for grossly unrealistic claims.

98. *Massachusetts Ploughman* 10 (Dec. 28, 1850): 1.

99. Millard Fillmore, "First Annual Message," Dec. 2, 1850, APP.

Chapter 3 · Economic Nationalism in the Greater Rural Northeast

1. Thomas Paine, *Common Sense* (Mineola, NY: Dover, 1997), 19, 21 (emphasis in original).

2. Diane Lindstrom, *Economic Development in the Philadelphia Region, 1810–1850* (New York: Columbia University Press, 1978), 3; Robert E. Lipsey, "US Foreign Trade and the Balance of Payments, 1800–1913," in *The Cambridge Economic History of the United States,* vol. 2, *The Long Nineteenth Century,* ed. Stanley L. Engerman and Robert E. Gallman (Cambridge: Cambridge University Press, 2000), 691; David R. Meyer, *The Roots of American Industrialization* (Baltimore, MD: Johns Hopkins University Press, 2003), 161.

3. See, especially, Sven Beckert, *The Monied Metropolis: New York City and the Consolidation of the American Bourgeoisie, 1850–1896* (Cambridge: Cambridge University Press, 2001); Andrew Dawson, *Lives of the Philadelphia Engineers: Capital, Class, and Revolution, 1830–1890* (Aldershot, UK: Ashgate, 2004).

4. This question has been raised and answered brilliantly for the late 1800s; see Richard Franklin Bensel, *The Political Economy of American Industrialization, 1877–1900* (Cambridge: Cambridge University Press, 2000).

5. On the downplaying of economic issues, see, for instance, Eric Foner, *Free Soil, Free Labor, Free Men: The Ideology of the Republican Party before the Civil War* (New York: Oxford University Press, 1995), 168–70. On expansive economic policy, see, among others, Heather Cox Richardson, *The Greatest Nation of the Earth: Republican Economic Policies during the Civil War* (Cambridge, MA: Harvard University Press, 1997).

6. For the economic interpretation, see Charles A. Beard and Mary R. Beard, *The Rise of American Civilization* (New York: Macmillan, 1930), 2:6–7. For two recent studies that give attention to agriculture in the lead-up to the Civil War, but largely take the idea of yeoman family farms for granted, see James L. Huston, *The British Gentry, the Southern Planter, and the Northern Family Farmer: Agriculture and Sectional Antagonism in North America* (Baton Rouge: Louisiana State University Press, 2015); Adam Wesley Dean, *An*

Agrarian Republic: Farming, Antislavery Politics, and Nature Parks in the Civil War Era (Chapel Hill: University of North Carolina Press, 2015).

7. Alan L. Olmstead and Paul W. Rhode, *Creating Abundance: Biological Innovation and American Agricultural Development* (Cambridge: Cambridge University Press, 2008); Meyer, *Roots of American Industrialization*, 1–12.

8. See Robin Einhorn, "Institutional Reality in the Age of Slavery: Taxation and Democracy in the States," *Journal of Policy History* 18 (Winter 2006): 21–43; Don E. Fehrenbacher, *The Slaveholding Republic: An Account of the United States Government's Relations to Slavery* (Oxford: Oxford University Press, 2002).

9. Margaret Ellen Newell, *From Dependency to Independence: Economic Revolution in Colonial New England* (Ithaca, NY: Cornell University Press, 1998), chaps. 3–5 ("hub of intercolonial trade," 75); John J. McCusker and Russell R. Menard, *The Economy of British America, 1607–1789* (Chapel Hill: University of North Carolina Press, 1985), chaps. 5, 9 ("tied . . . to the export sector," 206); Marc Egnal, *New World Economies: The Growth of the Thirteen Colonies and Early Canada* (New York: Oxford University Press, 1998), chap. 4 ("export-led boom," 59).

10. Lawrence A. Peskin, *Manufacturing Revolution: The Intellectual Origins of Early American Industry* (Baltimore, MD: Johns Hopkins University Press, 2003), 59, 63; James A. Henretta, "The War for Independence and American Economic Development," in *The Economy of Early America: The Revolutionary Period, 1763–1790*, ed. Ronald Hoffman, Russell R. Menard, and Peter J. Albert (Charlottesville: University Press of Virginia, 1988), 45–86.

11. For an example of the effect of western competition, see Andrew H. Baker and Holly V. Izard, "New England Farmers and the Marketplace, 1780–1865: A Case Study," *Agricultural History* 65 (Summer 1991): 41. Western competition reinforced earlier moves toward agricultural intensification and market reorientation; see Winifred Barr Rothenberg, *From Market-Places to a Market Economy: The Transformation of Rural Massachusetts, 1750–1850* (Chicago: University of Chicago Press, 1992), 211; Richard A. Wines, "The Nineteenth-Century Agricultural Transition in an Eastern Long Island Community," *Agricultural History* 55 (Jan. 1981): 52.

12. For the classic account of antebellum transportation, see George Rogers Taylor, *The Transportation Revolution, 1815–1860* (New York: Rinehart, 1951). For an account that emphasizes wagon transport and therefore road over canal construction, see Meyer, *Roots of American Industrialization*, 29–34, 141–55. For water links and mountain divides in world history, see James C. Scott, *The Art of Not Being Governed: An Anarchist History of Upland Southeast Asia* (New Haven, CT: Yale University Press, 2009), 16, 43–50.

13. James Tallmadge, *Address before the American Institute, at the Close of Its Fourteenth Annual Fair, on the 26th of October, 1841* (New York: Hopkins and Jennings, 1841), 3; Adams quoted in Andrew Shankman, *Crucible of American Democracy: The Struggle to Fuse Egalitarianism and Capitalism in Jeffersonian Pennsylvania* (Lawrence: University Press of Kansas, 2004), 224.

14. See, for instance, "Farming in Western New York," *Working Farmer* 11 (Feb. 1859): 36–37; "Price of Land," *Pennsylvania Farm Journal* 5 (Jan. 1855): 10–11.

15. Lindstrom, *Economic Development in the Philadelphia Region, 1810–1850*, 140–45; Roberta Balstad Miller, *City and Hinterland: A Case Study of Urban Growth and Regional Development* (Westport, CT: Greenwood Press, 1979), 95; Michael Conzen, *Frontier*

Farming in an Urban Shadow: The Influence of Madison's Proximity on the Agricultural Development of Blooming Grove, Wisconsin (Madison: State Historical Society of Wisconsin, 1971), 88–96.

16. Paul Wallace Gates, *The Farmer's Age: Agriculture, 1815–1860* (New York: Holt, Rinehart and Winston, 1960), 239–40, 250–52, 256, 261, 266, 267, 269; Jeremy Atack and Fred Bateman, *To Their Own Soil: Agriculture in the Antebellum North* (Ames: Iowa State University Press, 1987), 149; Eric Brunger, "Dairying and Urban Development in New York State, 1850–1900," *Agricultural History* 29 (Oct. 1955): 169–74; Clay McShane and Joel A. Tarr, *The Horse in the City: Living Machines in the Nineteenth Century* (Baltimore, MD: Johns Hopkins University Press, 2007), 130–33; William R. Baron and Anne E. Bridges, "Making Hay in Northern New England: Maine as a Case Study, 1800–1850," *Agricultural History* 57 (Apr. 1983): 165–80; Clarence H. Danhof, "Gathering the Grass," *Agricultural History* 30 (Oct. 1956): 172–73; Christopher Baas and Darrin Rubino, "The Most Successful Press in This or Any Other Country: The Material Culture of 19th-Century Beater Hay Presses in the Mid-Ohio Valley," *Material Culture* 45 (Spring 2013): 1–20; Robert Leslie Jones, "The Introduction of Farm Machinery into Ohio prior to 1865," *Ohio Archaeological and Historical Quarterly* 58 (1949): 1–20; Ulysses Prentiss Hedrick, *A History of Agriculture in the State of New York* (Albany: New York State Agriculture Society, 1933), 262, 386, 402.

17. Harold F. Wilson, *The Hill Country of Northern New England: Its Social and Economic History, 1790–1930* (New York: AMS Press, 1967), 75–94; Edwin C. Rozwenc, *Agricultural Policies in Vermont, 1860–1945* (Montpelier: Vermont Historical Society, 1981), 3–5; Martin Bruegel, *Farm, Shop, Landing: The Rise of a Market Society in the Hudson Valley, 1780–1860* (Durham, NC: Duke University Press, 2002), 75–79 ("mental horizon," 79); Reeve Huston, *Land and Freedom: Rural Society, Popular Protest, and Party Politics in Antebellum New York* (New York: Oxford University Press, 2000), 55; Miller, *City and Hinterland*, 92–93; Stevenson Whitcomb Fletcher, *Pennsylvania Agriculture and Country Life, 1840–1940* (Harrisburg: Pennsylvania Historical and Museum Commission, 1955), 265; Steven Stoll, *Larding the Lean Earth: Soil and Society in Nineteenth-Century America* (New York: Hill and Wang, 2002), 118–19; Robert Leslie Jones, *History of Agriculture in Ohio to 1880* (Kent, OH: Kent State University Press, 1983), 140–49; Clarence H. Danhof, *Change in Agriculture: The Northern United States, 1820–1870* (Cambridge, MA: Harvard University Press, 1969), 164–66.

18. Hal S. Barron, *Those Who Stayed Behind: Rural Society in Nineteenth-Century New England* (Cambridge: Cambridge University Press, 1984), 59–64; Olmstead and Rhode, *Creating Abundance*, 296–98 ("complete redesign," 302); Eric Carlos Stoykovich, "In the National Interest: Improving Domestic Animals and the Making of the United States, 1815–1870" (PhD diss., University of Virginia, 2009), chap. 1; Gates, *Farmer's Age*, 221–25.

19. Carol E. Brier, "Tending Our Vines: From the Correspondence and Writings of Richard Peters and John Jay," *Pennsylvania History* 80 (Jan. 2013): 91.

20. Constitution and minutes, ASNC-HSD, Sept. 16, 1837.

21. Olmstead and Rhode, *Creating Abundance*, 49–51, 60–61 ("grain yields would have plummeted," 41); Danhof, *Change in Agriculture*, 157; William Cronon, *Changes in the Land: Indians, Colonists, and the Ecology of New England* (New York: Hill and Wang, 1983), 153–55.

22. Bruegel, *Farm, Shop, Landing*, 75–76; Miller, *City and Hinterland*, 92–93; Jones, *History of Agriculture in Ohio to 1880*, 58, 63–64; Jones, "The Introduction of Farm Machinery into Ohio prior to 1865"; Harry N. Scheiber, *Ohio Canal Era: A Case Study of Government and the Economy, 1820–1861* (Athens: Ohio University Press, 1969), 321–33; Peter D. McClelland, *Sowing Modernity: America's First Agricultural Revolution* (Ithaca, NY: Cornell University Press, 1997), 94–120, 178, 190–93; Atack and Bateman, *To Their Own Soil*, 194, 251; Percy Wells Bidwell and John I. Falconer, *History of Agriculture in the Northern United States, 1620–1860* (Washington, DC: Carnegie Institution of Washington, 1925), 207–15.

23. *Annual Report of the Commissioner of Patents, for the Year 1847* (Washington, DC: Wendell and Van Benthuysen, 1848): 101.

24. Atack and Bateman, *To Their Own Soil*, 147, 248, 256; Gates, *Farmer's Age*, 233; Olmstead and Rhode, *Creating Abundance*, 263; Joan M. Jensen, *Loosening the Bonds: Mid-Atlantic Farm Women, 1750–1850* (New Haven, CT: Yale University Press, 1986), 79–141; Nancy Grey Osterud, *Bonds of Community: The Lives of Farm Women in Nineteenth-Century New York* (Ithaca, NY: Cornell University Press, 1991), 139–86; Sally McMurry, *Transforming Rural Life: Dairying Families and Agricultural Change, 1820–1885* (Baltimore, MD: Johns Hopkins University Press, 1995).

25. Elinor F. Oakes, "A Ticklish Business: Dairying in New England and Pennsylvania, 1750–1812," *Pennsylvania History* 47 (July 1980): 195–212.

26. Jensen, *Loosening the Bonds*, 79–83; McMurry, *Transforming Rural Life*, 59; Jones, *History of Agriculture in Ohio to 1880*, 182–85; Gates, *Farmer's Age*, 244–45.

27. McMurry, *Transforming Rural Life*, 24–38, 85–95 ("pervasive concern with system," 32; "dynamic innovativeness," 122); Jensen, *Loosening the Bonds*, 92–113; Huston, *Land and Freedom*, 48, 201; Jones, *History of Agriculture in Ohio to 1880*, 186, 190–91; Olmstead and Rhode, *Creating Abundance*, 331–39; Atack and Bateman, *To Their Own Soil*, 147–61; Gates, *Farmer's Age*, 241–46.

28. Atack and Bateman, *To Their Own Soil*, 228, 246, 250; Lindstrom, *Economic Development in the Philadelphia Region, 1810–1850*, 179. For a discussion of land values, see Peter H. Lindert, "Long-Run Trends in American Farmland Values," *Agricultural History* 62 (July 1988): 45–85.

29. Barron, *Those Who Stayed Behind*, chap. 3; Stoll, *Larding the Lean Earth*, 70; Mary Babson Fuhrer, *A Crisis of Community: The Trials and Transformation of a New England Town, 1815–1848* (Chapel Hill: University of North Carolina Press, 2014), 86–89; Miller, *City and Hinterland*, 139–42; Huston, *Land and Freedom*, 192, 202–3; Wilson, *The Hill Country of Northern New England*, 78–79; Danhof, *Change in Agriculture*, 107–14; Atack and Bateman, *To Their Own Soil*, 49–66, 100; Donald Hugh Parkerson, *The Agricultural Transition in New York State: Markets and Migration in Mid-Nineteenth-Century America* (Ames: Iowa State University Press, 1995), 133–36; Thomas Summerhill, *Harvest of Dissent: Agrarianism in Nineteenth-Century New York* (Urbana: University of Illinois Press, 2005), 44–45, 145–46; Lee A. Craig, *To Sow One Acre More: Childbearing and Farm Productivity in the Antebellum North* (Baltimore, MD: Johns Hopkins University Press, 1993), 102–4; Christopher Clark, *The Roots of Rural Capitalism: Western Massachusetts, 1780–1860* (Ithaca, NY: Cornell University Press, 1990), 137–39; Meyer, *Roots of American Industrialization*, 11.

30. *Working Farmer* 8 (Jan. 1857): 241; 8 (Feb. 1857): 265 (emphasis in original). On

hiring children of relatives and neighbors, see Parkerson, *Agricultural Transition in New York State*, 126–41.

31. Charles L. Flint, ed., *Abstract of Returns of the Agricultural Societies of Massachusetts, 1858* (Boston: William White, 1859), 41–42; Atack and Bateman, *To Their Own Soil*, 86–101; Bruegel, *Farm, Shop, Landing*, 104; Parkerson, *Agricultural Transition in New York State*, 126–41; Danhof, *Change in Agriculture*, 77–78. On the "agricultural ladder," see Foner, *Free Soil, Free Labor, Free Men*, 30–33; on a "competence" see Barron, *Those Who Stayed Behind*, 35–36.

32. Yasuo Okada, "Squires' Diary: New York Agriculture in Transition, 1840–1860," *Keio Economic Studies* 7 (1970): 78–98 ("good days work," 89).

33. See David C. Smith, "Middle Range Farming in the Civil War Era: Life on a Farm in Seneca County, 1862–1866," *New York History* 48 (Oct. 1967): 352–69; Baker and Izard, "New England Farmers and the Marketplace, 1780–1865"; Ronald D. Karr, "The Transformation of Agriculture in Brookline, 1770–1885," *Historical Journal of Massachusetts* 15 (Jan. 1987): 33–49; Adam Krakowski, "A Bitter Past: Hop Farming in Nineteenth-Century Vermont," *Vermont History* 82 (Summer–Fall 2014): 91–105.

34. Hinton Rowan Helper, *The Impending Crisis of the South: How to Meet It* (New York: Burdick Brothers, 1857), 48.

35. Douglas A. Irwin, *HSUS*, tables Ee446-457 and Ee569-589.

36. See, for instance, Sophus A. Reinert, *Translating Empire: Emulation and the Origins of Political Economy* (Cambridge, MA: Harvard University Press, 2011).

37. Frederic Hudson, *Journalism in the United States, from 1690 to 1872* (New York: Harper & Brothers, 1873), 319.

38. Stephen Haggard, *Developmental States* (Cambridge: Cambridge University Press, 2018). Also see the delineation of a "standard development model" in Robert C. Allen, *Global Economic History: A Very Short Introduction* (Oxford: Oxford University Press, 2011).

39. Drew R McCoy, *The Elusive Republic: Political Economy in Jeffersonian America* (New York: Norton, 1982).

40. Rebecca Harding Davis, "Life in the Iron Mills," *Atlantic Monthly* 7 (Apr. 1861): 430–51.

41. Peskin, *Manufacturing Revolution*, 65–92; Shankman, *Crucible of American Democracy*, 80.

42. Mathew Carey, *The New Olive Branch* (Philadelphia: M. Carey & Son, 1820), 172.

43. Mathew Carey, *Address Delivered before the Philadelphia Society for Promoting Agriculture, at Its Meeting, on the Twentieth of July, 1824* (Philadelphia: Mifflin & Parry, 1827), 11–12; Thomas Haines Dudley, *The Farmer Feedeth All: How Protection Affects the Farmer: An Address Delivered before the New Jersey State Agricultural Society, at Waverly, Sept. 22, 1882* (Philadelphia: Allen, Lane & Scott's Printing House, 1882), 5; Donald J. Ratcliffe, *The Politics of Long Division: The Birth of the Second Party System in Ohio, 1818–1828* (Columbus: Ohio State University Press, 2000), 59–61; Caleb B. Smith, *Effects of a Protective Tariff on Agriculture: Speech of Mr. Caleb B. Smith, of Indiana, on the Subject of the Tariff* (Washington, DC: J. & G. S. Gideon, 1844); E. B. Ward, "The Farmer and the Manufacturer, an Address Delivered at the Wisconsin State Fair, Madison, October 1, 1868," in *Transactions of the Wisconsin State Agricultural Society* 7 (Madison: Atwood &

Rublee, 1868), 452–69; David H. Mason, *How Western Farmers Are Benefitted by Protection* (Chicago, 1875); Thomas Haines Dudley, *Farmers and the Tariff: A Speech Delivered at the Meeting of the Farmers' Congress, Chicago, November 11, 1887* (New York: American Protective League, 1887).

44. Scott Reynolds Nelson, *A Nation of Deadbeats: An Uncommon History of America's Financial Disasters* (New York: Vintage Books, 2013), 61–78; Clyde A. Haulman, *Virginia and the Panic of 1819: The First Great Depression and the Commonwealth* (London: Pickering & Chatto, 2008); Daniel S. Dupre, "The Panic of 1819 and the Political Economy of Sectionalism," in *The Economy of Early America: Historical Perspectives and New Directions*, ed. Cathy D. Matson (University Park: Pennsylvania State University Press, 2006), 263–93.

45. Carey, *Address Delivered before the Philadelphia Society for Promoting Agriculture*; George Tibbits, *A Memoir on the Expediency and Practicability, of Improving or Creating Home Markets for the Sale of Agricultural Productions and Raw Materials, by the Introduction or Growth of Artizans and Manufacturers* (Albany, NY: Packard and Van Benthuysen, 1825).

46. N.B. [Nicholas Biddle] to Walter Lowrie, PSPA-UP, Feb. 22, 1822. Biddle appears to have sent nearly identical letters to James Monroe (Feb. 22, 1822), Mathew Carey (Feb. 4, 1822) and several others, including the agricultural reformer James LeRay de Chaumont (Feb. 4, 1822). See also Nicholas Biddle, *Address Delivered before the Philadelphia Society for Promoting Agriculture, at Its Annual Meeting, on the Fifteenth of January, 1822, by Nicholas Biddle, Esq.* (Philadelphia: Clark & Raser, 1822), 16.

47. Quoted in Tamara Plakins Thornton, *Cultivating Gentlemen: The Meaning of Country Life among the Boston Elite, 1785–1860* (New Haven, CT: Yale University Press, 1989).

48. *Memorial of the New York County Agricultural Society*, H. Doc. 28, 16th cong., 2nd sess. (Washington, DC: December 15, 1820), 6.

49. *Memorial of the Berkshire Agricultural Society of the Commonwealth of Massachusetts: January 22, 1821. Referred to the Committee on Manufactures* (Washington, DC: Gales & Seaton, 1821), 6; Mark Mastromarino, "Fair Visions: Elkanah Watson (1758–1842) and the Modern American Agricultural Fair" (PhD diss., College of William and Mary, 2002), 169, 207, 310–11.

50. *Rural Magazine and Farmer's Monthly Museum* 1 (Feb. 1819): 25; *American Farmer* 2 (June 9, 1820): 83; *Agriculturist's and Manufacturer's Magazine* 1 (Jan. 1820): 16, 18–21; Ratcliffe, *The Politics of Long Division*, 59; Murray Newton Rothbard, *The Panic of 1819: Reactions and Policies* (Auburn, AL: Ludwig von Mises Institute, 2007 [1962]), 218; William Frederic Worner, "Agricultural Societies in Lancaster County," *Historical Papers and Addresses of the Lancaster County Historical Society* 34 (1930): 278–80.

51. *American Farmer* 1 (1819): 247; other articles in the series appear on 206, 214, 216, 230, 272.

52. "Report of the Committee on Domestic Manufactures," Jan. 28, 1822, in ASBS-MMSL, volume titled "Communications to the Agricultural Society of Bucks County," 197.

53. *Memorial of the Berkshire Agricultural Society*; Mastromarino, "Fair Visions," 207, 310–11.

54. Ralph Waldo Emerson, "The Farmer and His Aides," in Charles Flint, ed.,

Abstract of Returns of the Agricultural Societies of Massachusetts, 1858 (Boston: William White, 1859), 18.

55. Donald B. Marti, *To Improve the Soil and the Mind: Agricultural Societies, Journals, and Schools in the Northeastern States, 1791–1865* (Ann Arbor, MI: University Microfilms International, 1979), 147. For evidence of rural tariff support, see Peskin, *Manufacturing Revolution*, chap. 6; Gates, *Farmer's Age*, 381; Huston, *Land and Freedom*, 55; Bruegel, *Farm, Shop, Landing*, 10, 77, 98–102; Malcom Rogers Eiselen, *The Rise of Pennsylvania Protectionism* (Philadelphia, 1932), 32, 46–52; Shankman, *Crucible of American Democracy*, 188–90, 210–13; Ratcliffe, *The Politics of Long Division*, 60–61; Jensen, *Loosening the Bonds*, 83.

56. Joseph Edwards to R. Ronaldson of Philadelphia, Sept. 3, 1849, DCIS-APS.

57. "The American Institute," *American Agriculturist* 1 (Aug. 1842): 129–30.

58. Richard E. Ela, "The Mechanical and Manufacturing Arts, Their Condition and Wants, and Relation They Sustain to the State Agricultural Society," *Transactions of the Wisconsin State Agricultural Society* 2 (Madison: Beriah Brown, 1853): 324.

59. Dupre, "The Panic of 1819 and the Political Economy of Sectionalism," 282–83.

60. H. Niles, *Agriculture of the United States, or, an Essay Concerning Internal Improvement and Domestic Manufactures, Shewing Their Inseparable Connection with the Business and Interests of Agriculture, in the Establishment of a Home-Market for Bread-Stuffs and Meats, Wool, Cotton, Flax, Hemp, &c., as Well as the Supplies That They Will Furnish in Aid of the Foreign Commerce of the United States* ([Baltimore, MD?], 1827), originally published in *Niles' Weekly Register*, Mar. 24, 1827, 49–58; Paul Keith Conkin, *Prophets of Prosperity: America's First Political Economists* (Bloomington: Indiana University Press, 1980), chaps. 4, 7; Michael Hudson, *Economics and Technology in 19th Century American Thought* (New York: Garland, 1975), chaps. 16–17.

61. *Mr. Clay's Speech on the Tariff: Or, The "American System," So Called, or, The Anglican System, in Fact, Introduced Here, and Perverted in Its Most Material Bearing upon Society, by the Omission of a System of Corn Laws, for the Protection of Agriculture* (Richmond, VA: Thomas W. White, 1827), 12–13, 18, 24.

62. Brian Schoen, *The Fragile Fabric of Union: Cotton, Federal Politics, and the Global Origins of the Civil War* (Baltimore, MD: Johns Hopkins University Press, 2009), 109–11; Norris W. Preyer, "Southern Support of the Tariff of 1816: A Reappraisal," *Journal of Southern History* 25 (Aug. 1959): 315; William W. Freehling, *Prelude to Civil War: The Nullification Controversy in South Carolina, 1816–1836* (New York: Harper & Row, 1966), 91–96.

63. *Mr. Clay's Speech on the Tariff*, 3, 25.

64. First petition: *American Farmer* 1 (Jan. 28, 1820): 348. Second petition: *Memorial of the Delegates of the United Agricultural Societies of Prince George, Sussex, Surry, Petersburg, Brunswick, Dinwiddie, and Isle of Wight. December 13, 1820. Referred to the Committee on Agriculture* (Washington, DC: Gales & Seaton, 1820), 3–4; *Memorial from the United Agricultural Societies of the State of Virginia: January 17, 1820, Referred to the Committee on Commerce* (Washington, DC: Gales & Seaton, 1820). For similar points, see "Remonstrance of the Virginia Agricultural Society of Fredericksburg," *American Farmer* 1 (Jan. 14, 1820): 333; and "An Address to the Public, from the Delegation of the United Agricultural Societies of Virginia," *American Farmer* 1 (May 19, 1820): 57–59. See also Dupre, "The Panic of 1819 and the Political Economy of Sectionalism," 287–91.

65. McCoy, *The Elusive Republic*, 84. See also Paul Finkelman, *Slavery and the Founders: Race and Liberty in the Age of Jefferson* (Armonk, NY: M. E. Sharpe, 1996), 22–32; John E. Crowley, *The Privileges of Independence: Neomercantilism and the American Revolution* (Baltimore, MD: Johns Hopkins University Press, 1993).

66. McCoy, *The Elusive Republic*, 137–39; Schoen, *The Fragile Fabric of Union*, 85–87, 96–97, 226–28; Haulman, *Virginia and the Panic of 1819*, 57.

67. *Report of the Committee on Agriculture, on the Memorial of the Delegates of the United Agricultural Societies of Sundry Counties of the State of Virginia* (Washington, DC: Gales & Seaton, 1821), 26, 28.

68. "Nathaniel Macon and Bartlett Yancey," *North Carolina University Magazine* 7 (Oct. 1857): 95–96.

69. Freehling, *Prelude to Civil War*, 109. On the politics of the Missouri Crisis, see John R. Van Atta, *Wolf by the Ears: The Missouri Crisis, 1819–1821* (Baltimore, MD: Johns Hopkins University Press, 2015); Matthew Mason, *Slavery and Politics in the Early American Republic* (Chapel Hill: University of North Carolina Press, 2006), chap. 8; Leonard L. Richards, *The Slave Power: The Free North and Southern Domination, 1780–1860* (Baton Rouge: Louisiana State University Press, 2000), chap. 3.

70. *American Farmer* 2 (Oct. 31, 1820): 242.

71. Mason, *Slavery and Politics in the Early American Republic*, 197–200; Harry Ammon, "The Richmond Junto, 1800–1824," *Virginia Magazine of History and Biography* 61 (Oct. 1953): 404, 407, 411; Don E. Fehrenbacher, *Constitutions and Constitutionalism in the Slaveholding South* (Athens: University of Georgia Press, 1989), 40–41, 48–49.

72. Randolph quoted in Padraig Riley, *Slavery and the Democratic Conscience: Political Life in Jeffersonian America* (Philadelphia: University of Pennsylvania Press, 2016), 128. For Taylor, see Stoll, *Larding the Lean Earth*, 71–73; Conkin, *Prophets of Prosperity*, chap. 3. Ruffin has received a lot of attention; see, among others, David F. Allmendinger, *Ruffin: Family and Reform in the Old South* (New York: Oxford University Press, 1990).

73. Schoen, *The Fragile Fabric of Union*, 110.

74. *Declaration of the Immediate Causes Which Induce and Justify the Secession of South Carolina from the Federal Union; And the Ordinance of Secession* (Charleston: Evans & Cogswell, 1860), 7–8; Freehling, *Prelude to Civil War*, 83, 106, 255, and throughout; Fehrenbacher, *Constitutions and Constitutionalism in the Slaveholding South*, 45–52.

75. A. P. Calhoun, "Address," in *History of the State Agricultural Society of South Carolina*, ed. W. A. Clark, W. G. Hinson, and D. P. Duncan (Columbia: R. L. Bryan Co., 1916), 102–21; Charles B. Dew, *Apostles of Disunion: Southern Secession Commissioners and the Causes of the Civil War* (Charlottesville: University Press of Virginia, 2001), 39–41.

76. Dupre, "The Panic of 1819 and the Political Economy of Sectionalism," 278.

77. Einhorn, *American Taxation, American Slavery*; Max M. Edling, *A Revolution in Favor of Government: Origins of the U.S. Constitution and the Making of the American State* (New York: Oxford University Press, 2003).

78. Daniel Peart, *Lobbyists and the Making of US Tariff Policy, 1816–1861* (Baltimore, MD: Johns Hopkins University Press, 2018).

79. Calhoun, "Address," 110.

80. *Mr. Clay's Speech on the Tariff*, 48.

81. See, especially, Michael F. Holt, *The Political Crisis of the 1850s* (New York: Norton, 1983).

82. Charles Grier Sellers Jr., "Who Were the Southern Whigs?," *American Historical Review* 59 (Jan. 1954): 338, 340, 344–45; J. Mills Thornton, *Politics and Power in a Slave Society: Alabama, 1800–1860* (Baton Rouge: Louisiana State University Press, 2014), 53 and throughout; Daniel Walker Howe, *The Political Culture of the American Whigs* (Chicago: University of Chicago Press, 1979), chap. 10.

83. Phillip W. Magness, "The American System and the Political Economy of Black Colonization," *Journal of the History of Economic Thought* 37 (June 2015): 187–202.

84. Amy S. Greenberg, *A Wicked War: Polk, Clay, Lincoln, and the 1846 U.S. Invasion of Mexico* (New York: Alfred A. Knopf, 2012), chap. 3.

85. George Winston Smith, *Henry C. Carey and American Sectional Conflict* (Albuquerque: University of New Mexico Press, 1951), 31–33.

Chapter 4 · Henry C. Carey and the Republican Developmental Synthesis

1. Henry C. Carey, "Money," *Merchants' Magazine and Commercial Review* 32 (Jan. 1855): 27.

2. LSM [Louisa S. McCord], "Carey on the Slave Trade," *Southern Quarterly Review* 9 (Jan. 1854): 115; "Review of the Southern Cultivator for July," *Southern Cultivator* 10 (Aug. 1852): 244.

3. For example, see William Terrell, *Letter from Dr. Terrell, to the Executive Committee of the Southern Central Agricultural Society* (Macon, GA: Southern Central Agricultural Society, 1854), Readex American Broadsides and Ephemera, accessed Jan. 4, 2018.

4. Quoted in Maris A. Vinovskis, "Horace Mann on the Economic Productivity of Education," *New England Quarterly* 43 (Dec. 1970): 563.

5. There has been substantial scholarship on Carey. See Paul Keith Conkin, *Prophets of Prosperity: America's First Political Economists* (Bloomington: Indiana University Press, 1980), chaps. 10–11; Stephen Meardon, "Henry C. Carey's 'Zone Theory' and American Sectional Conflict," *Journal of the History of Economic Thought* 37 (June 2015): 305–20; Stephen Meardon, "Reciprocity and Henry C. Carey's Traverses on 'the Road to Perfect Freedom of Trade,'" *Journal of the History of Economic Thought* 33 (Sept. 2011): 307–33; Adrian Johns, *Piracy: The Intellectual Property Wars from Gutenberg to Gates* (Chicago: University of Chicago Press, 2011), 309–25; Jeffrey P. Sklansky, *The Soul's Economy: Market Society and Selfhood in American Thought, 1820–1920* (Chapel Hill: University of North Carolina Press, 2002), chap. 3; Andrew Dawson, "Reassessing Henry Carey (1793–1879): The Problems of Writing Political Economy in Nineteenth-Century America," *Journal of American Studies* 34 (Dec. 2000): 465–85; Michael Perelman, "Henry Carey's Political-Ecological Economics: An Introduction," *Organization & Environment* 12 (Sept. 1999): 280–92; Rodney J. Morrison, *Henry C. Carey and American Economic Development*, Transactions of the American Philosophical Society (Philadelphia: American Philosophical Society, 1986). For aspects of Carey's business interests, see Anthony F. C. Wallace, *St. Clair: A Nineteenth-Century Coal Town's Experience with a Disaster-Prone Industry* (New York: Knopf, 1987), 184–200; David Kaser, *Messrs. Carey & Lea of Philadelphia: A Study in the History of the Booktrade* (Philadelphia: University of Pennsylvania Press, 1957). Older but still useful studies include Joseph Dorfman, *The Economic Mind in American Civilization, 1606–1865* (New York: A. M. Kelley, 1966), 2:789–804; Arnold W. Green, *Henry Charles Carey, Nineteenth-Century Sociologist* (Philadelphia: University of Pennsylvania Press, 1951); George Winston Smith, *Henry C. Carey*

and American Sectional Conflict (Albuquerque: University of New Mexico Press, 1951); A.D.H. Kaplan, *Henry Charles Carey: A Study in American Economic Thought* (Baltimore, MD: Johns Hopkins University Press, 1931).

6. Conkin, *Prophets of Prosperity*, 284.

7. Jesse Buel, *The Farmer's Companion, or, Essays on the Principles and Practice of American Husbandry* (Boston: Marsh, Capen, Lyon, and Webb, 1839), 21.

8. Clarence H. Danhof, *Change in Agriculture: The Northern United States, 1820–1870* (Cambridge, MA: Harvard University Press, 1969), 254; Stevenson Whitcomb Fletcher, *Pennsylvania Agriculture and Country Life, 1640–1840* (Harrisburg: Pennsylvania Historical and Museum Commission, 1950), 124–25.

9. Sally McMurry, *Transforming Rural Life: Dairying Families and Agricultural Change, 1820–1885* (Baltimore, MD: Johns Hopkins University Press, 1995), 29; Richard A. Wines, "The Nineteenth-Century Agricultural Transition in an Eastern Long Island Community," *Agricultural History* 55 (Jan. 1981): 54; Richard A. Wines, *Fertilizer in America: From Waste Recycling to Resource Exploitation* (Philadelphia: Temple University Press, 1985), 9–17; Steven Stoll, *Larding the Lean Earth: Soil and Society in Nineteenth-Century America* (New York: Hill and Wang, 2002), 25, 49–54; Danhof, *Change in Agriculture*, 49–52; G. E. Mingay, *The Agricultural Revolution: Changes in Agriculture, 1650–1880* (London: Adam & Charles Black, 1977), chap. 3.

10. On the recycling mentality, see Wines, *Fertilizer in America*. On urban fertilizers, also see Catherine McNeur, *Taming Manhattan: Environmental Battles in the Antebellum City* (Cambridge, MA: Harvard University Press, 2014), 101–9; Clay McShane and Joel A. Tarr, *The Horse in the City: Living Machines in the Nineteenth Century* (Baltimore, MD: Johns Hopkins University Press, 2007), 131–32; Joel A. Tarr, "From City to Farm: Urban Wastes and the American Farmer," *Agricultural History* 49 (Oct. 1975): 598–612.

11. On the manufacturing process, see McNeur, *Taming Manhattan*, 119–26; Wines, *Fertilizer in America*, 25–30.

12. "Poudrette as a Manure," *American Agriculturist* 2 (Apr. 1843): 25.

13. Buel, *Farmer's Companion*, 72.

14. *American Farmer* 4 (May 1849): 379; *Third Annual Report of the American Institute, on the Subject of Agriculture*, New York State Senate doc. no. 124 (Apr. 22, 1844): 134–37; *New and Improved Poudrette of the Lodi Manufacturing Company* ([New York], 1853), 2–3.

15. "The Feeding of Cities," *Working Farmer* 7 (Apr. 1855): 43.

16. Gregory T. Cushman, *Guano and the Opening of the Pacific World: A Global Ecological History* (Cambridge: Cambridge University Press, 2013); Edward D. Melillo, "The First Green Revolution: Debt Peonage and the Making of the Nitrogen Fertilizer Trade, 1840–1930," *American Historical Review* 117 (Oct. 2012): 1028–60.

17. See several undated items in Hare-APS, series 1, box 4 and series 2, boxes 9 and 12. For fish fertilizers in general, see Wines, *Fertilizer in America*, 87–95.

18. Lewis B. Nelson, *History of the U.S. Fertilizer Industry*, ed. J. Harold Parker (Muscle Shoals, AL: Tennessee Valley Authority, 1990), 45; Wines, *Fertilizer in America*, 87, 96–111.

19. Gouverneur Emerson, *Address Delivered before the Agricultural Society of Chester County, Pennsylvania, September 17, 1853* (Philadelphia: T. K. and P. G. Collins, 1853), 13; "Artificial Manures," *Genesee Farmer* 8 (Sept. 1852): 269.

20. Nelson, *History of the U.S. Fertilizer Industry*, 42–45, 100

21. James Rose Hubbard diary, 1855, Guilford Free Library, Guilford, CT.

22. Constitution and minutes, Aug. 13, 1859, ASNC-HSD; "The Progression of Primaries: Analysis of Soils and Fertilizers," *New England Farmer* 9 (Sept. 1859): 411; Stevenson Whitcomb Fletcher, *Pennsylvania Agriculture and Country Life, 1840–1940* (Harrisburg: Pennsylvania Historical and Museum Commission, 1955), 94.

23. L. H. Bailey, *The State and the Farmer* (New York: Macmillan, 1911), 59; Wines, *Fertilizer in America*, 7.

24. "Our Present System of Agriculture—Its Defects and Remedies," *Cincinnatus* 1 (Jan. 1856): 11; George E. Waring Jr., "Agricultural Features of the Census of the United States for 1850," reprinted in *Organization & Environment* 12 (1999): 306.

25. American Institute [of the City of New York], *Report on the Commercial Intercourse of the United States and Great Britain* (New York: Jared W. Bell, 1844), 11.

26. On American exceptionalism in this regard, see Dorothy Ross, *The Origins of American Social Science* (Cambridge: Cambridge University Press, 1991), chap. 2.

27. Thomas Malthus, *An Essay on the Principle of Population*, ed. Geoffrey Gilbert (Oxford: Oxford University Press, 2004); David Ricardo, *Principles of Political Economy and Taxation*, ed. E.C.K. Gonner (London: G. Bell and Sons, 1919), 44.

28. Friedrich List, *The National System of Political Economy*, trans. Sampson S. Lloyd (London: Longmans, Green, and Co., 1916), 104, 206. For the American influence on List, see Keith Tribe, *Strategies of Economic Order: German Economic Discourse, 1750–1950* (Cambridge: Cambridge University Press, 2007), 32–65.

29. Henry C. Carey, *Principles of Political Economy* (Philadelphia: Carey, Lea & Blanchard, 1837), 1:189.

30. Conkin, *Prophets of Prosperity*, 270–71.

31. Henry C. Carey, *The Past, the Present, and the Future*, Reprints of Economic Classics (New York: A. M. Kelley, 1967), 9–133 (quotations on 24, 48).

32. Henry C. Carey, *The Harmony of Interests: Agricultural, Manufacturing, and Commercial*, Reprints of Economic Classics (New York: A. M. Kelley, 1967), 86.

33. Joseph A. Schumpeter, *History of Economic Analysis*, ed. Elizabeth Boody Schumpeter (N.p.: Taylor & Francis e-Library, 2006), 491. While praising his vision, Schumpeter also deplored Carey's "technical deficiency" as an economist (492).

34. Carey, *The Past, the Present, and the Future*, 62 ("all soils"), 92 ("present limited knowledge"); Carey, *Harmony of Interests*, 86 ("better machinery"), 125 ("whole business").

35. Carey, *The Past, the Present, and the Future*, 284–314 (quotation on 306).

36. For Carey's ideas in agricultural addresses, see "Extracts from an Address Delivered by the Hon. Jeremiah S. Black, before the Somerset County Agricultural Society," *Pennsylvania Farm Journal* 5 (Jan. 1855): 21–22; Sidney George Fisher, *Address Delivered before the Montgomery County Agricultural Society at Their Annual Exhibition Held at Springtown, October 7th, 1859* (Philadelphia: James B. Chandler, 1859), 6–18. For Carey and the *New-York Tribune*, see Michael Perelman, *Marx's Crisis Theory: Scarcity, Labor, and Finance* (New York: Praeger, 1987), chap. 2. For influence abroad, see, for example, [Count] Kardoff-Wabnitz to Carey, May 15, 1876, Carey-HSP, box 19; Gordon Alexander Craig, *Germany, 1866–1945* (New York: Oxford University Press, 1978), 87. For Republicans, see Arthur M. Lee, "Henry C. Carey and the Republican Tariff," *Pennsylvania Magazine of History and Biography* 81 (July 1957): 280–302; George Winston Smith,

"Ante-Bellum Attempts of Northern Business Interests to 'Redeem' the Upper South," *Journal of Southern History* 11 (May 1945): 177–213. For Lincoln and Emerson, see below in this chapter.

37. "The Mineral and Other Resources of the West," *Hunt's Merchant Magazine* 30 (Mar. 1, 1854): 322.

38. David Lowenthal, *George Perkins Marsh, Prophet of Conservation* (Seattle: University of Washington Press, 2000); Stephen C. Trombulak, "Introduction," in *So Great a Vision: The Conservation Writings of George Perkins Marsh*, ed. Stephen C. Trombulak (Hanover, NH: Middlebury College Press, published by University Press of New England, 2001), ix–xviii; Richard W. Judd, "George Perkins Marsh: The Times and Their Man," *Environment and History* 10 (May 2004): 169–90.

39. George Perkins Marsh, *Address Delivered before the Agricultural Society of Rutland County, Sept. 30, 1847* (Rutland, VT: Herald Office, 1848), 6; George Perkins Marsh, *Man and Nature*, ed. David Lowenthal (Seattle: University of Washington Press, 2003), 29.

40. George Perkins Marsh, "The Study of Nature," in *So Great a Vision*.

41. Marsh, *Address Delivered before the Agricultural Society of Rutland County, Sept. 30, 1847*, 24.

42. Justus Liebig, *Familiar Letters on Chemistry and Its Relation to Commerce, Physiology and Agriculture*, ed. John Gardner (New York: D. Appleton & Co., 1843), 116. This essay is reprinted in *Working Farmer* 5 (Apr. 1853): 44.

43. Quoted in John Bellamy Foster and Fred Magdoff, "Liebig, Marx and the Depletion of Soil Fertility: Relevance for Today's Agriculture," in *Hungry for Profit: The Agribusiness Threat to Farmers, Food, and the Environment*, ed. Fred Magdoff, John Bellamy Foster, and Frederick H. Buttel (New York: Monthly Review Press, 2000), 49.

44. *Report of the Commissioner of Patents for the Year 1852: Agriculture* (Washington, DC: Robert Armstrong, 1853): 3–4.

45. "Our Present System of Agriculture—Its Defects and Remedies," 10. See also A Farmer, "The Study of Political Economy," *Merchants' Magazine and Commercial Review* 24 (Apr. 1851): 454, with replies by R.S. (June 1851): 704, and E.P.S., "Protection vs. Free Trade," 25 (July 1851): 67–68.

46. Horace Greeley, "Needs of American Agriculture," *Cincinnatus* 3 (Nov. 1858): 488.

47. Waring, "Agricultural Features of the Census of the United States for 1850," 306. For Carey and Liebig, see John Bellamy Foster, " 'Robbing the Earth of Its Capital Stock': An Introduction to George Waring's Agricultural Features of the Census of the United States for 1850," *Organization & Environment* 12 (Sept. 1999): 293–94.

48. Land for Agricultural Colleges, &c., to Accompany Bill H. R. No. 2," Apr. 15, 1858, 35th cong., 1st sess., House Report no. 261, p. 12.

49. Tarr, "From City to Farm," 598–600.

50. "Night Soil—Its Preparation, Use and Value in Agriculture," *American Farmer* 7 (Feb. 3, 1826): 362.

51. Dana Simmons, "Waste Not, Want Not: Excrement and Economy in Nineteenth-Century France," *Representations* 96 (Autumn 2006): 84–85.

52. Christopher Hamlin, *Public Health and Social Justice in the Age of Chadwick: Britain, 1800–1854* (Cambridge: Cambridge University Press, 1998), 237–40; Martin Melosi, *Pragmatic Environmentalist, Sanitary Engineer George E. Waring, Jr.* (Washington,

DC: Public Works Historical Society, 1977); Martin V. Melosi, *Garbage in the Cities: Refuse, Reform, and the Environment, 1880–1980* (College Station: Texas A&M University Press, 1981), 51–78.

53. A. Peysson, *Public Health and Agriculture* (Philadelphia: J. H. Jones, 1851), 4, 10.

54. *Philadelphia Press*, Sept. 19, 1857, 3, and Oct. 9, 1857, 2; *The Street Sweeping & Fertilizing Co. of Philadelphia: Incorporated by the State of Pennsylvania. Its Objects, Facilities and Prospects of Operation in the City of Philadelphia, and Other Cities and Towns of the United States. Charter Perpetual* (Philadelphia: King & Baird, 1857).

55. Victor Hugo, *Les Misérables*, trans. Lee Fahnestock and Norman MacAfee (New York: Signet, 2013), 1256–57; Donald Reid, *Paris Sewers and Sewermen: Realities and Representations* (Cambridge, MA: Harvard University Press, 1991), 20–21. My thanks to Simon Vezina for drawing my attention to Hugo's discussion of this topic.

56. Edward S. Morse, *Japan Day by Day, 1877, 1878–79, 1882–83* (Boston: Houghton Mifflin, 1917), 23–24; Yuko Tanaka, "The Cyclical Sensibility of Edo-Period Japan," *Japan Echo* 25 (Apr. 1998).

57. Wines, *Fertilizer in America*; Tarr, "From City to Farm."

58. H. C. Carey, *Principles of Social Science* (Philadelphia: J. B. Lippincott & Co., 1858), 1:34.

59. Michael Hudson, *America's Protectionist Takeoff, 1815–1914* (Dresden: ISLET, 2010), 155–74; Michael Hudson, *Economics and Technology in 19th Century American Thought* (New York: Garland, 1975), 212–27; Michael Hudson, "E. Peshine Smith: A Study in Protectionist Growth Theory and American Socialism" (PhD diss.: New York University, 1968). For biographical details, see also Frederick W. Seward, *Reminiscences of a War-Time Statesman and Diplomat, 1830–1915* (New York: G. P. Putnam's Sons, 1916), 85, 91–92; John Henry Hobart Peshine, *The Peshine Family in Europe and in America* (Santa Barbara, CA: Frank Morley, 1916), 80–81; Meryl Frank and Blake McKelvey, "Some Former Rochesterians of National Distinction," *Rochester History* 21 (July 1959): 22.

60. E. Peshine Smith, *A Manual of Political Economy* (New York: George P. Putnam & Co., 1853), iii.

61. Hudson, *America's Protectionist Takeoff, 1815–1914*, 159.

62. Hudson, *America's Protectionist Takeoff, 1815–1914*, 164–65. See Smith to Carey, Oct. 8, 1854, Carey-HSP, box 18.

63. Hudson, "E. Peshine Smith," 75–114. For references to Volta's work and to various agricultural chemists, see Smith, *Manual of Political Economy*, 24–26, 33, 36, 37, 41–42ff., 46, 51. For familiarity with Joule, see Smith to Carey, Dec. 28, 1854, Carey-HSP, box 18. As Hudson points out, Smith continued to work out his ideas after publication of the *Manual* in his correspondence with Carey.

64. The discussion in this paragraph draws on Bruce J. Hunt, *Pursuing Power and Light: Technology and Physics from James Watt to Albert Einstein* (Baltimore, MD: Johns Hopkins University Press, 2010), chaps. 1–3; Ronald E. Martin, *American Literature and the Universe of Force* (Durham, NC: Duke University Press, 1981), chaps. 1–3; Anson Rabinbach, *The Human Motor: Energy, Fatigue, and the Origins of Modernity* (New York: Basic Books, 1990), chap. 2.

65. Smith, *Manual of Political Economy*, 33.

66. Smith to Carey, Oct. 21, 1854, Carey-HSP, box 18.

67. Smith to Carey, July 13, 1855, Carey-HSP, box 18.

68. Smith to Carey, Feb. 21, 1857, Carey-HSP, box 18.

69. Hudson, *America's Protectionist Takeoff, 1815–1914*, 163; Smith to Carey, Oct. 11, 1855, Carey-HSP, box 18.

70. Smith to Carey, Feb. 22, 1854, Carey-HSP, box 18 ("certain orbit"; "question whether"); Smith, *Manual of Political Economy*, 35–36.

71. Smith, *Manual of Political Economy*, 71–72, 74.

72. Smith, *Manual of Political Economy*, 17. For a similar formulation, see Marsh, "The Study of Nature," 75.

73. Carey, *Principles of Social Science*, 1:35, 94, 95, 418.

74. Thomas D. Birch, "Toward a Better Order: The Economic Thought of Ralph Waldo Emerson," *New England Quarterly* 68 (Sept. 1995): 385–401; Kenneth Cameron, "Emerson's Second Merlin Song and Economist H. C. Carey," *Emerson Society Quarterly* 13 (1958): 65–83.

75. [Anna?] M. M. Storm to Carey, Aug. 29, 1862, Carey-HSP, box 18.

76. Charles Flint, ed., *Abstract of Returns of the Agricultural Societies of Massachusetts, 1858* (Boston: William White, 1859), 17–18.

77. Ralph Waldo Emerson, "Wealth," in *The Conduct of Life* (1860), The Complete Works of Ralph Waldo Emerson, http://www.rwe.org/iii-wealth.

78. Ralph Waldo Emerson, "Farming," in *Society and Solitude* (1870), The Complete Works of Ralph Waldo Emerson, https://www.rwe.org/chapter-vi-farming.

79. For Carey's influence, see Reinhard H. Luthin, "Abraham Lincoln and the Tariff," *American Historical Review* 49 (July 1944): 626–27.

80. Abraham Lincoln, *The Collected Works of Abraham Lincoln* (Springfield, IL: Abraham Lincoln Association, 1953), 3:478, http://quod.lib.umich.edu/l/lincoln.

81. Lincoln, *The Collected Works of Abraham Lincoln*, 3:479.

82. For example, see Buel, *Farmer's Companion*, 30.

83. Lincoln, *The Collected Works of Abraham Lincoln*, 3:474.

84. Lincoln, *The Collected Works of Abraham Lincoln*, 3:363.

85. For this reading, see Steven B. Smith, "Lincoln's Enlightenment," in *Principle and Prudence in Western Political Thought*, ed. Christopher Lynch and Jonathan Marks (Albany: State University of New York Press, 2016); John Sexton, "On Lincoln's 'Pragmatism,'" *American Political Thought* 2 (Spring 2013): 89–117.

86. Charles Postel, *Equality: An American Dilemma, 1866–1896* (New York: Farrar, Straus and Giroux, 2019), chaps. 1–3.

Chapter 5 · A Crisis of Agricultural Expertise

1. *Working Farmer* 9 (1857): 113 (emphasis in original). Because this chapter references a great many items from the farm press, citations are generally kept to the bare minimum of publication title, volume, year and page. This is usually sufficient to find the references with ease because agricultural journals, unlike newspapers, typically had few items to the page. Additional details are provided in cases where there might be any difficulty or ambiguity. Mapes elaborated his theory in many articles and comments in the *Working Farmer* from late 1856 onward. For fairly full statements, see *Transactions of the American Institute of the City of New York, for the Year 1856* (Albany: C. Van Benthuysen, 1857): 328–36; "Agriculture," in *The American Annual Cyclopædia and Register of Important Events of the Year 1861* (New York: D. Appleton & Co., 1864), 2–9.

2. *Working Farmer* 11 (1859): 1–2.

3. "Mapes' 'Progressive Primaries,'" *Genesee Farmer* 21 (1860): 170–71; "Report of Prof. S. W. Johnson, Chemist to the Society, for 1859," *Transactions of the Connecticut State Agricultural Society, for the Year 1859, with Report of the Annual Meeting, for 1860* (Hartford: Williams, Wiley and Turner, 1859), 47.

4. "The Late Professor James J. Mapes," *Horticulturist* 21 (Mar. 1866): 93; J. O. Barrett, "Progressive Primaries for Fruit Growing," in *Annual Report of the Minnesota State Horticultural Society* 14 (St. Paul: J. W. Cunningham, 1886): 184–88.

5. "Progression of Primaries," *Boston Journal of Chemistry* 6 (Aug. 1871): 18, referencing an article in the *Journal of Applied Chemistry*, probably the periodical of that name published in New York.

6. *Proceedings of the American Pharmaceutical Association at the Eighth Annual Meeting* (Boston: Geo. C. Rand & Avery, 1859), 373–74; Andrew Jackson Davis, *The Harbinger of Health, Containing Medical Prescriptions for the Human Body and Mind* (New York: C. M. Plumb & Co., 1865), 155.

7. Margaret W. Rossiter, *The Emergence of Agricultural Science: Justus Liebig and the Americans, 1840–1880* (New Haven, CT: Yale University Press, 1975); Emily Pawley, "Accounting with the Fields: Chemistry and Value in Nutriment in American Agricultural Improvement, 1835–1860," *Science as Culture* 19 (Dec. 2010): 461–82.

8. John S. Skinner, "Address on Agriculture," *Monthly Journal of Agriculture* 2 (Nov. 1846): 215; *Report of Commissioners concerning an Agricultural School, January 1851* (Boston, 1851), 5.

9. *The Plough, the Loom, and the Anvil* 6 (1853): 90.

10. Diary of William Claytor, 1849–1896, vol. 1, July 28, 1849, https://search.alexanderstreet.com/preview/work/bibliographic_entity%7Cbibliographic_details%7C4362149.

11. Reprinted from *New York Sun* as "Science Applied to Agriculture," *Working Farmer* 1 (1850): 181.

12. Paul Wallace Gates, *The Farmer's Age: Agriculture, 1815–1860* (New York: Holt, Rinehart and Winston, 1960), 316.

13. *American Agriculturist* 2 (1843): 318.

14. Rossiter, *Emergence of Agricultural Science*, 119–20; constitution and minutes, Oct. 18, 1849, ASNC-HSD.

15. Justus Liebig, *Familiar Letters on Chemistry and Its Relation to Commerce, Physiology and Agriculture*, ed. John Gardner (New York: D. Appleton & Co., 1843), 172; Justus Liebig, *Letters on Modern Agriculture*, ed. John Blyth (New York: John Wiley, 1859), 1.

16. Rossiter, *Emergence of Agricultural Science*, 40–46 (quotation on 46); Pawley, "Accounting with the Fields," 471–73.

17. Rossiter, *Emergence of Agricultural Science*; Benjamin Cohen, *Notes from the Ground: Science, Soil, and Society in the American Countryside* (New Haven, CT: Yale University Press, 2009), chap. 1; David B. Danbom, "The Agricultural Experiment Station and Professionalization: Scientists' Goals for Agriculture," *Agricultural History* 60 (Spring 1986): 246–55; Charles E. Rosenberg, "Rationalization and Reality in the Shaping of American Agricultural Research, 1875–1914," *Social Studies of Science* 7 (Nov. 1977): 401–22.

18. Rossiter, *Emergence of Agricultural Science,* 91–108.

19. Rossiter, *Emergence of Agricultural Science,* 109, 117–18.

20. *American Agriculturist* 2 (1843): 376, and 3 (1844): 71, 127, 256.

21. See, for example, Samuel W. Johnson, "Agricultural Charlatanry," *Cultivator* 1 (1853): 35–36.

22. "Analysis of Soils, Manures, &c.," *Cultivator* 7 (May 1850): 184; Pawley, "Accounting with the Fields," 476.

23. For Antisell's advertisements, see *American Agriculturist* 9 (May 1850): 199; for his credentials, see Thomas Antisell, *A Manual of Agricultural Chemistry, with Its Application to the Soils of Ireland* (Dublin: Hodges and Smith, 1845); *American Journal of Science and Arts* 26 (1858): 126, and 29 (1860): 112; for notices of Antisell's and Gardner's work with the American Agricultural Association, see *Transactions of the New York State Agricultural Society* 8 (Albany: Weed, Parsons and Co., 1848): 592; *American Quarterly Journal of Agriculture and Science* 1 (1845): 352; see also the respectful notice given to one of Gardner's scientific papers in the *Journal of the Franklin Institute* 13 (1847): 106–13.

24. "Our Present Volume," *American Agriculturist* 9 (Jan. 1850): 11; A. Hunter Dupree, *Science in the Federal Government: A History of Policies and Activities to 1940* (Cambridge, MA: Belknap Press, 1957), 152–53.

25. *New England Farmer* 17 (1839): 101, 300–301, 308–9.

26. *New England Farmer* 5 (1853): 116, 284; *Transactions of the Agricultural Societies of the State of Massachusetts for 1851* (Boston: Dutton and Wentworth, 1852), 398–99. On Nash, see Liberty Hyde Bailey, ed., *Cyclopedia of American Agriculture,* 4 vols. (New York: Macmillan, 1911), 4:370, 383–84; Robert S. Fletcher and Malcolm O. Young, eds., *Amherst College Biographical Record of the Graduates and Non-Graduates, Centennial Edition, 1821–1921* (Amherst, MA: The College, 1927).

27. *Monthly Journal of Agriculture* 2 (1847): 337, and 3 (1848): 315–16; *New England Farmer* 17 (1838): 101; *American Farmer* 4 (1848): 15.

28. *Ohio Cultivator* 6 (1850): 375; *Southern Planter* 9 (1849): 124–25, and 10 (1850): 107–8; *DeBow's Review* 2 (1852): 538.

29. Rossiter, *Emergence of Agricultural Science,* 121–22.

30. *New England Farmer* 5 (1853): 125 (emphasis in original); *Cultivator* 4 (1856): 244.

31. *Country Gentleman* 4 (July 1854): 5–6.

32. "An Address to the Members of the Society by James Worth, President, Delivered 8th May 1820," p. 4, ASBS-MMSL; Eaton quoted in Emily Pawley, "'The Balance-Sheet of Nature': Calculating the New York Farm, 1820–1860" (PhD diss., University of Pennsylvania, 2009), 141.

33. *Working Farmer* 1 (1849): 108, 137, and 2 (1859): 123.

34. *Working Farmer* 1 (1849): 154; *Monthly Journal of Agriculture* 1 (1845): 52. Examples could be multiplied; see Courtney Fullilove, "The Archive of Useful Knowledge" (PhD diss., Columbia University, 2009), 243–44.

35. *Ohio Cultivator* 9 (1853): 129 (emphasis in original); *Cultivator* 1 (1853): 266; *New England Farmer* 5 (1853): 205.

36. *Prairie Farmer* 13 (1853): 341.

37. See, for example, *Cultivator* 1 (1853): 266, 307.

38. *Report of Commissioners concerning an Agricultural School, January 1851*, 5–6 (emphasis added).

39. For favorable references to Mapes regarding his advocacy of soil analysis, see *American Farmer* 6 (1851): 351; *Maine Farmer*, July 15, 1852, 1.

40. The following discussion of Mapes's life is compiled from the World Biographical Information System Online, American Biographical Archive, series 1, microfiche 1068, frames 176–87; *Family Record* (1897): 33–35; John Howard Brown, *Lamb's Biographical Dictionary of the United States* (Boston: Federal Book Company of Boston, 1903), 351–52; Mark R. Finlay, "James Jay Mapes," in *ANB*; Williams Haynes, *Chemical Pioneers: The Founders of the American Chemical Industry* (New York: D. Van Nostrand Co., 1939), 74–87; Ethan Robey, "The Utility of Art: Mechanics' Institute Fairs in New York City, 1828–1876" (PhD diss., Columbia University, 2000), 135–38.

41. For Waring, see Richard Skolnick, "George E. Waring, Jr.: A Model for Reformers," *New-York Historical Society Quarterly* 47 (July 1963): 257–87; Albert Shaw, *Life of Col. Geo. E. Waring, Jr.: The Great Apostle of Cleanliness* (New York: Patriotic League, 1899); Martin Melosi, *Pragmatic Environmentalist, Sanitary Engineer George E. Waring, Jr.* (Washington, DC: Public Works Historical Society, 1977). For Quinn, see *The History of the New Jersey Agricultural Society: Early Attempts to Form a Society, Proceedings, Fairs, Activities and Accomplishments, 1781–1940* (Trenton, NJ: The Society, 1947), 41, 57–58; *Fourth Annual Report of the New Jersey State Agricultural Experiment Station for the Year 1883* (Vineland: Henry W. Wilbur, 1883): 5.

42. Reprinted in *American Farmer* 1 (1866): 84.

43. For instance, when Mapes reprinted one of Liebig's *Familiar Letters on Chemistry* in the *Working Farmer* he prefaced it by recommending that it "be studied by rote" (*Working Farmer* 5 [1853]: 43).

44. *Working Farmer* 2 (1851): 241.

45. C. M. Warren to Everett, July 13, 1854, Everett-HML; *Transactions of the American Institute of the City of New York for the Year 1854* (Albany: C. Van Benthuysen, 1855), 119.

46. For the history of the early American fertilizer and superphosphate industry, see Richard A. Wines, *Fertilizer in America: From Waste Recycling to Resource Exploitation* (Philadelphia: Temple University Press, 1985); K. D. Jacob, "History and Status of the Superphosphate Industry," in *Superphosphate: Its History, Chemistry, and Manufacture*, United States Department of Agriculture and Tennessee Valley Authority (Washington, DC: GPO, 1964), 19–94.

47. Harry A. Curtis, "Liebig and the Chemistry of Mineral Fertilizers," in *Liebig and after Liebig: A Century of Progress in Agricultural Chemistry*, ed. Forest Ray Moulton (Washington, DC: American Association for the Advancement of Science, 1942), 64–70.

48. *American Farmer* 6 (1850): 105–7.

49. *New and Improved Poudrette of the Lodi Manufacturing Company* ([New York, NY?: N.p.], 1853), 2–3, Library Company of Philadelphia.

50. *American Farmer* 4 (May 1849): 379; Lewis B. Nelson, *History of the U.S. Fertilizer Industry*, ed. J. Harold Parker (Muscle Shoals, AL: Tennessee Valley Authority, 1990), 45.

51. Previous examinations of this episode have not looked at Mapes's response; see Rossiter, *Emergence of Agricultural Science*, 149–56; Wines, *Fertilizer in America*, 101–3;

A. L. Demaree, "The Farm Journals, Their Editors, and Their Public, 1830–1860," *Agricultural History* 15 (Oct. 1941): 185.

52. *Genesee Farmer* 14 (1853): 281.

53. *Remarks on the Origin and Application of Guano. For Sale by Allen & Needles, Dealers in Oil and Guano, 22 and 23 South Wharves, Above Chestnut Street, Philadelphia* (Philadelphia: [Allen & Needles], [1849?]), 6, Library Company of Philadelphia.

54. "Report of Prof. S. W. Johnson, Chemist to the Society, for 1859," 41.

55. *Cultivator* 9 (1852): 365.

56. *Ohio Cultivator* 9 (1853): 129.

57. *Working Farmer* 11 (1859): 80.

58. Liebig, *Familiar Letters on Chemistry*, 55–60.

59. *Working Farmer* 10 (1858): 121.

60. "Agriculture," in *American Annual Cyclopædia and Register of Important Events of the Year 1861*, 2.

61. *Michigan Farmer* 12 (1854): 234. See also *Ohio Cultivator* 9 (1853): 83.

62. *Working Farmer* 13 (1861): 2.

63. *Working Farmer* 12 (1860): 49.

64. *Working Farmer* 1 (1849): 98; see also James Jay Mapes, "Inaugural Address, Delivered Tuesday Evening, Jan. 7, 1845, before the Mechanics' Institute, of the City of New York" (New York: Institute Rooms, 1845).

65. *Transactions of the American Institute of the City of New York, for the Year 1856*, 336.

66. "Report of Prof. S. W. Johnson, Chemist to the Society, for 1859," 47.

67. Rossiter, *Emergence of Agricultural Science*, 158–59; Alan I. Marcus, *Agricultural Science and the Quest for Legitimacy: Farmers, Agricultural Colleges, and Experiment Stations, 1870–1890* (Ames: Iowa State University Press, 1985).

68. Williams Haynes, *Chemical Pioneers: The Founders of the American Chemical Industry* (New York: D. Van Nostrand Co., 1939), 76.

69. This is the view given in Wines, *Fertilizer in America*, 96–101.

70. For biographical information, see Ezra S. Stearns, William Frederick Whitcher, and Edward Everett Parker, eds., *Genealogical and Family History of the State of New Hampshire* (New York: Lewis Publishing Co., 1908), 4:1799–801.

71. Henry F. French, "Chemical Fertilizers," *Transactions of the Massachusetts Horticultural Society, for the Year 1876*, part 1 (Boston: The Society, 1876), 113.

72. *New England Farmer* 9 (1859): 410.

73. *New England Farmer* 7 (1856): 271.

74. *New England Farmer* 9 (1859): 410.

75. See, for example, Ronald E. Martin, *American Literature and the Universe of Force* (Durham, NC: Duke University Press, 1981), chaps. 2–3.

76. Jackson's remarks are reprinted in the *Working Farmer* 12 (1860): 33.

77. *Transactions of the American Institute of the City of New York for 1856*, 335.

78. *New England Farmer* 9 (1859): 410.

79. "Profess J. J. Mapes," *Tiffany's Monthly* 3 (1857): 80.

80. *Transactions of the American Institute of the City of New York, for the Year 1856*, 336–37.

81. *Pennsylvania Farm Journal* 5 (1855): 88.

82. *Cultivator* 2 (1854): 235.

83. *Maine Farmer* 29 (July 11, 1861): 1.

84. George Edwin Waring, *The Elements of Agriculture: A Book for Young Farmers* (New York: Tribune Association, 1868), 7–8.

85. Bailey, *Cyclopedia of American Agriculture*, 4:379.

86. *Cincinnatus* 3 (Nov. 1858): 482–83.

87. *Cincinnatus* 1 (Jan. 1856): 10–12, and 2 (Jan. 1857).

88. *New England Farmer* 5 (May 1853): 205.

89. Cong. Globe, 35th Cong., 1st Sess., 1694.

90. Cong. Globe, 37th Cong., 2nd Sess., 1692.

91. James M. Swank, *The Department of Agriculture: Its History and Objects* (Washington, DC: GPO, 1872), 55.

92. Rossiter, *Emergence of Agricultural Science*, 149–71.

93. Rossiter, *Emergence of Agricultural Science*, 130; Roger L. Williams, *Evan Pugh's Penn State: America's Model Agricultural College* (University Park: Penn State University Press, 2018), chaps. 1–3; Mark R. Finlay, "The German Agricultural Experiment Stations and the Beginnings of American Agricultural Research," *Agricultural History* 62 (Spring 1988): 41–50.

94. *Pennsylvania Farm Journal* 5 (1855): 6, 36.

95. *The Agricultural College of Pennsylvania* (Philadelphia: William S. Young, 1862), 46–48.

96. Newspaper clipping, June 29, 1861, in clippings file, CCAS-CCHS.

97. *Transactions of the New York State Agricultural Society* 12 (Albany: C. Van Benthuysen, 1853): 9.

98. *Transactions of the New York State Agricultural Society*, 12:365.

99. *Pennsylvania Farm Journal* 5 (1855): 235.

100. *Farm Journal and Progressive Farmer* 6 (1856): 355.

101. *Working Farmer* 9 (1857): 8; *Farm Journal and Progressive Farmer* 6 (1856): 28.

102. *Maine Farmer,* June 11, 1857, 1.

103. *Valley Farmer* 9 (1857): 269. See also *New England Farmer* 9 (1857): 420.

104. *New York Times*, Sept. 18, 1866, 5; *Second National Trial of Mowers, Reapers, Horse Powers, Etc., at Auburn, 1866* (Albany, NY: Benthuysen, 1867).

105. Emily Pawley, "The Point of Perfection: Cattle Portraiture, Bloodlines, and the Meaning of Breeding, 1760–1860," *Journal of the Early Republic* 36 (Spring 2016): 37–72; Emily Pawley, "Cataloging Nature: Standardizing Fruit Varieties in the United States, 1800–1860," *Business History Review* 90 (Sept. 2016): 405–29.

106. Wines, *Fertilizer in America*, 126–35 (quotation on 128).

107. Quoted in Marcus, *Agricultural Science and the Quest for Legitimacy*, 42.

108. "Montrose Mowing Machine Trial," *Independent Republican* (Montrose, PA), Aug. 19, 1858, 2, and Sept. 9, 1858, 2; *Second Annual Descriptive and Illustrative Catalogue of Agricultural Implements & Machines: Manufactured at the Tioga-Point Agricultural & Junction Iron Works* (Elmira, NY: Daily Advertiser Steam Book and Job Press, 1859); see also Richard Lamb Allen, *Protest against the Report and Awards on the Field Trial of Reapers and Mowers, and Harvest Implements by the United States Agricultural Society, at Syracuse, July, 1857* (New York: N.p., 1858).

109. For the Allens' advocacy of agricultural colleges, see *American Agriculturist* 3

(Feb. 1844): 52; R. L. Allen, *Compend of American Agriculture* (New York: Saxton & Miles, 1846), 8–9.

110. Marcus, *Agricultural Science and the Quest for Legitimacy,* 42.

111. *Report of the Register of the Maryland Agricultural College, to the Board of Trustees; Act of Incorporation, with Amendments Thereto: List of Officers, and Names of Stockholders, with Number of Shares Held by Each* (Baltimore, MD: Samuel S. Mills, 1858), 23–29; for the advertisements of some of these firms, see unpaginated advertiser section in *DeBow's Review* 5, nos. 5 and 6 (May–June 1861); *American Farmer* 13 (July 1857): 39, and 14 (June 1859): 391, 394.

112. Alfred Charles True, *A History of Agricultural Education in the United States, 1785–1925* (New York: Arno Press, 1969), 66–67.

Chapter 6 · From "Private Enterprise" to "Governmental Action"

1. For doubts, see Donald B. Marti, "The Purposes of Agricultural Education: Ideas and Projects in New York State, 1819–1865," *Agricultural History* 45 (Oct. 1971): 279; Gould P. Colman, *Education and Agriculture: A History of the New York State College of Agriculture at Cornell University* (Ithaca, NY: Cornell University, 1963), 31; Eldon L. Johnson, "Misconceptions about the Early Land-Grant Colleges," *Journal of Higher Education* 52 (July 1981): 336, 338.

2. Nathan M. Sorber, *Land-Grant Colleges and Popular Revolt: The Origins of the Morrill Act and the Reform of Higher Education* (Ithaca, NY: Cornell University Press, 2018); Mary Summers, "Conflicting Visions" (unpublished doctoral dissertation in author's possession), chap. 4; M. Elizabeth Sanders, *Roots of Reform: Farmers, Workers, and the American State, 1877–1917* (Chicago: University of Chicago Press, 1999), 316–17; Edwin C. Rozwenc, *Agricultural Policies in Vermont, 1860–1945* (Montpelier: Vermont Historical Society, 1981), 20–21; Charles Postel, *The Populist Vision* (Oxford: Oxford University Press, 2007), 45–48; Alan I. Marcus, *Agricultural Science and the Quest for Legitimacy: Farmers, Agricultural Colleges, and Experiment Stations, 1870–1890* (Ames: Iowa State University Press, 1985), 36–38; Theodore Saloutos, "The Grange in the South, 1870–1877," *Journal of Southern History* 19 (Nov. 1953): 485–86.

3. Carl Kaestle, *Pillars of the Republic: Common Schools and American Society, 1780–1860* (New York: Hill and Wang, 1983), 13, 29; Patricia Cline Cohen, *A Calculating People: The Spread of Numeracy in Early America* (New York: Routledge, 1999), 12, 116–49.

4. Sun Go and Peter Lindert, "The Uneven Rise of American Public Schools to 1850," *Journal of Economic History* 70 (Mar. 2010): 2.

5. Jeremy Atack and Fred Bateman, *To Their Own Soil: Agriculture in the Antebellum North* (Ames: Iowa State University Press, 1987), 47.

6. Nancy Beadie, "Toward a History of Education Markets in the United States: An Introduction," *Social Science History* 32 (Spring 2008): 59–60; see also Donald Hugh Parkerson and Jo Ann Parkerson, *The Emergence of the Common School in the U.S. Countryside* (Lewiston, NY: E. Mellen Press, 1998), 23–26, 48–49.

7. "Manures—No. 1," *Working Farmer* 1 (Feb. 1849): 4.

8. J. M Opal, *Beyond the Farm: National Ambitions in Rural New England* (Philadelphia: University of Pennsylvania Press, 2008).

9. Isaac Phillips Roberts, *Autobiography of a Farm Boy* (Albany: J. B. Lyon Co., 1916), 66–67.

10. *Annual Report of the Regents of the University of the State of New York* 56 (Albany: E. Mack, 1843): 174, 181.

11. Petition, Feb. 15, 1838, McAllister-LCP, box 23, item no. 7375 F 52.

12. *Annual Report of the Regents of the University of the State of New York* 70 (Albany: C. Van Benthuysen, 1857): 20, 23.

13. Quoted in Maris A. Vinovskis, "Horace Mann on the Economic Productivity of Education," *New England Quarterly* 43 (Dec. 1970): 563.

14. "Improvement," *Working Farmer* 1 (Apr. 1849): 37.

15. Emily Pawley, " 'The Balance-Sheet of Nature': Calculating the New York Farm, 1820–1860" (PhD diss., University of Pennsylvania, 2009), 40–41, 54–55, 69–70.

16. "The County Fair," *Semi-Weekly Eagle* (Brattleboro, VT), Oct. 6, 1851, 2.

17. Sanders P. McComsey, ed., *A History of the Octoraro Farmers' Club, 1856–1946* (Christiana, PA: Madison E. McElwain, 1948). For a similar example, see *Essays and Discussion on Agriculture, before the Farmers' Club of Little Falls* (Little Falls, NY: D. Ayer, 1859).

18. "On Agricultural Schools," *Agricultural Museum* 2 (20 Mar. 1811): 294.

19. "An Agricultural College and Experimental Farm," *New York Daily Tribune*, Feb. 14, 1844, 1.

20. "Farm Schools," *New York Daily Tribune*, May 6, 1845, 2.

21. *Transactions of the Society for the Promotion of Useful Arts, in the State of New-York* (Albany: Websters and Skinners, 1819), vol. 4, pt. 2; Liberty Hyde Bailey, ed., *Cyclopedia of American Agriculture* (New York: Macmillan Co., 1911), 4:386–87.

22. Simeon De Witt, *Considerations on the Necessity of Establishing an Agricultural College, and Having More of the Children of Wealthy Citizens, Educated for the Profession of Farming* (Albany, NY: Websters and Skinners, 1819), 5, 25–26.

23. "Agricultural School," *Plough Boy* 4 (Dec. 10, 1822): 218.

24. Marti, "Purposes of Agricultural Education," 278.

25. "Agricultural School—Report of the Committee on the Memorial of the New-York State Agricultural Society," *New York Farmer* 6 (Apr. 1833): 100.

26. "State Agricultural Schools," *Workingman's Advocate* 4 (Apr. 13, 1833): 1.

27. Bailey, *Cyclopedia of American Agriculture*, 4:389–90; Harry J. Carman, "Introduction," in *Jesse Buel, Agricultural Reformer: Selections from His Writings*, ed. Harry J. Carman (New York: Columbia University Press, 1947), xxiv–xxv.

28. *Rural Magazine and Literary Evening Fireside* 1 (June 1, 1820): 206; Herbert Galen Lull, *The Manual Labor Movement in the United States*, Bulletin of the University of Washington 8 (Seattle, 1914); Joseph J. McCadden, *Education in Pennsylvania, 1801–1835 and Its Debt to Robert Vaux* (New York: Arno Press, 1969).

29. *First Annual Report of the Society for Promoting Manual Labor in Literary Institutions: Including the Report of Their General Agent, Theodore D. Weld. January 28, 1833* (New York: S. W. Benedict & Co., 1833); Paul Goodman, "The Manual Labor Movement and the Origins of Abolitionism," *Journal of the Early Republic* 13 (Oct. 1993): 355–88.

30. Lull, *Manual Labor Movement in the United States*, 381–86; H. G. Good, "Early Attempts to Teach Agriculture in Old Virginia," *Virginia Magazine of History and Biography* 48 (Oct. 1940): 347–50.

31. Robert Dale Owen, *Threading My Way: Twenty-Seven Years of Autobiography* (London: Trübner & Co., 1874), 121–49; John Rogers Commons et al., *History of Labour in the United States* (New York: Macmillan, 1918), 1:247–48; McCadden, *Education in Pennsylvania*, 67–68.

32. Marti, "Purposes of Agricultural Education," 273–74.

33. Morris to Philip Emanuel von Fellenberg (copy), Mar. 8, 1827, Morris-HSP; also J. S. Skinner to Morris, Apr. 14, 1827, and Morris to Skinner (copy), Apr. 16, 1827; *American Journal of Education* 3 (1828): 505–8, 568–71; *American Farmer* 9 (Feb. 15, 1828): 378; McCadden, *Education in Pennsylvania*, 59–61.

34. For "great objects," Morris to Jeremiah Warder (copy), Apr. 27, 1827, Morris-HSP; for "profits," R. A. Rose to Morris, June 12, 1828; for practical difficulties, Morris to Warder, Apr. 27, 1827; W. Chaderton to Morris, Sept. 25, 1827; Jonathan Roberts to Morris, Oct. 13, 1827.

35. John Griscom to Haines, July 21, 1829, Haines-APS, box 19, folder 246.

36. Nancy Beadie, *Education and the Creation of Capital in the Early American Republic* (Cambridge: Cambridge University Press, 2010), 249–53.

37. Jeffrey A. Mullins, "'In the Sweat of Thy Brow': Education, Manual Labor, and the Market Revolution," in *Cultural Change and the Market Revolution in America, 1789–1860*, ed. Scott C. Martin (Lanham, MD: Rowman & Littlefield, 2005), 170–71.

38. One proposal, for instance, explicitly envisioned a "School of Industry for the Poor" alongside the main institution. See Mrs. Warder to Morris, July 17, 1827, Morris-HSP.

39. Mullins, "'In the Sweat of Thy Brow.'"

40. "Associated Effort—Agricultural Fairs," *Cincinnatus* 2 (Oct. 1857): 407 (emphasis in original).

41. "Benefits of Agricultural Fairs," *New England Farmer* 2 (Nov. 9. 1850): 373.

42. "Aurora Agricultural Institute," *Cultivator* 2 (Apr. 1845): 119.

43. Elizabeth A. Osborne, ed., *From the Letter-Files of S. W. Johnson* (New Haven, CT: Yale University Press, 1913), 84–85.

44. "Farmer's College, College Hill, Ohio," *Country Gentleman* 4 (Sept. 7, 1854): 151.

45. *New-York Daily Tribune*, Feb. 5, 1844, 2, 4; Feb. 9, 1844, 2; Feb. 23, 1844, 2; Feb. 24, 1844, 8; Mar. 23, 1844, 3.

46. *New-York Daily Tribune*, May 7, 1845, 2; *Genesee Farmer* 6 (May 1845): 69; E. Merton Coulter, *Daniel Lee, Agriculturist: His Life North and South* (Athens: University of Georgia Press, 1972), 3–6.

47. "Western N.Y. Agricultural School," *New-York Daily Tribune*, Oct. 14, 1846, 3; see also Feb. 5, 1846, 3; May 16, 1846, 1; Coulter, *Daniel Lee, Agriculturist*, 7–8.

48. "Young Men's Agricultural Association and School," *Genesee Farmer* 8 (Jan. 1847): 10.

49. "Farm Schools," *New England Farmer* 4 (Apr. 1852): 185.

50. For examples, see *American Agriculturist* 2 (Sept. 1843): 183–84; *Working Farmer* 8 (1856): 26, and 9 (1857): 48, 171; Bailey, *Cyclopedia of American Agriculture*, 4:378; Rozwenc, *Agricultural Policies in Vermont, 1860–1945*, 51; James Hyatt, *Lime and Marl: Their Agricultural Uses* ([Germantown, PA: Mount Airy Agricultural Institute], 1848).

51. Pamphlet on the Orange County Scientific and Practical Agricultural Institute, dated Mar. 1846, and Memorial to National Convention of Farmers, Gardeners and Silk

Culturists, dated Oct. 1846, Darrach-YU, box 1; [James Darrach], "Agricultural Education," *Literary Record and Journal of the Linnaean Association of Pennsylvania College* 2 (Sept. 1846): 220–21; *Cultivator* 2 (Apr. 1845): 119; *Genesee Farmer* 6 (June 1845): 89.

52. Rev. John Johnson to Darrach, Jan. 12, 1848, Darrach-YU, box 1; Helena (White) Darrach, notebook with diary and commonplace entries, Dec. 21, 1854, Darrach-YU, box 10.

53. *Friends Weekly Intelligencer* 1 (Sept. 7, 1844): 192; *Friends' Intelligencer and Journal* 23 (June 22, 1895): 398. For similar examples, see *New Hampshire Sentinel*, Feb. 3, 1847, 3; *Erie Observer*, Nov. 6, 1847, 3; *Presbyterian Banner and Advocate* (Pittsburgh, PA), Sept. 26, 1857, 4; *Journal of the Seventh Senate of the State of New Jersey*, 75th sess. (Salem: Robert Gwynne, 1851): 157.

54. For examples, see Alfred Charles True, *A History of Agricultural Education in the United States, 1785–1925* (Washington, DC: GPO, 1929), 43; Bailey, *Cyclopedia of American Agriculture*, 4:368–69; Stanley M. Guralnick, *Science and the Ante-Bellum American College* (Philadelphia: American Philosophical Society, 1975), 132–33.

55. "Agricultural Education," *Bangor Daily Whig and Courier*, Nov. 8, 1851, 2.

56. This paragraph and the next are based on data from the annual reports of the Regents of the University of the State of New York for the years from 1843 to 1858 (the fifty-sixth through the seventy-first reports).

57. For trustees, see *The Cortland Academy Jubilee Celebrated at Homer, N.Y., July 7 & 8, 1846* (Syracuse, NY: Stoddard & Babcock, 1846), 35; H. C. Goodwin, *Pioneer History: Or, Cortland County and the Border Wars of New York* (New York: A. B. Burdick, 1859), 319. For county agricultural society officers, see the annual *Transactions of the New York State Agricultural Society*; Hamilton Child, *Gazetteer and Business Directory of Cortland County, N.Y., for 1869* (Syracuse, NY: Journal Office, 1869), 68–69.

58. "Agricultural Meeting in Homer," *Genesee Farmer* 7 (June 1846): 136; also see 6 (Dec. 1845): 179, and 8 (Jan. 1847): 11; *Cultivator* 3 (May 1846): 160; *Transactions of the New York State Agricultural Society* 7 (Albany: C. Van Benthuysen, 1848): 52.

59. Emily Dickinson, *The Letters of Emily Dickinson*, ed. Thomas Herbert Johnson and Theodora Van Wagenen Ward (Cambridge, MA: Harvard University Press, 1986), 180; John Adams Nash, *The Progressive Farmer* (New York: C. M. Saxton, 1853); Bailey, *Cyclopedia of American Agriculture*, 4:383–84.

60. Nancy Beadie and Kimberley Tolley, "A School for Every Purpose: An Introduction to the History of Academies in the United States," in *Chartered Schools: Two Hundred Years of Independent Academies in the United States, 1727–1925*, ed. Nancy Beadie and Kimberly Tolley (New York: RoutledgeFalmer, 2002), 3–18.

61. Benjamin Gue, *Diary of Benjamin F. Gue in Rural New York and Pioneer Iowa, 1847–1856*, ed. Earle D. Ross (Ames: Iowa State University Press, 1962), 19, 28.

62. Gue, *Diary of Benjamin F. Gue*, 56.

63. Nancy Beadie, "Internal Improvement: The Structure and Culture of Academy Expansion in New York State in the Antebellum Era, 1820–1860," in *Chartered Schools*, ed. Beadie and Tolley, 105–6.

64. Gue, *Diary of Benjamin F. Gue*, 51.

65. Gue, *Diary of Benjamin F. Gue*, 19, 23.

66. Benjamin F. Gue, "Origin and Early History of Iowa State College" (1891), typescript copy, Iowa State University Archives; Benjamin F. Gue, *Biographies and*

Portraits of the Progressive Men of Iowa (Des Moines, IA: Conaway & Shaw, 1899), 147–48.

67. Beadie, "Toward a History of Education Markets in the United States"; Beadie and Tolley, "School for Every Purpose."

68. Colman, *Education and Agriculture*, 50, 61.

69. Earle D. Ross, "The United States Department of Agriculture during the Commissionership: A Study in Politics, Administration, and Technology, 1862–1889," *Agricultural History* 20 (June 1946): 138.

70. But see Daniel J. Kevles, "A Primer of A, B, Seeds: Advertising, Branding, and Intellectual Property in an Emerging Industry," *UC Davis Law Review* 42 (Dec. 2013): 657–78.

71. Ray Palmer Baker, *A Chapter in American Education: Rensselaer Polytechnic Institute, 1824–1924* (New York: Charles Scribner's Sons, 1924), 3; Palmer Chamberlain Ricketts, *History of Rensselaer Polytechnic Institute, 1824–1914* (New York: John Wiley and Sons, 1914), 1–107.

72. Stephen Van Rensselaer to Samuel Blatchford, Nov. 5, 1824, and Minutes of the Board of Trustees, Dec. 29, 1824, both in "Early Documents of Rensselaer," accessed Sept. 14, 2010, http://www.lib.rpi.edu/dept/library/html/Archives/early_documents.

73. In addition to the school histories cited above, see Margaret W. Rossiter, *The Emergence of Agricultural Science: Justus Liebig and the Americans, 1840–1880* (New Haven, CT: Yale University Press, 1975), 51–52.

74. Rossiter, *Emergence of Agricultural Science*, 87.

75. Rossiter, *Emergence of Agricultural Science*, 129; Osborne, *From the Letter-Files of S. W. Johnson*, 69.

76. "County Agricultural Institutes," *Cultivator* 8 (Aug. 1851): 264.

77. Carl M. Becker, "Freeman Cary and Farmers' College: An Ohio Educator and an Experiment in Nineteenth Century 'Practical' Education," *Bulletin of the Historical and Philosophical Society of Ohio* 21 (July 1963): 154; Betty Ann Smiddy, ed., *A Little Piece of Paradise: College Hill, Ohio* (Cincinnati, OH: College Hill Historical Society, 2008), 26–28, 31, 99–102; Gail Deibler Finke, *College Hill* (Mount Pleasant, OH: Arcadia Publishing, 2004), 10, 24.

78. Carl M. Becker, "The Patriarch of Farmers' College: Dr. Robert H. Bishop," *Cincinnati Historical Society Bulletin* 23 (1965): 105.

79. Julianna Chaszar, "Leading and Losing the Agricultural Education Movement: Freeman G. Cary and Farmers' College, 1846–1884," *History of Higher Education Annual* 18 (1998): 42n14; Becker, "Freeman Cary and Farmers' College," 153–56; *A Plea for the Farmers' College of Hamilton, Ohio and for a Reformation in Collegiate Instruction: Being a Report to That Institution, Made July 17, 1850* (Cincinnati: Ben Franklin Printing House, 1850), 15; A. B. Huston, *Historical Sketch of Farmers' College* (Published by the Students' Association of Farmers' College, N.d.), 38–48.

80. *A Plea for the Farmers' College of Hamilton, Ohio and for a Reformation in Collegiate Instruction: Being a Report to That Institution, Made July 17, 1850* (Cincinnati: Ben Franklin Printing House, 1850), 14; "Farmers' College v. Cary," in *Reports of Cases Argued and Determined in the Supreme Court of Ohio*, vol. 35, new series (Cincinnati, 1880), 650–51.

81. Chaszar, "Leading and Losing the Agricultural Education Movement," 27. An

1847 law authorized the raising of new capital specifically to endow an agricultural professorship; see "Farmers' College v. Cary," 35:650–51.

82. Huston, *Historical Sketch of Farmers' College*, 50–51.

83. Becker, "Freeman Cary and Farmers' College," 160–65; Chaszar, "Leading and Losing the Agricultural Education Movement," 25–30; Murat Halstead, "The Story of Farmers' College," *Cosmopolitan* 22 (Jan. 1897): 284.

84. Smiddy, *A Little Piece of Paradise*, ii; Chaszar, "Leading and Losing the Agricultural Education Movement," 32–33.

85. Bailey, *Cyclopedia of American Agriculture*, 4:373.

86. *Plea for Farmers' College*, 5–6 (emphasis in original).

87. Quoted in Huston, *Historical Sketch of Farmers' College*, 52.

88. "Institutions for the Promotion of Scientific Agriculture—Proposed Advantages," *Cincinnatus* 1 (June 1856): 284; "Difficulties and Discouragements in the Establishment of Institutions for the Promotion of Scientific Agriculture—Plant to Be Pursued," *Cincinnatus* 1 (Apr. 1856): 162.

89. Charles Flint, ed., *Abstract of Returns of the Agricultural Societies of Massachusetts, 1858* (Boston: William White, 1859), 3.

90. *Report of the Commissioner of Patents for the Year 1852: Part II. Agriculture* (Washington, DC: Robert Armstrong, 1853), 9.

91. "Necessity for a School of Agricultural Instruction and Experiment," *Farm Journal and Progressive Farmer* 6 (Sept. 1856): 258.

92. "Our Present System of Agriculture—Its Defects and Remedies," *Cincinnatus* 1 (Jan. 1856): 11–12.

93. "Dedication of Polytechnic Hall," *Cincinnatus* 1 (Nov. 1856): 547.

94. For the terms of Farmers' scholarship stocks, see "Farmers' College v. Cary." For Genesee College, see Nancy Beadie, "From Academy to University in New York State: The Genesee Institutions and the Importance of Capital to the Success of an Idea, 1848–1871," *History of Higher Education Annual* 14 (1994): 14, 17; Beadie, *Education and the Creation of Capital in the Early American Republic*, 176–211, 268–70, 280–81, 299. For similar practices by other institutions, see Peter A. Browne, *An Essay on the Veterinary Art; Setting Forth Its Great Usefulness, Giving an Account of the Veterinary Colleges in France and England, and Exhibiting the Facility and Utility of Instituting Similar Schools in the United States* (Philadelphia: John Thompson, 1837), 21.

95. "Farmers' College v. Cary."

96. Beadie, "From Academy to University in New York State," 21–27 (quotation on 27).

97. Chaszar, "Leading and Losing the Agricultural Education Movement," 38; Becker, "Freeman Cary and Farmers' College," 173.

98. Huston, *Historical Sketch of Farmers' College*, 70–74. For the board's reasoning, see *Ohio Farmer* 14 (1865): 42–43, 84, 98, 100.

99. "Agricultural School in France—A State Agricultural School in New-York, &c.," *New-York Daily Tribune*, Feb. 9, 1847, 1; also see various newspaper clippings and pamphlets from the mid-1840s, AI-NYHS, box 461. The institute's officers were closely in touch with Darrach's Orange County school and must have been well informed of the difficulties. See T. B. Wakeman to Darrach, Apr. 10, 1846, and pamphlet dated March 1846, Darrach-YU, box 1.

100. "Agricultural College and Experimental Farm," *New-York Daily Tribune*, Jan. 28, 1848, 1.

101. "Agricultural Schools, &c.," *Working Farmer* 3 (June 1851): 79.

102. Henry Colman, *European Agriculture and Rural Economy from Personal Observation*, vol. 1 (London: Joseph Rogerson, 1844), 179–248; Henry Colman, *European Agriculture and Rural Economy from Personal Observation*, vol. 2 (Boston: Arthur D. Phelps, 1848), 412–41; Donald B. Marti, "The Reverend Henry Colman's Agricultural Ministry," *Agricultural History* 51 (July 1977): 531. Horace Greeley reprinted long parts of the reports on European agricultural schools. See, *New-York Daily Tribune*, Dec. 26, 1844, 4, and May 24, 1845, 2.

103. "Agricultural Statistics," *Working Farmer* 6 (1854): 126; see also 1 (1849): 100, 129–30; 3 (1851): 28.

104. Edward Hitchcock and Marshall P. Wilder, *Report of Commissioners concerning an Agricultural School, January 1851* ([Boston], 1851), 4, 8, 10, 69.

105. Henry Barnard, *National Education in Europe: Being an Account of the Organization, Administration, Instruction, and Statistics of Public Schools of Different Grades in the Principal States* (New York: Charles B. Norton, 1854), 3, 467.

106. Rozwenc, *Agricultural Policies in Vermont, 1860–1945*, 53; Harold Whiting Cary, *The University of Massachusetts: A History of One Hundred Years* (Amherst: University of Massachusetts, 1962), 15.

107. "Agriculture," *New York Times*, July 12, 1852, 2.

108. *Report of the Commissioner of Patents, for the Year 1850: Part II. Agriculture* (Washington, DC: Printers to the House of Reps., 1851), 148.

109. William Henry Seward, *The Works of William H. Seward*, ed. George E. Baker (Boston: Houghton, Mifflin, 1884), 3:181.

110. Hitchcock and Wilder, *Report of Commissioners concerning an Agricultural School*, 70.

111. For the repudiation, see Louis Hartz, *Economic Policy and Democratic Thought: Pennsylvania, 1776–1860* (Cambridge, MA: Harvard University Press, 1948); L. Ray Gunn, *The Decline of Authority: Public Economic Policy and Political Development in New York, 1800–1860* (Ithaca, NY: Cornell University Press, 1988).

112. *Report of the Register of the Maryland Agricultural College, to the Board of Trustees; Act of Incorporation, with Amendments Thereto: List of Officers, and Names of Stockholders, with Number of Shares Held by Each* (Baltimore, MD: Samuel S. Mills, 1858), 15; True, *History of Agricultural Education in the United States*, 66–67.

113. "The Pennsylvania Farm School," *Pennsylvania Farm Journal* 5 (Mar. 1855): 94 (emphasis in original); "Act of Incorporation of the Farmers' High School of Pennsylvania," *Pennsylvania Farm Journal* 5 (Mar. 1855): 94; True, *History of Agricultural Education in the United States*, 69.

114. "Farmers' High School of Pennsylvania," *Working Farmer* 9 (1857): 170–71; Michael Bezilla, *Penn State: An Illustrated History* (University Park: Pennsylvania State University Press, 1985), chap. 1, http://www.libraries.psu.edu/psul/speccolls/psua/pshistory/bezilla.html; James Howard Waring, *An Agricultural History of the Pennsylvania State College: Embracing a Brief Historical Sketch of Agricultural Education Both in Europe and in America, the Founding of the Farmers' High School of Pennsylvania, and the Development of the Pennsylvania State College from That Beginning until the Present Time* (N.p.: N.p.,

1919), 15–16; Stevenson Whitcomb Fletcher, *Pennsylvania Agriculture and Country Life, 1840–1940* (Harrisburg: Pennsylvania Historical and Museum Commission, 1955), 450–54.

115. Marti, "Purposes of Agricultural Education," 280; George Brayton et al., "Report of the Committee on Agriculture on So Much of the Governor's Message as Relates to an Agricultural College and Mechanical School, and on the Memorial of the State Agricultural Society on the Same Subject," in *Documents of the State Assembly of New York, Seventy-Fourth Session* (Albany: C. Van Benthuysen, 1851), 2:2.

116. Brayton et al., "Report of the Committee on Agriculture," 1–21 (quotation on 2).

117. "The Agricultural College," *New-York Daily Tribune*, May 20, 1851, 5; True, *History of Agricultural Education in the United States*, 50–51; Bailey, *Cyclopedia of American Agriculture*, 4:391.

118. John Mason Clarke, *James Hall of Albany: Geologist and Paleontologist, 1811–1898* (Albany, N.p., 1923), 190–203.

119. True, *History of Agricultural Education in the United States*, 50–53; Bailey, *Cyclopedia of American Agriculture*, 4:391–93; Marti, "Purposes of Agricultural Education," 281–82.

120. Daniel W. Lang, "The People's College, the Mechanics' Mutual Protection and the Agricultural College Act," *History of Education Quarterly* 18 (Autumn 1978): 295–304.

121. Daniel W. Lang, "Origins of the American Land Grant College Movement," *Higher Education Perspectives* 2 (Mar. 2006): 35–38; Walter Gable, "The Ovid Academy and the Seneca Collegiate Institute," Seneca County, NY, accessed July 7, 2011, http://www.co.seneca.ny.us/dpt-genserv-historian-seneca.php; Ulysses Prentiss Hedrick, *A History of Agriculture in the State of New York* (Albany: New York State Agriculture Society, 1933), 93–110.

122. "Gov. Hunt's Message," *New-York Daily Tribune*, Jan. 7, 1852, 4.

123. "State Appropriations for Colleges, *New-York Daily Tribune*, Jan. 29, 1852, 6.

124. "Gov. Hunt's Message," *New-York Daily Tribune*, Jan. 7, 1852, 4.

125. "Meeting of the 'People's College' Association," *New-York Daily Tribune*, Feb. 18, 1852, 6.

126. "An Agricultural College," *New-York Daily Tribune*, Jan. 18, 1856, 4; "From Washington," *New-York Daily Tribune*, Mar. 3, 1856, 4.

127. ["The education of farmers,"] *New-York Daily Tribune*, Nov. 25, 1856, 4; "From Washington," *New-York Daily Tribune*, Apr. 26, 1858, 6.

128. Colman, *Education and Agriculture*, 33; Lang, "Origins of the American Land Grant College Movement," 38–40, 43–44; Barbara H. Bell, "Charles Cook: The Father of Schuyler County," *Crooked Lake Review* 85 (Apr. 1995).

129. J[ohn]. W[hite]. Chickering to Brewer, Feb. 1, 1857, Brewer-YU.

130. "Resolution of the New York State Agricultural College Trustees," April 21, 1860, King-NYHS, box 2; William Kelly to King, June 4, 1860, and June 8, 1860, King-NYHS, box 2; Diedrich Willers, *The New York State Agricultural College, at Ovid, and Higher Agricultural Education: An Historical Paper Read at a Meeting of the Seneca County Historical Society, Held at Romulus, Sept. 5, 1906* (Geneva, NY: N.p., 1907), 6–7.

131. M. R. Patrick to King, June 20, 1860, King-NYHS, box 2.

132. William Kelly to King, Nov. 7, 21, and 30, 1860, King-NYHS, box 2.

133. John Seeley to King, Aug. 5 and 22, 1862, King-NYHS, box 2.

134. William Kelly to King, Feb. 18, 1861, and Nov. 20, 1862; King to F. S. Winston (copy), June 3, 1860; and "Summons for Relief by Romine Barnum," July 27, 1861, all in King-NYHS, box 2.

135. King to William Kelly (draft), Nov. 24, 1862, and Kelly to King, June 25, Aug. 9, and Nov. 26, 1862, King-NYHS, box 2.

136. Lang, "Origins of the American Land Grant College Movement," 44–48; Lang, "The People's College, the Mechanics' Mutual Protection and the Agricultural College Act," 306–17; Wayne E. Morrison, ed., *New York State Agricultural College, Ovid, Seneca Co., N.Y.: A History* (Ovid, NY: Wayne E. Morrison & Co., 1978), 43–44; Carl L. Becker, *Cornell University: Founders and the Founding* (Ithaca, NY: Cornell University Press, 1943), 160–61; Willers, *New York State Agricultural College, at Ovid, and Higher Agricultural Education*, 24.

137. See, for example, Cary, *University of Massachusetts*, 23.

138. "Farmers' High School of Pennsylvania," *Working Farmer* 9 (Oct. 1857): 170–71. For Vail's Westchester Farm School, see "Westchester County," *Working Farmer* 8 (Apr. 1856): 26, and 9 (Apr. 1857): 48.

139. "The People's College—Another Experiment—President Hopkins's Address," *Cincinnatus* 3 (Dec. 1858): 558–63.

140. *Report of the Commissioner of Agriculture for the Year 1865* (Washington, DC: GPO, 1866): 140.

141. "Industrial Education Convention," *Prairie Farmer* 14 (Oct. 1854): 365; Burt Eardley Powell, *The Movement for Industrial Education and the Establishment of the University, 1840–1870*, Semi-Centennial History of the University of Illinois (Urbana: University of Illinois, 1918), 77–78.

142. "The Agricultural Department of Our Government—Distribution of Seeds," *Cincinnatus* 2 (Jan. 1857): 4; petition of Farmers' College to Congress, Feb. 4, 1858, RG 233, SEN 35A-H17.4; F. C. Cary to Patent Office, Sept. 11, 1856, vol. 12 (1856), RG16.

Chapter 7 · Movement into Lobby

1. Henry Barrett Learned, *The President's Cabinet: Studies in the Origin, Formation and Structure of an American Institution* (New Haven, CT: Yale University Press, 1912), 295–301; Alfred Charles True, *A History of Agricultural Education in the United States, 1785–1925* (Washington, DC: GPO, 1929), 7.

2. George Washington, "Eighth Annual Message," Dec. 7, 1796, APP.

3. Franklin Knight, ed., *Letters on Agriculture from His Excellency, George Washington, President of the United States, to Arthur Young, Esq., F.R.S., and Sir John Sinclair, Bart., M.P.* (Washington, DC: Published by the Editor, 1847), 12.

4. Quotations in A. Hunter Dupree, *Science in the Federal Government: A History of Policies and Activities to 1940* (Cambridge, MA: Harvard University Press, 1957), 47; Courtney Fullilove, *The Profit of the Earth: The Global Seeds of American Agriculture* (Chicago: University of Chicago Press, 2017), 48–50; Kenneth W. Dobyns, *The Patent Office Pony: A History of the Early Patent Office* (Boston: Docent Press, 2016), 123–40; Paul Wallace Gates, *The Farmer's Age: Agriculture, 1815–1860* (New York: Holt, Rinehart and Winston, 1960), 360; Alfred Charles True, *History of Agricultural Experimentation and Research in the United States, 1607–1925: Including a History of the United States Department of Agriculture* (Washington, DC: GPO, 1937), 23–24.

5. True, *History of Agricultural Experimentation and Research in the United States, 1607–1925*, 24; Learned, *President's Cabinet*, 308–9; Dobyns, *Patent Office Pony*, 111–13.

6. Agriculture and Useful Arts, H.R. Rep. no. 25-655 (Mar. 7, 1838), 8–9.

7. True, *History of Agricultural Experimentation and Research in the United States, 1607–1925*, 24–27.

8. For example, J. K. Miller to Patent Office, June 12, 1848, and H. Meigs to Patent Office, Mar. 12, 1849, both in RG 16, vol. 1 (1839–49), entry P1-191-I.

9. Alan L. Olmstead and Paul Webb Rhode, *Creating Abundance: Biological Innovation and American Agricultural Development* (Cambridge: Cambridge University Press, 2008).

10. Learned, *President's Cabinet*, 312; Gates, *Farmer's Age*, 331.

11. Quoted in Dupree, *Science in the Federal Government*, 66.

12. Paul W. Gates, "Charles Lewis Fleischmann: German-American Agricultural Authority," *Agricultural History* 35 (Jan. 1961): 13–15.

13. "To the Farmers of the United States," *Western Farmer and Gardener* 2 (May 1841): 172–73; for previous discussion, see *Cultivator* 6 (1839): 147; 7 (1840): 190; 8 (1841): 52, 86. For other supporters, see *Cultivator* 9 (June 1842): 94; *Farmers' Register* (Petersburg, VA) 9 (Apr. 1841): 248–49; *Farmer's Cabinet and American Herd Book* 6 (1841–42): 135, 197–98; *American Agriculturist* 1 (1842): 4.

14. Gates, "Charles Lewis Fleischmann," 14.

15. Petition of Edwin Green, and Others, Praying the Establishment of an Agricultural and Mechanical Department of the Government, S. Doc. no. 25-418 (1838); Petition of Grafton Tyler, and Others, Praying the Establishment of a Department of the Government to Promote the Interests of Agriculture, of Science, and of the Mechanical and Fine Arts, S. Doc. no. 25-419 (1838); Memorial of Joseph L. Smith, and Others, Praying That the Committee on Agriculture Be Instructed to Make an Annual Report on the Agricultural Interests of the Union, S. Doc. no. 26-61 (1840); Petition of Joseph L. Smith and Others, Praying the Establishment of a Department of the Government, to Be Called the Department of Agriculture and Education, S. Doc. no. 26-181 (1840); Memorial of Joseph L. Smith and Others, Praying That the Committee on Agriculture Be Instructed to Make an Annual Report on the Agricultural Interests of the Union, S. Doc. no. 26-519 (1840); Joseph L. Smith, et Al.—Department of Agriculture, H. R. Rep. no. 27-595 (1842).

16. Report of the Commissioner of Patents, H.R. Doc. no. 27-74 (1842), 5.

17. "To the Farmers and Planters of Virginia," *Farmers' Register* 9 (Apr. 1841): 250.

18. Dupree, *Science in the Federal Government*, 66–90.

19. D. Jay Browne to Townshend Glover, Aug. 10, 1858, RG 16, vol. 20 (1858); True, *History of Agricultural Experimentation and Research in the United States, 1607–1925*, 334–36; James M. Swank, *The Department of Agriculture: Its History and Objects* (Washington, DC: GPO, 1872), 12–20. On imperial botanical gardens, see Richard Harry Drayton, *Nature's Government: Science, Imperial Britain, and the "Improvement" of the World* (New Haven, CT: Yale University Press, 2000).

20. Cong. Globe, 32nd Cong., 1st Sess., appendix, 494.

21. For instance, see "Senator Douglas," *Working Farmer* 3 (Nov. 1851): 202.

22. William Henry Seward, *The Works of William H. Seward*, ed. George E. Baker (Boston: Houghton, Mifflin, 1884), 3:186.

23. Cong. Globe, 32nd Cong., 1st Sess., appendix, 746.

24. Cong. Globe, 34th Cong., 1st Sess., 958.

25. "National Convention of Farmers and Silk Culturists," *American Farmer* 1 (Nov. 1846): 138; Circular for 1846, AI-NYHS, box 461; *Proceedings of the National Convention of Farmers, Gardeners and Silk Culturists* (New York: Joseph H. Jennings, 1846), 11–15; "Agriculture and the Government," *Working Farmer* 1 (Aug. 1849): 73.

26. Home Department, H.R. Rep. no. 30-66 (1849).

27. "A Look about Us," *Horticulturist* 4 (Apr. 1850): 441.

28. "Agricultural Bureau," *Maine Farmer* 17 (Dec. 20, 1849): 1; "Agricultural Bureau," 18 (Jan. 10, 1850): 1; "Bureau of Agriculture," *New England Farmer* 2 (Jan. 1850): 30; "The Home Department," *Working Farmer* 1 (1849): 49.

29. "Education and Choice of Profession," *Valley Farmer* 2 (Mar. 1850): 76.

30. Mary Rogers Cabot, "Governor Frederick Holbrook," in *Annals of Brattleboro, 1681–1895* (Battleboro, VT: E. L. Hildreth, 1922), 2:788–96; Jacob G. Ullery, *Men of Vermont: An Illustrated Biographical History of Vermonters and Sons of Vermont* (Battleboro, VT: Transcript Publishing Co., 1894), 198. Also see *Cultivator* 4 (Dec. 1847): 384; *Journal of Agriculture* (Boston) 1 (1851): 274. For Holbrook's authorship of the report, see *Cultivator* 6 (Dec. 1849): 362–63.

31. Resolutions of the Legislature of Vermont, Relative to the Establishment of an Agricultural Bureau, H. Misc. Doc. 31-2 (1849).

32. *Working Farmer* 1 (1850): 164–65; *New England Farmer* 2 (1850): 30.

33. *Transactions of the New Hampshire State Agricultural Society for 1850, 1851 and 1852* (Concord: Butterfield and Hill, 1853): 40; "Agricultural Bureau," *Michigan Farmer* 8 (Mar. 1850): 72; *Transactions of the State Agricultural Society of Michigan* (1851): 258.

34. Resolutions of the Legislature of Alabama, in Favor of the Establishment of a Bureau of Agriculture, S. Misc. Doc. 32-28 (1852); Resolutions of the Legislature of New Hampshire, in Relation to the Establishment of a Bureau of Agriculture in the Department of the Interior, S. Misc. Doc. 32-9 (1851); Resolutions of the Legislature of Florida, in Favor of the Establishment of a Bureau of Agriculture, S. Misc. Doc. 31-21 (1851); Resolutions of the Legislature of Rhode Island, in Favor of the Establishment of a Bureau of Agriculture, S. Misc. Doc. 31-73 (1850); Resolution of the Legislature of Pennsylvania, in Favor of the Establishment of a National Board of Agriculture, S. Misc. Doc. 31-107 (1850); Resolution of the Legislature of Tennessee, in Favor of the Establishment of an Agricultural Bureau, S. Misc. Doc. 31-65 (1849); *Minutes of the Votes and Proceedings of the Seventy-Fourth General Assembly of the State of New Jersey* (Freehold: Orrin Pharo, 1850), 494–97; *Transactions of the New York State Agricultural Society* 9 (Albany: Weed, Parsons and Co., 1849): 145; "Meeting of the Ken. Co. Ag. Society," *Maine Farmer* 18 (Feb. 21, 1850): 2; "Maryland State Agricultural Society," *American Farmer* 7 (Mar. 1852): 311.

35. See the numerous examples among the petitions referred to the Committee of Agriculture in the 31st and 32nd Congress, RG 233, HR 31A-G1.1 and HR 32A-G2.1.

36. Thomas W. Reece to A. J. Harlan, Dec. 22, 1849, RG 233, HR 31A-G1.1.

37. Petition from Northumberland County, PA, referred to House Committee on Agriculture, May 28, 1858, RG 233, HR 31A-G1.1.

38. Petitions from Pennsylvania, referred to committee on Feb. 19, 1852, in the folder marked "Establishment of an Agricultural Bureau in Washington," RG 233, HR 32A-G2.1.

39. F. J. Cope to Patent Office, Nov. 8, 1852, RG 16, vol. 2 (1849–59) (emphasis in original).

40. "Report of Secretary of the Interior," *American Quarterly Register and Magazine* 3 (Dec. 1849): 155–56; Zachary Taylor, "Annual Message," Dec. 4, 1849, APP.

41. "The General Government in Favor of Agriculture—at Last," *American Agriculturist* 9 (Feb. 1850): 56; "Aid to Agricultural Societies," *American Farmer* 5 (Jan. 1850): 247.

42. Message from the President of the United States, to the Two Houses of Congress, at the Commencement of the Second Session of the Thirty-First Congress, S. Exec. Doc. no. 31-1 (1850); Message from the President of the United States, to the Two Houses of Congress at the Commencement of the First Session of the Thirty-Second Congress, H.R. Exec. Doc. no. 32-2 (1851), pt. 1; Cong. Globe, 32nd Cong., 1st Sess., 13–14; Message from the President of the United States to the Two Houses of Congress, at the Commencement of the Second Session of the Thirty-Second Congress, S. Exec. Doc. no. 32-1 (1851), vol. 1, pt. 1.

43. Agricultural Bureau, H.R. Rep. no. 31-407 (1850); "Agricultural Interests in Congress," *Maine Farmer* 18 (Apr. 4, 1850): 1.

44. Cong. Globe, 31st Cong., 1st Sess., 734.

45. A Bill to Establish an Agricultural Bureau in the Department of the Interior, S. 203, 31st Cong. (1850); Cong. Globe, 31st Cong., 1st Sess., 769; 2nd Sess., 102, 145; Cong. Globe, 32nd Cong., 1st Sess., 80, 102, 225, appendix, 494; "An Agricultural Bureau," *Valley Farmer* 4 (Mar. 1852): 101–2; "An Agricultural Bureau," *Lancaster Intelligencer*, May 28, 1850, 2.

46. "The Agricultural Department," *American Farmer* 7 (May 1852): 391.

47. "State Agricultural Society," *Southern Planter* 12 (Feb. 1852): 50. For similar sentiments, see "The President's Message," *Richmond Enquirer*, Dec. 7, 1852, 2.

48. House Journal, 30th Cong., 1st Sess., vol. 43 (Mar. 17, 1848), 577–80. Separate volumes would, however, substantially increase the cost by doubling the amount of binding.

49. Cong. Globe, 31st Cong., 1st Sess., 474.

50. Cong. Globe, 31st Cong., 1st Sess., 503–4.

51. Cong. Globe, 31st Cong., 1st Sess., 473–75, 503–6. The support from both Democrats and Whigs, among northern representatives, suggests that the large print run really was intended for constituents and not merely as a patronage contract for a partisan printer.

52. Cong. Globe, 31st Cong., 1st Sess., 916–22.

53. Jas. P. Rounsiwell to Patent Office, Aug. 6, 1850, RG 16, vol. 2 (1849–52).

54. Cong. Globe, 33rd Cong., 1st Sess., 1146; 35th Cong., 1st Sess., 2241–42.

55. Cong. Globe, 32nd Cong., 1st Sess., 225, appendix, 491–95, 585–88, 746–48, 892–94; 33rd Cong., 1st Sess., 48.

56. Roswell S. Colt to D. S. Gregory, Apr. 1, 1848, and Charles Calvert to John G. Chapman, Jan. 8, 1849, in RG 233, HR 30A-G2.1; *American Farmer* 4 (Dec. 1848): 172; *Working Farmer* 1 (Apr. 1849): 33–34.

57. "The Agricultural Bureau—Agricultural Interests," *American Farmer* 5 (Mar. 1850): 311 (emphasis in original).

58. "Agricultural Bureau," *Michigan Farmer* 8 (Mar. 1850): 73.

59. "Agricultural Bureau," *Michigan Farmer* 9 (Jan. 1851): 17.

60. "Rough Notes, from the West," *Horticulturist* 4 (1850): 544; "Agriculture and the President," *Working Farmer* 3 (1852): 241.

61. *Journal of the United States Agricultural Society* 1 (Aug. 1852): 5.

62. "An Agricultural Congress," *American Farmer* 7 (Aug. 1851): 70–71.

63. "A National Congress of Agriculture," *The Plough, the Loom, and the Anvil* 4 (Aug. 1851): 97.

64. *Transactions of the Wisconsin State Agricultural Society* 2 (Madison: Beriah Brown, 1853): 122.

65. "A Congress of Agriculture," *Genesee Farmer* 12 (Aug. 1851): 177–78.

66. "National Agricultural Convention," *Cultivator* 9 (Mar. 1852): 120.

67. *The Plough, the Loom, and the Anvil* 4 (June 1852): 753–54; *Michigan Farmer* 10 (July 1, 1852): 201; *American Farmer* 7 (June 1852): 436; *Working Farmer* 4 (July 1852): 117; *Horticulturist* 6 (June 1852): 205.

68. James Grant Wilson and John Fiske, eds., *Appleton's Cyclopædia of American Biography* (New York: D. Appleton & Co., 1888), 3:265–66.

69. *Journal of the United States Agricultural Society* 1 (Aug. 1852): 7–20 (emphasis in original).

70. "National Agricultural Convention," *Working Farmer* 4 (Aug. 1852): 123.

71. On USAS Unionism, see Philip Mills Herrington, "The Exceptional Plantation: Slavery, Agricultural Reform, and the Creation of an American Landscape" (PhD diss., University of Virginia, 2012), 183–207. Though usually careful to avoid open partisanship, Wilder showed his hand in his 1856 presidential address by stating that the USAS represented "the American System"; see *Journal of the United States Agricultural Society* 4 (1856): 16–17.

72. See, for example, Wilder to King, Jan. 10, 1855, and Feb. 5, 1856, King-NYHS, box 1.

73. Wilder to King, Jan. 10, 1853, and May 2, 1856, King-NYHS, box 1.

74. For the "Great National Trial," see chapter 5.

75. See Herrington, "The Exceptional Plantation," 183–207.

76. *Journal of the United States Agricultural Society* 1 (1852): 6–7.

77. "Southern Agricultural Congress," *Southern Literary Messenger* 18 (Oct. 1852): 613–14. The following year, the southern convention proposed a uniquely southern agricultural university; see *Southern Cultivator* 12 (Jan. 1854): 28–29.

78. *Journal of the United States Agricultural Society* 1 (1852): 13; 4 (1857): 10–11; 7 (1860): 86–88, 192, 388.

79. *Journal of the United States Agricultural Society* 5 (1857): 39–40; *American Farmer* 13 (Oct. 1857): 133; *Monthly Bulletin of the United States Agricultural Society* 1, no. 5 (June 1858): 36; 1, no. 7 (Aug. 1858): 49–50; David R. Goldfield, *Urban Growth in the Age of Sectionalism: Virginia, 1847–1861* (Baton Rouge: Louisiana State University Press, 1977), 100.

80. *Monthly Bulletin of the United States Agricultural Society* 1, no. 8 (Sept. 1858): 60.

81. *Journal of the United States Agricultural Society* 2 (1854): 11–12, 23–28; 3 (1855): 32; Report: The Committee on Agriculture, to whom was referred the memorial of the Maryland State Agricultural Society, S. Rep. no. 33-262 (1854); Cong. Globe, 33rd Cong., 1st Sess., 1145.

82. For lobbying and congressional committees, see Daniel Peart, *Lobbyists and the Making of US Tariff Policy, 1816–1861* (Baltimore, MD: Johns Hopkins University Press, 2018).

83. "From Washington," *New-York Daily Tribune*, Mar. 5, 1856, 4.

84. *Journal of the United States Agricultural Society* 4 (1856): 8; "Obituary," *Annual Report of the Indiana State Board of Agriculture* 25 (Indianapolis: Wm. S. Burford, 1883): 623–25.

85. Cong. Globe, 34th Cong., 1st Sess., 1923–24; "Department of Agriculture," *American Farmer* 12 (Oct. 1856): 97–101.

86. *Journal of the United States Agricultural Society* 3 (1855): i; 4 (1856): 7–8; 5 (1857): 10–11.

87. "Sixth Agricultural Congress," *New-York Daily Tribune*, Jan. 15, 1858, 3.

88. Wilder to King, Dec. 29, 1856, King-NYHS, box 1. Also see Wilder to King, Dec. 18, 1856, King-NYHS, box 2, in folder marked "Undated misc. MSS, newspaper clippings, etc."

89. Benjamin French, *Witness to the Young Republic: A Yankee's Journal, 1828–1870*, ed. Donald B. Cole and John J. McDonough (Hanover, NH: University Press of New England, 1989), 246 (emphasis in original).

90. *Journal of the United States Agricultural Society* 3 (1855): 23; 5 (1857): 3; 7 (1859): 7, 10; Joseph P. McKerns, "Benjamin Perley Poore," *ANB*.

91. J. B. Turner, "A View from Illinois—The Farmers' Great Want," *Cincinnatus* 3 (Feb. 1858): 78.

92. *Journal of the United States Agricultural Society* 1 (1853): 7, 13, 16–17; Lyman Carrier, "The United States Agricultural Society, 1852–1860: Its Relation to the Origin of the United States Department of Agriculture and the Land Grant Colleges," *Agricultural History* 11 (Oct. 1937): 285–86.

93. Cong. Globe, 32nd Cong., 1st Sess., appendix, 746.

94. Cong. Globe, 34th Cong., 1st Sess., 532, 958–61, 1198–1200, 1992–94; F. G. Cary to Patent Office, Aug. 21, 1856, and Sept. 11, 1856, RG 16, vol. 12 (1856).

95. "Doings at the Patent Office," *New England Farmer* 8 (Aug. 1856): 364–65; *Journal of the United States Agricultural Society* 5 (1857): 3; *Monthly Bulletin of the United States Agricultural Society* 1, no. 2 (Mar. 1858): 13.

Chapter 8 · The Sectionalization of National Agricultural Policy

1. Clark Kerr, *The Uses of the University* (1963), 5th ed. (Cambridge, MA: Harvard University Press, 2001), 35.

2. Cong. Globe, 35th Cong., 2nd Sess., 718.

3. See James M. McPherson, "Antebellum Southern Exceptionalism," in *Major Problems in the Civil War and Reconstruction: Documents and Essays*, ed. Michael Perman and Amy Murrell Taylor (Boston: Wadsworth Cengage Learning, 2011), 41–49.

4. "An Important Subject," *Prairie Farmer* 2 (Oct. 28, 1858): 281.

5. David Morris Potter, *The Impending Crisis, 1848–1861*, ed. Don E. Fehrenbacher (New York: HarperCollins, 1976), 43.

6. Don E. Fehrenbacher, *The Slaveholding Republic: An Account of the United States Government's Relations to Slavery* (Oxford: Oxford University Press, 2002).

7. Cong. Globe, 35th Cong., 1st Sess. (Mar. 4, 1858), 962.

8. This paragraph is based on my research in the files of the House and Senate Committees of Public Lands, RG 233, HR 30A-G19.3, HR 33A-G20.3, HR 35A-G20.1, SEN 35A-H17.4. Also see Yonatan Eyal, "Trade and Improvements: Young America and the Transformation of the Democratic Party," *Civil War History* 51 (Sept. 2005): 245–68; James Warren Oberly, *Sixty Million Acres: American Veterans and the Public Lands before the Civil War* (Kent, OH: Kent State University Press, 1990); Paul W. Gates, *History of Public Land Law Development* (Washington, DC: GPO, 1968); Vernon Carstensen, ed., *The Public Lands: Studies in the History of the Public Domain* (Madison: University of Wisconsin Press, 1968).

9. *Journal of the United States Agricultural Society* 4 (mislabeled as vol. 3): 23 (emphasis in original); Burt Eardley Powell, *The Movement for Industrial Education and the Establishment of the University, 1840–1870* (Urbana: University of Illinois, 1918).

10. *DeBow's Review* 13 (Dec. 1857): 639.

11. *Journal of the United States Agricultural Society* 4 (1856): 22–23, 78–80 (emphasis in original).

12. *Journal of the United States Agricultural Society* 5 (1857): 61–66; George E. Waring, *The Elements of Agriculture: A Book for Young Farmers, with Questions Prepared for the Use of Schools* (New York: D. Appleton, 1854).

13. *Journal of the United States Agricultural Society* 4 (1856): 7; 5 (1857): 10.

14. Cong. Globe, 34th Cong., 1st Sess., 530.

15. Cong. Globe, 35th Cong., 1st Sess., 1697.

16. Resolutions of the Legislature of Michigan, in Favor of a Donation of Land for the Endowment of the Michigan Agricultural College, S. Misc. Doc. no. 35-157; Memorial of Members of the Board of Education of the State of Michigan and of the Faculty of the Agricultural College of That State, Praying a Donation of Land for the Agricultural College, S. Misc. Doc. no. 35-7; *Ohio Cultivator* 16 (Jan. 15, 1858): 25; *Maine Farmer* 26 (Feb. 4, 1858): 1.

17. *American Farmer* 8 (Jan. 1858): 227; *Working Farmer* 10 (Feb. 1858): 36–37.

18. Constitution and minutes, Feb. 27, 1858, ASNC-HSD.

19. Resolutions of the Legislature of the State of New Jersey, Asking for a Donation of Public Lands for Agricultural Colleges, H.R. Misc. Doc. no. 35-118; Resolutions of the State Agricultural Society of New York, for the Distribution of a Portion of the Public Lands to the States and Territories, for the Benefit of Agricultural Colleges Therein, H.R. Misc. Doc. no. 35-99; Resolution of the Legislature of the State of Rhode Island and Providence Plantations, in Favor of a Donation of Public Lands to the Several States and Territories to Aid and Encourage Scientific Education in Agriculture and the Mechanic Arts, S. Misc. Doc. no. 35-183; Preamble and Resolution of the Kentucky Agricultural Society, in Relation to the Appropriating of a Portion of the Public Domain for School Purposes, H.R. Misc. Doc. no. 35-82.

20. Paul Wallace Gates, *The Farmer's Age: Agriculture, 1815–1860* (New York: Holt, Rinehart and Winston, 1960), 379.

21. Cong. Globe, 35th Cong, 1st Sess., 32–33, 36–37, 52.

22. Lands for Agricultural Colleges, &c., H.R. Rep. no. 35-261.

23. Gates, *Farmer's Age*, 374–75.

24. Michael Todd Landis, *Northern Men with Southern Loyalties: The Democratic Party and the Sectional Crisis* (Ithaca, NY: Cornell University Press, 2014), 60.

25. Message from the President of the United States, Returning to the Senate the Bill Entitled "An Act Making a Grant of Public Lands to the Several States for the Benefit of Indigent Insane Persons," with a Statement of the Objections Which Have Required Him to Withhold from It His Approval, S. Ex. Doc. no. 33-56.

26. Quoted in David L. Lightner, "Ten Million Acres for the Insane: The Forgotten Collaboration of Dorothea L. Dix and William H. Bissell," *Illinois Historical Journal* 89 (Spring 1996): 28.

27. Message from the President of the United States (Dix bill veto message), 7–8; Taney, *Scott v. Sandford (TANEY, C. J., Opinion of the Court)*, 60 U.S. 393.

28. Cong. Globe, 35th Cong., 2nd Sess., 714–15.

29. Lands for Agricultural Colleges, &c., 1–2.

30. Lands for Agricultural Colleges, &c., 6–14.

31. Coy F. Cross, *Justin Smith Morrill: Father of the Land-Grant Colleges* (East Lansing: Michigan State University Press, 1999), 79–83; Cong. Globe, 35th Cong., 1st Sess., 1692–97.

32. Kenneth C. Martis, *The Historical Atlas of United States Congressional Districts, 1789–1983* (New York: Free Press, 1982), 90–91, 248, 264; US Census 1860, 412–38.

33. *New-York Daily Tribune*, Apr. 23, 1858, 4; *Chicago Tribune* Apr. 27, 1858, 2.

34. *Valley Farmer* 10 (Apr. 1854): 113–14.

35. *American Farmer* 13 (1858): 366.

36. *American Farmer* 13 (June 1858): 403; *Cincinnatus* 3 (1858): 83–86; 273–74; *Michigan Farmer* 16 (May 1858): 128–30; Gates, *Farmer's Age*, 377–78.

37. Joseph R. Williams, "Address," in *Transactions of the New York State Agricultural Society* 18 (Albany: Charles Van Benthuysen, 1859): 32–60; *New York Times*, Oct. 9, 1858, 5. The address was published as a pamphlet, and excerpts from it circulated widely. See *American Farmer* 12 (Dec. 1858): 722–34; *Valley Farmer* 10 (Dec. 1858): 1–5; Joseph R. Williams, *Address Delivered before the N.Y. State Agricultural Society* (Albany: C. Van Benthuysen, 1858).

38. Williams, "Address," 35, 37, 42, 44, 56 (emphasis in original).

39. "Educated people" in Williams, "Address," 59; Andrew P. Calhoun, "Col. A. P. Calhoun's Address," in *History of the State Agricultural Society of South Carolina*, ed. W. A. Clark, W. G. Hinson, and D. P. Duncan (Columbia: R. L. Bryan Co., 1916), 102–21 (quotations on 110, 115, 116, 117, 119).

40. Cong. Globe, 35th Cong., 2nd Sess., 712–13.

41. Cong. Globe, 35th Cong., 2nd Sess., 718, 722, 786.

42. Cong. Globe, 35th Cong., 2nd Sess., 719.

43. Cong. Globe, 35th Cong., 2nd Sess., 187, 724, 852.

44. *New-York Daily Tribune*, Feb. 4, 1859, 5.

45. Cong. Globe, 35th Cong., 2nd Sess., 720–22.

46. Cong. Globe, 35th Cong., 2nd Sess., 857.

47. Brown to Brewer, May 19, 1858, Brewer-YU.

48. Cong. Globe, 35th Cong., 1st Sess., 2230; 35th Cong., 2nd Sess., 851.

49. Gregory T. Cushman, *Guano and the Opening of the Pacific World: A Global Ecological History* (Cambridge: Cambridge University Press, 2013), 23–74; Edward D. Melillo, "The First Green Revolution: Debt Peonage and the Making of the Nitrogen Fertilizer Trade, 1840–1930," *American Historical Review* 117 (Oct. 2012): 1028–60;

Vaclav Smil, *Enriching the Earth: Fritz Haber, Carl Bosch, and the Transformation of World Food Production* (Cambridge, MA: MIT Press, 2004), 39–43.

50. *Third Annual Report of the American Institute, on the Subject of Agriculture,* New York S. Doc. no. 124 (Apr. 22, 1844), 8; Jimmy M. Skaggs, *The Great Guano Rush: Entrepreneurs and American Overseas Expansion* (New York: St. Martin's Press, 1994), 4–15.

51. Gates, *Farmer's Age,* 327.

52. Weymouth T. Jordan, "The Peruvian Guano Gospel in the Old South," *Agricultural History* 24 (Oct. 1950): 212.

53. Skaggs, *Great Guano Rush,* 17–34; Kenneth E. Shewmaker, "'Untaught Diplomacy': Daniel Webster and the Lobos Islands Controversy," *Diplomatic History* 1 (Oct. 1977): 321–40.

54. *Prospectus of the American Guano Company* (New York: John F. Trow, 1855).

55. Skaggs, *Great Guano Rush,* 53–55; Courtney Fullilove, "The Archive of Useful Knowledge" (PhD diss., Columbia University, 2009), 247–50.

56. *American Farmer* 11 (Jan. 1856): 203–4.

57. Trade between the United States and the Republic of Peru, H.R. Rep. no. 33-347; Constitution and minutes, Mar. 15, 1856, ASNC-HSD; *American Farmer* 11 (Apr. 1856): 306; *Journal of the United States Agricultural Society* 2 (1854): 20; *DeBow's Review* 20 (June 1856): 745; Skaggs, *Great Guano Rush,* 11–15; Shewmaker, "'Untaught Diplomacy,'" 323–25.

58. *Journal of the American Geographical and Statistical Society* 1 (June 1859): 188; *United States Statutes at Large* 11 (1855–59): 119–20; Christina Duffy Burnett, "The Edges of Empire and the Limits of Sovereignty: American Guano Islands," *American Quarterly* 57 (Sept. 2005): 788.

59. Cong. Globe, 34th Cong., 1st Sess., 1699.

60. Virginia Mason, *The Public Life and Diplomatic Correspondence of James M. Mason: With Some Personal History* (Roanoke, VA: Stone Printing and Manufacturing Co., 1903), 68.

61. Robert W. Young, *Senator James Murray Mason: Defender of the Old South* (Knoxville: University of Tennessee Press, 1998), 65–66.

62. Cong. Globe, 33rd Cong, 2nd Sess., 244–48, 916–19; 34th Cong, 1st Sess., 1797–99 (quotation on 1798); Elmer Plischke, *U.S. Department of State: A Reference History* (Westport, CT: Greenwood Press, 1999), 125–27; Matt Karp, "Slavery and American Sea Power: The Navalist Impulse in the Antebellum South," *Journal of Southern History* 77 (May 2011): 283–324.

63. "Home Department," *Southern Planter* 17 (Jan. 1857): 7.

64. Gautham Rao, "The Federal *Posse Comitatus* Doctrine: Slavery, Compulsion, and Statecraft in Mid-Nineteenth-Century America," *Law and History Review* 26 (Spring 2008): 23–25.

65. On this point, see Paul Finkelman, *Slavery and the Founders: Race and Liberty in the Age of Jefferson* (Armonk, NY: M. E. Sharpe, 1996), chap. 1.

66. Walter Johnson, *River of Dark Dreams: Slavery and Empire in the Cotton Kingdom* (Cambridge, MA: Harvard University Press, 2013), chap. 8.

67. James Oakes, *Freedom National: The Destruction of Slavery in the United States, 1861–1865* (New York: W. W. Norton, 2013).

68. Cong. Globe, 35th Cong., 2nd Sess., 716, 719 (emphasis added).

69. "Letter from Washington," *Alexandria Gazette*, Jan. 23, 1857, 2.

70. Cong. Globe, 34th Cong., 1st Sess., 1198 (May 13, 1856).

71. Cong. Globe, 34th Cong., 1st Sess., 1992–93 (Aug. 8, 1856). See also the suggestion to form agricultural societies for this purpose in "Foreign Seeds and Grains," *Lehigh Register*, Mar. 28, 1855, 2.

72. Robert W. Scott to Patent Office, Jan. 2, 1857, RG 16, vol. 15 (1857).

73. For similar impressions, see Courtney Fullilove, *The Profit of the Earth: The Global Seeds of American Agriculture* (Chicago: University of Chicago Press, 2017), 52.

74. Henry F. French to Patent Office, Aug. 3, 1853, RG 16, vol. 3 (1852–53); J. H. Frazer to Patent Office, Mar. 20, 1855, RG 16, vol. 6 (1854–55); John Harrold to Patent Office, Feb. 12, 1855, RG 16, vol. 6 (1854–55).

75. Cong. Globe, 35th Cong., 1st Sess., 2242. For an example of demand for the reports from Mississippi, see M. W. Philips to Patent Office, Aug. 31, 1852, RG 16, vol. 2 (1849–52).

76. On this point, see Thomas Clingman's remarks in Cong. Globe, 34th Cong., 1st Sess., 1198 (May 13, 1856).

77. Joseph Henry to Charles Mason, Jan. 31, 1856, RG 16, vol. 10 (1856).

78. Fullilove, *Profit of the Earth*, 50–52.

79. All the following in RG 16: G. Libbern to Patent Office, June 2, 1854, vol. 5 (1854); D. Jay Browne to Patent Office, Oct. 6, 1854; John Y. Mason to Patent Office, Dec. 13, 1854; William L. Marcy to Patent Office, Jan. 8, 1855, vol. 6 (1854–55); Townsend Glover to Patent Office, Dec. 24, 1856; J. C. Dobbin to Patent Office, Nov. 3, 1856, vol. 12 (1856); D. Jay Browne to Townsend Glover, Aug. 10, 1858, vol. 20 (1858), RG16; Charles Mason, *Life and Letters of Charles Mason, Chief Justice of Iowa, 1804–1882*, ed. Charles Mason Remey (Washington, DC: N.p., 1939), 2:160.

80. All the following in RG 16: Orange Judd to Patent Office, July 10, 1856, vol. 11 (1856); Fowlers & Wells to Patent Office, June 15, 1855, vol. 7 (1855); Henry F. French to Patent Office, Nov. 16, 1857, vol. 17 (1857); Edmund Ruffin to Patent Office, Oct. 25, 1854, vol. 5 (1854).

81. Kenneth W. Dobyns, *The Patent Office Pony: A History of the Early Patent Office* (Boston: Docent Press, 2016), 142–47 (quotation on 146); Mason, *Life and Letters of Charles Mason, Chief Justice of Iowa, 1804–1882*, 154; "Patent History Materials Index—Extracts from the Diaries of Commissioner Charles Mason," University of New Hampshire School of Law, IP Mall, entry dated Nov. 14, 1856, accessed August 24, 2016, https://ipmall.law.unh.edu/content/patent-history-materials-index-extracts-diaries-commissioner-charles-mason.

82. Corey M. Brooks, *Liberty Power: Antislavery Third Parties and the Transformation of American Politics* (Chicago: University of Chicago Press, 2016), 220; Oakes, *Freedom National*, 30; Sarah T. Phillips, "Antebellum Agricultural Reform, Republican Ideology, and Sectional Tension," *Agricultural History* 74 (Autumn 2000): 799–822.

83. Charles B. Dew, *Apostles of Disunion: Southern Secession Commissioners and the Causes of the Civil War* (Charlottesville: University Press of Virginia, 2001), 33, 101. On the abolitionist mail controversy of the 1830s, see Richard R. John, *Spreading the News: The American Postal System from Franklin to Morse* (Cambridge, MA: Harvard University Press, 1995), 257–80.

84. Hinton Rowan Helper, *The Impending Crisis of the South: How to Meet It* (New

York: Burdick Brothers, 1857), 51–52. The book that sparked controversy was an abridged version, in which the same passage recurs: Hinton Rowan Helper, *Compendium of the Impending Crisis of the South* (New York: A. B. Burdick, 1860), 29.

85. Phillips, "Antebellum Agricultural Reform, Republican Ideology, and Sectional Tension," 818.

86. "Home Department," *Southern Planter* 17 (Jan. 1857): 6.

87. John C. Underwood to Henry Carey, Nov. 6, 1860, Carey-HSP, box 19; William W. Freehling, *The South vs. the South: How Anti-Confederate Southerners Shaped the Course of the Civil War* (Oxford: Oxford University Press, 2001), 25; Eric Foner, *Free Soil, Free Labor, Free Men: The Ideology of the Republican Party before the Civil War* (Oxford: Oxford University Press, 1995), 123; Oakes, *Freedom National*, 32–33; Brooks, *Liberty Power*, 118. On slavery's decline in Maryland, see Barbara Jeanne Fields, *Slavery and Freedom on the Middle Ground: Maryland during the Nineteenth Century* (New Haven, CT: Yale University Press, 1985).

88. Benjamin Hallowell, *Autobiography of Benjamin Hallowell* (Philadelphia: Friends Book Association, 1884), 162–66; A. Glenn Crothers, *Quakers Living in the Lion's Mouth: The Society of Friends in Northern Virginia, 1730–1865* (Gainesville: University Press of Florida, 2012), 217–18. For Calvert, see Ira Berlin and the Students of History 429, "Knowing Our History: African-American Slavery and the University of Maryland" (College Park: University of Maryland, 2009), http://cdm16064.contentdm.oclc.org /cdm/ref/collection/p266901coll7/id/2614.

89. Gates, *Farmer's Age*, 378–79.

90. Advisory Board of Agriculture, H.R. Exec. Doc. no. 35-56; *Journal of the United States Agricultural Society* 4 (1856): 7–8, 254–69; 7 (1859–60): 9, 18, 86–88, 192, 388.

91. *American Farmer* 14 (Mar. 1859): 275.

92. *Journal of the United States Agricultural Society* 7 (1859): 18–19, 89–97.

93. Quoted in Julianna Chaszar, "Leading and Losing the Agricultural Education Movement: Freeman G. Cary and Farmers' College, 1846–1884," *History of Higher Education Annual* 18 (1998): 36.

94. Cong. Globe, 35th Cong., 2nd Sess., 256, 268; *DeBow's Review*, 26 (1859): 237, 608.

95. William G. Whiteley to Patent Office, May 6 and June 4, 1858, RG 16, vol. 20 (1858), and Jan. 6, 1859, vol. 21 (1859–60).

96. Cong. Globe, 35th Cong., 2nd Sess., 716 (emphasis added).

97. *Chicago Tribune*, Feb. 11, 1859, 2. See also *New-York Daily Tribune*, Feb. 17, 1859, 4, and Feb. 28, 1859, 4; *Philadelphia Press*, Feb. 22, 1859, 2; *Pittsburgh Daily Gazette*, Feb. 25, 1859, 1.

98. Brown to William Brewer, May 19, 1858, Brewer-YU.

99. Cong. Globe, 35th Cong., 2nd Sess., 1412–13.

100. *New-York Daily Tribune*, Feb. 28, 1859, 4.

101. *Chicago Tribune*, Mar. 1, 1859, 2.

102. *Philadelphia Press*, Feb. 22, 1859, 2, and Feb. 28, 1859, 2.

103. *National Era*, Apr. 21, 1859, 1.

104. Abraham Lincoln, "First Annual Message," Dec. 3, 1861, APP.

105. *Journal of the United States Agricultural Society* 10 (1862): 13–14, 22–24.

106. Cong. Globe, 37th Cong., 2nd Sess., 751, 855–57.

107. An Act to Establish a Department of Agriculture, H.R. 269, 37th Cong. (1862); A Bill to Establish a Department of Agriculture, S. 249, 37th Cong. (1862).

108. Cong. Globe, 37th Cong., 2nd Sess., 1690.

109. Cong. Globe, 37th Cong., 2nd Sess., 2014.

110. Cong. Globe, 37th Cong., 2nd Sess., 1690–92, 1756; Lincoln, "First Annual Message."

111. Committee Report on Establishment of Department of Agriculture, H.R. Rep. no. 37-21.

112. "Directors, 1840–1865," U.S. Census Bureau, http://www.census.gov/history /www/census_then_now/director_biographies/directors_1840_-_1865.html; *Journal of the United States Agricultural Society* 1 (Aug. 1853): 19.

113. Cong. Globe, 37th Cong., 2nd Sess., 1755–57, 2014–17, 2216.

114. Cong. Globe, 37th Cong., 2nd Sess., 2187, 2248–50, 2275–77, 2328–29, 2394–96, 2440–43, 2625–34, 2769–70 (1862); quotations on 2187, 2395, 2276, respectively.

115. Earle D. Ross, "The United States Department of Agriculture during the Commissionership: A Study in Politics, Administration, and Technology, 1862–1889," *Agricultural History* 20 (June 1946): 136.

116. *Annals of Congress*, 14th Cong., 2nd Sess., 502; "Nathaniel Macon and Bartlett Yancey," *North Carolina University Magazine* 7 (Oct. 1857): 94–95; A. V. Dicey, *Introduction to the Study of the Law of the Constitution*, 6th ed. (London: Macmillan and Co., 1902), 145.

117. Jon Grinspan, "'Young Men for War': The Wide Awakes and Lincoln's 1860 Presidential Campaign," *Journal of American History* 96 (Sept. 2009): 357–78.

118. "Home Department," *Southern Planter* 17 (Jan. 1857): 6.

Epilogue

1. "What Has Government Done for Agriculture?" *Working Farmer* 6 (Nov. 1854): 207–8; Robert Charles Winthrop, *American Agriculture: An Address Delivered before the Bristol County Agricultural Society, on Occasion of the Their Annual Cattle Fair at Taunton, Oct. 15, 1852* (Boston: John Wilson and Son, 1853).

2. *Report of the Commission on the Bureau of Statistics of the Treasury Department* (Washington, DC: GPO, 1877).

3. *The Story of U.S. Agricultural Estimates* (Washington, DC: GPO, 1969).

4. Alan L. Olmstead and Paul W. Rhode, *Arresting Contagion: Science, Policy, and Conflicts over Animal Disease Control* (Cambridge, MA: Harvard University Press, 2015), 9.

5. For the USDA's reputation for competence and impact, see Daniel P. Carpenter, *The Forging of Bureaucratic Autonomy: Reputations, Networks, and Policy Innovation in Executive Agencies, 1862–1928* (Princeton, NJ: Princeton University Press, 2001).

6. Frederick J. Turner, "Social Forces in American History," *American Historical Review* 16 (Jan. 1911): 223.

7. Gabriel N. Rosenberg, *The 4-H Harvest: Sexuality and the State in Rural America* (Philadelphia: University of Pennsylvania Press, 2015).

8. John M. Gaus and Leon O. Wolcott, *Public Administration and the United States Department of Agriculture* (Chicago: Public Administration Service, 1940), 3–13; Henry Barrett Learned, *The President's Cabinet: Studies in the Origin, Formation and Structure of*

an American Institution (New Haven, CT: Yale University Press, 1912), 292–345 (esp.
334); Lloyd Milton Short, "The Development of National Administrative Organization
in the United States" (PhD diss., University of Illinois, 1923), 374–94 (esp. 380–81);
William Lawrence Wanlass, *The United States Department of Agriculture: A Study in
Administration* (Baltimore, MD: Johns Hopkins Press, 1920), 9–32 (esp. 21–22). There
appears to be only one article that tries to arrive at some general claims about the period
of the "commissionership" from 1862 to 1889. It is largely concerned with the relationship
between scientists and administrators within the department. See Earle D. Ross, "The
United States Department of Agriculture during the Commissionership: A Study in
Politics, Administration, and Technology, 1862–1889," *Agricultural History* 20 (June
1946): 129–43.

9. Kenneth Finegold and Theda Skocpol, *State and Party in America's New Deal*
(Madison: University of Wisconsin Press, 1995); Elisabeth S. Clemens, *The People's Lobby:
Organizational Innovation and the Rise of Interest Group Politics in the United States, 1890–
1925* (Chicago: University of Chicago Press, 1997); Carpenter, *Forging of Bureaucratic
Autonomy*; Adam D. Sheingate, *The Rise of the Agricultural Welfare State: Institutions and
Interest Group Power in the United States, France, and Japan* (Princeton, NJ: Princeton
University Press, 2001).

10. See, for example, Roger L. Ransom and Richard Sutch, *One Kind of Freedom: The
Economic Consequences of Emancipation* (Cambridge: Cambridge University Press, 2001).

11. Charles A. Beard and Mary R. Beard, *The Rise of American Civilization* (New
York: Macmillan, 1930), 2:3–51.

12. Barrington Moore, *Social Origins of Dictatorship and Democracy: Lord and Peasant
in the Making of the Modern World* (Boston: Beacon Press, 1967), 111–58.

13. Later geohistorical concepts such as the "urban frontier" and "nature's metropolis"
complicated the Turnerian picture. See Richard C. Wade, *The Urban Frontier: The Rise
of Western Cities, 1790–1830* (Cambridge, MA: Harvard University Press, 1959); William
Cronon, *Nature's Metropolis: Chicago and the Great West* (New York: W. W. Norton,
1991). My own contribution, "the Greater Northeast," is intended to emphasize that not
only were there cities in the West, there were farms in the East.

14. For influential formulations, see Richard L. McCormick, *The Party Period and
Public Policy: American Politics from the Age of Jackson to the Progressive Era* (New York:
Oxford University Press, 1986); Stephen Skowronek, *Building a New American State:
The Expansion of National Administrative Capacities, 1877–1920* (Cambridge: Cambridge
University Press, 1982).

15. This argument is best made in Michael F. Holt, *The Political Crisis of the 1850s*
(New York: Norton, 1983). For a brilliant recent application, see Corey M. Brooks,
Liberty Power: Antislavery Third Parties and the Transformation of American Politics
(Chicago: University of Chicago Press, 2016).

16. Eric Foner, *Free Soil, Free Labor, Free Men: The Ideology of the Republican Party
before the Civil War* (Oxford: Oxford University Press, 1995), 59.

17. See, for example, Foner, *Free Soil, Free Labor, Free Men*, 224–25. The discussion
here suggests that Radical Republicans turned to Unionism instrumentally in order to
attack slavery, but that "moderates and conservatives" did the opposite and were fundamentally committed to Unionism. It is hard, then, to say which of the two is more basic
and, indeed, Foner observes that Lincoln synthesized the two. For an argument that

288 Notes to Page 218

Lincoln was a nationalist first, see Dorothy Ross, "Lincoln and the Ethics of Emancipation: Universalism, Nationalism, Exceptionalism," *Journal of American History* 96 (Sept.
2009).

18. Eric Foner, *Reconstruction: America's Unfinished Revolution, 1863–1877* (New York:
Harper & Row, 1988), 124–75.

19. David Montgomery, *Beyond Equality: Labor and the Radical Republicans, 1862–
1872* (New York: Knopf, 1967).

20. Foner, *Reconstruction*, 460–511. The coalitional purpose of ideological construction defines a space of political possibility constrained by the limits of the plausible and
the need to differentiate one party from the other. Foner's concept of ideology therefore
helps explain the Republicans' shifting fortunes within the party system. Also see
Heather Cox Richardson, *The Greatest Nation of the Earth: Republican Economic Policies
during the Civil War* (Cambridge, MA: Harvard University Press, 1997); Heather Cox
Richardson, *The Death of Reconstruction: Race, Labor, and Politics in the Post–Civil War
North, 1865–1901* (Cambridge, MA: Harvard University Press, 2001).

21. Foner is well aware that "in ante-bellum America, the word 'labor' had a meaning
far broader than its modern one" (*Free Soil, Free Labor, Free Men*, 15), and he has many
discussions that acknowledge the influence of small-holding craftsmen and farmers. All
the same, the analytic approach remains largely urban and worker-centered. This is evident, for instance, in discussions of the tariff and homestead policies from the perspective
of their effects on workers, rather than farmers, and more fundamentally from a reliance
on big city newspapers.

22. See, especially, Sean Wilentz, *Chants Democratic: New York City and the Rise of
the American Working Class, 1788–1850* (New York: Oxford University Press, 1984); Sven
Beckert, *The Monied Metropolis: New York City and the Consolidation of the American
Bourgeoisie, 1850–1896* (Cambridge: Cambridge University Press, 2001). Foner's own
earlier study of Thomas Paine in revolutionary Philadelphia suggests an origin point for
free labor ambiguities; see Eric Foner, *Tom Paine and Revolutionary America* (New York:
Oxford University Press, 2004).

23. Karl Marx, *Capital: A Critique of Political Economy* (Chicago: Charles H. Kerr &
Co., 1909), 1:186–87. Reflecting on his breakthrough monograph twenty-five years later,
Foner explicitly locates "the forthright articulation of an ideology of free labor" in the
northern response to proslavery critiques of urban working conditions (*Free Soil, Free
Labor, Free Men*, xx).

24. Winifred Barr Rothenberg, *From Market-Places to a Market Economy: The Trans-
formation of Rural Massachusetts, 1750–1850* (Chicago: University of Chicago Press, 1992);
Christopher Clark, *The Roots of Rural Capitalism: Western Massachusetts, 1780–1860*
(Ithaca, NY: Cornell University Press, 1990); Allan Kulikoff, *The Agrarian Origins of
American Capitalism* (Charlottesville: University Press of Virginia, 1992); Martin Bruegel,
Farm, Shop, Landing: The Rise of a Market Society in the Hudson Valley, 1780–1860 (Dur-
ham, NC: Duke University Press, 2002); Hal S. Barron, *Those Who Stayed Behind: Rural
Society in Nineteenth-Century New England* (Cambridge: Cambridge University Press,
1984).

25. See, especially, James A. Henretta, "Families and Farms: Mentalité in Pre-
industrial America," *William and Mary Quarterly* 35 (Jan. 1978): 3–32; Michael Merrill,
"Cash Is Good to Eat: Self-Sufficiency and Exchange in the Rural Economy of the United

States," *Radical History Review* 3 (1977): 42–71. The political implications were drawn out in the subsequent debates over the antebellum "market revolution," but farmers remained in the mold of the Jeffersonian agrarian ideal. At most, they chose a party but did not otherwise organize independently. See Charles Grier Sellers, *The Market Revolution: Jacksonian America, 1815–1846* (New York: Oxford University Press, 1991); Daniel Walker Howe, *What Hath God Wrought: The Transformation of America, 1815–1848* (Oxford: Oxford University Press, 2007). Work on New York's anti-rent movement offers a partial exception; see, especially, Reeve Huston, *Land and Freedom: Rural Society, Popular Protest, and Party Politics in Antebellum New York* (New York: Oxford University Press, 2000).

26. Mark Cowling and James Martin, eds., *Marx's Eighteenth Brumaire: Postmodern Interpretations* (London: Pluto Press, 2002), 100–101. For Marx, this meant that French peasants could only conceive of government as a central authority, above and beyond them. American farmers are usually seen as tending toward the opposite extreme, perpetually favoring the devolution of powers to the locale.

27. Sally McMurry, *Transforming Rural Life: Dairying Families and Agricultural Change, 1820–1885* (Baltimore, MD: Johns Hopkins University Press, 1995); Paula Baker, *The Moral Frameworks of Public Life: Gender, Politics, and the State in Rural New York, 1870–1930* (New York: Oxford University Press, 1991); Clemens, *People's Lobby.* Also see Joan M. Jensen, *Loosening the Bonds: Mid-Atlantic Farm Women, 1750–1850* (New Haven, CT: Yale University Press, 1986); Sally McMurry, *Families and Farmhouses in Nineteenth-Century America: Vernacular Design and Social Change* (New York: Oxford University Press, 1988); Nancy Grey Osterud, *Bonds of Community: The Lives of Farm Women in Nineteenth-Century New York* (Ithaca, NY: Cornell University Press, 1991); Deborah Fink, *Agrarian Women: Wives and Mothers in Rural Nebraska, 1880–1940* (Chapel Hill: University of North Carolina Press, 1992); Mary C. Neth, *Preserving the Family Farm: Women, Community, and the Foundations of Agribusiness in the Midwest, 1900–1940* (Baltimore, MD: Johns Hopkins University Press, 1998).

28. See, especially, Amy Dru Stanley, *From Bondage to Contract: Wage Labor, Marriage, and the Market in the Age of Slave Emancipation* (Cambridge: Cambridge University Press, 1998).

29. See, for instance, Walter Johnson, *Soul by Soul: Life inside the Antebellum Slave Market* (Cambridge, MA: Harvard University Press, 1999); Richard Holcombe Kilbourne, *Slave Agriculture and Financial Markets in Antebellum America: The Bank of the United States in Mississippi, 1831–1852* (London: Routledge, 2006); Calvin Schermerhorn, *The Business of Slavery and the Rise of American Capitalism, 1815–1860* (New Haven, CT: Yale University Press, 2015).

30. James Oakes, "Capitalism and Slavery and the Civil War," *International Labor and Working-Class History* 89 (Spring 2016): 195–220; John J. Clegg, "Capitalism and Slavery," *Critical Historical Studies* 2 (September 2015): 281–304; James Oakes, *Freedom National: The Destruction of Slavery in the United States, 1861–1865* (New York: W. W. Norton, 2013).

31. Foner, *Free Soil, Free Labor, Free Men*, 28.

32. Elliott West, *The Last Indian War: The Nez Perce Story* (Oxford: Oxford University Press, 2011).

33. "Agriculture, as Connected with Mechanics and Engineering," newspaper clipping in Everett-HML.

34. William E. Gienapp, *The Origins of the Republican Party, 1852–1856* (New York: Oxford University Press, 1987).

35. Daniel Peart, *Lobbyists and the Making of US Tariff Policy, 1816–1861* (Baltimore, MD: Johns Hopkins University Press, 2018); Margaret Susan Thompson, *The Spider Web: Congress and Lobbying in the Age of Grant* (Ithaca, NY: Cornell University Press, 1986).

36. I have been particularly influenced here by these articles: Paula Baker, "The Domestication of Politics: Women and American Political Society, 1780–1920," *American Historical Review* 89 (June 1984): 620–47; Elisabeth S. Clemens, "Organizational Repertoires and Institutional Change: Women's Groups and the Transformation of U.S. Politics, 1890–1920," *American Journal of Sociology* 98 (Jan. 1993): 755–98; Mary Hershberger, "Mobilizing Women, Anticipating Abolition: The Struggle against Indian Removal in the 1830s," *Journal of American History* 86 (June 1999): 15–40.

37. Charles Postel, *Equality: An American Dilemma, 1866–1896* (New York: Farrar, Straus and Giroux, 2019), 11.

38. *Minutes of the Votes and Proceedings of the Seventy-Fourth General Assembly of the State of New Jersey* (Freehold: Orrin Pharo, 1850), 496; "Agriculture and the Government," *Working Farmer* 1 (June 1849): 73.

39. Ross, "The United States Department of Agriculture during the Commissionership," 136.

40. Abraham Lincoln, "Fourth Annual Message," accessed Sept. 1, 2019, APP.

41. US Department of Agriculture, *Monthly Report of the Condition of the Crops for September, 1863* (Oct. 1863), 2, http://archive.org/details/monthlyreportofd1863unit.

42. This had been true since the days of the Patent Office's Agricultural Division and helps explain the remarkable number of agricultural societies established in western states with relatively few Euro-American settlers. See, in addition to table 2.5, Fred Kniffen, "The American Agricultural Fair: Time and Place," *Annals of the Association of American Geographers* 41 (Mar. 1951): 44; Merrill E. Jarchow, "Early Minnesota Agricultural Societies and Fairs," *Minnesota History* 22 (Sept. 1941): 249–69.

43. All the following in RG 16: George Fisher to Patent Office, Sept. 8, 1853, vol. 4 (1853), 103; George Fisher to Patent Office, Feb. 17, 1855, vol. 6 (1854–55), 1004. For similar examples, see W.H.L. Smith to Patent Office, Feb. 15, 1855, vol. 6 (1854–55), 998; Albert C. Ingham to Patent Office, Oct. 28, 1853, vol. 4 (1853), 711; John Harold to Patent Office, Feb. 12, 1855, vol. 6 (1854–55), 984.

44. US Department of Agriculture, *Monthly Report of the Condition of the Crops for July, 1863* (August 10, 1863), 1, http://archive.org/details/monthlyreportofd1863unit; *List of Agricultural Colleges, and of Farmers' Clubs, and Agricultural, Horticultural, and Pomological Societies on the Books of the Department of Agriculture, June 1, 1872, Together with the Name of the President and Secretary of Each* (Washington, DC: GPO, 1872); *List of Agricultural Societies, and Farmers' Clubs, Established to Promote the Agricultural, Horticultural, and Pomological Interests of the Farmer, on the Books of the Department of Agriculture, July 4, 1876, Being the Centennial Year of American Independence, Together with a List of Agricultural Colleges* (Washington, DC: GPO, 1876).

45. When the USDA began issuing monthly reports on crop conditions in 1863, it noted that it had "no means" other than seeds and reports "to pay for interrogatories necessary to procure information." See US Department of Agriculture, *Monthly Report*

of the Condition of the Crops for June, 1863 (July 10, 1863), 3, http://archive.org/details /monthlyreportofd1863unit.

46. Quoted in Oliver Hudson Kelley, *Origin and Progress of the Order of the Patrons of Husbandry in the United States: A History from 1866 to 1873* (Philadelphia: J. A. Wagenseller, 1875), 13.

47. Postel, *Equality*, 17–47.

48. Thomas A. Woods, *Knights of the Plow: Oliver H. Kelley and the Origins of the Grange in Republican Ideology* (Ames: Iowa State University Press, 1991), 38–39, 97. Some Granges, like the earlier agricultural societies, established themselves on the basis of annual fairs aimed at promoting adoption of new technologies. See Warren J. Gates, "Modernization as a Function of an Agricultural Fair: The Great Grangers' Picnic Exhibition at Williams Grove, Pennsylvania, 1873–1916," *Agricultural History* 58 (July 1984): 262–79.

49. Woods, *Knights of the Plow*.

50. Postel, *Equality*, 63.

51. Kelley, *Origin and Progress*, 30. Also see Solon Justus Buck, *The Granger Movement: A Study of Agricultural Organization and Its Political, Economic and Social Manifestations, 1870–1880* (Cambridge, MA: Harvard University Press, 1913), 58, 64.

52. Woods, *Knights of the Plow*, 29, 99; Kelley, *Origin and Progress*, 36, 54–55, 196; Buck, *Granger Movement*, 44, 46.

53. Postel, *Equality*, 21; Theodore Saloutos, *Farmer Movements in the South, 1865– 1933* (Lincoln: University of Nebraska Press, 1960), 33–35.

54. Postel, *Equality*, 43, 76–79 (quotations on 90, 105).

55. Quoted in *Story of U.S. Agricultural Estimates*, 32.

56. Saloutos, *Farmer Movements in the South*, 32. In 1867, the department sent Theodore Peters, a farm editor closely involved with the New York State Agricultural Society and the People's College effort, on a fact-finding mission (*Story of U.S. Agricultural Estimates*, 27).

57. Postel, *Equality*, 80, 82, 108.

58. Quoted in Kathleen Mapes, *Sweet Tyranny: Migrant Labor, Industrial Agriculture, and Imperial Politics* (Urbana: University of Illinois Press, 2009), chaps. 31–32, and in general, chaps. 1, 5. Also see Kristin L. Hoganson, *The Heartland: An American History* (New York: Penguin Press, 2019), 173–74.

59. These were not exactly new associations. For an early American example of racialized science, see Joyce E. Chaplin, *Subject Matter: Technology, the Body, and Science on the Anglo-American Frontier, 1500–1676* (Cambridge, MA: Harvard University Press, 2001).

60. This point was suggested to me by my colleague, Kenneth Hamilton.

61. Stefan Link and Noam Maggor, "The United States as a Developing Nation: Revisiting the Peculiarities of American History," *Past & Present* 246 (February 2020): 269–306.

62. M. Elizabeth Sanders, *Roots of Reform: Farmers, Workers, and the American State, 1877–1917* (Chicago: University of Chicago Press, 1999); Monica Prasad, *The Land of Too Much: American Abundance and the Paradox of Poverty* (Cambridge, MA: Harvard University Press, 2012).

63. William J. Novak, "The Myth of the 'Weak' American State," *American Historical Review* 113 (June 2008): 752–72; Ariel Ron and Gautham Rao, "Introduction: Taking Stock of the State in Nineteenth-Century America," *Journal of the Early Republic* 38 (Spring 2018): 61–66; Stephen Skowronek, "Present at the Creation: The State in Early American Political History," *Journal of the Early Republic* 38 (Spring 2018): 95–103; Richard R. John, "The State Is Back In: What Now?," *Journal of the Early Republic* 38 (Spring 2018): 105–18.

64. Among the many examples of these kinds of formulations, see Christopher Howard, *The Hidden Welfare State: Tax Expenditures and Social Policy in the United States* (Princeton, NJ: Princeton University Press, 1999); Suzanne Mettler, *The Submerged State: How Invisible Government Policies Undermine American Democracy* (Chicago: University of Chicago Press, 2011); Brian Balogh, *A Government out of Sight: The Mystery of National Authority in Nineteenth-Century America* (Cambridge: Cambridge University Press, 2009); Timothy Mitchell, "Society, Economy and the State Effect," in *The Anthropology of the State: A Reader*, ed. Aradhana Sharma and Akhil Gupta (Malden, MA: Wiley-Blackwell, 2006), 169–86; James T. Sparrow, William J. Novak, and Stephen W. Sawyer, eds., *Boundaries of the State in U.S. History* (Chicago: University of Chicago Press, 2015); Damon Mayrl and Sarah Quinn, "Beyond the Hidden American State: Classification Struggles and the Politics of Recognition," in *The Many Hands of the State: Theorizing Political Authority and Social Control*, ed. Kimberly J. Morgan and Ann Shola Orloff (Cambridge: Cambridge University Press, 2017); Elisabeth S. Clemens, "Lineages of the Rube Goldberg State: Building and Blurring Public Programs, 1900–1940," in *Rethinking Political Institutions: The Art of the State*, ed. Ian Shapiro, Stephen Skowronek, and Daniel Galvin (New York: New York University Press, 2006), 380–443.

Primary Sources

Three sets of primary sources underpin this study: the publications and internal records of agricultural journals and societies that allow me to reconstruct the agricultural reform movement; works on political economy that shape my conception of the ideology I call the Republican developmental synthesis; and the federal government records that tell the story of agricultural policy's sectionalization in the 1850s. Newspaper accounts and personal papers are also crucial. Each of these sets of sources was accessed both in print and online, occasionally by microfilm. This is a good place to again acknowledge the work of many librarians and archivists who helped me get my hands on the necessary materials.

For the agricultural journals—besides physical copies, which I consulted at various libraries and archives—the best database is ProQuest's American Periodicals Series Online, though some journals that play an important part in this book, such as James J. Mapes's *Working Farmer* and John S. Skinner's shorter-lived *Monthly Journal of Agriculture*, are not included there. For newspapers, I relied most heavily on Readex's America's Historical Newspapers for earlier periods and on ProQuest's Historical Newspapers and Penn State University's Pennsylvania Civil War Era Newspaper Collection for later periods. The Internet Archive, Google Books, and HathiTrust Digital Library were essential supplements for all printed sources, especially for the reports and transactions of agricultural societies and farmers' clubs, and for state laws.

For federal records, I used the *Congressional Globe* through the Library of Congress's "A Century of Lawmaking for a New Nation" website, and I accessed committee and Patent Office reports through ProQuest's Congressional database and Readex's U.S. Congressional Serial Set. Manuscript records at the National Archives were also key, especially the correspondence volumes of the Patent Office's "Agricultural Department" in record group 16 and the petitions referred to the Public Lands and Agricultural Committees of the 30th through 36th Congresses, held at the Center for Legislative Archives in record group 233.

Manuscript records for key agricultural reform people and organizations are surprisingly rare. Many of my most important finds occurred at small county historical societies and town libraries. Although seldom extensive, these collections sometimes include membership lists that, when matched to manuscript census data through Ancestry.com, provide evidence of the agricultural reform movement's socioeconomic base. The following collections were especially valuable in this regard: Middlesex Agricultural Society Records, 1803–

92, Concord Free Public Library, Concord MA; Fairfield County Agricultural Society Records, 1840–51 (MS B90), Fairfield Museum and History Center, Fairfield, CT; Communications to the Agricultural Society of Bucks County, 1820–23 (BM-B-428) and Bucks County Agricultural Society Charter and Member List (BM-E-14), Mercer Museum and Library, Doylestown, PA; Records of the American Institute of the City of New York for the Encouragement of Science and Invention (MS 17), New-York Historical Society.

Insight into the ways that agricultural reformers and organizations operated came especially from the following collections: John Alsop King Papers and Henry O'Reilly Papers, New-York Historical Society; William H. Seward Papers (microfilm), William H. Brewer Papers, and Darrach Family Papers, Yale University; Anthony Morris Family Papers, Historical Society of Pennsylvania, Philadelphia; Delaware County Institute of Science Minutes and Papers, circa 1833–73, American Philosophical Society, Philadelphia; Jacob Cist Papers (collection 152), Academy of Natural Sciences, Philadelphia; Philadelphia Society for Promoting Agriculture Records (ms. coll. 92), University of Pennsylvania; Agricultural Society of New Castle County Records, 1836–72 (ms. book box 92), Historical Society of Delaware, Wilmington, DE. In addition, I read numerous farmers' diaries, journals, and account books at the archives mentioned above, as well as at the Chester County (PA) Historical Society, the Maine Historical Society, and the Guilford (CT) Free Library.

The parts of the book that deal with the history of economic thought were researched primarily at the Library Company of Philadelphia, the Hagley Museum and Library, the Historical Society of Pennsylvania, and the University of Pennsylvania's Rare Books and Manuscripts Library. I used the first two for their collections of pamphlets and monographs, the latter two for their collections, respectively, of Henry Charles Carey's correspondence and of his personal library, which is commingled with that of his friend and fellow political economist, Stephen Colwell.

Secondary Sources

This study began from questions about the origins and early policies of the Republican party. The most important works on this topic, for my purposes, are Eric Foner, *Free Soil, Free Labor, Free Men: The Ideology of the Republican Party before the Civil War* (Oxford: Oxford University Press, 1995); William E. Gienapp, *The Origins of the Republican Party, 1852–1856* (New York: Oxford University Press, 1987); Michael F. Holt, *The Political Crisis of the 1850s* (New York: Norton, 1983); Richard Franklin Bensel, *Yankee Leviathan: The Origins of Central State Authority in America, 1859–1877* (Cambridge: Cambridge University Press, 1990); Sven Beckert, *The Monied Metropolis: New York City and the Consolidation of the American Bourgeoisie, 1850–1896* (Cambridge: Cambridge University Press, 2001); Heather Cox Richardson, *The Greatest Nation of the Earth: Republican Economic Policies during the Civil War* (Cambridge, MA: Harvard University Press, 1997); Leonard L. Richards, *The Slave Power: The Free North and Southern Domination, 1780–1860* (Baton Rouge: Louisiana State University Press, 2000). For important recent contributions, see James Oakes, *Freedom National: The Destruction of Slavery in the United States, 1861–1865* (New York: Norton, 2013); Corey M. Brooks, *Liberty Power: Antislavery Third Parties and the Transformation of American Politics* (Chicago: University of Chicago Press, 2016); James L. Huston, *The British Gentry, the Southern Planter, and the Northern Family Farmer: Agricul-*

ture and Sectional Antagonism in North America (Baton Rouge: Louisiana State University Press, 2015); Adam Wesley Dean, *An Agrarian Republic: Farming, Antislavery Politics, and Nature Parks in the Civil War Era* (Chapel Hill: University of North Carolina Press, 2015).

There is an extensive social science literature on the history of American politics, often referred to as American political development or APD. Key works for me are Stephen Skowronek, *Building a New American State: The Expansion of National Administrative Capacities, 1877–1920* (Cambridge: Cambridge University Press, 1982); Theda Skocpol, *Protecting Soldiers and Mothers: The Political Origins of Social Policy in the United States* (Cambridge, MA: Harvard University Press, 1992); Richard Franklin Bensel, *The Political Economy of American Industrialization, 1877–1900* (Cambridge: Cambridge University Press, 2000); Elisabeth S. Clemens, *The People's Lobby: Organizational Innovation and the Rise of Interest Group Politics in the United States, 1890–1925* (Chicago: University of Chicago Press, 1997); M. Elizabeth Sanders, *Roots of Reform: Farmers, Workers, and the American State, 1877–1917* (Chicago: University of Chicago Press, 1999); Adam D. Sheingate, *The Rise of the Agricultural Welfare State: Institutions and Interest Group Power in the United States, France, and Japan* (Princeton, NJ: Princeton University Press, 2001); Daniel P. Carpenter, *The Forging of Bureaucratic Autonomy: Reputations, Networks, and Policy Innovation in Executive Agencies, 1862–1928* (Princeton, NJ: Princeton University Press, 2001). This body of work builds on the "party period" school of political history: Richard L. McCormick, *The Party Period and Public Policy: American Politics from the Age of Jackson to the Progressive Era* (New York: Oxford University Press, 1986); Joel H. Silbey, *The American Political Nation, 1838–1893* (Stanford, CA: Stanford University Press, 1991); Ronald P. Formisano, *The Transformation of Political Culture: Massachusetts Parties, 1790s–1840s* (New York: Oxford University Press, 1983); Michael F. Holt, *The Rise and Fall of the American Whig Party: Jacksonian Politics and the Onset of the Civil War* (New York: Oxford University Press, 1999).

More recent political histories have both drawn on and challenged the above works and have particularly emphasized state capacity as opposed to the party system. Influential for me: Richard R. John, *Spreading the News: The American Postal System from Franklin to Morse* (Cambridge, MA: Harvard University Press, 1995); William J. Novak, *The People's Welfare: Law and Regulation in Nineteenth-Century America* (Chapel Hill: University of North Carolina Press, 1996); Robin L. Einhorn, *American Taxation, American Slavery* (Chicago: University of Chicago Press, 2006); Mark Wilson, *The Business of Civil War: Military Mobilization and the State, 1861–1865* (Baltimore, MD: Johns Hopkins University Press, 2006); Gabriel N. Rosenberg, *The 4-H Harvest: Sexuality and the State in Rural America* (Philadelphia: University of Pennsylvania Press, 2015); Alan L. Olmstead and Paul W. Rhode, *Arresting Contagion: Science, Policy, and Conflicts over Animal Disease Control* (Cambridge, MA: Harvard University Press, 2015); Padraig Riley, *Slavery and the Democratic Conscience: Political Life in Jeffersonian America* (Philadelphia: University of Pennsylvania Press, 2016).

The theory and history of the public sphere and print culture also shaped my approach, although my engagement in this case has been patchy. See, especially, Michael Warner, *Publics and Counterpublics* (Cambridge, MA: MIT Press, 2002); Michael Warner, *The Letters of the Republic: Publication and the Public Sphere in Eighteenth-Century America* (Cambridge, MA: Harvard University Press, 1990); David M. Henkin, *The Postal Age: The Emergence of*

Modern Communications in Nineteenth-Century America (Chicago: University of Chicago Press, 2006); David M. Henkin, *City Reading: Written Words and Public Spaces in Antebellum New York* (New York: Columbia University Press, 1998).

No history of the United States before the Civil War (or any era, really) can ignore the centrality of slavery. Because this book aims to explicate the political economy of the antebellum period, I have paid most attention to the recent surge in histories of slavery and capitalism: Gavin Wright, *Slavery and American Economic Development* (Baton Rouge: Louisiana State University Press, 2006); James Oakes, *The Ruling Race: A History of American Slaveholders* (New York: Knopf, 1982); Walter Johnson, *Soul by Soul: Life inside the Antebellum Slave Market* (Cambridge, MA: Harvard University Press, 1999); James L. Huston, *Calculating the Value of the Union: Slavery, Property Rights, and the Economic Origins of the Civil War* (Chapel Hill: University of North Carolina Press, 2003); Adam Rothman, *Slave Country: American Expansion and the Origins of the Deep South* (Cambridge, MA: Harvard University Press, 2005); Sean P. Adams, *Old Dominion, Industrial Commonwealth: Coal, Politics, and Economy in Antebellum America* (Baltimore, MD: Johns Hopkins University Press, 2004); John D. Majewski, *A House Dividing: Economic Development in Pennsylvania and Virginia before the Civil War* (Cambridge: Cambridge University Press, 2000); John Majewski, *Modernizing a Slave Economy: The Economic Vision of the Confederate Nation* (Chapel Hill: University of North Carolina Press, 2009); Brian Schoen, *The Fragile Fabric of Union: Cotton, Federal Politics, and the Global Origins of the Civil War* (Baltimore, MD: Johns Hopkins University Press, 2009); Sven Beckert, *Empire of Cotton: A Global History* (New York: Alfred A. Knopf, 2014); Edward E. Baptist, *The Half Has Never Been Told: Slavery and the Making of American Capitalism* (New York: Basic Books, 2014); Sven Beckert and Seth Rockman, eds., *Slavery's Capitalism: A New History of American Economic Development* (Philadelphia: University of Pennsylvania Press, 2016); Matthew Karp, *This Vast Southern Empire: Slaveholders at the Helm of American Foreign Policy* (Cambridge, MA: Harvard University Press, 2016); Caitlin Rosenthal, *Accounting for Slavery: Masters and Management* (Cambridge, MA: Harvard University Press, 2018).

For essential recent works on non-slave agriculture in the nineteenth century, see Emily Pawley, *The Nature of the Future: Capitalism, Agriculture, and Science in the Antebellum North* (Chicago: University of Chicago Press, 2020); Courtney Fullilove, *The Profit of the Earth: The Global Seeds of American Agriculture* (Chicago: University of Chicago Press, 2017); Alan L. Olmstead and Paul W. Rhode, *Creating Abundance: Biological Innovation and American Agricultural Development* (Cambridge: Cambridge University Press, 2008); Steven Stoll, *Larding the Lean Earth: Soil and Society in Nineteenth-Century America* (New York: Hill and Wang, 2002). Still essential are Clarence H. Danhof, *Change in Agriculture: The Northern United States, 1820–1870* (Cambridge, MA: Harvard University Press, 1969); Paul Wallace Gates, *The Farmer's Age: Agriculture, 1815–1860* (New York: Holt, Rinehart and Winston, 1960). For a general overview, see David B. Danbom, *Born in the Country: A History of Rural America* (Baltimore, MD: Johns Hopkins University Press, 1995).

A longstanding debate about the American "transition to capitalism" shaped numerous historical studies of nineteenth-century rural communities. Several articles lay out key positions within this debate: Michael Merrill, "Cash Is Good to Eat: Self-Sufficiency and Exchange in the Rural Economy of the United States," *Radical History Review* 3 (1977):

42–71; James A. Henretta, "Families and Farms: Mentalité in Pre-industrial America," *William and Mary Quarterly* 35 (January 1978): 3–32; Winifred B. Rothenberg, "The Market and Massachusetts Farmers, 1750–1855," *Journal of Economic History* 41 (June 1981): 283–314; Richard Lyman Bushman, "Markets and Composite Farms in Early America," *William and Mary Quarterly* 55 (July 1998): 351–74; Naomi R. Lamoreaux, "Rethinking the Transition to Capitalism in the Early American Northeast," *Journal of American History* 90 (September 2003): 437–61. The most important monographs to come out of this tradition were especially attentive to rural gender dynamics. See, especially, Sally McMurry, *Transforming Rural Life: Dairying Families and Agricultural Change, 1820–1885* (Baltimore, MD: Johns Hopkins University Press, 1995); Sally McMurry, *Families and Farmhouses in Nineteenth-Century America: Vernacular Design and Social Change* (New York: Oxford University Press, 1988); Nancy Grey Osterud, *Bonds of Community: The Lives of Farm Women in Nineteenth-Century New York* (Ithaca, NY: Cornell University Press, 1991); Joan M. Jensen, *Loosening the Bonds: Mid-Atlantic Farm Women, 1750–1850* (New Haven, CT: Yale University Press, 1986); Christopher Clark, *The Roots of Rural Capitalism: Western Massachusetts, 1780–1860* (Ithaca, NY: Cornell University Press, 1990); Donald Hugh Parkerson, *The Agricultural Transition in New York State: Markets and Migration in Mid-Nineteenth-Century America* (Ames: Iowa State University Press, 1995); Martin Bruegel, *Farm, Shop, Landing: The Rise of a Market Society in the Hudson Valley, 1780–1860* (Durham, NC: Duke University Press, 2002); Thomas Summerhill, *Harvest of Dissent: Agrarianism in Nineteenth-Century New York* (Urbana: University of Illinois Press, 2005); Mary Babson Fuhrer, *A Crisis of Community: The Trials and Transformation of a New England Town, 1815–1848* (Chapel Hill: University of North Carolina Press, 2014).

For the institutions of the agricultural reform movement—the societies, journals and fairs—see Tamara Plakins Thornton, *Cultivating Gentlemen: The Meaning of Country Life among the Boston Elite, 1785–1860* (New Haven, CT: Yale University Press, 1989); Donald B. Marti, *To Improve the Soil and the Mind: Agricultural Societies, Journals, and Schools in the Northeastern States, 1791–1865* (Ann Arbor, MI: Published for the Agricultural History Society and the Dept. of Communication Arts, New York State College of Agriculture and Life Sciences, Cornell University by University Microfilms International, 1979); Donald B. Marti, *Historical Directory of American Agricultural Fairs* (New York: Greenwood Press, 1986); Mark Mastromarino, "Fair Visions: Elkanah Watson (1758–1842) and the Modern American Agricultural Fair" (PhD diss., College of William and Mary, 2002); Wayne Caldwell Neely, *The Agricultural Fair* (New York: Columbia University Press, 1935); Albert Lowther Demaree, *The American Agricultural Press, 1819–1860* (New York: Columbia University Press, 1941).

Finally, for the history of American economic thought in this period, see, especially, Michael Hudson, *America's Protectionist Takeoff, 1815–1914* (Dresden: ISLET, 2010), and the articles of Stephen Meardon: "Henry C. Carey's 'Zone Theory' and American Sectional Conflict," *Journal of the History of Economic Thought* 37 (June 2015): 305–20; "Reciprocity and Henry C. Carey's Traverses on 'the Road to Perfect Freedom of Trade,'" *Journal of the History of Economic Thought* 33 (September 2011): 307–33; "From Religious Revivals to Tariff Rancor: Preaching Free Trade and Protection during the Second American Party System," *History of Political Economy* 40 (January 2008): 265–98; "How TRIPs Got Legs:

Copyright, Trade Policy, and the Role of Government in Nineteenth-Century American Economic Thought," *History of Political Economy* 37 (January 2005): 145–74. Also see Paul Keith Conkin, *Prophets of Prosperity: America's First Political Economists* (Bloomington: Indiana University Press, 1980); Michael Hudson, *Economics and Technology in 19th Century American Thought* (New York: Garland, 1975); Joseph Dorfman, *The Economic Mind in American Civilization, 1606–1865,* 5 vols. (New York: A. M. Kelley, 1966).

Page numbers in *italics* refer to figures, tables, and maps.

CPSIA information can be obtained
at www.ICGtesting.com
Printed in the USA
BVHW041934200123
656741BV00003B/23